AF846878

Arrows of Desire

Praise for *Arrows of Desire*

'Thirty-six striking essays, across a breathtaking range of subjects and in a dizzying register of moods and tones, at once brilliant and revelatory. *Arrows of Desire* offers us the extraordinary and exceptional from Peter Wollen's considerable output. Untimely meditations at once flamboyant and outstanding, with memorable and arresting insights on art, cinema, culture. The book highlights, if there was ever a doubt, that Wollen was one of Britain's formidable post-war intellectuals. An unsung hero to many of my generation, who left us way too soon.'
John Akomfrah

'For any cinephile or citizen who believes that cinema can be something other than a costly instrument serving ideologies and propaganda – and instead become an arsenal of critical ideas, acts of rebellion and constructive proposals – the writings of curator and filmmaker Peter Wollen serve as a historical touchstone and source of theoretical fuel. *Arrows of Desire* can be placed alongside the works of Germaine Dulac, S. M. Eisenstein, Dziga Vertov, Maya Deren, Amos Vogel, Jonas Mekas, Guy Debord, Jean-Luc Godard, Danièle Huillet, Jean-Marie Straub, Nagisa Ōshima, Glauber Rocha, Med Hondo, Adachi Masao, Harun Farocki, Ing Kanjanavanit, Nick Deocampo, The Otolith Group, Khadijeh Habashneh and of course, Laura Mulvey. Together and alongside others – each in their own way and on their own front – they have fought, and continue to fight tenaciously, for cinema to realize itself as an experimental and revolutionary art form.'
Nicole Brenez

'Peter Wollen enjoyed something too many theorists lack: a grace in the art of writing.'
Raymond Bellour

'This thrilling book does more than confirm Peter Wollen's place as perhaps the most incisive thinker to triangulate cinema, art and politics in the post-1968 period: by collecting lesser-known texts and astutely contextualising them, it reveals Wollen's daring, interdisciplinary expansiveness. With a critical and passionate gaze, Wollen meets his changing times in essays full of historical consciousness and conviction, launching arrows that sail into the darkness of our present with a shock of illumination. If this first book is anything to go by, the next two volumes of these previously uncollected writings can't come soon enough.'
Erika Balsom

Arrows of Desire

Selected Writings 1963–2002

Peter Wollen

Edited by Kodwo Eshun, Oliver Fuke
and Nicolas Helm-Grovas

VERSO
London • New York

First published by Verso 2026
© Peter Wollen 1963–2002
Introduction © Kodwo Eshun 2026
Frida Kahlo and Tina Modotti © Peter Wollen and Laura Mulvey 1983
Trialogue © Kodwo Eshun, Oliver Fuke and Nicolas Helm-Grovas 2026

All rights reserved

The publisher expressly prohibits the use of artificial intelligence in the composition of its publications, as it prohibits the use of those publications to develop AI technologies

The manufacturer's authorized representative in the EU for product safety (GPSR) is LOGOS EUROPE, 9 rue Nicolas Poussin, 17000, La Rochelle, France
Contact@logoseurope.eu

The moral rights of the authors have been asserted

1 3 5 7 9 10 8 6 4 2

Verso
UK: 6 Meard Street, London W1F 0EG
US: 207 East 32nd Street, New York, NY 10016
versobooks.com

Verso is the imprint of New Left Books

ISBN-13: 978-1-83674-117-6
ISBN-13: 978-1-83674-119-0 (US EBK)
ISBN-13: 978-1-83674-118-3 (UK EBK)

British Library Cataloguing in Publication Data
A catalogue record for this book is available from the British Library

Library of Congress Cataloging-in-Publication Data
A catalog record for this book is available from the Library of Congress

Typeset in Minion Pro by MJ & N Gavan, Truro, Cornwall
Printed in the UK by CPI Group (UK) Ltd, Croydon, CR0 4YY

Contents

II. Anti-Imperialisms

List of Plates

The place from which we fire our arrows …

Kodwo Eshun

The history of Cinema is like that of Revolution in our time, a chronicle of hopes and expectations, aroused and suspended, tested and deceived.
– Annette Michelson, *Film and the Radical Aspiration*[1]

J. B. Priestley the writer came to stay here in 1933. And one day, quite by accident, he stumbled into a school in the centre of the city. 'There's something very moving about these children,' he wrote. 'A film producer could make a film of exceptional interest about them.'
– John Akomfrah, *A Touch of the Tar Brush* (1992)[2]

The thirty-seven essays, articles, diagrams, proposals, lecture notes, letters, reviews and poetry chosen for *Arrows of Desire: Selected Writings 1963–2002* reveal the consistency, contestation, commitment and surprise that animate the work of Peter Wollen. As with the forthcoming companion volumes *Knight's Moves* and *Fire and Ice*, *Arrows of Desire* brings together previously uncollected and inaccessible writings, drawing attention to the exigencies and the vicissitudes of anti-imperialism, feminism, the politics of identity and the avant-garde unfamiliar to those whose knowledge of Wollen's writing extends as far as 'Godard and Counter-Cinema: *Vent d'Est*' (1972) or 'The Two Avant-Gardes' (1975). That unfamiliarity might

1 Annette Michelson, 'Film and the Radical Aspiration', *Film Culture* 42 (Fall 1966), 404.

2 Michael O'Pray, programme notes on *A Touch of the Tar Brush* by John Akomfrah, in *Arrows of Desire: The Second ICA Biennial of Independent Film and Video* (Institute of Contemporary Art, 1992), 19. See also Peter Wollen, 'The Cosmopolitan Ideal in the Arts', in George Robertson, Melinda Mash, Lisa Tickner, Jon Bird, Barry Curtis and Tim Putnam (eds), *Travellers' Tales: Narratives of Home and Displacement* (Routledge, 1994), 193.

well be a side effect of Wollen's fidelity to Pandora's virtues: compulsive curiosity, inveterate epistemophilia, indefatigable indisciplinarity, joy in learning, *le gai savoir*.[3] Wollen died in December 2019, after the onset of Alzheimer's disease at the age of sixty-five forced his retirement from public life in 2005. Peter Wollen was born in 1938 in Walthamstow, East London, the first child of Winifred Wollen, a teacher, and Douglas Wollen, a Methodist minister. Wollen's writing for *New Left Review* published, initially, under the name of Lee Russell, in the mid 1960s, *Screen* in the 1970s and *Framework* in the 1980s initiated intense debate in the nascent field of film studies. Wollen had already gained recognition, in film circles, for co-writing Antonioni's 1975 film, *The Passenger*; by the 1980s, he had become known, in contemporary art circles, for co-curating 'Frida Kahlo and Tina Modotti' in 1982, the first major international exhibition of those now canonical artists, and, not without controversy, for 'On the Passage of a Few People through a Rather Brief Moment in Time: The Situationist International, 1957–1972' in 1989, the first international exhibition devoted to Situationist art.

Determined to write his first book before turning thirty, Wollen produced *Signs and Meaning in the Cinema*, a field-defining text republished in five different editions between 1969 and 2013.[4] With Laura Mulvey, he wrote and directed six films that included the British feminist avant-garde landmark *Riddles of the Sphinx* in 1977. In 1987, he directed *Friendship's Death*, his singular feature film, adapted from his science fiction fable published in *Bananas*, Emma Tennant's literary magazine, in 1976. Starring Tilda Swinton as an alien android from the Procyon star system stranded in Amman, Jordan, during the so-called Black September of 1970, *Friendship's Death* derived, in part, from Wollen's experience as a political journalist; it remains painfully resonant. Besides poetry, theory, fiction, lectures, film and television scripts, Wollen wrote hundreds of essays and articles for independent magazines, academic journals and exhibition catalogues while working as a freelance lecturer, teaching at Essex, Northwestern, Columbia, NYU, Brown, San Francisco State, Simon Fraser and elsewhere on short-term contracts before moving to Los Angeles in 1988 to work at the Department of Film and Television at University of California, Los Angeles, first as a visiting lecturer and from 1993 as tenured professor.

---

3 Laura Mulvey, 'Pandora's Box: Topographies of Curiosity', *Fetishism and Curiosity* (British Film Institute, 1996), 53–64.

4 Leslie Dick, 'Editorial Note', in Peter Wollen, *Signs and Meaning in the Cinema*, 5th edition (British Film Institute, 2013), 253.

The title of *Arrows of Desire* situates the reader in the early 1990s, beyond the historical moment of 'counter-cinema'. It refers to 'Arrows of Desire: The Second ICA Biennial of Independent Film and Video' that opened at the Institute of Contemporary Arts at The Mall in Central London in 1992.[5] 'Arrows of Desire' featured thirty films and videos selected by Wollen that exemplified the state of the avant-garde in Britain under the Conservative regime of John Major. Wollen's title quotes the poetic image that ends the second line of the fourth verse of William Blake's Preface to *Milton: A Poem in Two Books*, orchestrated by Elgar for the hymn *Jerusalem*. It responds to the title of Hugh Hudson and David Puttnam's Oscar-winning *Chariots of Fire* (1981) that cited the martial phrase concluding the fourth line of *Jerusalem*'s fourth verse, sung, then, and now, by exultant Union Jack-wearing audiences attending the so-called Last Night of the Proms at London's Albert Hall. Against the 'Puttnamist' vision of British cinema, Wollen positioned 'Arrows of Desire' as a 'counterblast' to the 'completely decadent English chauvinism' of *Chariots of Fire*, a rejection of its decade-long influence on British cinema, a riposte to its craven desire for Hollywood recognition[6] and a counter-claim on the 'tradition of Blake in all its visionary intransigence'.[7]

If we create a hypothetical transect across the five programmes of 'Arrows of Desire', what do we find? Alia Syed's *Fatima's Letter* (1992), a poetic documentary of 'glimpses and glances and telling details'. *A Touch of the Tar Brush* (1992), John Akomfrah's meditation on the 'old-established cosmopolitan mixed-race community of Liverpool' as the 'forgotten utopian image of a possible Britain'. Robert Crusz's *Inbetween* (1992), in which the director confronts his 'identity as a diasporic film-maker'. The 'blazon of gay erotic registers' of Constantine Giannaris's *Caught Looking* (1992). The 'fatality of disability' of Jacquie Duckworth's *A Prayer Before Birth* (1991), documented in 'images unsparing and

---

5 After the ICA, 'Arrows of Desire' subsequently toured to Manchester, The Hague, Cesena, Venice, Tokyo, Kyoto, Nagoya, Fukuoka, Hong Kong 'and many other parts of the world' under the British Council's title of 'New Directions in Film and Video: An International Tour'.

6 Wollen recalled that *Chariots of Fire* was Derek Jarman's 'most hated film'. See Peter Wollen, 'The Last New Wave: Modernism in the British Films of the Thatcher Era', in Lester Friedman (ed.), *Fires Were Started: British Cinema and Thatcherism* (Wallflower Press, 2006), 38.

7 Ibid. 'Puttnamism' refers to 'British' movies such as *Gandhi*, *Local Hero*, *The Killing Fields*, *Another Country*, *Absolute Beginners*, *Revolution* and *The Mission*, movies financed by *Chariots of Fire*'s producer David Puttnam between 1983 and 1986.

undespairing'. These independent, experimental films and videos attested to 'a new vision of British culture' that refused to be 'constrained by the oppressive myths of Britishness'.[8]

The title of *Arrows of Desire* invokes this historical moment of cultural contention. In quoting a lesser-known curatorial project, *Arrows of Desire* aims to complicate our habitual understanding of Wollen's aesthetico-political imagination. If we approach the diagrams in the plate section of *Arrows of Desire* as *Denkbilder* or images of Wollen's thought, they provide us with entry points into the critical, political, artistic and historical inquiries of this book. Each diagram enables us to attend to the dialects and the creoles of political journalism, cultural criticism, film theory, film lectures and exhibition proposals pursued by Wollen. *Arrows of Desire* is divided into three sections: 'Counter-Cinema and Beyond', 'Anti-Imperialisms', and 'The Continent'. The first and second sections of this introductory essay analyse Wollen's diagram tracing the history of experimental film and the texts in 'Counter-Cinema and Beyond'; the third and the fourth sections explicate his shot plans for *Friendship's Death* and the writings of 'Anti-Imperialisms'; the fifth and sixth sections elucidate the diagram for 'The Continent'; this ambitious, unrealised curatorial project to reconceive American modern art provides the title for the final section, bringing untranslated and inaccessible essays together with proposals and outlines for completed and unmade exhibitions and films.

Counter-Cinema and Beyond 1: A force field in which judgements matter

> *Once upon a time, way back in the seventies, it was possible to speak of 'two avant-gardes' that posited a binarism of form and content. Times have changed, and along with them, categories of concern.*
>
> – B. Ruby Rich, 'The Authenticating Goldfish: Re-Viewing Film and Video in the Nineties'[9]

8 'Arrows of Desire' in this volume, 121.

9 B. Ruby Rich, 'The Authenticating Goldfish: Re-Viewing Film and Video in the Nineties', in Elisabeth Sussman et al. (eds), *1993 Biennial Exhibition* (Whitney Museum of Modern Art in association with Harry N. Abrams, 1993), 90.

> *Consider working the situation backwards and attempt to recreate a 'real' location solely with the information given by the film; very rapidly that real landscape would be full of voids and blanks, and grossly ill-fitting details.*
>
> – Peter Greenaway, *The Stairs: Geneva The Location / Genève Le Cadrage*[10]

Peter Wollen's untitled and undated diagram on the history of experimental film, produced, perhaps, around 1999, offers a point of departure for the texts assembled in 'Counter-Cinema and Beyond'. The ellipse of names that appears in the lower part of the drawing provides one of many competing foci of attention. These names compress the diagram's nominative connectivity into a centripetal ellipse that congregates the handwritten capitalised names of CONNER and JARMAN above addition signs, with JARMAN accompanied by a question mark at its left, on the vertical axis – and WARHOL and GODARD on the horizontal axis. Above GODARD is the title *Made in USA*; beneath is *Femme mariée.* These surnames and film titles are set within red-and-black-ruled quadrangles connected by horizontally spaced lines that form an ellipsoid around the term 'Artists and Film', above which is the name Nauman in parenthesis and below which the underlined term 'Pop Art'. Describing an elliptical orbit are the names and the movements of FARBER, CORNELL, DEREN, BRAKHAGE, STRUCTURAL FILM, GREENAWAY, LANDSCAPE FILM, FLUXUS and LETTRISM. Wollen's diagram can be understood as a factory that visualises his thought at work.[11]

Perhaps Wollen produced this diagram for his lectures in the Critical Studies programme at the Department of Film and Television at UCLA. In 1999, close to the time, perhaps, of his diagram, the essay 'Perhaps…' recalled the critical possibilities enabled in the late 1960s in London by Wollen and his allies at the British Film Institute's Education Department for rethinking the revolutionary Soviet cinema of the 1920s. The impact of Wollen's essay 'Eisenstein's Aesthetics' in *Signs and Meaning in the Cinema* (1969) stemmed from the ways in which it situated Eisenstein's films within the 'much wider context' of artistic modernism, thereby opening the 'narrow context' of orthodox film history to the promises and the problematics of contemporary theory. 'Eisenstein's Aesthetics' combined three approaches to intermediality: the intermedial art history

10 Peter Greenaway, *The Stairs: Geneva The Location / Genève Le Cadrage* (Merrell Holberton, 1994), 77.

11 Wollen, *Signs and Meaning*, 5th edition, 141. For the diagram on the history of experimental film, see the plate section in this volume.

pioneered by Camilla Gray in *The Russian Experiment in Art: 1863–1922*; the intermedial aesthetics initiated by Eisenstein in his extensive writings on cinema; and the essayistic intermediality proposed by Jean-Luc Godard in his writings for *Cahiers du Cinema* and in his films. 'Eisenstein's Aesthetics' announced nothing less than a 'new kind of film history' that emphasised film as an intermedial artform located 'at the crossroads of literature, music, theater and painting.'[12]

Wollen's approach to film history was intellectual rather than academic; the collective invention of film theory in Britain was undertaken by his friends and colleagues, a generation of freelance writers with undergraduate degrees rather than university lecturers with postgraduate qualifications. This partially explains why Wollen's essays tend not to mention their sources, nor provide, with specific exceptions, footnotes. The Wollen text is allusive, assertive, polemical, partisan, provocative, importunate, imperative, impassioned, intent, always, on persuasion. It deploys the registers of the meticulous, the generalised, the recondite, the vanguardist and the dithyrambic. It aims to rally its readers to its cause. It describes 'the bloodless transfer of power to the Bloomsbury group.' It champions 'the attempt, inspired by Godard, to build a bridgehead to a radicalised European art cinema.' It notes how 'photography struggled to conquer territories prima facie denied it.'[13] It recounts its 'contribution toward an uprising in film studies.'[14]

What Wollen advanced in 'Eisenstein's Aesthetics', recollected in 'Perhaps…', and revisited in the fictional dialogue of 'Afterword: Lee Russell Interviews Peter Wollen' (1997) was a critical argument for film not as mass media, nor as communication, but as an art, indeed as *the* artform of the twentieth century, characterised by its intermediality, definable through its polymorphousness and understandable through its heterogeneity.[15] In 'Knight's Moves' (2002), Wollen condenses this far-reaching argument into the position that there 'can be no distinct ontology of film, only a range of possibilities.'[16] Wollen's 'Reply to Sitney' (1982) goes further by drawing out the ethico-political repercussions of

12 'Perhaps…' in this volume, 130. See also Camilla Gray, *The Russian Experiment in Art: 1863–1922* (Harry N. Abrams, 1970), 271.

13 Wollen, 'The Last New Wave', 33; and 'Arrows of Desire', 114; and Peter Wollen, 'Photography and Aesthetics', in *Readings and Writings: Semiotic Counter-Strategies* (Verso, 1982), 178. Originally published in *Screen* 19:4 (Winter 1978–9), 9.

14 Peter Wollen, 'Thinking Theory', *Film Comment* (July 1988), 50.

15 Wollen, 'Afterword: Lee Russell Interviews Peter Wollen', in *Signs and Meaning*, 5th edition.

16 'Knight's Moves' in this volume, 144.

deontologising film: 'It's simply wrong to restrict the history of film to film alone as though it was sealed off from the other arts or other intellectual and social currents.'[17]

These statements assert a position, a belief and a value system that persist across Wollen's entire body of work. By emphasising its intermedial relations rather than its essential nature, Wollen sought to expand the imagination of cinema to the scale visualised in his diagram of experimental film. The title of *Zorns Lemma* written above the rectangle that contains the words ZOO, GREENAWAY and LANDSCAPE FILM alludes to the connections between Hollis Frampton's *Zorns Lemma* (1970), Greenaway's *A Zed & Two Noughts* (1985) and the tradition of landscape film exemplified in the experimental films of Chris Welsby. Perhaps Wollen used his diagram to envision an exhibition on the serial logics of landscape cinema. According to Wollen, what differentiated a Welsby film such as *Wind Vane* (1972) from Frampton's *Ordinary Matter (Hapax Legomena V)* (1972) or Greenaway's *Windows* (1975), however, was not its style or content but its exploitation of the possibilities of film locked in and by the technology of industrial cinema. Welsby's modifications of the standardised cinematic apparatus enable film to capture a 'whole range of meteorological phenomena' from the sun path to wind force to tidal motion that directs the cinematographic process itself.[18]

A Welsby film such as *Anemometer* (1974) announces a 'different kind of relationship' between science and art in which 'observation is separated from surveillance and technology from domination.'[19] The technopolitical stakes of this divorce become clearer in the context of Wollen's essay 'Cinema and Technology: A Historical Overview' (1980). The 'dominant and cohesive mode of representation', argues Wollen, is a 'specious unity'.[20] If we link this critique to Wollen's diagram, it becomes possible to account for the capacity of experimental film to extricate the 'forms of matter taken by the technical apparatus' from the 'interface where the economies of capital and libido interlock.'[21] Wollen uses Welsby's films to rethink experimental film as a technopoetic practice capable of interrupting and intervening in the historico-technical processes of

17 'Reply to Sitney' in this volume, 92.

18 'Landscape, Meteorology, and Chris Welsby' in this volume, 84.

19 Ibid., 85.

20 Peter Wollen, 'Cinema and Technology: A Historical Overview', in *Readings and Writings: Semiotic Counter-Strategies* (Verso, 1982), 177. Originally published in Stephen Heath and Teresa de Lauretis (eds), *The Cinematic Apparatus* (Macmillan, 1980).

21 Wollen, 'Cinema and Technology', 176.

the industrialization of vision and thought. Wollen's writing resonates, tantalisingly, at this point, with Harun Farocki's cine-investigations into operational images 'that do not represent an object but rather are part of an operation' in films such as *As You See* (1986), *Images of the World and the Inscription of War* (1988) and *Eye/Machine I–III* (2000–2003).[22]

Counter-Cinema and Beyond 2: So that only the stars remain inaccessible

> *Struggle______a film about struggle   a struggle about film   unity of theory & practice*
>
> – Peter Wollen, 'Jean-Luc Godard: *Wind from the East*'[23]

> *The antithesis is the battle between two plenitudes set ritually face to face like two armed warriors.*
>
> – Roland Barthes, *S/Z*[24]

Wollen often takes aim at the arguments for ontological purification advanced by specific critics. Such critics play the role of intimate enemies, to use the formulation of Ashis Nandy.[25] Intimate, because their work becomes the object of ongoing scrutiny against which Wollen's arguments take shape. Wollen makes these figures a subject for his antithetical thought: André Bazin, whose writings 'remained hostile throughout to experimental film' and whose criticism and theory revealed him to be 'a conservative';[26] P. Adams Sitney, whose writing 'remains wedded to a very traditional Romanticism' and whose essay 'Structural Film' 'outraged' Wollen in its 'near-total consignment of European film-makers after 1943 to oblivion';[27] Clement Greenberg, whose insistence on 'the triumph of

22 Harun Farocki, 'Phantom Images', *Public* 29 (2004), 17. See also Antje Ehmann and Kodwo Eshun (eds), *Harun Farocki: Against What? Against Whom?* (Koenig Books/Raven Row, 2009), 211–12, Jussi Parikka, *Operational Images: From the Visual to the Invisual* (University of Minnesota Press, 2023), 11–25, 99–110 and 217–19 and Nora M. Alter, *Harun Farocki: Forms of Intelligence* (Columbia University Press, 2024), 162–74.

23 'Jean-Luc Godard: *Wind from the East*' in this volume, 64.

24 Roland Barthes, *S/Z*, trans. Richard Miller (Hill and Wang, 1974), 27.

25 Ashis Nandy, *The Intimate Enemy: Loss and Recovery of the Self under Colonialism* (Oxford University Press, 1983).

26 Peter Wollen, 'Introduction to *Citizen Kane*', and '"Ontology" and "Materialism" in Film', in *Readings and Writings*, 53, 192. Originally published in *Film Reader* 1 (1975), and *Screen* 17:1 (1976).

27 Wollen, '"Ontology" and "Materialism" in Film', 193; 'The Avant-Gardes: Europe and America', in this volume, 86.

modern American painting' required the suppression of 'all consciousness of its debt to Mexico and the artists of the Pacific North-West'.[28] Other objects of critique include T. J. Clark, David Puttnam and, amusingly, the Evangelists. Against those figures of antipathy, we can see figures of affinity from whom Wollen learns and whose strategies he acknowledges, frequently, but not, however, uncritically: Sergei Eisenstein, who 'still has an enormous amount to teach us';[29] Jean-Luc Godard, whose 'heterogeneity' continues to provoke 'critical uncertainty and mutability';[30] Bertolt Brecht, for whom 'knowledge always took precedence over imagination';[31] Viktor Shklovsky, the champion of the 'unmotivated device' and the 'knight's move';[32] Yvonne Rainer, whose films are 'riddles that have no simple answer'.[33] Other elective figures of affinity include Alfred Hitchcock, Chantal Akerman and André Breton.

The poles of attraction and antagonism highlight a style of argumentation that frequently departs from an oppositional structure. 'The Two Avant-Gardes' begins with the declaration that 'Film history has developed unevenly, so that in Europe today there are two distinct avant-gardes.'[34] Point 1 of '*Passion* 1' (1983) asserts 'Two passions: the passion for justice and the passion for art' while point 19 declares 'Two realms: the aesthetic and the political (modern versions of the sacred and the secular)'.[35] In conversation with Ilona Halberstadt in 1993, Wollen speaks of the 'two poles of attraction' of the media world and the art world.[36] On rereading these texts, what becomes clear, however, is the degree to which these polarities function as starting points that set in motion a process that acts back upon and breaks down those initial extremes. We can see this dialectical process at work in the reiterated introduction and conclusion of the film script for *Frida Kahlo and Tina Modotti* (1983): 'Two choices for women: the personal, the traditional sphere of women, their suffering,

---

28 'The Continent – Notes to a Sketch for an Exhibition' in this volume, 300.

29 Wollen, 'Eisenstein's Aesthetics', in *Signs and Meaning*, 5th edition, 57.

30 'L'Eternel Retour' in this volume, 111.

31 Wollen, '"Ontology" and "Materialism" in Film', 201.

32 'Knight's Moves', 140, 147.

33 Peter Wollen, 'Counter-Cinema and Sexual Difference', in Kate Linker (ed.), *Difference: On Representation and Sexuality* (The New Museum of Contemporary Art, 1985), 37. Forthcoming in Peter Wollen, *Fire and Ice*, ed. Kodwo Eshun, Oliver Fuke and Nicolas Helm-Grovas (Verso).

34 Peter Wollen, 'The Two Avant-Gardes', in *Readings and Writings*, 92. Originally published in *Studio International* 190 (1975).

35 '*Passion* 1' in this volume, 96.

36 'The Avant-Gardes', 86; 'Interview on "Arrows of Desire", ICA Biennial of Film and Video' in this volume, 124.

their self-image. On the other hand, the political, the renunciation of home and family to produce images dedicated to social change. Frida Kahlo and Tina Modotti both provoke and defy such neat categorisation.'[37] Adversarial thought tends to incite critical unease. Then again, if 'counter-aesthetics, too, can harden into a system of dualistic opposition', as Laura Mulvey warned in 'Changes: Thoughts on Myth, Narrative and Historical Experience' in 1987 then so, too, could the counter-position to counter-aesthetics.[38] When B. Ruby Rich asserted, in 1993, that the '"two avant-gardes" posited a binarism of form and content', what becomes clear is the extent to which the notion of the two avant-gardes, like that of counter-cinema, had, over two decades, fused into one misremembered critical cliché similar to that of Mulvey's 'male gaze' or Said's 'Orientalism' or Gilroy's 'Black Atlantic': concepts rendered as *idées fixes* whose citation functioned as a prelude to their ritualised dismissal.

Bringing texts on experimental film written in London in the 1970s and writings on 'Arrows of Desire' for the 1990s together with unpublished lecture notes on Godard prepared during Wollen's time at Northwestern University between 1972 and 1974, the section titled 'Counter-Cinema and Beyond' situates the idea of counter-cinema within a longer *durée* that aims to complicate critical condescension.[39] Across these lecture notes, Wollen disassembles Godard's films directed prior to and under the aegis of the Dziga Vertov Group into 'analytic re-expositions' that articulate the metaphorical risks, ideological promises and political stakes operative throughout Godard's equations, analogies, comparisons and transpositions between global struggles for cultural revolution and cinemarxist struggles for an anti-imperialist cinema.[40]

---

37 Laura Mulvey and Peter Wollen, *Frida Kahlo and Tina Modotti* script, in Oliver Fuke (ed.), *The Films of Laura Mulvey and Peter Wollen: Scripts, Working Documents, Interpretation* (BFI Bloomsbury Publishing, 2023), 157.

38 Laura Mulvey, 'Changes: Thoughts on Myth, Narrative and Historical Experience', *Visual and Other Pleasures* (Indiana University Press, 1989), 164. First published as 'Changes' in *Discourse* 7 (Spring 1985) without the quoted sentence and republished with the relevant sentence in *History Workshop Journal* 23:1 (1987).

39 The Wollen archives at the British Film Institute contain lecture notes on *Breathless* (1960), *My Life to Live*, (1962), *Les Carabiniers* (1963), *La Chinoise* (1967) and *Weekend* (1967).

40 The term 'cinemarxism' takes seriously the implications of the graffiti-slogan-portmanteau-neologisms of CINEMAR sprayed by Anne Wiazemsky in blue letters on a white and dark blue wall and CINEMARXISM sprayed in black letters on a grey corrugated fence in the first and fourth chapters, 'The Stones Rolling' and '1 plus 1 makes 2', of *One Plus One* aka *Sympathy for the Devil* (1968). See also Jacques Rancière, 'The Red of *La Chinoise*: Godard's Politics', in Jacques Rancière, *Film Fables*, trans. Emiliano Battista (Berg, 2006), 143–57.

Wollen argues that making films that are 'primarily theoretical – i.e. they are directed towards the conscious minority'– aggravates those bourgeois critics who insist that 'work on the theory of cinema' should not be 'regarded as a political task'.[41] For Wollen, however, the significance of *Le Gai Savoir* (1968), *British Sounds* (1969) and *Wind from the East* (1969) lies in the way each film, in its struggle within and between images, sounds, colours, voices and noises, dramatises 'what has been learned theoretically'. To encounter *Le Gai Savoir* as 'a film for semiologists ... a film about signs' is to be confronted, as a theorist preoccupied with meaning and signs in cinema, with the question of what, why and how films can and should be made, with theory.[42] The 'Lecture Notes' on 'Jean-Luc Godard: *British Sounds*' make clear the extent to which the Dziga Vertov Group's aggressive reinvigoration of 'the place of film as "political work"' compelled Wollen to face the question of the relations that mediate between theoretical practice, collective practice and political work. By critically comparing LEF or the Left Front of the Arts in the Soviet Union in the 1920s with the League of Left-Wing Writers led by Lu Hsun in the Republic of China in the 1930s, Wollen sought to pose the history of Marxist collective practice as an urgent question for the 1970s. The tragic fate of Mayakovsky, who committed suicide in 1930 when Stalin turned the doctrine of 'social command' against LEF, provided a historical warning for undertaking collective work under the political directives of the Party. The impact of the Dziga Vertov Group, by contrast, stemmed from its capacity to work collectively outside and against the authority of the Parti communiste français.

These comparisons between LEF, then, and Godard, now, afford the possibility of reading the 'Lecture Notes' on Godard in dialogue with the 'Introduction to Two Mayakovsky Scenarios' of 1971. When Wollen argues that Mayakovsky was 'not just a revolutionary movie-maker but also a theorist interested in the nature of film',[43] we can hear the Godardian emphasis on the place of cinema as theoretical work as it informs the reception of LEF in early 1970s Britain.[44] To read 'Jean-Luc Godard:

41 'Jean-Luc Godard: *British Sounds*' in this volume, 61.

42 'Jean-Luc Godard: *Le Gai Savoir*' in this volume, 51.

43 'Introduction to Two Mayakovsky Scenarios' in this volume, 47.

44 'Documents from *Lef*' prepared by Richard Sherwood, 'Documents from *Novy Lef*' prepared by Ben Brewster in *Screen Reader 1 Cinema/ Ideology/ Politics* (The Society for Education in Film and Television, 1977), 256–89, 290–331. Originally published in *Screen* 12:4 (Winter 1971), 25–58, 59–102. See also Viktor Shklovsky, *Mayakovsky and his Circle*, ed. and trans. Lily Feiler (Dodd, Mead & Company, 1972) and *Coiled Verbal Spring: Devices of Lenin's Language*, ed. and intro. Sezgin Boynik (Rab-Rab Press, 2016).

Counter-Cinema' is to encounter an alternative version of 'Godard and Counter Cinema: *Vent d'Est*' (1972) that envisions the libidinal cost of collective practice exacted on Godard by the Dziga Vertov Group. The Group film, suggests Wollen, engages in the struggle to collectively produce the 'theoretical principles' required for the 'procedures of film-making'. This struggle requires Godard to 'dissolve' his subjectivity by 'subordinating' himself, as an individual filmmaker, to the principles that inform those procedures. What sustains collectivisation, then, is Godard's willingness to 'desubjectivise' himself by committing to the process of transforming theoretical preoccupations into 'trans-subjective principles' enacted by and sustained through the will of the group.

Wollen contrasts those collective principles that subordinated the subjective with the expansive, personal energies of early 1990s audiovisual culture, which he characterises as 'a force field, in which judgements matter'.[45] He uses the occasion of 'Arrows of Desire' to provide a cognitive map for the 'multi-channel' culture of the 1990s that can no longer be understood in terms of the 'central cleavage' between the 'clearly coded mainstream and avant-garde' which characterised the 1970s. The 1990s, argues Wollen, requires artists, critics and curators to navigate an 'expanded spectrum' of image-making activities, that demands, in turn, a shift in the 'categories of concern', to use B. Ruby Rich's term, for evaluating independent and experimental film and video in and beyond Britain.[46] The ambition to acknowledge this transformation of the categories of the 'political' animates the curatorial project of 'Arrows of Desire'. In Wollen's hands, the medium of the biennial becomes the vehicle for announcing an artistic 'changing of the guard' in which one generation passes the torch to another. 'Arrows of Desire' recognises the 'coming of age' of an independent avant-garde for the 1990s whose politico-poetic preoccupations would be overshadowed, one year later, by the crossover impact of Douglas Gordon's *24 Hour Psycho* (1993).

To comprehend the significance of 'Arrows of Desire', however, requires a shift away from the presupposition of intergenerational succession towards the actuality of intergenerational divergence registered in the distance between the concerns of the generation of Peter Wollen, Laura Mulvey and Ilona Halberstadt that struggled for *Screen*, the Independent Film-Makers' Association and The Other Cinema in 1977[47] and the

45 'Interview on "Arrows of Desire"', 127.

46 'Arrows of Desire', 114.

47 For the generation of Mulvey, Wollen and Halberstadt, critical events included the 'Theory of Avant-Garde Film Practice Seminar' at the London Film-Makers'

generation of Alia Syed, John Akomfrah and Robert Crusz that struggled for *Ten.8*, *Third Text* and the First National Black Art Convention at Wolverhampton Polytechnic on 28 October 1982.[48] Wollen spoke of the films and videos selected for 'Arrows of Desire' as 'a montage of politics'. This reversal of the familiar notion of the politics of montage anticipates Hito Steyerl's formulation of the 'montage of the political' in 'The Articulation of Protest' (2002). The ambition to think 'about art and politics together', argues Steyerl, is 'usually treated in the field of political theory' in which 'art often appears as its ornament'.[49] Steyerl reverses this habitual perspective to ask what happens when artistic practice makes a claim upon contemporary politics. 'What if', she asks, 'we conversely relate a reflection about a form of artistic production, namely the theory of montage, to the field of politics? In other words, how is the political field edited, and which political significance could be derived from this form of articulation?'[50]

Steyerl's questions allow us to think of Wollen's formulation as an enquiry into the ways in which montage edits the political field. Wollen develops this notion by describing the interlinked yet differentiated political concerns of the films and videos of 'Arrows of Desire'. These concerns indicate the relations between art and politics that inform Wollen's selection and programming for the Biennial. The criteria for those selections and the implications of those programmes provide the terms for the account of the discussion between Halberstadt and Wollen that concludes this essay.

Co-operative from 10 to 11 February 1976 and the International Forum on Avant Garde Film at the thirtieth Edinburgh International Film Festival from 30 August to 3 September 1976. For the generation of Syed, Akomfrah and Crusz, critical events included 'The Thin Black Line' at the ICA from 15 November 1985 to 26 January 1986, the Cultural Identities conference at the Commonwealth Institute in March 1986 and the Black Film/British Cinema conference at the ICA on 31 January 1988. See Mark Webber (ed.), *Shoot Shoot Shoot: The First Decade of the London Film-Makers Co-operative* 1966–76 (LUX, 2016), 231–3, 242–5, *Edinburgh '76 Magazine Number 1 Psycho-analysis/ Cinema/ Avant-Garde* and 'Independent Film-Making in the 70s: 1976: IFA Conference Organising Committee', in Margaret Dickinson (ed.), *Rogue Reels: Oppositional Film in Britain* (BFI, 1999), 126–36.

48 See Kobena Mercer (ed.), *ICA Documents 7: Black Film British Cinema*, 1988, *Undercut: The Magazine for London Film-Makers' Co-Op* 17 (Spring 1988) and Alice Correia (ed.), *What Is Black Art?* (Penguin Books, 2022).

49 Hito Steyerl, 'The Articulation of Protest', in *The Wretched of the Screen* (Sternberg Press, 2012), 79.

50 Ibid.

Anti-Imperialisms 1: The profane substructure for the sacred and holy superstructure

> *I proceeded to make this film, built a large studio in Kyoto, constructed a jungle labyrinth and trained the fine actors for many months to recreate this story ...*
>
> – Josef von Sternberg, *The Saga of Anatahan* (1953)

> *You could say something about the British signals operation at Akrotiri.*
>
> – Friendship in *Friendship's Death* (1987)[51]

If we study the diagrams for *Friendship's Death* (1987) together with Wollen's conversation with Simon Field published in 1987 as 'Two Weeks on Another Planet', we begin to see how the annotated shot plans indicate the making of *Friendship's Death* on the sets of the Amman hotel rooms constructed at Elstree Studios in Borehamwood, Hertfordshire. Wollen's responses enable us to undertake a speculative reading of those diagrams. The black rectangles with arrowed lines indicate the 'camera positions that have been worked out during rehearsals' by Wollen and cinematographer Witold Stok. The eleven pages of green lines ruled left and the eight pages ruled right mark out the 'light drawn on the rehearsal room floor' to 'show where the light fell'. The red lines and arrows that point towards shaded circles and reverse from empty circles indicate the positions worked out by Wollen with actors Tilda Swinton and Bill Paterson that suggest how 'their performances were choreographed to show a series of different views of the rooms'.[52]

51 On first watching *Friendship's Death* in 2016, the scene in which Friendship passes her signal intercept on to Sullivan attracted my attention for the way in which Tilda Swinton pronounces the name 'Akrotiri'. I did not know, then, of the existence of RAF Akrotiri, the surviving consequence of British colonialism, in Southern Cyprus. The name of Akrotiri, now, in 2026, indicates 'the 518 publicly available Intelligence, Surveillance and Reconnaissance flights undertaken by the Royal Air Force from RAF Akrotiri to the Occupied Palestinian Territory between 3 December 2023 and 27 March 2025'. According to the *UK Royal Air Force's Surveillance Flights over the Occupied Palestinian Territory Examined*, the report authored by the London-based research charity Action on Violence for the media organisation Declassified UK, grave concerns remain about 'the purpose of these sorties and the UK's continued sharing of intelligence with Israel within the context of its destruction of occupied Gaza, the International Court of Justice's investigation of Israel for genocide and the International Criminal Court's issuing of arrest warrants for Benjamin Netanyahu and Yoav Gallant for war crimes and crimes against humanity against the Palestinian people'.

52 See *Friendship's Death* diagrams in the plate section in this volume.

These diagrams depict the relations between camera positions, lighting direction and furniture drawn and annotated by Wollen with instructions, queries and notes in red, green, blue and black ink. By rearranging the levels of lighting so that it 'changes, according to which room you are in, whether the window is open or whether there are shutters or blinds, according to the time of day' before moving to 'paraffin lamps, to candles, to darkness',[53] it becomes possible to speculate that Wollen used *Friendship's Death* to reimagine Hitchcock's experiment with the so-called 'light organ' to artificially create 'the changing time of day' for *Rope* (1948).[54] Connecting the 'insistent visibility' of the 'filmic device(s)' of *Friendship's Death* with the argument of 'Knight's Moves' (2002) in which Wollen cites Shklovsky's assertion that 'we are reading a fiction that we cannot mistake for reality', allows us to situate *Friendship's Death* within the tradition of experimental cinema that confronts us with the reflexive awareness that 'the film has been constructed'.[55] Three levels of estrangement emerge from reading these plans together with 'Two Weeks on Another Planet' and 'Knight's Moves'. What *Friendship's Death* lays bare, first, is not merely a discrete cinematographic device. Rather, the figure of Friendship acts as the focal point on which the devices of costume, lighting and cinematography converge. Insofar as the character of Friendship operates, secondly, as a 'common protagonist' or a 'threading device', to use Shklovsky's terminology, for *Friendship's Death*, we could say that 'she' lays bare the artifice of the genre of science fiction. By inputting the fictional devices of the android and the alien – distinct conceptions with particular genealogies and specific proleptic affordances – into one 'interlocking system', *Friendship's Death* uses the tradition of the extraterrestrial to estrange the idea of the android and the fantasy of the android to unsettle the fiction of the extraterrestrial.

This has significant implications for the mode of address of *Friendship's Death*. Instead of visualising the Palestinian Resistance Movement through the normative perspectives imposed by the standardised format of television reportage or 'fast-paced, objectionably violent' Hollywood adventure films such as *Black Sunday* (1977) and *Delta Force* (1986) that depicted Palestinians as 'murderous terrorists whose only victims are innocent civilians',[56] here Amman becomes the fictional setting for a close

53 'Two Weeks on Another Planet' in this volume, 229.

54 'Knight's Moves', 153.

55 Ibid., 147.

56 Edward W. Said, 'Review of *Wedding in Galilee* and *Friendship's Death*', in *The Politics of Dispossession: The Struggle for Palestinian Self-Determination 1969–1994* (Chatto & Windus, 1994), 131. First published in *The Nation*, 28 May 1988.

encounter with an alien android whose anomalous presence alienates the monopoly of reportage and the dominance of the action film over the audiovisual narration of Palestinian existence. *Friendship's Death* recreates eight fateful days in September 1970 as an 'unclassified and unsettled' time-space that unfolds in an epistemic climate of fiction suspended between 'concept and drama'.[57] The reciprocal interlock between Friendship as an (in)existent entity and the studio settings of Amman hotel rooms during armed conflict redirects the artifice of the studio picture towards the mediality of historical memory.

From this perspective, *Friendship's Death* can be situated, thirdly, within the 'model of a studio picture' in the tradition of von Sternberg's *The Saga of Anatahan* (1953) or Fassbinder's *The Bitter Tears of Petra von Kant* (1972) which works by taking 'something that at first sight doesn't seem like a studio project, like a war' to recreate it within the studio that 'you are trapped inside'.[58] Replacing the location shoot with the studio set exposes the intermediation of historical events, media spectacles and popular memory through the manipulation of the special affects of disorientation, distantiation and scalarity. *Friendship's Death* uses these epistemic torques to transmute the 'human tragedy of Palestine', in the words of Edward W. Said, into the 'quasimystical celebration of sacrifice and elegiac immobilization'.[59]

The 'political dimension of the estrangement' created by laying bare these artistic devices enables us to see *Friendship's Death* as a project that brings together preoccupations that recur across the writings in 'Anti-Imperialisms'. Wollen's commitment to anti-imperialism appears throughout his chosen genres of political journalism, cultural criticism, filmmaking and poetry writing. Analysing these articles is less a question, however, of identifying the specific ways in which they deploy the concepts of imperialism proposed in the various Marxisms of Luxemburg, Bukharin, Lenin, Mariátegui, Mao, Nkrumah, Tito, Fanon, Althusser, Godard, Guevara, Debray, Kanafani, Cabral or Sankara, than a matter of discerning the changing continuities of an anti-imperialist reading practice capable of estranging the presuppositions that guide the received wisdoms provided by the creoles, the pidgins and the dialects of white British journalism.

The essay 'Contradiction' (1972), however, stands out from other articles for its focus on the life cycle of the historical concept of contradiction,

57 Simon Hammond, 'Knight's Moves: Peter Wollen', *New Left Review* 124 (July/August 2020), 39.

58 'Two Weeks on Another Planet', 230.

59 Said, 'Review of *Wedding in Galilee* and *Friendship's Death*', 135.

beginning with Hegel's *Science of Logic* (1816) and Marx's *A Contribution to the Critique of Political Economy* (1859) and concluding with Lenin's *Philosophical Notebooks* (1914–16) and Mao Tse-tung's *On Contradiction* (1936). The theoretical 'weapon' of contradiction, argues Wollen, enables the masses to gain traction on the 'many new and unexpected transformations' that are 'visibly shifting' in the world in 1971. Wollen invites the New Left readers of *7 Days* to use contradiction as an 'instrument' to help force global imperialism to its 'breaking point'. Wollen's phrase is quite precise; a breaking point is a moment of potential transformation that depends on the 'mutually exclusive opposites' of the Easter Offensive of the People's Army of Vietnam against the Army of the Republic of Vietnam and the United States in March 1972, the armed insurrection of the People's Liberation Front against the Bandaranaike government of the Dominion of Ceylon in April 1971 and the protest marches of the Northern Ireland Civil Rights Association against internment in Derry in January 1972.[60]

To analyse opposing forces at the point of breaking suggests that the use value of contradiction stems from its capacity to exert pressure upon its object of analysis. The impact of *Friendship's Death* lies in its reimagining of the unremembered breaking point of September 1970 through methods of defamiliarisation particular to science fiction. *Friendship's Death* looks back at the eight days leading up to the 'September War' of 1970 – when the political order of the planet turned on the balance of forces in Amman – as a crisis of dual power in which the Jordanian army that controlled the hills and the countryside moved against the Palestinian Resistance Movement in control of the refugee camps and downtown sections of the city.[61] As the 'crux' on which the stability of the whole region depended, the national existence of the Palestinians, argued Edward Said in 1971, could be said to constitute an 'extra-dimensionality' capable of exerting pressure on the interlocking forces that produced, and continues to produce, Palestinian existence as a 'virtual nexus of oppressions' simultaneously 'imperialist, racial, native and foreign'.[62] The obduracy of this nexus of oppression that detains, disperses and exiles Palestinians, with the aid of the reactionary Arab regimes of the Middle East and their

60 'Contradiction' in this volume, 221–5.

61 'Two Weeks on Another Planet', 226–32. See also Edward W. Said, 'The Palestinians: One Year since Amman', in *The Politics of Dispossession*, 27 and Alberto Toscano, 'After October, Before February: Figures of Dual Power', in Fredric Jameson, *An American Utopia: Dual Power and the Universal Army*, ed. Slavoj Zizek (Verso, 2016), 216–19.

62 Said, 'The Palestinians: One Year since Amman', 28.

powerful allies, since 1947, confronts New Left movements, then and now, with the task of building and sustaining anti-imperialist partisanship with the Palestinian struggle for self-determination.[63] Such anti-imperialism is inseparable from internationalist solidarity that requires what Fred Halliday, Wollen's colleague at *New Left Review*, called 'a political element, of *helping* those who need support, and an *instructive* element, of learning from the study of other struggles', both of which are founded, in turn 'on the *material sharing of interests* that unites the oppressed of different countries, just as the rulers of these countries share common interests which underlie their own competition'.[64]

We can see *Friendship's Death* and Michel Khleifi's *Wedding in Galilee* (1987) as film fables that widen Palestine's militant cinematic tradition through defamiliarising its commitment to documenting the largely masculine work of armed resistance.[65] Reading Wollen's brief 'Introduction to *Wedding in Galilee*' alongside Edward Said's reviews of *Friendship's Death* and *Wedding in Galilee*, it becomes clear that Khleifi's sustained attention to Palestinian women, to 'their hopes and fears, their strength', constitutes a cinematic revolution in the history of Palestinian cinema inaugurated by the documentaries of Mustafa Abu Ali made under the auspices of the Palestinian Film Unit dedicated to the witnessing of people's theatre, rallies, posters, satirical cartoons and testimonies.[66] In the 'Introduction to *Wedding in Galilee*', Wollen declares himself to be 'profoundly moved', in unexpected ways, by his encounter with Khleifi's film. The texts assembled in 'Anti-Imperialisms' suggest that this response might emerge from Wollen's concern to fashion a vocabulary complex enough to account for the intranational and international instabilities that emerge from the contradictions of semi-colonial dictatorship, colonial insurgency, postcolonial unification, counter-revolutionary repression and dual-power conflict. What comes after the repression of the Shah's regime in the semi-colony of Iran, the guerrilla rebellions against the British armed forces in the Radfan Mountains in the Federation of South Arabia, the popular uprising

63 Said, 'How to Answer Palestine's Challenge', 139.

64 Fred Halliday, *Arabia without Sultans: A Political Survey of Instability in the Arab World* (Vintage Books, 1974), 6.

65 Said, 'How to Answer Palestine's Challenge', 136.

66 Reem Shilleh and Mohanad Yaqubi, 'Reflections on Palestinian Militant Cinema', in Marco Scotini and Elizabetta Galasso (eds), *Politics of Memory: Documentary and Archive* (Archive Books, 2014), 93–103, Nadia G. Yaqub, *Palestinian Cinema in the Days of Revolution* (University of Texas Press, 2018) and Khadijeh Habashneh, *Knights of Cinema: The Story of the Palestine Film Unit*, trans. Samirah Alkassim and Nadine Fattaleh (Palgrave Macmillan, 2023).

that establishes the People's Republic of Zanzibar in the early 1960s, the formation of the United Republic of Tanganyika and Zanzibar, the anti-communist military massacre in the Republic of Indonesia in the mid 1960s, the Palestinian liberation movement assailed by the armed forces of Jordan's Hashemite monarchy in the early 1970s, the Iran-Iraq War of the 1980s and the First Gulf War between the Republic of Iraq and the United States in the early 1990s? What follows from these conflicts between tribal insurgents, occupying forces, civilian governments, authoritarian military rule, autocratic regimes and resistance movements?

Are they extensions, expansions, contractions or reversals of the struggles for independence? The local consequences of imperial frameworks that play out within the borders of the new polity? Struggles for liberation from or for the independence of the new state? The volatility of political transformation invites Wollen, under his nom de plume of Lucien Rey, to declare his allegiances in a vocabulary conscientious enough to register the necessity of partisanship. 'Iran Today – and Tomorrow?' (1965) concludes with the declaration that Iran's 'apparent somnolence hides frustrated energies which, when they are released, will sweep away the Shah and its tyranny'.[67] 'Guilt by Association' (1966) ends with the assertion that a 'new phase of the struggle has opened' for the Iranian oppressed 'to develop their own strategy of liberation'.[68] 'The Revolution in Zanzibar' (1964) closes with the contention that the 'revolution goes on, at a new level'.[69] The poem 'Iraq' (1991–1992) begins with the image of Baghdad as the 'city given no chance to heal, wounded city where brother killed brother' that evokes the Iranian Air Force strikes on Baghdad during the war between Iran and Iraq of 1980 to 1988.[70]

These conjunctural conclusions stand at the threshold between the reconstruction of past events and the prospect of political change. We can see this in 'Dossier of the Indonesian Drama' (1966) where the anti-communist massacre of 1965 perpetrated by the 'extreme right wing Muslim and Christian mobs' incited by the Indonesian military under the rule of General Suharto requires a forensic mode of narration. Benedict Anderson and Ruth McVey's initial report, *A Preliminary Analysis of the October 1, 1965, Coup in Indonesia*, popularly known as the Cornell paper, comprehensively reconstructed the attempted military coup of October 1965 to assess the chain of events that 'triggered off the political

67 'Iran Today – and Tomorrow' in this volume, 190.
68 'Guilt by Association' in this volume, 195.
69 'The Revolution in Zanzibar' in this volume, 163.
70 'Iraq' in this volume, 235.

oscillations of the last six months with some degree of detachment, the first shock past'.[71] To protect Anderson and McVey's identities from the military, Wollen, writing as Lucien Rey, undertook what Perry Anderson describes as 'an original redaction of the Cornell document entirely in his own words'.[72] Rey reassembled the events that led to the 'properly planned, organized and executed' massacre of half a million of Indonesia's Communist Party and its sympathisers. 'Dossier of the Indonesian Drama' begins by drawing attention to the 'vacuums' formed by the attempted physical obliteration of the Communist Party. It concludes by invoking the consolation of a vision that 'our' imagination will, in time, be able to 'recrystallize' in a future which cannot be glimpsed, now, in a present rendered obscure by the 'opacity' of the ruins of the Partai Komunis Indonesia.[73]

The essays on Iran that Rey wrote for *New Left Review* – 'Persia in Perspective', 'Persia in Perspective 2', 'Iran Today – and Tomorrow?' and 'Guilt by Association' – the third and fourth of which are reprinted in 'Anti-Imperialisms', allow us to grasp the political significance of Tehran for Rey. These writings emerged from time Wollen spent in Pich-e Shemiran in downtown Tehran AWOL from British military service in the winter of 1960, an experience, he reflected in a conversation with Mulvey published in 2008, that 'had an important political effect on me'.[74] Tehran brought Wollen face to face with the 'true impact of the West as imperialism brutally imposing itself and distorting Persian history'. It challenged the Eurocentric insistence on imperialism as a 'cultural and technological cornucopia voluntarily available to progressive-minded Persians'.[75] To contest the imperialist lie of cornucopia with the truth of imperialist imposition required an analysis capable of challenging imperialism's distortion of the truth with the truth of imperialism's distortion. Tehran, it could be said, taught Wollen the dialectics of anti-imperialism.

---

71 'Dossier of the Indonesian Drama' in this volume, 196.

72 For further details, see Kodwo Eshun, '"Aliens wherever they have to go": *Friendship's Death*', in Oliver Fuke (ed), *The Films of Laura Mulvey and Peter Wollen: Scripts, Working Documents, Interpretation* (Bloomsbury, British Film Institute, 2023), 274–5n7.

73 'Dossier of the Indonesian Drama', 208.

74 Laura Mulvey and Peter Wollen, 'From Cinephilia to Film Studies', in Lee Grieveson and Haidee Wasson (eds), *Inventing Film Studies* (Duke University Press, 2008), 224. Wollen made a short return visit to Tehran in 1964. See Hammond, 'Knight's Moves: Peter Wollen', 8, 13.

75 Lucien Rey, 'Persia in Perspective (Part I)', *New Left Review* I/19 (March/April 1963), 32–55, and 'Persia in Perspective (Part II)', *New Left Review* I/20 (Summer 1963), 69–98.

Between 1964 and 1965, Wollen lived in Milan and Rome where he wrote three substantive essays on the new Labour government of 1964 for *International Socialist Journal*. Those essays – 'Labour's First Spring Budget', 'The Pound Sterling' and 'The Crisis in Sterling' – the third of which is reprinted in 'Anti-Imperialisms', constitute a sustained critique of Harold Wilson's Labour Party. In these texts, Rey brought his attack on imperialism, honed in Tehran, to bear on Britain's economic crisis.[76] 'The Crisis in Sterling' (1965) offers critical insights into Rey's participation in the New Left rejection of the Parliamentary Labour Party. Rey's account of the so-called sterling crisis discloses the limitations of British Labourism. Instead of seizing on the crisis to advance the socialist transformation of the British economy, the Wilson government burdened itself with saving the 'Sterling Area' for capitalism. Labour's course of action, argues Rey, was determined, to a large extent, by the demands of the City of London, governed in its turn by the pressures of the 'world monetary system' on the British empire, to which the Labour Party, like its enemies in the Conservative and Unionist Party, pledged its allegiance:

> Just halfway through its glorious first hundred days, what is already clear is the extent to which the Labour government has capitulated to the City and to the international bankers. The stability of the world monetary system and the place of sterling in it are to have priority over any other objectives. The Sterling Area is, of course, nothing else than the modern and morbid form of the British Empire. It is the profane substructure for the sacred and holy superstructure of the Commonwealth. It is to save the Sterling Area that British troops are fighting in South Arabia and Borneo and Buccaneer fighter planes are sent to South Africa. Every time a Radfan [sic] tribesman is shot or a Singapore student imprisoned, sterling is a little safer.[77]

Rey deploys three analytical operations here. First, he devalues the obsequious terminology of the 'crisis in sterling'. Translating the polite vocabulary of the so-called Sterling Area into the frank language of the 'British Empire' enables his analysis to scale from the critique of Labour's fealty to the City of London to the indictment of the world monetary

76 Lucien Rey, 'Labour's First Spring Budget', *International Socialist Journal* 2:9 (June 1965), 364–70, and 'The Pound Sterling', *International Socialist Journal* 2:11/12 (September–December 1965), 597–609.

77 'The Crisis in Sterling' in this volume, 173. See also Halliday, *Arabia without Sultans*, 207–33.

system. Second, he challenges the orthodox journalistic separation between foreign and domestic policy by connecting the metropolitan sphere of the City to the military operations undertaken by British armed forces against Radfani tribal rebels in the Radfan mountains in the Federation of South Arabia, the decision of the Labour government to honour its arms contract with the apartheid regime of South Africa in November 1964 and the arrest and detention of students at Nanyang University in Singapore for so-called communist subversive acts in June 1964. Third, Rey demystifies the profits generated by oil operations in Aden to expose the colonial structure of the British economy.

The essay 'Aden' deciphers the euphemism of 'British interests' in the Middle East in terms of oil wealth valued at 'roughly £100 million per year to Britain's balance of payments plus column'. Rey's critique of the 'scaling-up of military operations against tribesmen' that shows 'British "decolonisation" in a cruel light' is redirected towards the colonial metropole so as to pose two fundamental questions: 'Finally, what is Britain's stake in the Middle East? Can it be dispensed with without radical social change in Britain itself?'[78] If the economy of the British state depended on the oil wealth derived from the Middle East, then the decolonisation of the Middle East entailed the transformation of the British state.

Rey's questions redirect Fanon's defamiliarising insight that Europe is 'literally the creation of the Third World' towards apprehending Britain as the creation of the Middle East.[79] Fanon's critique enables us to grasp Europe as the overdeveloped yet dependent outcome of the Third World. Such an insight, however, is not phenomenologically available to those subjected to capitalist extraction by imperialist occupation; it has to be theoretically produced by anti-colonial analysis in the face of the political and economic forces committed to preventing the remaking of Britain.

Turning to the less-known writings of Lucien Rey allows us to situate his critiques within *New Left Review*'s wider project of internationalist anti-imperialism. Rey's essays contributed to the New Left's 'very vigorous rejection' of British Labour politics. His texts participated in the challenge to the parochial culture of the British Left advanced by *New Left Review*'s translations of Sartre, Lévi-Strauss, Gramsci, Althusser, Lacan, Brecht, Benjamin, Adorno and others.[80] Notwithstanding Tom

78 'Aden' in this volume, 170.

79 Frantz Fanon, *The Wretched of the Earth*, trans. Constance Farrington (Penguin Books, 1967), 81 and Frantz Fanon, *The Wretched of the Earth*, trans. Richard Philcox (Grove Press, 2004), 58.

80 See *New Left Review* I/18 (January/February 1963). See also Mulvey and Wollen, 'From Cinephilia to Film Studies', 224.

Nairn's influential analysis of 'the stale fungus of Powellism' in 1970, the success of *New Left Review*'s commitments to Guevarist anti-imperialism and European Marxism worked, perversely, to inhibit and postpone the journal's necessary critique of the 'oppressive racial settlement' that inscribed 'all public practices from the labour market to the town hall' with the 'structured secondariness' of British segregation.[81]

Anti-Imperialisms 2: The first shock past

> *Imperialism has laid its body over the world, the head in Eastern Asia, the heart in the Middle East, its arteries reaching Africa and Latin America. Wherever you strike it, you damage it, and you serve the World Revolution.*
>
> – Ghassan Kanafani, *The 1936–39 Revolution in Palestine*[82]

> *KNIGHT: 'Independence. What nonsense. We hypnotize them. We rob them…' Pages of it. 'They should strip us naked at the airport, put jewelry in our noses, give us a blowpipe and wattle hut, and invite us to live in the jungle. Why not? That would be Africanization.' (He looks up.) Is he joking there?*
>
> – Mark Peploe, Peter Wollen and Michelangelo Antonioni, *The Passenger*[83]

Protracted national liberation struggles against settler occupations continued across three continents throughout the early and middle 1970s, and into the 1980s and 1990s; at the same time, however, fissiparous intranational conflicts fractured the body politic of newly independent nation-states. Localised, ongoing regional wars at the borders within and beyond these new states problematised the capacity of the New Left to

81 Tom Nairn, 'Enoch Powell: The New Right', *New Left Review* I/61 (May/June 1970), 3–27. See also Manifesto for New Times, 'The New Times', in Stuart Hall and Martin Jacques (eds), *New Times: The Changing Face of Politics in the 1990s* (Verso, 1990), 28, originally published as *The Manifesto for New Times*, Communist Party of Great Britain, June 1989 and subsequently amended by the Communist Party executive committee as *Manifesto for New Times: A Strategy for the 1990s* (The Communist Party in association with Lawrence and Wishart, 1990), 20 and Stuart Hall, Chas Critcher, Tony Jefferson, John Clarke and Brian Roberts, *Policing the Crisis: Mugging, the State and Law and Order* (The Macmillan Press, 1978), 339-48.

82 Ghassan Kanafani, *The 1936–39 Revolution in Palestine* (Committee for a Democratic Palestine, 1972), 65.

83 Mark Peploe, Peter Wollen and Michelangelo Antonioni, *The Passenger* (Grove Press, 1975), 78.

adjudicate upon the distinctions between liberation, unification, repression, exploitation, independence and dependency. In the early 1970s, Wollen used his experience as a political journalist who was not, crucially, an accredited member of 'the international press corps' to portray the figure of the male, white First World journalist as a vehicle for the quandaries of solidarity. The screenplay for *The Passenger* (Michelangelo Antonioni, 1975) exhibits the persona of the 'international' reporter that embodies the ethico-political predicaments compounded by the political fractures within newly independent states that exacerbate the hostilities that preceded their formation. *The Passenger* dramatises the malaise of the 'postcolonial hangover' experienced by the no-longer-leftist but not-quite-rightist white male journalist. Jack Nicholson's David Locke holds back the temptation to declare his disappointment in and distaste for his work, his life, his marriage and himself, and makes do, instead, with pursing his lips in an I-could-have-told-you-as-much moue at the Third World for not living up to his expectations. Locke finds himself in situations that demand impartiality but preclude neutrality, that require partisanship but inhibit allegiance. Each 'professional' compromise impedes and encroaches on his sense of political capacity, expressing itself in grimaces, winces and smirks of obsequiousness, obnoxiousness and politesse that speak of disaffection, disdain, despair, dissociation and disenchantment.

Suffused with what Thomas Elsaesser calls 'an almost physical sense of inconsequential action, of pointlessness and uselessness', Locke exits from the impasse of political journalism into the new identity of Robertson, the unctuous gunrunner, thereby ensnaring himself further in the efforts of 'people fighting a secret war in an obscure part of the world'.[84] Locke is a creature hoist by his own petard, the object of a script written by the Chadian state, subject to a death sentence dictated by the sinister Mr. President to which he resigns himself with the fatalism of a man exasperated by his own existence.

Locke, suggests Wollen in 'Two Weeks on Another Planet', finds himself 'confused about his own role in relation to the reality he's supposed to be reporting'; this confusion between character, conduct and occupation engenders a series of 'ontological problems' that problematise his whiteness, his authority and his masculinity.[85] If the fiction of Locke

84 Peploe, Wollen and Antonioni, *The Passenger*, 110. See also Thomas Elsaesser, 'The Pathos of Failure: American Films in the 1970s: Notes on the Unmotivated Hero' (1975) in Thomas Elsaesser, Alexander Horwath and Noel King (eds), *The Last Great Picture Show: New Hollywood Cinema in the 1970s* (Amsterdam University Press, 2004), 282.

85 'Two Weeks on Another Planet', 228.

explores ontological insecurity, and the figure of Sullivan in *Friendship's Death* enacts the epistemological improbability of the professional reporter 'confused about his own role in relation to the extra-terrestrial', we can begin thinking of autobiography as the narrative mode in which the problem of being enters into dialogue with the difficulty of knowing and the insight of not-knowing.

The adult Wollen uses autobiography in his unpublished essay 'John Wesley' to report on the childhood of Young Mr. Wollen. Autobiography, in this sense, can be understood as a practice of life-writing that takes on the dimension of 'a life's work' that may, in the words of Hannah Arendt, 'be unknown to the one who presents it'.[86] In 'John Wesley', Wollen confronts the ways in which his childhood values provided a pattern for his adult actions. Wollen's mother, Winifred, a teacher, and his Methodist minister father, Douglas, were socialist pacifists.[87] Upon retirement, Douglas Wollen became the curator of Wesley's Chapel, the 'principal shrine' of Methodism, at 49 City Road in Shoreditch, East London. Wollen, perhaps inevitably, declared himself to be 'a renegade, an unbeliever and an unrepentant sinner'.[88] Perhaps inevitably, because his upbringing in a 'devout Methodist household' guaranteed that he would eventually reject the Christianity he imbibed from his parents 'without any conscious effort on my part'.[89]

As Wollen recounts the process of reading Theodore W. Jennings's *Good News to the Poor: John Wesley's Evangelical Economics*, he records his increasing appreciation for his father's rejection of the Methodist establishment. As he comprehends his father's evangelical radicalism, he narrates the process by which he comes to understand that his repudiation of his parents' faith reenacted his father's militant Methodism. Methodism, concedes Wollen, exerted 'its influence on the ways in which

86 Roy Grundmann and Fatima Naqvi, 'The Actor as Author: An Interview with Alexander Horwath', *Cineaste* 1:3 (Summer 2025), 7.

87 Winifred Wollen can be seen in the role of Louise's mother in the tenth sequence of 'Louise's Story' in *Riddles of the Sphinx* (1977). See Kimberley Lamm, *Riddles of the Sphinx* (BFI Publishing, 2025), 77. See also Neil Genzlinger, 'Peter Wollen, Who Wrote a Film Theory Bible, Is Dead at 81', *The New York Times*, 26 December 2019. See also Ian Christie, 'Peter Wollen', *The Guardian*, 8 January 2020. Douglas Wollen recounted his life and work as a Methodist minister in Ronald Fraser's series of articles on work published in *New Left Review* and assembled in *Work Volume 2: Twenty Personal Accounts* in 1969. See 'Douglas Wollen, Methodist Minister', in Ronald Fraser, ed., *Work Volume 2: Twenty Personal Accounts* (Penguin Books and New Left Review, 1969), 240–56.

88 'John Wesley' in this volume, 238.

89 Ibid.

I rebelled, however much I might disown it'.[90] This retroactive awareness of an influence that provides the idiom for subsequent rebellions confronts Wollen with an ex post facto understanding of the structure of disavowed inheritance that points, perhaps inevitably, towards the blindness and insight of generational temporality.

This style of rebellious will reemerges in Wollen's recourse to the pseudonyms of Lucien Rey in his writing for *New Society*, *International Socialist Journal*, *New Left Review* and *7 Days* and Lee Russell for *New Left Review*. Bringing these names into relation with each other is not only a matter of drawing the attention of those familiar with the texts of Russell to the essays published under the name of Rey, necessary as that is. Rather, this act of nominative *Risorgimento* enables a closer reading of the heteronymic strategy deployed by Wollen. Doubling nomination enables Wollen to dissociate himself from himself, twice over. Each name puts a distance between each of his names, creating the impression of two writers at work in unrelated fields, both of whom turn out to be proxies protecting each from the other and Wollen from both. The pragmatic protections provided by these pseudonyms do not elucidate the reasons for their peculiar connotations of Swissness, Frenchness and Americanicity.[91] The more you look at each name, however, the more they appear to announce the arbitrariness of *all* nomination. To name oneself Lucien Rey or Lee Russell or, finally, Lewis Rodia, is to call attention to one's selves in ways that exceed the practical need for dissimulation.[92] It is as if the recurring initials of L. R. transform the necessity for subterfuge into the ludic expression of (im)proper names that flout, flaunt and fictionalise the name of the father. Those initials hold out the promise of hidden readings, covert meanings and latent analogies detectible beneath the surface of histories, geographies and vocabularies traditionally segregated from each other.

---

90 Ibid.

91 See the Trialogue in this volume, 319–41. According to Simon Hammond 'the alias was devised by NLR editor Roger Murray, intended to be of suitably ambiguous nationality, definitely not British. Lucien Goldmann and Fernando Rey may have provided subliminal inspiration.' Hammond, 'Knight's Moves: Peter Wollen', 9.

92 Wollen recalled the provenance of Lee Russell to Serge Guilbaut and Scott Watson in January 2001: 'Lee, that was one of the pen-names William Burroughs had used – right? William Lee! Russell probably came from Bertrand Russell. I don't know, something like that!' See Serge Guilbaut and Scott Watson, 'From an Interview with Peter Wollen', *Last Call* 1:3 (Spring 2002). Oliver Fuke notes the name of Lewis Rodia adopted by Wollen for his work as script doctor on the screenplay for *Melancholia* directed by Andi Engel in 1989. The name Rodia alludes to Simon Rodia, the Italian artist responsible for building Nuestro Pueblo or Watts Towers in Watts, Los Angeles, which can be seen on the front cover of Don Cherry's album *Brown Rice* in 1975. Oliver Fuke, 'Introduction', in Fuke (ed.), *The Films of Laura Mulvey and Peter Wollen*, 13n4.

'He That Shall Come' (1963), Rey's review of Vittorio Lanternari's *The Religion of the Oppressed: A Study of Modern Messianic Cults* (1963) for *New Society* concludes with a critique of analogy. Rey takes Lanternari to task for succumbing to the temptation of comparison. Lanternari, he argues, 'risks an analogy between the messianism of colonized peoples in the 19th century and the messianism of the New Testament itself'. What is more, he evades the two 'crucial points' that follow from this equivalence. First, he misattributes Christ's class position to the rural masses rather than the urban artisanate. And second, he overlooks the historical evidence that Christ's position could be seen as 'favouring the Romans'.[93] This evidence must have impressed Wollen because he returned, after eight years, to the crucial point that Christ could be seen as having supported the occupying forces of Roman imperialism. Readers that picked up a copy of the Christmas 1971 edition of *7 Days* found themselves staring at the soulful expression of Sebald Beham's *The Head of Christ Crowned with Thorns* (c. 1520), headlined by the question: 'Was Christ a Collaborator?' Wollen picks up the thread of his 1963 review by situating the petty bourgeois class position of the historical Jesus within the context of the 'national liberation struggle' of the Jewish masses against Roman imperial occupation.[94] He narrates Jewish resistance to Roman rule from 63 BC to 70 AD in the style of Gillo Pontecorvo's *The Battle of Algiers* (1966), with Jesus in the role of Ali La Pointe, except in reverse.[95] He critiques the 'fawning' Gospel writers for separating Jesus from the militant kidnappings of the Zealots, whom he compares to Uruguay's Tupamaros, and for picturing Jesus as a 'passive collaborator' with the Romans to distance him from 'the fate of the Jewish people'.[96]

Analysing the Gospels as Christian propaganda enables Wollen to rewrite the historical life of Jesus from the perspectives of three political actors: the ideologues of the Gospels, the procurators of the Roman occupation and the differentiated forces of Jewish resistance. 'Was Christ a Collaborator?' deploys a mode of militant anachronism that resembles the politicised science fiction of Peter Watkins's *Culloden* (1964) in which rebel Jacobite Highlanders speak direct to camera on the battlefields of

93 'He That Shall Come' in this volume, 158.

94 'Was Christ a Collaborator?' in this volume, 219. The article was prefaced with the following questions: 'What was the political situation in Palestine when Christ was born? What were his class origins and how did they affect his teachings? What are the unanswered questions about his role in the struggle against Rome? At this time of feasting and goodwill, it seems appropriate to ask WAS CHRIST A COLLABORATOR?'

95 Thanks to Tobi Haslett for the first part of this analogy.

96 'Was Christ a Collaborator?', 210.

Culloden Moor in 1746 before their rout by the battalions of the British royal army. This anti-imperialist perspective exposes the Bible as a partisan project that continues to shape the imagination of readers in the Christmas of 1971. Wollen opens up (the) time (of reading) as a terrain of struggle in which Christmas provides a critical opportunity for interrogating the hegemony of the Gospels. 'Was Christ a Collaborator?' succeeds, above all, in transforming the political life of historical Jesus into a matter of contemporary concern. The ideology of Christianity ceases to be a theological question; it becomes, to the surprise, surely, of those reading *7 Days*, then, as a newspaper in 1971, and now, online in 2026, a living political question that requires its readership to choose a side in the 'struggle of mutually exclusive opposites'.[97]

The Continent 1: To understand the mechanisms in which we are still caught

> *Finally,* Que Viva Mexico!, *this history of the change of cultures, presented not vertically (in years and centuries), but horizontally (as the geographical coexistence of the most diverse stages of culture) ...*
>
> – Sergei Eisenstein, *Immoral Memories: An Autobiography*[98]

> Between the Haida totem and its creator; between the Chrysler building and its creator there is an uncrossed ocean of difference and a bond.
>
> – Kenneth Lawrence Beaudoin, *Eight and a Totem Pole*[99]

The diagram for the unrealised exhibition titled 'The Continent' can be read as a curatorial argument in eleven rectangles. Wollen's line of reasoning for 'The Continent' emerges in the outlined, numbered, titled and arrowed quadrilaterals that lead from 1. INTRODUCTION TO THE MEXICAN RENASCENCE to 10. NORTHWEST COAST RENASCENCE

97 Thanks to Jessica Lehman via Jacob Bolton for the formulation of 'time as a terrain of struggle' at the 'Future Matters Symposium on Simulation and Forecasting', Centre for Research Architecture, 15–16 May 2025. *7 Days* can be read online in the archive of publications sustained by the Barry Amiel and Normal Melburn Trust, at banmarchive.org.uk/7-days.

98 Sergei M. Eisenstein, *Immoral Memories: An Autobiography*, trans. Herbert Marshall (Peter Owen, 1985), 260.

99 Kenneth Lawrence Beaudoin, *Eight and a Totem Pole*, exhibition catalogue (Gallery Neuf, 14 April–8 May 1946). From the papers of Peter Busa, quoted in Sandra Kraskin, *The Indian Space Painters: Native American Sources for American Abstract Art* (Sidney Mishkin Gallery, City University of New York, 1991), 8.

via 5. RIVERA-KAHLO CIRCLE. Each oblong contains the surnames – Barrer, Baziotes, Nevelson, Busa – and the proper names – George Biddle, Willie Seaweed, Charlie Edenshaw – of the proposed artists and the titles of significant exhibitions in chronological order – 41. MOMA Indian Art of the United States show 'with Navajo sand painter'; 46. '8 and a Totem Pole show' (Galerie Neuf); 47. The Ideographic Picture Show – to which 'The Continent' responds. Within and adjacent to rooms 1, 5 and 10, we can read annotations such as '*Research Problem* The South West and O' Keefe' or 'Thought is needed as to how present MURALS – by film, photography, sketches, documents.'[100]

These questions, observations and reminders can be read together with 'The Continent – Notes to a Sketch for an Exhibition' for what would have become 'The Continent'.[101] Why the discussions between Wollen, curator Elizabeth Sussman and then Whitney Museum of American Art director David Ross throughout 1992 and 1993 did not progress towards the opening of 'The Continent' remains unclear. Naming the final section of *Arrows of Desire* after 'The Continent', however, draws attention to the hidden labour of this ambitious, unremembered project. *Avant-textes* such as the working documents for 'The Continent' and the outline for the unrealised film 'Eisenstein in Mexico' offer a series of insights, moreover, into the 'non-corpus' of abandoned projects that illuminate, in turn, the guiding principles, operative logics and political stakes of Wollen's curatorial thought throughout the 1980s and 1990s.[102]

Whatever the reason for its non-appearance, 'The Continent' stands as the apex in Wollen's curatorial practice that begins with 'Frida Kahlo and Tina Modotti' (with Laura Mulvey) at the Whitechapel Gallery in East London in 1982 and 'V. Komar and A. Melamid' (with Mark Francis) at the Fruitmarket Gallery in Central Edinburgh in 1985, intensifies with 'Posada: Messenger of Mortality' at the Museum of Modern Art, Oxford, in 1989 and 'On the Passage of a Few People through a Rather Brief Moment in Time: The Situationist International, 1957–1972' (with Mark Francis) at the Musée National d'Art Moderne at Centre Georges Pompidou in Paris in 1989, continues with 'Arrows of Desire: The Second ICA Biennial of Independent Film and Video' at the Institute of Contemporary Arts at the Mall in Central London in 1992, 'Addressing the Century: Art and Fashion' at the Hayward Gallery in South London in

---

100 'The Continent – Sketch for an Exhibition' in the plate section of this volume.

101 'The Continent – Notes to a Sketch for an Exhibition', 299–301.

102 See Michael Witt, *Jean-Luc Godard's Unmade and Abandoned Projects* (Bloomsbury Academic, 2025), 1–17.

1998 and the North America section of 'Global Conceptualism: Points of Origin, 1950s–1980s' at the Queens Museum in New York in 1999 and concludes with 'EAST 2001', selected with Mary Kelly, at Norwich Gallery, Norwich School of Art and Design in 2001.

That Wollen did not train as an art historian, curator or film programmer suggests that his approach to exhibition making and film programming did not rest on institutional experience or disciplinary expertise as much as curatorial strategies that entailed 'critique and counter-argument and reformulation'.[103] Making exhibitions enabled Wollen to transpose his arguments from the analytic mode of theory to the intermedial ontology of film to the montagic staging of exhibitions and back again. The research conducted by Wollen and Mulvey for 'Frida Kahlo and Tina Modotti' generated two essays, the second of which appeared as the catalogue essay that provided specific sentences, in turn, for the script of *Frida Kahlo and Tina Modotti* (1983) which adapted, in a further turn, some of the exhibition's montage strategies for documentary.[104] Bringing the socialist formalism of Modotti together with the symbolic self-portraiture of Kahlo, Wollen and Mulvey's exhibition sought to juxtapose images that could 'spark off a new line of thought or argument' in the 'mind of the spectator'.[105] The goal was to confront the historical forms of the Mexican avant-garde with the political questions of the contemporary feminist avant-garde. As Wollen wrote in 'Mexico/ Women/Art' (1979), to 'think about the future of the avant-garde' means 'thinking about its past, not as antiquarianism or archaeology, but to understand the mechanisms in which we are still caught'.[106]

The ambition to expose the structures of the past that condition the meanings of the present reappears in 'Eisenstein in Mexico' (1985), Wollen's unrealised proposal for a film on Eisenstein's unfinished film *Que Viva Mexico* (1930–1932). Wollen's cine-investigation into the absent presence of *Que Viva Mexico* can be understood as a case study for the

103 Wollen, 'Afterword: Lee Russell Interviews Peter Wollen', 231.

104 'Frida Kahlo and Tina Modotti' was shown at Whitechapel Art Gallery from 26 March to 2 May 1982; Haus am Waldsee, Berlin, from 14 May to 11 July 1982; Kunstverein, Hamburg, from 29 July to 12 September 1982; Kunstverein, Hannover, from 26 September to 7 November 1982; Kulturhuset, Stockholm, from 19 November 1982 to 30 January 1983; and Grey Art Gallery, New York University, New York, from 1 March to 16 April 1983. The tour concluded at the Museo Nacional de Arte, Mexico City, from 1 June to 31 August 1983.

105 'Frida Kahlo and Tina Modotti' in this volume, 252. First published in Laura Mulvey and Peter Wollen, 'Frida Kahlo and Tina Modotti', in Mark Francis (ed.), *Frida Kahlo and Tina Modotti* (Whitechapel Art Gallery, 1982), 7–27.

106 Peter Wollen, 'Mexico/ Women/ Art', in *Readings and Writings*, 113.

revolutionary significance of so-called shadow or phantom cinema[107] that would have contrasted 'scenes from the film at sketch stage and the development of Eisenstein's pictorial ideas' with the drawings Eisenstein made in Mexico, the murals of David Alfaro Siqueiros, José Clemente Orozco and Diego Rivera and the Mexican photographs by Tina Modotti and Edward Weston from Anita Brenner's 1929 book *Idols Behind Altars*,[108] some of which were displayed at the Whitechapel with the surviving footage of *Que Viva Mexico* filmed by Eduard Tisse.

'Eisenstein in Mexico' convenes a meeting among surviving media to stage a visual study, theorised by Nicole Brenez as 'a study of the image by means of the image itself'[109] that tests the capacities of the images Eisenstein would have used, not to remake *Que Viva Mexico*, but to confront its incomplete past with its unfinished future. The contrast between its forcibly negated existence and its influential afterlife would have brought audiences face to face with the economic and political forces exercised by Eisenstein's enemies to prevent its completion. Unrealised projects such as 'Eisenstein in Mexico' require an intertemporal reading practise to dramatise their past potential future. Understanding the proleptic implications of 'The Continent' entails reading unmade and made texts together so that the preparatory proposals of 'The Continent' enter into dialogue with the catalogue essay 'Introduction to *J. G. Posada, Messenger of Mortality*' for the exhibition 'Posada: Messenger of Mortality' in 1989. Wollen concludes his essay on Posada by addressing critics and curators:

> As we look at Posada, or graffiti artists, or the Kalighat painters and Battala print-makers of Calcutta, painters from Shaba or Huxian, *haj* murals or barber-shop signs, we should take care not to deracinate the work, remove it mentally from its context. Instead, we should use the work to question

107 James Fenwick, Kieran Foster and David Eldridge (eds), *Shadow Cinema: The Historical and Production Contexts of Unmade Films* (Bloomsbury Academic, 2021), 1–16.

108 According to Patricia Albers, Anita Brenner selected seventy photographs for *Idols Behind Altars* as illustrations of 'a spiritual inventory of what Mexican life is'. See Patricia Albers, *Shadows, Fire, Snow: The Life of Tina Modotti* (University of California Press, 2002), 158.

109 Nicole Brenez, 'Harun Farocki and the Romantic Genesis of the Principle of Visual Critique', in Ehmann and Eshun (eds), *Harun Farocki: Against What?*, 129, Nicole Brenez, 'Recycling, Visual Study, Expanded Theory – Ken Jacobs, Theorist or the Long Song of the Sons', in Michele Pierson, David E. James and Paul Arthur (eds), *Optic Antics: The Cinema of Ken Jacobs* (Oxford University Press, 2011), 161–74 and Nicole Brenez, *On the Figure in General and the Body in Particular: Figurative Invention in Cinema*, trans. Ted Fendt (Anthem Press, 2023), 149–70.

> the institutions and parameters of the Western world, to question its hierarchies, its values, its motives and its cults.[110]

Wollen cites the genres of Huxian peasant painting and Shaba paintings analysed by Guy Brett in *Through Our Own Eyes: Popular Art and Modern History* (1987) to draw attention to the twentieth-century counterparts of Posada.[111] Art criticism, he argues, should not decontextualise, analogise or typologise the popular art of the Third World. It should aim, instead, at the ruthless critique of the structures, values, presuppositions and motivations, not just of the Western art world but of the Western *world* as such. These far-reaching calls for the transvaluation of Western values reappear in the proposals for 'The Continent' not in the form of Santiago patchwork pictures or the Battala printmakers of Calcutta, important as those are. Rather, 'The Continent' sought to challenge the institutions, parameters, hierarchies, motives and cults of the Western world by presenting the muralists of the Mexican Renaissance and their American acolytes alongside the mid-twentieth-century sculptures of Mungo Martin and Willie Seaweed and the sculptures of Bill Reid and Robert Davidson that launched the Northern Northwest Coast Renaissance in British Columbia during the late 1960s and the 1970s.

We can connect this wide-ranging interrogation of Western institutions to Wollen's insistence, in the essay 'Mexico/Women/Art', that 'most of the discussion of the avant-garde is both Eurocentric (or North Americanocentric) and male-centric'.[112] Wollen built upon this preliminary yet fundamental insight in his curatorial selections for the North America section of 'Global Conceptualism: Points of Origin, 1950s–1980s' at the Queens Museum of Art in New York in 1999. The undated 'Exhibition Notes' for 'Global Conceptualism: North America' reveal the extent to which Wollen exercised his curatorial prerogative to make space for works that addressed 'social issues' or fell 'outside mainstream definitions' of Conceptual Art, or both, by excluding artists whose work had already been presented at the '1965–1975: Reconsidering the Object of Art' exhibition at the Museum of Contemporary Art in Los Angeles in 1995. Of the artists proposed by Wollen, 'women artists make up 50 percent of my choices, artists with Native American or non-western backgrounds

110 'Introduction to *J.G. Posada, Messenger of Mortality*' in this volume, 292. First published as Peter Wollen, 'Introduction', in Julian Rothenstein (ed.), *J. G. Posada, Messenger of Mortality* (Redstone Press and South Bank Centre,1989), 14–23.

111 Guy Brett, *Through Our Own Eyes: Popular Art and Modern History* (New Society Publishers, 1987), 11–109, 130–54.

112 Wollen, 'Mexico/Women/Art', 110.

over a third, "collective" artists nearly one third and Canadian artists one quarter'.[113] Those percentages indicated Wollen's ambition to rewrite the canon of 'conceptual art'. The quotation marks around 'conceptual art' announced his desire to distance the North America section from the conceptualist canon by opening his section to the 'great variety of ways' in which cultural work by the People of Kitwancool in British Columbia or the Workers Art Coalition projects of Faith Ringgold or Robert Huot might be understood as 'conceptual art'.[114]

One senses the institutional pressures that constrained Wollen's curatorial objectives; comparing the exhibition notes and the actual exhibition reveals that eight of the artists already selected for '1965–1975: Reconsidering the Object of Art' reappeared in the North America section of 'Global Conceptualism' despite Wollen's declared intention to exclude them to make space for 'very little known' works of art marginalised by the art market. This discrepancy between intention and execution indicates the extent to which Wollen's ambitions exceeded and exposed the limits of American institutions throughout the 1990s.

This becomes clearer still when we compare the title of 'The Continent' with that of the recent exhibition 'Vida Americana: Mexican Muralists Remake American Art, 1925–1945' at the Whitney Museum of Modern of Art, New York, in 2020, which resembles 'The Continent' in scale, if not in scope. The title of 'Vida Americana: Mexican Muralists Remake American Art, 1925–1945' makes the argument that the Mexican muralists recreated an entity already constituted as American art. The title of 'The Continent', by contrast, questions the epistemological borders that secure the political coherence of the geographical entity designated as America. Wollen proposed a number of alternate titles and subtitles for 'The Continent'. One title, 'TOTEM AND TABU: OR HOW AMERICA

113 '1965–1975: Reconsidering the Object of Art' at the Museum of Contemporary Art in Los Angeles ran from 15 October 1995 to 4 February 1996. See 'Global Conceptualism: North America – Exhibition Notes' in this volume, p. x. Of the twenty artists in Wollen's 'suggested preliminary list', nine were white American men, ten were women, three had 'non-Western backgrounds', one had a 'Native-American' background, four were Canadian and five worked in collectives. There was a noticeable discrepancy between the initial proposal and the eventual realisation, in which eight of the twenty artists proposed in Wollen's preliminary list had works selected. Of the twenty-five artists in the North America section of the final exhibition, eleven were women, no artists 'with Native American backgrounds' were selected, four artists with 'non-Western backgrounds' were selected, five artists were Canadians and two worked in collectives. Wollen selected just two African American artists in his preliminary list while the final exhibition contained just one African American artist. See the editorial note accompanying 'Global Conceptualism: North America – Exhibition Notes' for the final artist list.

114 'Global Conceptualism', 316.

STOLE MODERN ART FROM ITSELF', announced a theft perpetrated by America on 'itself'. Should a second subtitle, Wollen asked himself, be written as 'FROM ITSELF' or 'FROM ITS OWN OTHER'? In these doubled readings of the psychic lives of 'America' and the split identities of 'Modern Art', we see Wollen rehearsing ways of dismantling the grammar of possessive individualism to make way for vocabulary that foregrounds questions of larceny, indebtedness and acknowledgement.[115]

The Continent 2: To question the institutions and parameters of the Western world

> *Always, when the words 'art' and 'artistic' are applied to my photographic work, I am disagreeably affected.*
>
> – Tina Modotti, 'On Photography'[116]

> *I think that within the black community and within the art world as well, you do become partially invisible because of having a disability ... but within the avant-garde there is a community there which you can fit into. You're not so much an outsider, there. There is a place there where you can actually discuss ideas and look at the bizarre nature of, let's say, sexuality and masculinity and race.*
>
> – Donald Rodney in *Three Songs on Pain, Light and Time* (1995)[117]

To analyse the paintings of Pollock, argues Wollen, is to 'see a debt to muralism, especially Orozco, a debt to the North American Indian heritage, and a specific debt to Siqueiros from whom he acquired a version of experiment in art, consolidated for him later by another Latin American, Matta Echaurren.'[118] These overt debts stand in for an indebtedness hidden in the 'indecipherable marks and trails' of *Mural* (1944). According to Clement Greenberg, *Mural* proved Pollock not only the 'strongest painter

115 Both subtitles allude to Freud's title *Totem und Tabu: Einige Ubereinstimmungen im Seelenleben der Wilden und der Neurotiker* and both transform the title of Serge Guilbaut's *How New York Stole the Idea of Modern Art: Abstract Expressionism, Freedom, and the Cold War*, trans. Arthur Goldhammer (University of Chicago Press, 1983). See 'The Continent – Sketch for an Exhibition' in this volume, 299.

116 Tina Modotti, 'On Photography', in *Frida Kahlo and Tina Modotti* (Whitechapel Gallery, 1982), 28.

117 Donald Rodney in Edward George and Trevor Mathison, *Three Songs on Pain, Light and Time* (Black Audio Film Collective, 1995). See also David Marriott, *Of Effacement: Blackness and Non-Being* (Stanford University Press, 2024), 323–48.

118 'The Continent – Sketch for an Exhibition' in this volume, 300.

of his generation and perhaps the greatest since Miró' but also the 'greatest painter this country had produced'.[119] Greenberg treats *Mural* as an origin myth upon which he erects the edifice he calls American modern art. If we read the outlines for 'The Continent' (1992–3) together with 'The Triumph of American Painting: "A Rotten Rebel from Russia"' (1993) and the previously untranslated 'Masculinity: Siqueiros and Pollock' (1995), we find Wollen embarking on an exposé of the structures of surrogation and suppression that support the foundation and erection of Greenberg's edifice.[120] Wollen's investigation draws on the speculative anthropology of patriarchy in *Totem and Taboo: Some Points of Agreement between the Mental Lives of Savages and Neurotics* (1913) in which Freud traces 'the sources, known and unknown, of religion, morality and society' back in time to the 'primaeval' murder of the 'primal father' by his sons; a crime whose 'most ruthless suppression', he insists, must nonetheless 'leave room for distorted surrogate impulses and for reactions resulting from them'.[121]

'Masculinity: Siqueiros and Pollock' and 'The Triumph of American Painting' rely on a close reading of *Jackson Pollock: An American Saga*, Steven Naifeh and Gregory White Smith's 934-page mythobiography. The starting point for *Mural*, according to Naifeh and Smith, lies in Pollock's 'vision' of 'a stampede'. Naifeh and Smith trace this vision to the memory of a 'mustang huntin' trip to Cain Springs Canyon in Nevada in the autumn of 1926 undertaken by the fourteen-year-old Pollock and his friends. In an interview, Robert Cooter, Pollock's teenage friend, told Naifeh and Smith, 'We killed a few. We just walked off and left them. They were beautiful horses and I can't believe we could just shoot them and walk off. But we did. And I'm ashamed of it to this day.' Naifeh and Smith treat Pollock's 'vision' as an origin myth for *Mural* in which he transforms 'a chaos of haunches and legs and unfurled manes charging across the canvas in graphic black panic' until 'the images began to change, overlap, combine and obliterate one another'.[122]

Wollen, by contrast, emphasises Pollock's 'part in the slaughter of beautiful, long maned, terrified animals' and his remorse for the 'cruel and tragic event in which he was implicated'. By 'obliterating every identifiable

---

119 Steven Naifeh and Gregory White Smith, *Jackson Pollock: An American Saga* (Clarkson N. Potter, 1989), 496, 472.

120 Peter Wollen, 'The Triumph of American Painting: "A Rotten Rebel from Russia"', in *Raiding the Icebox: Reflections on Twentieth-Century Culture* (Verso, 1993), 72–119.

121 Sigmund Freud, *Totem and Taboo, The Standard Edition of the Complete Psychological Works of Sigmund Freud*, vol. 13 (Hogarth Press, 1955), 159.

122 Naifeh and White Smith, *Jackson Pollock*, 112–13, 467–8.

image' of those wild horses until the 'last fragments of recognizable images disappeared', Pollock's marks expunge 'every trace of his shame'.[123] *Mural* enacts the suppression of a crime scene. Its trails stand in for the recognisable images of the stampede and testify, simultaneously, to the unending labour of eradication. The illegibility of each mark, each indecipherable visual neologism, speaks of 'distorted surrogate impulses' and the 'reactions resulting from them'.[124] Wollen puts *Jackson Pollock: An American Saga* on the couch to write a case study of the psychic life of *Mural* mediated through the genres of biography, art history and art criticism that uphold American art's 'suppression of all consciousness of its debt'.

Untranslated texts like 'Masculinity: Siqueiros and Pollock', unrealised exhibitions like 'The Continent' and unmade films such as *Eisenstein in Mexico* encourage a speculative analysis that mines their subjunctive potential. To do justice to the final section of 'The Continent', however, requires us to attend to the curatorial projects completed by Wollen. That entails redirecting our attention towards the afterlives of actually existing exhibitions such as 'Frida Kahlo and Tina Modotti'. Looking back on that exhibition from a twenty-year distance in 2003, Wollen assessed his role in the making of the phenomenon he named 'Fridamania'.[125] The conjunction of the opening of 'Frida Kahlo and Tina Modotti' at the Grey Art Gallery and Study Center at New York University with the publication of Hayden Herrera's *Frida: A Biography of Frida Kahlo* in 1983 'sparked off' an interest within the United States that fed into the existing enthusiasm for Kahlo in Mexico and in Europe, which, in turn, intensified the fascination with Kahlo. Wollen's term implicitly acknowledged that the success of 'Frida Kahlo and Tina Modotti' had, despite its curatorial intentions, elevated Kahlo at the expense of Modotti. It could be argued, however, that the arguments on women's art Mulvey and Wollen hoped to generate did, in fact, take place; just not in the way they intended or imagined. History, as Wollen stated, often, plays strange tricks. Instead of sparking ideas through juxtaposition, ideas on feminist aesthetics were channelled through curatorially unforeseeable artistic encounters with Kahlo's project of 'intense self-investigation and self-exposure'.[126]

In 1997, Sonia Boyce recalled her visit, as a Fine Art undergraduate in her final year at Stourbridge College of Art, to see 'Frida Kahlo and

123 'Masculinity: Siqueiros and Pollock', 306.

124 Freud, *Totem and Taboo*, 159.

125 Peter Wollen, 'Fridamania', *New Left Review* 22 (July/August 2003), 119–30. See also Laura Mulvey, *Kahlo/Modotti – 40 Years Later* (Harun Farocki Institut, 2024), 3–16.

126 Wollen, 'Mexico/ Women/ Art', 110.

Tina Modotti': 'After I saw the Whitechapel exhibition', Boyce stated, 'I finally bought a copy of the catalogue and became very "involved" with the work of Frida Kahlo. Most notably, *My Grandparents, My Parents and I.*' Sonia Boyce is one of the few artists to speak of the 'Frida Kahlo and Tina Modotti' catalogue even as she fails to mention Mulvey, Wollen or Modotti. Of the twenty-three Kahlo paintings reproduced in the Whitechapel catalogue, is it not intriguing, moreover, that the painting that preoccupied Boyce was actually unavailable for the exhibition?[127] The catalogue's reproduced image of Kahlo as a colossal youth holding 'the crimson ribbon' or the 'bloodline', to quote Hayden Herrera, that 'supports her family tree as easily as if it were the string of a prized balloon' became an object of profound contemplation for Boyce.[128] From the sustained study of the genealogical symbolism of Kahlo's *My Grandparents, My Parents and I (Family Tree)* (1936) emerged the vertiginous familial space of Boyce's *She Ain't Holdin' Them Up, She's Holdin' On (Some English Rose)* (1986).[129] It is not that Sonia Boyce actively rejected the counter-curatorial strategy of Mulvey and Wollen; rather, the encounter between the contemporary artist and the historical image operates in and through artistic agency that selectively reorders and reevaluates the past in the service of the present.

The use value of 'Frida Kahlo and Tina Modotti' persists beyond the 1980s and 1990s into the present. Upon leaving the main exhibition space of *Donald Rodney: Visceral Canker* at the Whitechapel Gallery in March 2025, visitors encountered a monitor that showed Black Audio Film Collective's *Three Songs on Pain, Light and Time* (1995)[130] in which Rodney, seated in his wheelchair in a darkened library, recalled his initial encounter with the work of Frida Kahlo through his friendship with Boyce:

> It was Sonia, Sonia Boyce, who mentioned Frida Kahlo to me. Frida Kahlo was crippled but that didn't stop her from being a highly political artist. Not just about the situation of her people but about herself, she did

127 Gilane Tawadros, *Sonia Boyce: Speaking in Tongues* (Kala Press, 1997), 11. See also Frida Kahlo, 'My Grandparents, My Parents and I (Family Tree)', in *Frida Kahlo and Tina Modotti*, 40.

128 Hayden Herrera, *Frida: The Biography of Frida Kahlo* (Bloomsbury, 2003), 8.

129 Sonia Boyce in Lizzie Carey-Thomas (ed.), *Migrations: Journey into British Art* (Tate, 2012), 114. The most striking detail in this disconcerting pastel drawing, however, is the miniature hammer and sickle at the centre of the neckline of Boyce's patterned dress that alludes to the blood red hammer and sickle emblazoned on Kahlo's plaster corset.

130 'Donald Rodney: Visceral Canker' at the Whitechapel Gallery, 12 February to 4 May 2025. *Three Songs on Pain, Light and Time* was directed by Trevor Mathison and Edward George for Black Audio Film Collective in 1995 for Arts Council England.

> very powerful work about her place within society as a woman and also she used her disability and images of her disability as a metaphor for the crippling effect of those forces on her culture.[131]

Rodney transforms the 'corporeal symbolism' of Kahlo's *The Broken Column* (1944) in ways unavailable to Boyce, Wollen or Mulvey.[132] The darkened X-ray crayoned landscape of Rodney's *Britannia Hospital III* (1987) magnifies Kahlo's metaphorically condensed political body into a monumental malediction on the malign body politic of Thatcherite Britain. Rodney and Boyce's works bear differential witness to the critical role of 'Frida Kahlo and Tina Modotti' for the artistic formation of generational consciousness in 1980s Britain. David Scott defines a generation as a 'particular social institution of time' shaped by the 'distinctive formative experiences' of a shared relation to an event.[133] Rodney and Boyce's mediated meetings with Kahlo constituted two such formative experiences that engendered structures of feeling from which these artists constituted themselves as a generation that would, in time, designate itself as the British Black Art Movement.[134]

A montage of politics

> *For us, 1981 was a profoundly empowering moment, mobilising energies and creating an optimistic mood about our capacities and abilities to challenge our conditions of existence. That feeling of empowerment came from the collective identity we constructed for ourselves as black gay men, enabling us to overcome both the marginality we experienced as black people and the individual isolation we felt as gay people.*
>
> – Kobena Mercer and Isaac Julien, *Race, Sexual Politics and Black Masculinity: A Dossier*[135]

131 Donald Rodney at 04:05 to 05:23 of *Three Songs on Pain, Light and Time.*

132 John Berger, 'Frida Kahlo', in Tom Overton (ed.), *Portraits: John Berger on Artists* (London and New York: Verso, 2017), 336.

133 David Scott, 'The Temporality of Generations: Dialogue, Tradition, Criticism', *New Literary History* 45:2 (Spring 2014), 161, 174.

134 In a communication dated 12.02.2025, John Akomfrah explained that he had visited 'Frida Kahlo and Tina Modotti'. See also Rita Keegan's self-portrait *Homage to Frida Kahlo*, 1987, in Rita Keegan, Mathew Harle and Ego Ahaiwe Sowinski (eds), *Mirror Reflecting Darkly: The Rita Keegan Archive* (Goldsmiths Press, 2021), 52.

135 Kobena Mercer and Isaac Julien, 'Race, Sexual Politics and Black Masculinity: A Dossier', in Rowena Chapman and Jonathan Rutherford (eds), *Male Order: Unwrapping Masculinity* (Lawrence and Wishart, 1988), 98.

Fatima, are we all fleeing to the land of the sailors?

– Alia Syed, *Fatima's Letter* (1992)

To think of a generation as a distinctive socio-temporal institution enables us to conclude by returning to 'Arrows of Desire', the project with which this essay begins and from which this book takes its title. At a certain point in Halberstadt and Wollen's conversation on the making of 'Arrows of Desire', the question of the relation between art and politics develops into a divergence over the direction of the left under Thatcherism that exposes the political purpose, promise and project of the Second ICA Biennial. When Halberstadt asks Wollen to elucidate the 'relation between art and politics in your selections' by explaining whether those selections 'reflect the general malaise, the fragmentation of political groups' or point towards 'a certain new optimism' for the British left, Wollen replies by pointing to the politics of AIDS of Newby's *Relax* and Marshall's *Robert Marshall*, the Green politics of Stones's *History of Disaster With Marvels*, the politics of ethnicity of Akomfrah's *A Touch of the Tar Brush* and Crusz's *Inbetween* and the politics of family values of Rimminen and Roche's *The Stain*.[136] He then acknowledges the political feelings that may inform Halberstadt's questions:

> But maybe what you're hinting at is that these are all concerns of the kind that used to be called 'single issue' politics, and that there isn't any cohesive sense here of politics as a master-narrative, as historically totalising. Or, put another way, isn't it just postmodern politics and is that real politics at all, in the traditional sense? Look at the way you couple 'fragmentation' with 'general malaise'... I don't think that the unity imposed on diverse issues by traditional left politics was necessarily a good thing. I'm happy with a montage of politics. It's more realistic.[137]

Although Wollen and Halberstadt belong to the same generation of 1968, their dialogue indicates distinct responses to the post-communist conjuncture of the early 1990s. Halberstadt's questions express a widely felt pessimism at the defeat of state socialism, the collapse of communist

136 'Interview on "Arrows of Desire"', 127.

137 Ibid. In 'Our Post-Communism: The Legacy of Karl Kautsky', Wollen argues that 'socialists should accept that it may be better to have a realistic hope, however historically distant, than a false hope based on a deformed foreshortening, however immediate and close at hand it may appear to be'. Peter Wollen, 'Our Post-Communism: The Legacy of Karl Kautsky', *New Left Review* I/202 (November/December 1993), 93.

parties, the death of 'traditional left politics' and the winning of social democracy for Thatcherite neoliberalism. It is this pessimism that prompts Halberstadt to ask whether Wollen's criteria for selection emerges from 'a certain new optimism' at the prospects of the left.

In contrast to Halberstadt's despair at the 'general malaise' of socialism, Wollen speaks from a commitment to the left politics of 1981. He questions the unspoken assumptions at work in her queries by voicing the misgivings he hears in Halberstadt's words. These concerns with AIDS or ethnicity or family values or Green politics: Don't they amount to yet more 'single issue' politics? Haven't we had enough political fragmentation? Wollen's reply probes the assumption that a single issue can neither provide the basis for a 'cohesive sense' of politics proper nor supply a 'master-narrative' that comprehends history as a totality. At this point, Wollen issues a challenge to Halberstadt: 'Look at the way you couple "fragmentation" with "general malaise".' What if the unity that 'traditional left politics' imposed on the diverse issues of AIDS or ethnicity or family values or Green politics, argues Wollen, wasn't necessarily a 'good thing', for them or anyone else? What if the political struggles around those issues experienced traditional left politics as a duty that required them to postpone their concerns in the interests of the unity of class struggle? From the perspectives of those struggles, what you call fragmentation would then feel more like pluralism. Which would not necessarily be 'a bad thing'. Or would it?

It is as if the process of selecting thirty films and videos from 'maybe three hundred' videos and films has drawn Wollen into alignment with the politics of identity of the generation born, politically speaking, in the flames of 1981, and out of alignment with the political common sense of his own generation of 1968. The implications of Wollen's realignment can be posed in oppositional terms: Do the politics of identity extend and expand the struggles undertaken in the name of Marxism? Or do they betray socialism and intensify the break-up of Marxism? To put it another way: Should Marxism serve the needs of struggles around the politics of identity? Or should those struggles work in the service of socialism?

The films and videos selected by Wollen make his position clear. 'Arrows of Desire' can be understood as a manifesto in the form of a biennial, a declaration of New Times for independent film and experimental video. Wollen's notion of the montage of politics enables him to sidestep the posture of lament invoked in the leftist vocabulary of fragmentation and malaise, to acknowledge rather than decry the proliferation of actually existing political struggles in Britain, to listen to the ways in which the 'personal political stances' of Crusz, Akomfrah, Marshall, Finch, Rimminen and Roche 'reverberate' with other videos, films or animations in ways that are neither 'single issue' nor, indeed, 'issue-led' but are, instead, differentially connected in and through struggle.

The montage of the political is the name Wollen gives to the curatorial strategy of using the differences between videos to enable connections between them. Using the medium of the film programme to curate audiovisual coalitions, Wollen focuses on the concrete concerns that revitalise the specific relations between the personal and the political. Relations that renew feminism's insistence on the personal as the political by expanding the 'politics of the personal' defined by Laura Mulvey as politics 'allotted by history and ideology, by oppression and exploitation, not subject to specialisation, expertise or education'.[138] The politics of the personal converge with the collective politics of identity described by Kobena Mercer and Isaac Julien and theorised by John Akomfrah. Such a convergence confounds 'our traditional understanding of what counts as "international" or "British"' in ways inadequately 'captured by terms such as "multi-cultural"' or 'even hybridity'.[139] Wollen's approach to 'Arrows of Desire' is guided by the ways in which the experimental films and independent videos he encounters generate categorical quandaries that contest the idea of the nation as an 'imaginary bounded entity' and problematise the vocabulary of the postcolonial. These works, simultaneously 'very cosmopolitan and very local', complicate the distinctions between the former and the latter in ways that undermine definitive understandings of either.[140] These definitional dilemmas indicate the destabilising effects engendered when the politics of the personal meets the politics of identity.

John Akomfrah draws a critical distinction between identity politics and the politics of identity that helps clarify the repercussions of this meeting. Where identity politics functions, according to Akomfrah, as a 'descriptive category' that makes '*a priori* as well as *a posteriori* assumptions about the location of identities' according to 'the "teleological arc"' implied by that category, the politics of identity, in contrast, is 'almost always "mired" in an attempt to foreground the theoretical, cultural,

---

138 Laura Mulvey, 'Introduction', *Visual and Other Pleasures* (Indiana University Press, 1989), viii.

139 Homi Bhabha, 'Signs Taken for Wonders: Questions of Ambivalence and Authority under a Tree outside Delhi, May 1817', in Henry Louis Gates, Jr. (ed.), *"Race," Writing and Difference* (University of Chicago Press, 1986), 173. First published in *Critical Inquiry* 12:1 (Autumn 1985), 154.

140 Wollen, 'The Cosmopolitan Ideal in the Arts', 193–4.

and psychoanalytic implications' entailed by 'any invocation of the term identity'.[141]

The capacity of *Fatima's Letter* or *A Touch of the Tar Brush* or *Inbetween* to frustrate assumed categories of Britishness and thwart traditional understandings of experimental film and independent video indicates the complexities to which Akomfrah alludes when he writes of the 'mire' brought about by the political invocation of the theoretical, cultural or psychoanalytic implications of identity. Wollen not only concedes these difficulties; he affirms them. When it comes to the politics of identity, Wollen speaks from the position of an initiate. When it comes to the montage of politics, however, he speaks from the perspective of an adept. The montage of the political, then, is Wollen's curatorial method for coming to terms with the dialectical and intergenerational challenges issued by the politics of identity and the politics of the personal to the politics of Marxism and the politics of socialism.

What Wollen learned in the process of curating 'Arrows of Desire' enables us to return, once more, to the montage of the political that resounds in the closing lines of the poem 'Iraq' written around the same time as 'Arrows of Desire'. Lines that register the scenes and the signs of Operation Desert Storm and Operation Epic Fury. Lines that allude to the monstrous times and malevolent spaces of the multiple genocides in which this book was edited.[142] Lines that invoke the lure and the threat of anticipatory obedience under which this book was revised. Lines received by interpretive communities that will gather, in time, around readings generated by these texts. Communities that will meet in the left of night and the dawn of dusk to confront and contest the continuities and metamorphoses of colonial occupation and imperial impunity: 'Think of the polls, the votes. Think of the flag. Think of the reeds, the body in the bag.'[143]

141 John Akomfrah, 'Memory and the Morphologies of Difference', in Scotini and Galasso (eds), *Politics of Memory*, 23–4.

142 I owe this formulation to Avi Varma, *Theory of Grasses*, PhD Thesis, Goldsmiths, University of London, 2025.

143 'Iraq', 237.

I

Counter-Cinema and Beyond

Introduction to Two Mayakovsky Scenarios

Mayakovsky was fascinated by the cinema all his life. His sister describes how, when he was a teenager, 'the cinema attracted him most of all; in one evening he was capable of sitting through three different programmes one after another. Because he was short of money, he would sometimes sneak in without paying and often get into trouble for this. But he would sacrifice everything for the cinema.' He wrote his first script in 1913, soon after he had come in contact with the Futurists for the first time. It was about a Futurist poet (Mayakovsky had a constant tendency to write himself into films as the hero) and never got made. The same year he appeared in an independent Futurist film with a number of other poets and painters and also wrote his first film criticism, which concentrated on attacking the theatre and theatre-based movies.

Mayakovsky's next wave of interest and activity in the cinema came immediately after the Revolution. In 1918 Mayakovsky wrote and starred in three movies for a private film company, Neptune. The first, an adaptation of Jack London's novel *Martin Eden*, shifted from California to Moscow with the hero changed into a Futurist poet. The second was another adaptation, of an Italian story about a delinquent who falls in love with a schoolteacher and gets killed in a gang fight defending her honour. The producers insisted on a religious ending which Mayakovsky managed to get cut out later when the industry was nationalised. The third project, *Shackled by Film*, was the most ambitious; it is the first version of *Heart of the Screen*, which is printed here, but less critical of the movie industry and more traditionally romantic in its conception of the love between the hero (an artist rather than a sign painter) and the star, played by Lily Brik.

Mayakovsky was dissatisfied with all the Neptune films. They were written and made in two weeks each and the director, Turkin, was out of sympathy with Futurism in general and Mayakovsky in particular. He showed no interest in the experiments which Mayakovsky wanted to introduce – 'Having familiarised myself with the technical side of film-making, I wrote a script on a par with our innovatory literary work. The production by Neptune made a shameful mess of it.'

Mayakovsky retreated from the cinema again after this experience, though he did write a polemical article, 'Cinema and Cinema', in 1922, attacking the capitalist cinema for which he had worked and hailing a new revolutionary cinema, which would spell the end of the old commercial spectacle, destroy aesthetics and root out emotions and plots to replace them with ideas and with reality. He worked briefly with Lunacharsky on plans to reorganise the nationalised film industry, but did no actual film work. Then in 1927 he was invited to write a number of scripts for VUFKU, the Ukrainian state film company. He wrote nine, of which only two were produced, both after re-writing by others. *Heart of the Screen* (not made) was one of this series and also *How Are You?*, which Mayakovsky himself thought the most important. He himself described its reception at Sovkino, where he read the scenario:

> The assembly listened gloomily. Comrade Yefremov rushed away (ill?) at the beginning of the second part.
>
> Afterwards, discussion. I can only report the essence of this from my own notes; unfortunately no stenographic record was made of this proud occasion, inspiring the entertainment industry to new heights.
>
> Comrade Trainin: I know of two types of scenario; one deals with the cosmos in general, the other – with man in the cosmos. The scenario we've heard conforms to neither type. To speak of it at once is difficult, but it seems clear that it passes the ideological test.
>
> Comrade Shvedchikov: Art is a reflection of reality. This scenario does not reflect reality. We don't need it. Orientate yourself to *The Tailor from Torzhok*. This is an experiment and we have to be self-supporting.
>
> Comrade Yefremov (who came back as Trainin began his speech): Never in all my life have I heard such nonsense.
>
> The Comrade Secretary looked around the circle of executives and then took the floor: The scenario will not be understood by the masses!
>
> Comrade Kuleshov (while the discussion goes on): How can you talk with such people? See what I mean? After their speeches my head will ache for two weeks!
>
> The scenario is not accepted by Sovkino.

After this experience (*How Are You?* had been through three drafts and was to have been directed by Kuleshov) Mayakovsky gave up writing for the cinema, though he intervened polemically in debate, denouncing Sovkino for underestimating the masses and considering them fit for nothing better than costume epics. He consistently supported experimental and newsreel directors, such as Esther Shub. In 1928, during his visit to Paris, he wrote Lily Brik that 'of the arts, I can stand to look at only movies – there I go every day'. One of his last projects, *Moscow is Burning*, is a kind of tribute to the cinema, which contains not only simultaneous three-screen projection, but episodes modelled directly on the cinema – Shub, Eisenstein, and American chase and slapstick movies. Cinema struck Mayakovsky as the most modern and contemporary art and he approached it as a modernist. It influenced his own work enormously: plays like *The Bath-House* and *The Bedbug* were both based on rejected scripts, his poems were influenced stylistically by his scenarios. It is a tragedy he never had the chance to influence the movies, by getting his scripts made as he wanted, even or at all. Today, when directors and critics are turning back more and more to Russian cinema of the twenties, we can learn from Mayakovsky as we can from Eisenstein or Dziga Vertov: like them he was not just a revolutionary movie-maker but also a theorist interested in the nature of film.

* * *

Introduction to translations of two film scenarios by Vladimir Mayakovsky, How Are You? *and* Heart of the Screen, *both 1927, both unrealised. Published in* Screen *12:4 (Winter 1971), a special issue on Soviet film in the 1920s.*

Jean-Luc Godard: *Le Gai Savoir*

Godard different from other experimental directors in that he began his career in the legitimate feature film & still keeps himself in that tradition. The distribution of his films, for instance, has been quite different from most other 'experimental' directors. He has used 'stars' from the mainstream commercial cinema (Léaud, Gian Maria Volonté) ... (Jane Fonda, Yves Montand) even in experimental films. But reverse direction from a Buñuel or a Clair or Warhol, Harrington, etc.

Godard b. Paris 1930. Childhood, education Switzerland. Anthropology at the Sorbonne. Visits to Cine-clubs. First writing on cinema.
Brazil – anthropology.
Return – founding *Cahiers* (Hans Lucas).
Shot his first short in 1954. (Switzerland).
Return. Wrote regularly for *Cahiers*. More short films.
Then 1959: *Breathless*.

In a certain sense, Godard was an experimental director from the start & it is difficult to place the pivotal moment when he broke with mainstream cinema.

Already in *Breathless* there are completely heterodox features: Michel & Patricia visit a cinema to see *Westbound*, but the words on the sound track are not Burt Kennedy but poetry by Aragon & Apollinaire.

A few features of his early films:
Mixing fiction with 'real life', especially in interviews.
Using chapter structure to break down narrative.
'Factual' voice-over commentary. Dubbing characters in different voices.

Use of writing: book titles, postcards, graffiti, intertitles (Belmondo).
Use of quotation – dialogue & images, including whole sequences.
Reading, recitation.
Digressions – often little mimes or street theatre plays.
Willful camera movements. (Champs-Élysées in *Breathless*) ... 360° pan, etc.
Direct address to camera (Belmondo in *Breathless*).
Film within film (false dialogue, repeated shots. Lumière: Superboy).
Use of posters, picture postcards, etc. in close-up. Comic books. (Intra/extra-diegetic.)
Repetition of images. Reverse time-flow (*Weekend*).
Rapid cutting (gunfire in *Vivre sa vie*. Cf Eisenstein, Brakhage).
Subjective camera with camera movement.
Duration: shots held unexpectedly long.
Shots of backs of characters' heads (*Vivre sa vie* beginning).
Interference with stock: printing on negative – *Carabiniers* fireworks, *Alphaville*, Science fiction short in omnibus film.
Process of production: projection (*Carabiniers*), camera in *Chinoise* & *Far From Vietnam* – NB photography & acting in *Le Petit Soldat* – sound technician in *La Chinoise*. Filmmaking in *Contempt*.

Other devices follow *Le Gai Savoir*: scratching on film, etc.

The point I want to make is that almost all the 'experimental' devices in *Le Gai Savoir* can be traced back to devices used in earlier films, often within a narrative context. But, except for *Far From Vietnam*, *Le Gai Savoir* is the first film to drop narrative altogether. (Except of an extremely schematic kind – night-long student discussions spread through the time of a university course – 1st year, 2nd year, etc.) It is also the first film to make the possibility & meaning of these devices, the explicit subject of the film. No longer secondary to the dramaturgy as stylistic features or inserts or digressions, but the content of the film itself. Reflexiveness becomes primary theme of film.

Le Gai Savoir was commissioned by French Government TV in 1967 (Policy – cf. Rossellini's *Louis XIV*) – a modern *Emile*, film on the educational system. Clearly this is the starting point, except that the film turns out to be about cinematic & political education, rather than orthodox academic education.

Three films immediately before: *La Chinoise, Far From Vietnam, Weekend.* Foolhardy act to commission the film. Not that this was later to stop London Weekend – *British Sounds*, or RAI – *Struggle in Italy*.

Began shooting in December '67. Chronology somewhat unclear. Refused by French TV, re-edited during & after May 1968. Sold back to Godard. Finally released June 69 at the Berlin Festival.
Presumably studio sequences earliest. Inserts & additional sound track later.

Le Gai Savoir has to be seen in two ways.

First, three unities. Theory & practice.
Politics & cinema.
Content & form.
Each of these is seen not simply as combining automatically, but as combining only with difficulty (with struggle). It is true that all practice contains an implicit theory, all cinema contains an implicit politics, all form contains an implicit content & vice versa – but Godard wanted to make these relations explicit, i.e. to find the correct cinema for his kind of politics, etc. Revolution in one must mean a revolution in the other. A new kind of discourse must be new both in form/content, politics/cinema, theory/practice.

2. Necessity of going back to zero. To find the correct relationships (synthesis) it was necessary to go back to the beginning (analysis). NB this is in itself a difficult process – a process of *dissolution*, as he says in the film. It is not simply starting again. In fact the film is not itself a step on the new path, but the process of struggle to arrive back at the zero point, at nothing.

The process of dissolution, of analysis, is one of separating the basic elements of cinema & experimenting with their re-combination. The whole film is a struggle to find these elements & to try ways of combining them.

Because film is an audiovisual medium, these elements comprise both images & sounds. Also time, movement, and *emotion*.

Godard said *Le Gai Savoir* is a film for semiologists. It is a film about signs, about language (verbal & cinematic). In order to find a new voice, it is first necessary to understand how signs work.

A. Verbal language. Sound track

Different elements: dialogue (direct speech, indirect speech, recitation).
singing, music.
voice off, clear & jammed. Coherent & incoherent/ fragmentary.
noises-off (gunfire, applause, etc.).
All these elements are combined. Numerous levels on the sound track. The basic dialogue is constantly accompanied by reminders of the political world outside, especially May '68, through the radio voice ... and reminded of censorship & suppression of discourse by jamming.

Silence is also used as a feature of construction – both in the minute's silence for Black Panthers and in the use of silence to convey the existence of censorship. External uses of silence. Internal use: part of meditation on relationship between sound track & image track.
Other devices on the sound track – use of tape playback in scene with old man, who begins a dialogue with himself.
Use of pantomime – the scenes where he speaks from behind her & vice versa: again a comment on censorship (as well as subjectivity).
[We are all German Jews. Attempts to repeat exact sound of Anne & Michel – Pentagon.]
[Demented strip-cartoons.]

Imperialist film section: throttles her to make her repeat his sound.

Also decomposition of language itself:
puns (lost or travestied on the subtitles).
breakdown of words into constituent parts/phonemes television, cinema, etc. – like trans-sense poetry.
anagrams – Afranics, or through the use of underlined letters in graffiti.
neologisms – Mi so to di man. Her whole nonsense sequence in front of the Incredible Hulk.

word associations, with the child & the old man
consecutive words: a blow is an irrefutable philosophical argument (Hegel).
alphabet primer: words the letters stand for

There is a whole analogy running through the film between money – a sign of labour/value – and words. Financial crisis/linguistic crisis. Banks lending money, dictionaries lending words. Means of exchange – need for a new system of exchange: economics & semiology.

Intermediary between sound track & image track is writing: increasingly important feature of Godard's films. (Cf. *Weekend*) Listening/reading/seeing.

Elements of *Cinétracts*, made in '68. Film posters made of superimposition of news photographs with handwritten slogans. Influence of Chinese large-character posters (cultural revolution). Acrostics & ideograms: attempt to fabricate ideograms within a photographic/alphabetic culture.

These ideographic images contain puns & form independent sequences. NB too use of print as background allusion – words written in handwriting on book covers & pages of print. Sometimes with deletions & additions, to alter the sense.

B. Images

Film goes back to the first image: Niépce's first photograph of rooftop through a window very blurred. (Silent – first image silent. Photography before recording – cf. *Letter To Jane*).

Use of stills as illustration, both in this instance & for example John Ford to illustrate Imperialist Cinema. Allen Ginsberg, Biafran children, etc.

[SITUATIONISM MAOISM]
[Continuity *Made in USA*.]

Basically three kinds of footage:
Studio shots (Léaud/Berto).
Documentary of crowds in the street.

Inserts – stills. (With or without writing.)
*Image track equivalent of silence: blank screen.

*Inserts come from an amazing variety of different kinds of source & visual codes: comic books, cartoons, ads, fashion magazines, pornographic magazines, news photographs, portrait photographs, reproductions of works of art (Vermeer, etc.), posters (Dylan, Esso Tiger), book covers, newsprint, handwriting (Che), diagrams, flags, maps.

NB also collage elements – superimposition of a Dubuffet on a photograph, giant razor blade (like an Oldenburg monument).
Slogans & messages superimposed. NB too tinting, esp. red as in red pens, red flag flying over the Sorbonne. [CINÉ-TRACTS]
Stills function as illustrations (direct or ironic), intertitles & independent sequences.

The other kind of insert is documentary footage – difficult to decide whether it is specific or universal. In fact this ambiguity itself seems to express Who are the crowd – i.e. who are the public (cinematically), who are the masses (politically)?
Other features of the image track – destruction of the frame, as when Léaud & Berto crouch down beneath it, cigarette smoke comes up. Look offscreen, as though at film we are watching.

Cinematic references mostly come in the dialogue: *Great Dictator*, *Lola Montès* ... Bertolucci, Straub, Glauber Rocha contrasted with Bresson, Bergman, Antonioni.

Clapperboard.

But NB foreshadowing *Weekend*, different kinds of film – sometimes exact, like the experimental film sequence with the animated graphics; sometimes simply an allusion or representation, like psychological or imperialist film.

Also, of course, allusions to TV ... both the representation of two TV sets, large & small, with camera moving in to the TV image, and numerous hostile observations on sound track, including talking about & to the audience.

C. Sound-image relationships

Increasing preoccupation of Godard's. Image and sound continuities different & often contradictory.

Most clear-cut example: alternation of silence & blank screen.
Blank screen particularly important: Godard's wish to interrupt the flow of images. Ideological effect of TV based on uninterrupted presentation, without either silence or blankness. No time for reflection.

Priority of sound track – image in itself meaningless, given its content by the words which accompany it. Role of images in advertising, consumer society & political propaganda part of an integrated process. First task of de-construction, dismantling of this repressive/ideological discourse is separation of words & images so that each can be considered separately.

As well as separating them out, contradictions. Colour sequence.
Berto describing herself: discussion on obviousness – when is it obvious people are lying. When they are talking about what we can't see? When they are talking about what we can see but deceiving us about it by their verbal description.
Vice versa, can we deceive people through images, though we speak the right words?

NB this leads to another use of blank screen by Godard – to indicate that he has been unable to find the right images. Often blank screen foreshadows the moment when it will be filled by images of the process of production, for instance (*Struggle in Italy*).

Finally a few other points about the dramaturgy (the acting so to speak).
Playing representative symbolic characters: Emile & Patricia (Lumumba, Cultural Revolution, *Breathless*) – trend which began with *Carabiniers* (Brecht, *Ubu*).
Whole pattern of repetitions & variations of posture & direction as well as allusions based on puns (nuclear umbrella, consciousness reflector, cycles & topological surfaces, etc.). Symbolic use of dress: tricolour.
Also one Maya Deren-like shot in which they repeat themselves.

Theatre is reduced to the most schematic form possible – in characterisation & gesture & relation to camera. Yet at the same time the film is also a kind of love story, since language (verbal & cinematic) involves emotion as well as concepts. Long lyrical passages & sentimental moments (stroking hair, etc.). Still something of spontaneity within the schematic framework.

Conclusion: Godard differs from most of the American experimental cinema we have seen, in that the content of his films is not simply reflexive. He wants his films to be revolutionary both in their ideas about the cinema & in the ideas they express through the cinema. In this way he is closer to Buñuel/Dalí or Vertov (as he acknowledges). Although he uses almost every device used by Americans (& devices they don't use) he does this not simply to foreground the process of production or the process of signification in itself, but as part of a struggle against another cinema, another reality – not subjective, but objective. Cinema is not an end in itself, but a necessary detour.

* * *

Lecture notes, c. 1972–1974. Square brackets indicate handwritten additions to typewritten notes. From a course at Northwestern University, Illinois, where Wollen taught in the Department of Radio, Television and Film in 1972–73 and 1973–74 at the invitation of Paddy Whannel. Previously unpublished.

The lecture notes reproduced in this book are taken from a course that also includes an introduction to Godard and lectures on Breathless, Vivre sa vie, Les Carabiniers, La Chinoise, *and* Week-end.

Jean-Luc Godard: *British Sounds*

The film obviously ought to be called *British Sounds*, because this expresses Godard's purpose (Worker's Sounds, Student Sounds, Revolutionary Sounds, etc.). American title distorted (cf. *Her/My Life to Live*).

Made in Britain in February 1969 for London Weekend TV. This was a commercial TV company, which had the franchise for the London commercial channel over the weekend. 'Any Godard film is an event, certain to arouse controversy', or words to that effect. In reality, the project was the brain-child of Tony Garnett & his group, who had made their reputation doing socially-relevant plays on the BBC, then switched to Weekend as part of the packaging over the grant of the franchise – to give Weekend an added cultural respectability in its application to the ITA [Independent Television Authority]. In fact, they did not last long at Weekend and the main focus of their activities switched to movies as Kestrel productions, especially Ken Loach: *Poor Cow*, *Kes*, *Family Life* (*Wednesday's Child*). Garnett & others were/are Marxists, but of a different complexion from Godard.

Godard had already had *Le Gai Savoir* banned by French TV, but the British companies prided themselves on being more liberal than the (Gaullist) French. Nevertheless *British Sounds* wasn't shown. Instead they adopted a curious compromise. They showed the film to an invited audience (film critics, TV people, motor industry workers, students, etc.) & then filmed the discussion of the film, with a few clips from it as illustration, like on a talk show.

Ironically – almost everybody agreed the film would be unintelligible to the workers, etc., but this didn't stop the TV company from banning it.

Since making *Weekend*, a lot had happened in Godard's career. Early in '68 he had made *Le Gai Savoir* which prophetically focused on the character of education in France (capitalist system in general).

Then May '68, Godard worked on *Cinétracts*. Impetus from Chris Marker, collaboration with the Poster Workshops (collection at Northwestern). Collective/anonymous works, but Godard's *Cinétracts* are easy to recognise. Stills – mostly of the CRS (special riot police), intercut with graffiti, acrostics, etc. Equivalent of leaflets protesting police brutality.

Also shot *A Film Like the Others* about this time, which I haven't seen, but has a minimum of camera movement & editing/a maximum of political discussion.

Then went to England (late summer, after de Gaulle's reconsolidation of power) to make *One Plus One*, with the Rolling Stones, taking up the limits of 'youth revolution' from *Weekend* & with a strong black politics angle, built around Frankie Dymon. Then to America where he made *1 AM* with Leacock & Pennebaker, before returning to Britain. After *British Sounds* he went to Italy. *Pravda* in Czechoslovakia. I am not sure I am right, but I think his latest film, *Tout va bien*, was the first film made in France since May '68. If so, his period of artistic-cinematic exile was simultaneously a period of real exile.

May '68 had a decisive impact on Godard (October Revolution on Eisenstein). Intensely politicising experience but also, like all defeats, with a de-politicising aspect as well, pushing him towards a more or less desperate 'gauchisme'/ultra-leftism: to which he was probably temperamentally disposed anyway. In January '69, asked whether he had broken with Romanticism, he replied: 'Maybe not. Not that much. Romanticism? Misdirected, maybe.'

Before confronting the political questions, I want to compare the film with *Vivre sa vie*, made only seven years before. Great changes, but also great similarities. (In making criticisms of Godard, I think people ought to bear in mind the timescale of Godard's work; from *Vivre sa vie* to *British Sounds* is seven years; from *British Sounds* another seven years on takes us to 1976. Seven years isn't a long time in a director's work; Godard is still only in his forties. Patterns of continuity & discontinuity. Difficulty of prediction. Going through a second autodidactic period – the first was spent in the Cinémathèque and in the pages of *Cahiers*, the second in the Dziga Vertov collective and films.)

a. Commentary, voice-off. The prostitution sequences, read from Marcel Sacotte's book, which compose the sound track of Chapter 8. Obviously this has extended enormously in *British Sounds*, so there is an entirely independent sound track for most of the film. In fact there are a number of variations in relationship between sound & image.

1. The British Motor Corporation plant. Like *Vivre sa vie*, tracking shot with commentary over.
2. The woman sequence. Same, with some variations. Multiple sound track in which the man's voice (why?) drowns out the woman's voice.
3. BMC shop stewards. Direct sounds, but with camera *off* speaker.
4. TV speech. Sound, but parody. [With *sotto voce* (like *La Chinoise*).] Students. Normal sound-image relationship.

'This film is a sound which is opposing another sound: it is a revolutionary sound which is opposing a reactionary sound. But inside the film itself, there on the film-stock, this is expressed in the dialectics of the struggle between images and sounds.'

Godard seemed to work on the principle that sounds were more important than images; that they were less liable to expropriation or manipulation. (Adding a sound track/adding an image track.) [How to build an image. Pseudo-nature vs. construction (Eisenstein etc.).]

b. Absence of fiction, documentary 'real-life' material. In *British Sounds*, this is the majority of the film, whereas in *Vivre sa vie* there is the prostitution sequence, which is false-documentary (something like the woman in *British Sounds*) and the Brice Parain discussion, which is enlarged into the shop stewards discussion. Then there are the long sequences of the BMC plant & the Essex University Campus. (Shot in different styles. BMC plant – long tracking shot – *Weekend*, cars, etc. – & Essex more a vérité style.)

But this turn to reality is coupled with a new critique of photography, as an invention of the bourgeoisie, an essential element in the construction of the mass culture which goes with the single world market.

c. Chapter Structure. *British Sounds* maintains the same kind of chapter structure as *Vivre sa vie*, though this is not signaled quite so explicitly. As I said about *Vivre sa vie*, the film is showing a series of events, rather than telling a story. Perhaps now, it is a series of images, rather than a series of events.

In *British Sounds*, the different chapters are clearly contrasted with each other. Students vs. workers. Both vs. revolutionaries (which remains symbolic – the *Wind from the East*). The TV speech vs. the shop stewards discussion. As in *One Plus One*, Godard does not attempt to sum everything up into a single whole. Recognition of the fragmentary & contradictory nature of the film itself. He protested the Stones 'being emphasised over all the others in the film'. 'It is unfair, not from a personal point of view, but from a political point of view, unfair to the Black people.' 1 + 1 = ? ....

d. Digressions. By *British Sounds*, it is really impossible to say what a digression is and isn't. Is the child's history lesson a digression, because it never corresponds to anything precise in the image? Or is it a dimension of the film which exists only on the sound track? The dissolution of the priority of the narrative has reached the point where the film is seen as a system of separate but complementary-contradictory discourses.

e. Inter-titles. These began with the chapter-headings in *Vivre sa vie*, expanded a lot in *Les Carabiniers* (the postcards) and still further in *La Chinoise* – the running intertitles with one word added each time. In *British Sounds*, you just get the single word or phrase & you have to read it at intervals, disjunctively – 'a good comrade is more eager to go where the difficulties are greatest, etc.' – with some words (such as eager) repeated several times.

The intertitles have become graffiti – starting from Garce in *Vivre sa vie*, then exploding in *Pierrot le Fou* – OAS is written on the wall, Belmondo's notebook. New impulse in the *Cinétract* (need for compression). Ford usa = for- us-. (In *One Plus One* you see them being written on the wall with a paint spray, as in May '68. Again some element of prophesy in Godard.)

f. Other breaks in continuity. In *Vivre sa vie* commented on repeated shot of Joan of Arc, & there are a number of repeated shots in *British Sounds*, including repetition from different angle of girl painting poster: Why Are We Here? (very Godardian slogan) intercut with silent colour shots of workers, blacks, etc.

NB also switch into b/w for the TV sequence. NB the use of Picasso's *Guernica* as a pictorial quote & the various revolutionary songs (*Ciao, Bella Ciao*, etc.) as musical quotes. Cut to Chinese poster like in *La Chinoise*.

The quotations & aphorisms, maxims, too are centripetal as in *La Chinoise*; reflections on the theory of cinema on the sound track, especially in the People's Poster Brigade sequence (another echo of May).

g. Estrangement effects. The most curious of these are obviously the separation of voice & image in the shop steward's discussion, and also, especially, the Women's Liberation sequence – both the deliberate over-emphasis of woman-as-image and also the actress's repetition of the commentary over the telephone: She says ?we or I ... etc.

NB too, the way the man's voice drowns out the woman's.

h. Foregrounding of camera-movements. Talking about *Vivre sa vie* I mentioned the 'very deliberate and noticeable camera movements' – e.g. the formal silhouettes at the beginning, the sequence in the record-shop. Even more explicit in *British Sounds*.

Strangely, only one point when there is direct address to camera (leaving aside the TV sequence proper) is in one of the insertions, of workers who notice the camera & wave to it.

i. Didacticism vs. entertainment. Very strong – explicit in the child's history lesson, implicit in the whole approach to cinema. Little Red Book's influence as well. This didacticism has two aspects. First, there is a political didacticism – rather elementary, and indeed – as suggested by the child's lesson – so elementary as to be at a childish level.

Secondly there is a cinematic didacticism – teaching/learning the science of images. 'A science of the image exists, comrades. Let us start to construct it. Here are a few starting points for reference. Materialism/dialectics. Documentary/fiction ... etc...' This didacticism is elementary in a different, purer sense: trying to discover what has been invented – the elements of cinema. (Eisenstein).

I would like to go on now to say something about the politics of *British Sounds* & late Godard, taking up what was begun – maybe a little prematurely – talking about *La Chinoise*. I don't mean the politics in the sense of manifest content, which is both schematic & eclectic, but in the sense of the place of film as 'political work'.

6 heads: the question of propaganda, the 'social command', the legacy of Stalinism, the cultural revolution, the role of intellectuals, collective work (concept of a front), revolutionising one's own work practice...

I am not really trying to expound Godard's own point of view, or my own – I am trying to pose some classical problems of Marxism in such a way that you can see how Godard relates to them. The general discourse within which Godard carries on his specific discourse – a Marxist-Leninist discourse.

1. Propaganda. Classical Marxist theory, beginning with Plekhanov, the founder of Russian Marxism & endorsed by Lenin, etc., sees three distinct levels of work in literature the arts:
   Theory, propaganda, agitation.

   Theory is directed towards cadres, what Godard calls the 'conscious minority' & it is at a high level of abstraction/conceptual elaboration. (Scientific work, production of concepts.) In Lenin's words – no revolutionary theory, no revolutionary practice. Engagement in theoretical disputes which were fundamentally inner-party disputes or at least directed towards the conscious minority.

   Propaganda is directed towards the masses in general – as well as a party theoretical magazine, there are broad general newspapers, etc., which directed outside, towards the general public. Convey political education, instruction on the general line of the party, expose material, etc.

   Agitation is directed towards a specific situation, here & now, involving a specific section of the masses and it is designed to promote immediate action: posters, leaflets, etc.

   A lot of the complaints against Godard are that his films are no good for agitation, (though cf. *Cinétracts*) or for propaganda. In reality, it is clear that his films from '68 to the present have been primarily theoretical – i.e. they are directed towards the conscious minority. This is quite explicit in the statement about *Wind from the East*.

   On the other hand, they have a lot of propaganda & even agitational material in them & I think this leads to confusions – in effect, this material is more like the story in the early films & is disrupted in a similar way. It is wrong to look simply for the 'content' of the movie in Godard, because that isn't what it's about.

   The main point is that the relation between theory, propaganda & agitation is complex. If you look at Marx or Lenin (or Mao) you find some works which are more or less purely theoretical (*Capital*, *Materialism & Empirio-Criticism*, *On Contradiction*), others which are mixed (*Imperialism*), are propaganda (*The Communist Manifesto*), are agitation, etc.

   There is nothing peculiar about Godard, except insofar as work on the theory of cinema is not regarded as a political task. He obviously thinks it is.

2. 'Social command'. Godard has all along resisted the idea of the 'social command'. This began with Mayakovsky & LEF – artist following party directives – and was incorporated, in a kind of parody form, into Zhdanov's 'socialist realist' platform of the thirties – party-mindedness, drawing on Lenin's 1905 text on *Party Organisation & Party Literature*.

   It has been Godard's position throughout that artistic work should be politicised not simply by following party directives (the Stalinist model) but by constant learning/doing (The important thing is to be good at learning) and by collective work, based on what has been learnt theoretically. Only after a certain amount of knowledge has been accumulated is it right to move on from theoretical work (for a minority) to propaganda work (for the masses). In the case of cinema, theoretical work is at the front, because nothing much has been done, except by Eisenstein, Vertov, etc.

3. Legacy of Stalinism. Obviously the example of what happened to the artists of the twenties is in the forefront of Godard's mind. The doctrine of the 'social command' turned against its originators. The Mosfilm = Hollywood equation is recurrent in Godard's mind. You see this same strand of thought in a different (pre-political) form in the story of the *Man On The Moon* in *Pierrot*. Evidently China turns into the contrasting third factor for Godard. He was very impressed by the complete cessation of film production during the Cultural Revolution, the decision to break with Russian-type films & start afresh.

   A film like *Pravda*, made in Czechoslovakia, is very similar to *British Sounds*, except that it is about betrayal & the contrast between words & deeds. (The three voices: the imperialist, the voice of the boss – the revisionist – the deformed, betrayed voice of the masses – the militant film, 'The screen is simply a blackboard or wall in a classroom that presents the concrete analysis of a concrete situation.' Cf. *East Wind*.)

   Revisionism = Moscow Communism, the French Communist Party, etc.

4. The Cultural Revolution. Lenin-Mao. (Talked about apropos of *La Chinoise*.) Three points of great important. The rejection of the past, i.e. Moscow-Hollywood – the idea that a cultural revolution is as important as a political revolution (or nearly so) & the connection with Godard's analysis of Stalinism – the idea that the people must act on their own initiative & the party must be dismantled – 'It is right to rebel' applies equally to the party bureaucracy – Bombard Headquarters!

(Of course the Chinese now point to leftist excesses during the Cultural Revolution, especially in the field of foreign policy.)

5. The Role of Intellectuals. After May, Godard had a crisis about the character of the intellectual & in *One Plus One* he actually said a revolutionary intellectual must cease to be an intellectual in order to be a revolutionary. Later he modified this to 'give up being an intellectual in the way that the bourgeois conceives of an intellectual'.

   The role of the intellectual in politics has always been a difficult problem. Lenin's view was that anybody – whether of student or worker origin – who had mastered a certain level of theoretical work automatically became an intellectual. I.e. party cadre = intellectual. He thought that the resistance of the bourgeois intelligentsia to Marxism & the attraction of Marxism to the masses, would be reflected in the composition of the party intelligentsia. In reality, there were many difficulties & to the end of his life he was preoccupied by the problem of the 'limited horizons' of proletariat vs. instability, opportunism, etc. of intellectuals.

   Obviously there is a sense in which Godard is a typical unsteady & sloganeering intellectual, but in the absence of a mass proletarian revolutionary movement, it is difficult to see how this could be otherwise.

6. Finally, there is the question of the front. Godard sees himself as part of a revolutionary front, rather than a unified party, within which there are contradictions which must be open rather than suppressed & handled via criticism, self-criticism, collective discussion, etc. (Despite Godard's arrogance, he has always been willing to criticise himself & admit mistakes.)

   Moreover, in Godard's view, a front should not simply be a façade for some other organisation which manipulates it, like a lot of Communist Party fronts. Model: Lu Hsun in China in the thirties.

I have tried to sketch in some of the context in which Godard has worked out his political position on filmmaking, which I think is quite coherent & sustained. Naturally, this doesn't mean it is right, but it does mean it has to be respected.

* * *

Lecture notes, c. 1972–1974. See previous bibliographic note to 'Jean-Luc Godard: Le Gai Savoir'. *Previously unpublished.*

Jean-Luc Godard: *Wind from the East*

[Struggle_________a film about struggle, a struggle about film
Unity of theory & practice   Self-criticism / transformation]

First, I should point out that due to a technical error, one sequence got cut out in projection: Quite a crucial sequence.

Shot of film crew (sound man, camera, etc.).
Voice-over: In ten seconds you will be looking at a character on a bourgeois film screen. He is a Western character from a psychological drama, a thriller, a historical film...
Actor talks directly to camera.
VO: He says he is in the dark... He says there's an old man sitting in the fifth row... There's a good-looking girl at the back... He asks her to join him on the screen... A wonderful summer day... Sunshine... Truth.
Camera zooms back to show waterfall, pool, people diving & swimming – a pastoral idyll.
Then back to sound engineer.
Struggle against bourgeois concept of representation. Wrest the means of production from the hands of the dominant ideology. That is the most we can do. The most is to be able to say: This image is red.
Red screen.
then
Learn... education... etc.

* * *

Made in May '69, released 1970.
Original idea (attributed to Cohn-Bendit) was to transpose the events of May '68 into a Western. I.e. a kind of allegory, involving typical Western characters – the banker, the sheriff, the goldmine workers, the schoolteacher, etc., & a typical Western town as Paris.

This project still forms the skeleton of the movie, which becomes a kind of extended & inter-connected interrogation of both the May events & the Western genre. In effect, this implies a process of self-interrogation on the political task of making this film – *Wind From The East* – which is itself interrogated, recapitulated, transformed on screen.

I thought the best way of going about talking about *Wind From The East* was simply to go through the film offering some notes & observations on each sequence – rather than trying to offer some kind of unified explanation. This might be best, if only because of the overload of information there is in the film. A kind of analytic re-exposition.

1. Opening sequence:
Image of couple in chains. Sequence from the 'Western' – costume fiction. Its function in the narrative is more or less unintelligible. Instead, by the absence of activity, it throws us back on to *the sound track*. This also comes from the Western. It is a mixture of words which might come from a Western with contemporary political comment, Alcoa, etc., juxtaposed with Dodge City. As in *One Plus One* – a kind of composite text, in which parody & allegory are combined, the allegory at the surface.

This leads on to the question of *lies & stammering*. Cf. the end of *British Sounds*: the voice of the imperialist & the voice of the revisionist. In *Wind From The East*, the revolutionary voice is a stammering voice.

Uncertain, fragmentary, self-questioning – in a sense, this is the typical Godardian voice, searching for the truth, struggling to communicate. A kind of patchwork of phrases & questions, contrasted with the fluency & self-assurance of the lying discourse.

Godard begins with a question: 'What Is To Be Done?' Again, a typical Godardian question: *Why? What are we doing here?* Where are we going? Etc. This time with a political resonance. *What Is To Be Done?* is the name of one of the fundamental texts of Lenin, written in 1902 during the internal struggles within the Russian Social Democratic Party. It is the text which charts out the course of the future Bolshevik section of the RSDP, forerunner of the Bolshevik Party: CPSU (B).

Godard interprets the question in the sense of starting from scratch, going back to the beginning (cf. *British Sounds*) – not choosing a path, but *making* a path. [Reinventing the cinema.]

He directs the question to himself as a Leninist filmmaker. What kind of film should a militant filmmaker make?

The film now switches from the Western/meta-Western to an inquiry into the history of political cinema.

Image-track: actors making up. This is familiar territory – the distrust of fiction, the servility of actors – it goes right back to *The Little Soldier*.

On the sound track the anti-fictional polemic is presented through Vertov & against Eisenstein (reflects debates & polemics in LEF. Mayakovsky).

Sound track attacks Stalin. The conjunction of Maoism with anti-Stalinism, as I've suggested before, is important to Godard. It will explain the conflict over Stalin & Mao which comes later.

There is also an attack on *Pontecorvo* [Algiers/Africa: White Christians], which also prefigures later sequences.

Acting/lying. The sequence of actors making-up is intercut with a shot of the trade union official (the revisionist) reading from a paperback by Waldeck Rochet, the leader of the French Communist Party. I.e. the party is falsely acting the part of being Marxist & revolutionary, posing as revolutionary.

I.e. imperialists – liars.
Revisionists = liars + actors. (Mask, disguise.)

Another current: the mask of the Indian (reminds us of the end of *Pierrot*) – primary colours, contrasted with the mask of the girl with the simpering smile. What does this mean?

Control over camera connected with control over wealth. Shot of the ruling-class girl eating (with the cavalryman), then filming. Both these shots are repeated later in the film.

The film now returns to the 'Western' – political interrogation, taking up the problems raised by the words spoken by the stammering voices in the first sequence – strike, social democracy, repression, etc.

First chapter is the Strike.
Sound track: an account of a strike & strike tactics.
Image track: centres on the role of the union delegate. This time the equation acting + lying is expressed in terms of *false translation*. He acts as intermediary between the Indian & the Cavalryman, falsely translating the Indian's words, from revolution to economist demands ('a kopeck added to a ruble' as Lenin puts it in *What Is To Be Done?*).

Translation = treason. Traduttore = traditore. I.e. translation is always deceptive. In reality there are two untranslatable monologues in society – the discourse of the masses, the discourse of the bosses. All 'translation' attempts to reduce these irreconcilables to a common discourse, meeting on common ground, 'I think we can reach an agreement.'

Similarly in the cinema. Two discourses: Hollywood-Mosfilm & revolutionary cinema. What is the voice of revolutionary cinema (the cinematic equivalent of Marxism-Leninism). Pontecorvo etc. are the cinematic equivalents of the Union Official – translating the revolution into the cinematic terminology & language of Hollywood.

The antagonisms between the Indian & the Cavalryman are irreconcilable. The impossibility of true translation implies the inevitability of violence. Image track: Indian throwing rock – Cavalryman picking up gun. Union Official trying to mediate & pacify.
We now hear the voice of the Union Official, reading from Waldeck Rochet's book – this time we hear his voice. Intercut on sound track with the revolutionary voice saying 'That's false.'

Next we return to the question *What Is To Be Done?*
Students have escaped from the procession. Student-worker cooperation. *Left-Wing Communism, An Infantile Disorder* – used by the PCF against

students entering the factory. Cf. Cohn-Bendit's book: *Right-Wing Communism: A senile disorder.*

A young man & woman (Wiazemsky) are now contrasted with the other woman & with the Union Official.
Return to the parody-allegory kind of speech. She is identified with fascism, he is identified with revisionism, collaborating with chauvinism, Nazism, Gaullism & US imperialism (Dulles).

NB on image track. Red = blood, recurrent motif of the film. Red flag stained with blood of martyrs. (Cf. end of *British Sounds*). Search for image.

Next sequence is the General Assembly (Mass Meeting). This follows a narrative logic. The strike is led by the Union Delegate, who tries to monopolise its 'speech', talking only to the boss in private. Therefore the active minority (identified with students) must call a mass meeting, so that the workers can express themselves publicly.

However, the mass meeting instead concerns the film – the character of the next sequence 'Repression' – the forcible silencing of the masses.

The 'Italians' – who are Maoists – suggest the image of Stalin – Wanted For Murder By The Capitalists (Western allegory).
The discussion is about Stalin: whether he should be put together with Mao or not. The Italian Maoists (Serve The People! – Gian Maria Volonté) adopt the orthodox Maoist position. Godard adopts the anti-Stalinist position.
Image-track: confused camera movements.
Sound track: confused voices.
The question of Stalin is not settled (Godard's position) – on the images Stalin's face is alternately crossed out & not crossed out.
Stalin is also contrasted with Vertov.

The sequence ends with the statement: It's not the correct image, it is only an image.
We then move on to Godard's image of repression (rather than Volonté's): the Cavalryman brutalising the Indian in front of the waterfall.
Symbolic image, paralleled by symbolic examples of repression on the sound track (all by the right wing).

We now move on to the next chapter. Repression leads not to collapse but intensification of the strike: the active strike.
The sound track discusses student-worker relations further, then explains an active strike – instead of withholding their labour, the workers go on running the factory by & for themselves.
Formal shots on the images, which throw attention back onto the sound track.
Second voice on the sound track points out the limitations of the active strike & calls for the overthrow of the State as the strategic goal. (This is in line with the content of Lenin's *What Is To Be Done?*, the main theme of which, besides the need for theory, is the primacy of politics over economic struggle: the overthrow of Tsarism as the principal goal.)

The intensified active strike, leads to intensified repression: The Police State – i.e., a kind of spiral effect, leading to more abrupt confrontations, more violence.
Image of Cavalryman & Wiazemsky. She refuses to speak to him – refusal of dialogue. Instead violence. Blood. Symbolic red.
[Cavalryman on the water – jerky violent movements, like those of blows. Kind of mimetic symbolism.]

The first story is now over – it has ended in defeat, the establishment of a police state. However, the revolutionaries are victorious on a symbolic level. There will be another struggle – they will recognise each other by the symbolic red of the blood. (Something mystical about this.)

We now shift focus from the story (of May '68) to the film. Criticism of the film – being out of touch with the people. Poster-and-slogan style. Mechanical quoting from the Chinese instead of analysing one's own concrete situation. Rhetoric rather than science.
Image track: shots of people at work, in slums, etc.
These images are criticised as being simply verité/TV news pictures.
Return to interrogation of the cinema & the Western.

Theory A.
Sequence of the Cavalryman & the Indian.
Critique of Hollywood-Mosfilm & of Cuban & Algerian cinema.
Attack on underground cinema: 'A cinema which claims it has been liberated by poetry & art. A cinema without taboos, except against the class struggle.'

Then the parody of Glauber Rocha, with Glauber Rocha himself – a cinema of return to the 'popular', folklore, legend, intuitive energy & rebellion (cf. Pasolini).
Then the sequence of the waterfall.

This series of sequences is an *extension of the digression about acting.* A more direct questioning of the cinema itself, going back to the Lumière sequence in *Les Carabiniers* & putting it in a political & ideological framework. *Destruction of the illusory space of the screen.*

Conclusion: back to beginning, need to learn.
Taking up themes of *Le Gai Savoir* – learning in terms of the Maoist formula – Struggle, Self-Criticism, Change.
Attack on Althusser (*How To Read Capital*).
Long section about music (the student with a recorder).
Medicine (barefoot doctors vs. improved hospitals).
Hammer & sickle decapitating woman reading Proust.
Real education through political action: strikes at Fiat & Pirelli.

The basic form of these sequences comes from Chinese Street Theatre (*Pierrot*, *La Chinoise*) – sketches in poster-and-slogan style.
Illustrative diagrams rather than illusory space, story. Contrasted both with the Hollywood & Glauber Rocha & documentary footage.

The critique of the theory of filmmaking is now followed by a critique of the practice of filmmaking (making this particular film). Also return to a reflection on May '68.

Workers' Control (i.e. autonomy). Union Official vs. Delegate. Ringleader vs. Instigator. Mass Meeting vs. General Assembly. Occupation & Work-in vs. Active Strike.

Turin '19. Turin Soviets. Barcelona '37. Budapest '56. Paris '68. Workers councils, soviets, workers' control, self-management.

Sound track – criticism of Yugoslav self-management. Lenin & the works opposition. Reintroduction of market relations.

Image-track: mutilated film of the meeting of the workers on the film.

Two points about this:
1. First time film mutilated (negative shots, black leader, before). But unlike in experimental film (Brakhage, etc.) it obviously has a symbolic meaning of negation, rather than either reproducing inner vision or simply foregrounding film material.
2. Critique of workers' control of production of *Wind From The East*. This amounts to a self-justification by Gorin & Godard against Volonté & the Italians. (Godard's voice on the sound track.)

Now returns to the history of photography. The political role of the film is more important than the wishes of those working on it.

History of photography echoes *British Sounds* – invention in 19th century. Image-track, shot of Indian. Visual equation camera & gun. How to use the camera as a weapon.

The film now returns to the original story where it left off, with defeat. After the Police State it adds the words Armed Struggle (i.e. a further intensification of struggle).

Then follows the bomb-manufacturing sequence.
1. Clearest example of screen as blackboard. 'Educational' film.
2. Equation of violence with terrorism. In line with Godard's whole view of the gratuitousness of violence.
[Nihilism, anarchism, Nihilo-Maoism.]

Finally there are the two closing sequences.
1. Sexual division (man-woman) & division of labour – of repression. Woman identified with being well-behaved, conformist, family life, etc. Man identified with crude brutality, physical coercion, aggression.

Interesting example of use of direct address. Cf. *Pierrot*.

This sequence ends with black leader & then a return to the question, What Is To Be Done? this time answering it in general political terms; struggle against peaceful coexistence, mediation (regulation of relations), revisionism, etc.

Image track – a kind of illustration of the words, with flashbacks at relevant moments (lies – woman being made up; solidarity – revisionist talking to Cavalryman, ignoring Indian). Leading up to the conclusion – The East Wind & The West Wind – which once again states the major theme of struggle, antagonistic forces, impossibility of compromise.

It's been a long way from *Bonjour tristesse* to *Wind From The East* – a kind of journey from Hollywood to anti-Hollywood via art cinema. Yet despite the cinematic distance travelled, I think something coherent of Godard remains constant throughout.

* * *

Lecture notes, c. 1972–1974. See previous bibliographic note to 'Jean-Luc Godard: Le Gai Savoir'. *Previously unpublished.*

Jean-Luc Godard: Counter-Cinema

I want to talk about the idea of a counter-cinema in Godard & at the same time show the continuities as well as the discontinuities in his work. The way I want to do this is to take seven features of Godard's cinema which contrast with an 'orthodox' narrative cinema. In a sense, the seven deadly sins of the cinema v. seven cardinal virtues.

Fiction v. reality. Actors wearing make-up, telling a story, inhabiting a fictional world v. real life, the breakdown of representation, truth.

Narrative transitivity v. intransitivity. [Linear or transitive narrative vs. non-linear kind.] Sequence of events causally related in linear time v. episodic construction, gaps, ellipses, digressions.

Identification v. estrangement effects. (Empathy, emotional involvement with a character vs. direct address, voice-over, multiple & split characters.)

Single diegesis v. multiple diegesis. [Breaking through framework of narrative altogether, single.] (A unitary homogeneous story world v. heterogeneous worlds. Rupture between different codes & different channels.)

Transparency v. foregrounding ('Language wants to be overlooked': Siertsema v. making the mechanics of the film-text visible and explicit. Production. [Lack of matching between sound track & image track.]

Closure v. aperture. [Closed v. opened work.] (A self-contained object, harmonised within its own limits v. open-endedness, overspill, intertextuality: allusion, quotation, parody. [Reference back and outside itself.]

Pleasure v. unpleasure. (Entertainment, aiming to satisfy the spectator v. provocation, aiming to dis-satisfy & hence change the spectator. Didacticism.)

Obviously these seven features overlap & inter-relate, but I have tried to separate them for analytic purposes.

1. Fiction v. reality

Godard was never really satisfied with the 'pure' fiction film. From the start he wanted an impure cinema, with mixture of documentary & essay-ism. [Influence of Rouch. Later Brecht. Narrative vs. discursive, expository mode.]

Even *Breathless* has this side to it. Location-shotting: the de Gaulle/Eisenhower motorcade. Essay-ism contained within the dialogue.
A crucial step away from fiction comes with *Vivre sa vie* in 1962.
The whole film is very Rossellini-an in texture – the key section is Chapter 8, when the statistical & factual information on prostitution from Marcel Sacotte's book is presented in voice-over commentary – though cast (typically) in the form of an interview. [*2 or 3 Things* takes this further; sociological study & fiction.]

The point of implosion I think comes in *La Chinoise*, again in an interview – the long interview between Veronique (Anne Wiazemsky) and Francis Jeanson on the train. Interviews & 'guest spots' had appeared before in Godard – Brice Parain in *Vivre sa vie*. But in *La Chinoise* the interview is clearly marked off from the rest of the film – stylistically, in the way it is shot on the moving train, with natural greens & browns of the countryside, Jeanson & Veronique seen in silhouette. Dramatically, the fact that Jeanson talks about his own political career & record with evident seriousness, posing a different kind of problem to those we have encountered earlier (despite Omar Diop). Out of *Alice in Wonderland* & into May '68.

Afterwards, of course, the essayism becomes explicit & gradually takes over whole films. 'Characters' become spokesmen or 'reciters' of political theory & analysis. Fiction simultaneously expands & contracts – costume characters in *Weekend* & *East Wind* & the deconstruction of what they represent. [Almost no dialogue – at most various forms of alternating monologue.] [*East Wind*: polemic against Eisenstein. Not just documentary: wish to analyse and re-synthesise.]

Tout va bien marks a return to fiction – or at least to peaceful coexistence of fiction with essayism. Mediated, as in earlier films, through quotation and interview.

2. Narrative transitivity v. intransitivity

If we go back to *Breathless* the move to narrative intransitivity is there in embryo – the digression: interview at Orly. Stories & anecdotes – recounting the plot of *Wild Palms*, Belmondo's story about the couple in the South of France, etc. By *Vivre sa vie* the narrative structure is seriously assaulted. The digressions are much longer & extrinsic to the film: Brice Parain, the mime of the child with the balloon, the long quote from a woman's magazine. And the chapter structure is used to produce gaps & ellipses which are often bridged in an unorthodox way. Chapter 11 ends with Brice Parain discussing true love & Chapter 12 is about love. Chapter 4 ends with the question 'What are you going to do?' Chapter 5 introduces the young man. [*2 or 3 Things* – digression.] [Thematic links. On the street (illegible). His *death*. Joan of Arc. Porthos. Oval Portrait.] [*Tout va bien* relatively orthodox.]

The dissolution of narrative can be traced quite easily up to *East Wind* which is built on an explicit deconstruction. By this time narrative & digression have exchanged places. The film has an argumentative, rhetorical structure, numbered 1-7 with subsidiary sections, Theory A & Theory B. [Rhetoric, History, Allegory, Struggle, Self-Criticism, Transformation.] The narrative 'story' which has so many ellipses that it becomes unintelligible is set like a digression in the disposition of the argument.

3. Identification v. estrangement

From the start Godard was obsessed with acting & it becomes one of the main topics of his films. [Deception v. sincerity.] Similarly right from the beginning there is direct address to the spectator – the opening car sequence of Belmondo driving to the south & talking directly to the spectator. Insulting those who don't agree with him. In *Breathless* too he already dubs Belmondo's voice with his own (shorts; Belmondo's national service) & appears himself. Melville in the interview.
[Dubbed too as *2/3 Things*.]

The interview is one of the most interesting & central features of Godard's work. Almost every film has an interview, setting off actor against real person, idea of questioning to get at truth rather than fiction. A key interview, of course, is the interview with the actor in *Une femme mariée*, which centres around the problem of true speech, lying speech & theatrical speech. This same distinction surfaces later in *East Wind* – the distinction between the lying voice, the 'acting' 'deceptive' voice & the stammering voice of truth. Typically it is the 'theatrical' voice – that of revisionism – which comes in for the most virulent attack.

Interviewing, of course, is the purest form of linguistic demand – and the demand Godard is always making is for the truth. And the truth cannot, by definition, be spoken by an actor. Actors are people whose profession is to lie on demand. Cf. acting v. photography dialogue in *Le Petit Soldat*. [Truth 24 frames per second.] Later photography itself comes to be seen as a form of deception – one irreducible in the cinema. [Way to truth through lies.] [*2 or 3 Things* – start – this is Marina Vlady, this is Juliette Jeanson (Brecht).]

The other ways in which Godard tried to de-mystify acting are through direct address (*Breathless* – *Weekend*; like a lot of devices, changing from a gag to a crucial structural feature). *Tout va bien*: through dissociating the image of the actor or speaker from the voice on the sound track. Dubbing in his own voice (*Vivre sa vie*). *British Sounds*, where there are a number of sequences where image track & sound track are dissociated – shop stewards' discussion where camera is never on speaker. Women's liberation sequence, with exaggerated 'image' of women & multiple sound track – actress's repetition of commentary over telephone. Man's voice drowning out women. In fact only in the student sequence is there a normal sound-image relationship. Effect of this of course is to destroy unity of characters.

Through dissociation of sound, direct address, unmotivated behaviour or dialogue, use of deliberate 'types' (in *Les Carabiniers* [*Tout va bien*, case study in *Vivre sa vie*]), interrogation of characters, etc., Godard breaks up the psychological reality of screen protagonists. More radical than Brecht.

4. Single diegesis v. multiple diegesis

Again this begins as early as *Breathless* – scene in which they go in to see Budd Boetticher's *Westbound*, in which the dialogue is no longer Burt Kennedy's but consists of part of a poem by Aragon & two lines of dialogue which I think are from Apollinaire. Of course this is still contained within a film-within-a-film. There is a similar discrepancy (less extreme) in *Vivre sa vie* – last shot of *Joan of Arc* excerpt repeated twice – and in Mexico cinema in *Les Carabiniers* of course the pseudo-Lumière films are deliberatively demystified. (Superboy dialogue.) Mixing fictional, real, historical worlds. [Framing story in *Tout va bien* – filmmaking.]

Another device for breaking up the homogeneity of the screen world is the constant channel & code-switching from seeing/watching to reading. This begins with the use of book titles within the diegesis (in the shorts, Leviné's 'We are all dead men on parole' in *Breathless*, the book-title dialogue in *Une femme est une femme*, *2 or 3 Things*), then is transmuted into chapter headings (*Vivre sa vie*) and intertitles in *Les Carabiniers* (quotes from Germans at Stalingrad, Napoleon's armies in Spain, written as postcard messages from characters, on intertitles, in the same handwriting that the credits are in – ie. three separate sources superimposed). Intertitles then revert back into graffiti – in notebooks (*Pierrot*) or on walls (*One Plus One* – NB 'found' graffiti – *Vivre sa vie*). Then the graffiti merge with the intertitles – the *Cinétracts*. By *East Wind*, written messages are proceeding word by word cumulatively through the film on intertitles, demanding two levels of reading – instantaneous & retrospective.

Contradictions between sound track & image track [first really explored in *2 or 3 Things*], which dominate in *Le Gai Savoir*, *British Sounds*, *Pravda*, etc. *Struggle in Italy*, *East Wind* all go over the same image track, substituting a different sound track. This is done not to give multiple point of view (*Kane*, *Rashomon*, *Barefoot Contessa*, *Liberty Valance*) but to contest the status of the image track as such, necessarily ideological in its single reproduction of a homogeneous world. One world of perception v. two worlds of discourse (Althusser).

5. Transparency v. foregrounding

In the early films, the devices are foregrounded within the text. In *Breathless* the slow 180-degree pan across the Champs-Élysées, pausing a moment on the Arc de Triomphe, clearly a forerunner [360 *2 or 3 Things*] of the famous 720-degree pan/reverse pan in *Weekend*. Cf. also the stammering, stuttering images in *Vivre sa vie* during gunfire sequence (based on *October* – Brakhage). Switch to subjective camera during the dance in the room with the pool table. (Happiest moment for Nana – shots of blank wall.) Could reiterate endless formal devices – shots in silhouette (special lighting effects), oscillating pans, shots held unexpectedly long, etc. In *Les Carabiniers* we get for the first time interference with the stock – sequence with the fireworks printed in negative. Use of special stock to get look of silent film, intercut with old newsreel footage. The end of *Alphaville* also goes into negative.

The most radical act of this kind is in *East Wind* where Godard scratches the stock. Bringing him alongside developments in American 'experimental' cinema. Difference – American filmmakers – reduction of film to optical substrate – film in the projector, the frame, film as material to be worked on (Landow, Brakhage). In a sense foregrounding of 'noise' and then structuring according to some calculus or random coding principle. Godard seems to be looking for an iconic expression of negation. Ambition to turn films into pictography runs up against absence of negation. By running the sequence through twice, erasing it the second time, he produces a virtual negation. (Workers' control sequence, accompanied on sound track by a critique of workers' control, implicitly as it operated in *East Wind*, explicitly as it operates in Yugoslavia.) Film-writing & film-reading, rather than expanding object and modes of perception.

The other kind of foregrounding of the process of production consists of filming the film being made. *Les Carabiniers* demystifies the process of projection in the pseudo-Lumière sequence. *La Chinoise* & *Far From Vietnam* show the camera. In *La Chinoise* we see the cameraman filming

(Coutard) during the interview with Léaud about acting (itself a repeat of *Une femme mariée*). Also shots of the sound technician. This fits in with the designation of *La Chinoise* at the beginning as a film in the making. Cf. *One Plus One*.

In *East Wind* this kind of foregrounding is emphasised very strongly. Cf. the scene in which the actor addresses the spectator directly, inviting them up onto the screen. Shot of film crew. Voice-over: In ten seconds you will be looking at a character on a bourgeois film screen. He is a Western character from a psychological drama, a thriller, a historical film… He says he is in the dark, he says there's an old man sitting in the fifth row … good-looking girl at the back … he asks her to join him on the screen… A wonderful sunny day… Sunshine… Truth.
Camera pulls back showing waterfall, pool, people diving & swimming. Cut to sound engineer. Struggle against bourgeois concept of representation. Wrest the means of production from the hands of the dominant ideology. That is the most we can do. The most is to be able to say: This image is red.
Red screen.

Not necessary to expand on the purpose of this – relates to estrangement effects, code-switching, deconstruction of fiction, etc. [*Tout va bien*.]

6. Closure v. aperture

Godard was obsessed by quotation right from the beginning – from all the different forms of discourse. Literary quotes, musical quotes, pictorial quotes, and – of course – cinematic quotes. *Breathless* – Monogram Pictures, Bogart, *Bonjour tristesse*, etc. Whole sections of other movies are incorporated – the 'Tell me lies' sequence from *Johnny Guitar* inserted into *Le Petit Soldat*.

In the same way that the interrogation of acting or the narration of digressions move out from the primary narrative to become structural principles of the film, so also quotation becomes a structural principle. The quotations begin to carry the characters rather than vice versa, so that actors simply become 'reciters' [Brecht], voices speaking quoted passages – cf. the garbage truck sequence in *Weekend*, almost all of *One Plus One*. Godard's text becomes a montage of other texts, other voices.

There is no longer a single discourse with a single subject, but a multitude of separate, fragmented & contradictory discourses. Godard's own 'voice' is absent, his subjectivity becomes a location, a position in the intertextual multiple discourse. Conversely, the 'spectator' too has to abandon his own habitual role & find his own position. What began as a jackdaw mentality, then became a kind of polyphony (Pound or Joyce) ends up as a complete re-textualization. [*East Wind*: parody Western, Glauber Rocha, quotations: Waldeck Rochet, etc.] [In *Tout va bien* too Xs speak dialogue taken directly from books.]

7. Finally, pleasure v. unpleasure

Obviously Godard has led an increasingly virulent onslaught on the 'entertainment' cinema: Hollywood/Mosfilm. *Breathless* begins with insulting spectator. Taste for scandal & provocation. The turning point is *Les Carabiniers*. It is difficult to remember the scandal it created, extent to which it was seen as a provocation.

* * *

INSERT: It is not necessary to stress how this kind of provocation & didacticism has intensified in Godard's work. One point should be made – perhaps pleasure v. unpleasure is the wrong way of putting it. The aggressivity towards the spectator clearly has a sado-masochistic component which may, of course, be pleasurable. Indeed the whole of Godard's revolutionary stance is infected with a fascination with violence – obviously there from the very beginning. *East Wind* is very typical with its phantasies of blowing up shoppers in supermarkets, massacring trade union officials, etc. – out of any strategic context.

* * *

Godard's career seems to me to show continuities & constant factors quite as powerful as the apparent bewildering changes he has gone through. *British Sounds*, say, is not so far removed from *Vivre sa vie*, *East Wind* from *Les Carabiniers*. *Tout va bien* seems to mark a deliberate return & recognition of continuity.

In general I would say the development of Godard's cinema has been in the slow & uneven theorising of personal idiosyncrasies & traits and incorporating them into a highly theoretical model of what a revolutionary cinema should be. In the process Godard's dissolved his own subjectivity

& subordinated himself to theoretical principles & procedures of film-making. Repetition compulsion is still at work but is mastered not by seeing his films as a series of personal explorations but by transforming his own obsessions and compulsions into trans-subjective principles. Working-through in the real sense of the term.

* * *

Lecture notes, c. 1972–1974. See previous bibliographic note in 'Jean-Luc Godard: Le Gai Savoir*'. These notes closely follow Wollen's essay of the same period, 'Counter Cinema:* Vent d'Est*', first published in* Afterimage *4 (Autumn 1972), and republished as 'Godard and Counter Cinema:* Vent d'Est*', in* Readings and Writings: Semiotic Counter-Strategies *(New Left Books, 1982). Previously unpublished.*

Landscape, Meteorology, and Chris Welsby

Landscape painting developed relatively late in the history of Western art. Even when, in the seventeenth and eighteenth centuries, landscape painters such as Claude and Salvator Rosa (and the now-forgotten Both and Berchem) acquired great renown, their prestige never matched that of figure and history painters. Moreover, they painted exclusively 'ideal landscapes', constructed in the studio and using direct sketches from nature simply as source material to be adapted, composited and improvised upon at will. Their landscapes were invariably given some dramatic or mythological pretext whereby human figures would provide a point of interest. Topographical landscape painting took even longer to develop and was granted very low prestige indeed. Derived from the urban vedutisti tradition, it hardly surfaced at all until the whole attitude to landscape so changed during the nineteenth century.

It is worth remembering that even a 'modernist' critic like Baudelaire, writing in the Salon of 1859, says of Boudin's landscape sketches which he had seen, 'He knows quite well that all this will have to be turned into a picture, by means of the poetic impression recalled at will; and he lays no claim to be offering his notes as pictures' – this after Baudelaire's complaint that 'a mind which is absorbed in taking notes has no time to abandon itself to prodigious reveries'.[1] Nonetheless, he was intrigued that 'on the margin of each of these studies, so rapidly and so faithfully sketched from the waves and the clouds (which are of all things the most inconstant and difficult to grasp, both in form and in colour), he has inscribed the date, the time and the wind: thus for example, 8th October, midday, North-West

1 Charles Baudelaire, 'The Salon of 1858', *Art in Paris 1845–1862* (Phaidon, 1965), 199–200.

wind'. Indeed, Baudelaire goes on to comment that the accuracy of 'these meteorological beauties' could be verified as to season, time and wind.

The introduction of the concept of 'meteorology' into discourse on landscape was quite novel. The essential physical basis for modern meteorology had only been established at the end of the previous century (Lavoisier's discovery of the true nature of atmospheric air in 1783; Dalton's explanation of variations of water vapour in the atmosphere in 1800) and the first great compilation of weather observations was made during the Napoleonic period. Luke Howard's *The Climate of London* came out in 1820, Maury's maps of wind-fields in 1848. Gradually a new scientific basis for the observation of landscape was established, casting doubt on the old poetic and pastoral categories, challenging artists either to assimilate the new mode of observation or hold fast to their prodigious reveries.

This new mode of observation had been prefigured, of course, by Constable. During a lecture given in 1836 Constable commented on a painting by Ruisdael he had copied a few years previously:

> This picture represents an approaching thaw. The ground is covered with snow, and the trees are still white; but there are two windmills near the centre; the one has sails furled, and is turned in the position from which the wind blew when the mill left off work; the other has the canvas on the poles, and is turned another way, which indicates a change in the wind. The clouds are opening in that direction, which appears by the glow in the sky to be the south (the sun's winter habitation in our hemisphere), and this change will produce a thaw before morning. The concurrence of these circumstances shows that Ruisdael understood what he was painting.[2]

It is in this tradition that Chris Welsby's landscape films must be placed. The invention of photography (near contemporary of meteorology and soon of course to become an essential instrument of it) and subsequently film offered the artist entirely new opportunities, new ways of integrating scientific observations with poetic impressions. It is worth remembering that 1878, the year in which Muybridge's famous photographs of Leland Stanford's horses were published in the *Scientific American*, was also the year in which Monet moved to Vétheuil, where he began to paint in series, mooring his boat on the Seine opposite the island of Saint-Martin to record the scene at every hour of the day and each season of the year. He had a slotted box made to hold a number of canvases, changing from

2 John Constable, Lecture III, 'The Dutch and Flemish Schools', *John Constable's Discourses* 14 (Suffolk Records Society, 1970), 64.

one to the next as the light changed throughout the day (seldom staying on one canvas for more than half an hour). Eventually he reached a point where he would have as many as one hundred canvases under way, of a single subject. Muybridge's analytic photography provided a method of capturing the very sequence of instantaneities which came at the same time to obsess Monet.

It is significant that Muybridge's work was rediscovered by artists in the late 1960s, at the same time that 'land art' was developed.[3] In Welsby's work we find Muybridge's analytic serialisation of time applied, through the mediation of meteorological investigation, to a revived non-painterly interest in landscape. Through control over the temporal sequence (time-lapse, shutter-speed) of photography and the spatial orientation and movement of the camera and its associated equipment (especially the mount and panning head), Welsby is able to capture through the cinematographic process itself changes in the seasons, the position of the sun, the force of the wind, the movement of the tides: a whole range of natural and meteorological phenomena. Moreover, these phenomena themselves are structured serially: we can envisage the sequence of seasons, for instance, as being itself a sequence of temporal modules.

In addition, the techniques developed by Welsby made it possible for there to be a direct ('indexical' in the semiotic terminology of Peirce) registration of natural phenomena on film. Thus, camera movement could be determined by wind direction after a wind vane was linked to the panning head on the tripod. Natural processes were no longer simply recorded from outside, as objects of observation; they could be made to participate in the scheme of observation itself. The point of observation was no longer the external 'Archimedean' point of the artist's own consciousness. Furthermore, the automatic procedures of science and technology, instead of being inflicted on nature in order to dominate it, were directed by nature itself. The promise at the heart of Welsby's work is that of a new type of relationship between science and nature and between subject and object of observation. The Romantic cult of nature, which made it possible for landscape painting to flourish in the nineteenth century more than ever before, grew up alongside and in reaction against the technological destruction of nature which accompanied the industrial revolution. The danger, of course, was that our culture would

3 Cf., for instance, Dan Graham, 'Muybridge Moments', *Arts* (February 1967), and Mel Bochner, 'The Serial Attitude', *Artforum* (December 1967). Jan Dibbets's work is probably most comparable to Welsby's, though Dibbets uses sequential photography more for optical and spatial effect rather than indexical and temporal.

simply become increasingly split, as art set itself up against science and science was applied and developed divorced from any concern over value. Welsby's work makes it possible to envisage a different kind of relationship between science and art, in which observation is separated from surveillance and technology from domination. The late development of landscape art means that its particular history may only now be really beginning, as it enters a new post-painterly phase.

* * *

First published as 'Introduction to Chris Welsby: Films/Photographs/ Writings', *edited by David Curtis (Arts Council of Great Britain, 1980). Republished as 'Landscape, Meteorology, and Chris Welsby' in* Millennium Film Journal, *16–18 (Fall 1986/Winter 1987).*

The Avant-Gardes: Europe and America

Autobiography: five years ago (1975) I wrote an article on 'The Two Avant-Gardes' for *Studio International*. My main purpose was to outline somewhat schematically (though with the usual prudent provisos) two distinct types of film avant-garde. I am not going to quote or summarise the article but instead give something more like its subtext – the polemical drift running beneath the surface. I wanted to bring together two poles of attraction: New York and Paris (a characteristically British ambition perhaps). New York stood for modernism. In film terms: New American Cinema, Sitney's 'structural film' and its European counterparts, and analogues associated with the Co-op movement. Paris stood for May '68 and theory. In film terms: Godard, Straub-Huillet, Jancsó, Oshima – what I dubbed the 'second' avant-garde, the group of filmmakers pushed critically by *Cahiers* (long an important point of reference for me).

Part of my purpose, I think I should add, was to go beyond the controversy between Sitney and Le Grice over priority between US and European 'structural' filmmakers, of which I was all too aware. Naturally I was outraged by Sitney referring to Europe as 'the outlands' and his near-total consignment of European filmmakers after 1943 to oblivion. I thought Le Grice, the Heins and others were right to stress the autonomy and variety of European avant-garde film. Nonetheless it still seemed to me that New York was the ideological centre for this type of avant-garde – if only because New York had become the centre of the art world and this avant-garde was closely tied to visual art in its latest phases. The terms in which this avant-garde was discussed were crucially dependent on Greenbergian modernism and its transposition into minimalism, conceptualism, etc. (more of this later). I wanted to broaden the discussion to include both avant-gardes – and at the same time 'bury' the Europe-America polarisation by displacing it into a subtext.

I ended the article by expressing the hope that the two avant-gardes might converge. There were three reasons for wanting a convergence. (Though apparently historical, the article was in reality extremely programmatic in its strategy.) First, I was laying the theoretical foundations I felt were necessary for the Independent Film-Makers Association, recently established in Britain. My aim (not only mine, of course) was to avoid both the US model – complete lack of contact between avant-garde and political filmmakers – and the German model – initial co-operation followed by destructive splits. The design was that the IFA should be able to bring together 'militant' (Newsreel, Cinema Action) filmmakers with 'formalist' (Co-op) filmmakers. For this, the old slogan of 'new content, new forms' needed reviving and amplifying. Second, I was looking forward to our (Laura Mulvey and myself) next film, *Riddles of the Sphinx*, which we conceived of as an attempt to combine the two avant-gardes, a possibility we saw as signposted by the work of Yvonne Rainer in the US and Chantal Akerman in Europe. Third, I wanted to push the magazine *Screen*, with which I was associated, away from a univocal 'Parisianism' towards a more cosmopolitan stance. (A 'Parisianism' I was partly responsible for having introduced, though I had backed Peirce rather than Saussure from the start, something I felt increasingly thankful for as I read more post-Chomsky linguistics.)

The aim then was to combine New York modernism with Parisian ('68) theory. Things look rather different nowadays. Modernism is in disarray and '68 has led to unanticipated disavowals and reinterpretations: the rollback has begun. *Cahiers* has even reverted to its old pre-'68 cinephilia, bracketing off the intervening period as a time of aberration and excess. The way in which I saw things five years ago begins to look naive – or at least ill-starred. Nonetheless I think the underlying impulse was sound. What needs much more careful and searching treatment is the exact nature both of modernism and of 'new French theory' – and consequently of the avant-gardes associated with them.

I now see the history of the avant-garde in the visual arts – primarily painting, secondarily film – rather differently. I think that here too we should distinguish two separate trends. One (which I think of as 'modernism') is concerned with reflexiveness (film as film, film about film) and semiotic reduction (foregrounding one category of signifier, or, more radically, of the material substrate; movement towards suppression or suspension of the signified). The other (which I think of as 'avant-garde') is not purist, rejects ontological presuppositions or investigations, and is concerned with semiotic expansion (mixed media, montage of different codes, signs and semiotic registers, heterogeneity of signifiers and signifieds). It was 'modernism' which became dominant in the US in the post-war epoch, after the suppression of the avant-garde (especially in Germany and the USSR) prior to the trough of the thirties. Yet in the USA too both strands were always present: witness the Greenberg-Fried polemic against Duchamp and 'theatricality', or the Sitney-Maciunas polemic on 'structural' film.

In fact, it is clear that the Fluxus movement had a very important role (hardly acknowledged still) in the history of post-war art. It served, for instance, as the vehicle of transmission for Cage's ideas and his example to all the other arts. If we look at US 'structural' film and its own history more closely we find that both Landow and Sharits were directly involved with Fluxus; Tony Conrad too worked closely with La Monte Young. The influence of Fluxus was helped, I think, by the fact that it combined a strong element of semiotic reduction (absurd or minimal signifieds, 'literalness') with a strong element of semiotic expansion (mixed media, movement out of art museums into public space, lack of any painterly purism).

Fluxus was also able to take root in both the US and Europe. The ground was prepared by the same tendencies which surfaced as DIAS [Destruction in Art Symposium] in London and the 'material-aktion' in Austria and Germany, both of which had close ties with the beginnings of the Co-op movements and 'structural film' in their countries. Evidently Fluxus, like 'classical' Dadaism, was not a movement which could endure or consolidate. All the same, it alerts us to the possibility that New American Cinema was not necessarily concerned either with 'metaphors of mind' (Sitney) or with 'film as film' (Le Grice) except as one aspect of its development – a development, moreover, which was not simply towards an end-point along a line of progressive ontological purification.

Otherwise, in fact, one can hardly hope to make sense of Landow or even Snow. It is all very well pointing out the way in which *Film in Which There Appear Edge Lettering, Sprocket Holes, Dirt Particles, Etc.* foregrounds the material substrate of sprocket-holes, etc. (yet dust takes us back to Duchamp) but it seems inadequate for coping with *Wide Angle Saxon*, let alone Landow's latest film which heads off from the marriage-broker jokes in Freud's *Wit and the Unconscious*. Similarly it is clear that the leading interpreters of 'structural' film were much happier with the *Wavelength*, *Back and Forth*, *Région Centrale* trilogy than they were with

Rameau's Nephew, which again only makes sense within a Duchampian rather than Greenbergian tradition. (It is interesting too to see how Le Grice deals with Kren – consistently emphasising 'work on the signifier' rather than the almost unavoidable nature of the 'signifieds'.)

The conclusion I reach is that the New American Cinema and its European counterparts formed by no means a unitary movement, but represented two opposing tendencies which have been with modernism and the avant-garde ever since the 'natural' Renaissance scope of relations between signifier and signified was overthrown by Cubism. One tendency reflects a preoccupation with the specificity of the signifier, holding the signified in suspense or striving to eliminate it. The other has tried to develop new types of relation between signifier and signified through the montage of heterogeneous elements. It is clear that it is the second tendency which is 'convergent' with Godard and Straub-Huillet, and which in the long run must hold hopes of much greater potential. It is modernism which has run its course, not the avant-garde (though a crisis of one is necessarily a crisis for the other).

This brings us back to the second avant-garde and Paris. Looking back on what I wrote in 1975 I sense that I already felt disappointed with the outcome of Godard's adventures in the wilderness. It had seemed to me at first, as it did to many (witness *Cahiers* and *Cinéthique*) that Godard's trajectory was that of '68. The 'theoretical' accompaniment to this view came from *Tel Quel* with its attempt to elaborate theoretical positions which would bring together Marxism, psychoanalysis, semiotics and the avant-garde. (Or should I say Althusserianism, Lacanianism, 'sémanalyse' and a certain tradition of the avant-garde: Artaud, Joyce, etc.) Again, in retrospect, it is easy to see that the 'new French theory' was more complex than it looked at first – and like New American Cinema, it contained different trends, mutually inconsistent and contradictory, even more acutely perhaps.

There are three (very bare) points I would like to make. First, the *Tel quel* position was basically – like Situationism – a prolongation of the dissident surrealist tradition (Artaud rather than Buñuel, Bataille rather than Breton, Mao rather than Trotsky, etc.). As such, 1968 was both its crown and its wreath. Second, a great deal of 'new French theory' turned out to be 'old German theory' in origin: not simply Marx and Freud, but also Nietzsche, Husserl, Heidegger and so on. Again, it looks now like part of the lengthy process of French digestion of German thought – and, as such, much closer to Sartre than anyone was prepared to admit. Third, and this is the most pertinent point, the revival of semiotics turned out to be anti-scientific rather than scientific. Responsibility here, of course, falls on the very figures who inaugurated semiotics with such brave flourishes of scientificity: Barthes and Kristeva. Partly this turn against science was due to the pressure of the dissident surrealist and German idealist traditions that I have mentioned above. Partly it was due to an epistemological failure to accept the role of an empirical component in any science without it falling into empiricism – Althusser's failure, in particular, compounded by an accelerating philosophical fascination with language, text, discourse, etc., completely divorced from any theory of reference. Thirdly, and this is connected with the preceding point, there were serious weaknesses inherent in the fundamental work of Saussure: for instance, his lack of any real theory of syntax, thrown into an appallingly revealing light by Chomsky, and his ambivalence about the place of reference in his theory of the sign.

In making these (regrettably sweeping) criticisms, I should stress that I believe the project of semiotics is more important to defend now than ever before – as the wave of 1968 recedes, ever more attacks are made on semiotics, in the hope that its supposed weaknesses will cause it to collapse and the whole enterprise can be forgotten. The alternatives, of course, are new waves of Anglo-Saxon empiricism and impressionism. Fortunately too the semiotics of film (Metz, Bellour and others) was much less damaged by the anti-scientific reversal I have described than the project of semiotics in general. The problem of film semiotics has been twofold: the failure, building on a Saussurean base, to find flexible enough concepts to extend the scope of semiotics beyond the classical codes of Hollywood and art cinema, certainly in any way which could feed directly into filmmaking, and secondly a tendency to look for general theories of the cinematic sign (or 'dispositif' or 'imaginaire') rather than stressing the plurality and heterogeneity of film – as Metz himself at one stage correctly emphasised.

The failure to develop a theory of semiotics in relation to the film avant-garde was particularly unfortunate because it was here that the influence of Barthes, Kristeva, etc., in their later phases made itself increasingly felt. Eventually semiotics began to turn into an explicitly and militantly anti-scientific (let alone non-scientific) project. In fact *Screen* in England was not totally immune from this kind of slippage as it attempted to synthesise a post-*Cahiers* politique with the semiotic theory from which it had become divorced in France.

The project of a film semiotics capable of dealing with the problems of the avant-garde began to seem more and more Utopian, a vain struggle to hold back the tide of irrationalism. In fact, it was in the area of feminist filmmaking and feminist film theory that the line was best held. Feminism, of course, was itself in part a product of the political and intellectual upheavals emblematically associated with 1968. Feminism also demanded a critique of image and narrative in dominant forms of cinema which inflected it towards the avant-garde. As yet there are only the beginnings of a breakdown of the division into two avant-gardes and separation of avant-garde from theoretical work, but it is in and in relation to feminist film that the convergence is most marked. Many recent films have been made in a context where feminist theoretical writing has provided background and encouragement for film.

P.S. Since writing these lines my prediction of continuing attacks on semiotics has been amply fulfilled – Anderson, Brownlow, Durgnat and of course the MacCabe affair (itself foreshadowed by Durgnat's malign call for a struggle against semiotic infiltration of the universities and cultural institutions). While these particular attacks lack any intellectual credibility (Durgnat's, the most ambitious, opportunistically invokes both Popper and Thompson as guarantors of the most ideal scientific and scholarly empiricism he so deliriously travesties in his own work) there is plenty to worry about when you consider the political situation, ripe for a resurgence of neo-McCarthyism designed to wipe out the aftermath of '68. What is especially worrying is to find a 'progressive' journal like *Cineaste* launching a campaign against 'structuralist' Marxism and avant-garde film, using non-Marxists to trash enemies on the Marxist left, while cosying up obsequiously to establishment critics like Canby and Sarris.

On the other hand, it is reassuring that these attacks emanate above all from a pre-'68 generation attempting to turn back the clock. There is another important angle of approach to the present situation. Although, as I pointed out earlier, modernism and Parisian theory are both in disarray, it is possible to see filmmakers and theorists in Britain as inheritors, not of these two tendencies, but of the possibilities to develop them. Having spent the '70s turning between different points of intellectual and aesthetic attraction, the time is now ripe for a British independent film culture to explore the intellectual and aesthetic background of the '70s for its (their) own purposes. (March 1981)

* * *

Essay published in Framework *14 (Spring 1981).*

Reply to Sitney

Briefly,

1) I didn't pretend to Olympian detachment but made it quite clear that I was being partisan and polemical – just as partisan and polemical as Sitney is.
2) It stands to reason that my theoretical approach to film converges with my practice as a filmmaker. It would be strange if it didn't. This isn't careerism, it's consistency. You might as well call *Metaphors on Vision* careerist on the grounds that it serves Brakhage's filmmaking purposes.
3) My point about recent work by Landow and Snow was not that Sitney could not possibly write about these films – of course he has – but that he could not write about them in the same terms as he wrote about structural film. The new last chapter of *Visionary Film* is fine in itself, but I don't think that it respects the schema of developments that structured the first edition of the book.
4) Sitney's attempt to stay consistent gets him into trouble. It's not really possible to limit Duchamp's impact to that of *Anémic Cinéma* or to ignore the many non-filmic ways in which Duchamp's influence was transmitted. It's simply wrong to restrict the history of film to film alone as though it was sealed off from the other arts or other intellectual and social currents.
5) The main influences on my work have not been French – Peirce, Propp, Eisenstein, Freud, etc. I have never written of Barthes except critically and comparatively little about any other French theorist.
6) I don't see any future in trying to revive the sterile Europe vs. America debate. I admire the work of Welsby and Wyborny but I don't believe

in the 'authentic avant-garde tradition' of Kubelka, Isou, Lemaître, Hanoun. How are Kubelka and Hanoun part of the same tradition?

7) It is the Roussel side of Landow's work which appeals to me – not the Christian logos.
8) No apologies for harping on '68.
9) Sitney drags *The Cinematic Apparatus* into the discussion just to fling a few rocks at de Lauretis and Heath. What he says isn't relevant to what I wrote there.
10) However reluctantly, I'm ready to grant Brakhage his place in history. When will Sitney do the same for Godard?

* * *

Reply to letter from P. Adams Sitney in response to 'The Avant-Gardes: Europe and America' (1981), both letters published in Framework *18 (1982), 57–8.*

The original issue of Framework *printed 'Lumet' instead of 'Lemaître' in Wollen's reply. This typographical error has been corrected.*

Passion 1

First thoughts (I need – and want – to see the film again).

1. Two passions: the passion for justice and the passion for art. Justice: the woman shop floor worker fired without compensation. Art: the great masterpieces of the past. A disparity therefore between a passion which society values and a passion which society devalues.

2. The two passions are structurally separate. The passion for art is embedded, as a studio TV feature (shot on video), within an exterior story. The interface is provided by the director and by the fact that the factory is used as a recruiting ground for TV extras. Two different kinds of work, two different kinds of factory. (Film/TV studio as factory, as in Shklovsky's *Third Factory*, a very Godardian book.)

3. An interrogation of the relations between love and work. In two senses: work as a form of love (perhaps this is what art is or aspires to be) and work as repression, displacement and 'perversification' of the erotic.

4. The interior story (or rather non-story) consists of a series of *tableaux vivants*, simulations of great masterpieces of the past: Rembrandt, Goya, Delacroix, Greco. The passionate sight-seer in the imaginary museum.

5. Memories/comparisons. Ruiz's *L'hypothèse du tableau volé*. Rainer's *Lives of Performers*: the closing sequence, in which the performers

recreate stills from *Pandora's Box*. Laguna Beach, where masterpieces are reproduced as tableaux on carnival floats.

6. Irony of Godard's tableaux. As in other examples, the tableau consists of *freezing* (cf. Rainer especially). Bodies in movement are immobilised. But in *Passion*, conversely, the look, which is frozen in the Rainer, now moves. Moreover, it moves not simply through space exterior to the tableau, but into it and within it.

7. A second level of memories/comparisons. Coppola's *One from the Heart*, Syberberg's *Parsifal*, Snow's *Presents*, the opening sequences. Movements into and through a set.

8. Penetration. The frame of a painting is not simply a rectangle inscribed round it, separating it from the plane surface of the wall. There is a second, virtual frame which demarcates imaginary from real space, co-extensive with the picture surface itself, a kind of veil or hymen, to use Derrida's favoured term. Whereas movement of the look (the camera's look) outside alters the first frame (the margin), movement of the look inside is an act of penetration, a metaphoric tearing of the veil.

9. The film culminates with the defloration of a virgin, intercut with the camera's movement into and through the tableau of El Greco's *Assumption of the Virgin Mary*. This is the moment when interior and exterior non-story and story most converge and interpenetrate.

10. Through the film the virgin stutters (the voice of the working class, a metaphor Godard has used before) but at the end, she changes register to recite the *Agnus Dei*, token of redemption.

11. The tableau has other erotic dimensions. There is a strain of Orientalism: one of the nineteenth century's favourite subjects, the harem. Again, of course, the motif of penetration. The forbidden look, the law of the Father (the sultan), the phantasy of replacing the Father in his absolute power and promiscuity, the fascination with the other.

12. Penetration, voyeurism, fetishism. Memories of the pornographic tableau in *Slow Motion* (a tableau which is set in movement by its director). The frozen moment of the fetish.

13. A third level of memory/comparison. Fleischer's *Fantastic Voyage*. The same phantasy of penetration, entry into and movement through an impossible/imaginary space, the voyage through the body. Godard's voyage through the body of the Virgin Mother?

14. Interior and exterior: studio and location: art and nature: construction and discovery. The interior non-story takes place in a studio set, the realm of dioramas, models, costumes and make-up. Masquerade. Time frozen: the tableau. Time past: the great masterpiece. Time further past: the subject of the masterpiece. Time frozen: the sacred.

15. The exterior story takes place in the factory, the TV studio, the motel and the roads between. Time is flowing forward, constantly changing in its rhythm and tempo. There are slow passages, then bursts and flurries of activity. Musical time, yet the contingent (aleatory) music of Cage, rather than the 'necessary' music of Mozart, which dominates the film.

16. Painting and music. Lessing's 'Laocoon', space and time, eye and ear, the look and the voice. In *Passion* there are two distinct registers both of space and time.

17. Typically Godardian moments: cars which bang into each other, sudden outbursts of violence which erupt almost arbitrarily, cuffs and boxes on the ear, violent gestures without violent effects (not even, in *Passion*, the red of 'blood'). Brusque kisses in parked cars. Crazy chases around factory machinery. Like the pinball games Godard's characters love to play: people bouncing here and there, lights flashing, trajectories destined to run out of control.

18. Two destinations. The interior non-story is destined for Hollywood (world capital of the fetish). The exterior story is destined for Poland (world capital of injustice to the working class).

19. Two realms: the aesthetic and the political (modern versions of the sacred and the secular). More than in any previous Godard film (even *One Plus One*) these two realms seem counterposed. The director must make a choice.

20. Narrative. Godard constantly exclaims against the concept of the script, the pre-determined storyline, which he sees as a kind of Law, the Producer's Law, which the Director must transgress. Godard pays for his transgression by being threatened and victimised by the Hollywood Producer (abstract or concrete). The relation of cinema to narrative still seems problematic and confused to Godard: he does not see stories as a tribute to the Public, as he sees stars.

21. A last personal note. I am surprised how close *Passion* is to the model of counter-cinema that I put forward more than ten years ago after seeing *Vent d'est*. It seems the road to a revolutionary cinema is still one that runs through a maze, however clearly the sign posts are lettered.

* * *

Essay on Passion *(Jean-Luc Godard, 1982), published in* Framework *21 (Summer 1983).*

L'Eternel Retour

In 1923, Jean Cocteau gave a lecture at the Collège de France, entitled 'On an Order Considered as an Anarchy', during the course of which he named Erik Satie and Pablo Picasso as his masters.[1] He went on: 'How many times have I heard Satie and Picasso reproached for not knowing where they are going. One day Picasso is giving up Cubism. The next, Satie is starting to regress. Yet, wonder of wonders, both of them are treated as if they were absolute beginners [translation mine].' Jean-Luc Godard's development has followed much the same pattern. His films have changed genre and style at an alarming rate, moving from Nouvelle Vague innocence to an embittered avant-gardism and thence to his idiosyncratic 'late' style. Beginning, in the Nouvelle Vague days, with a turbulent mélange of Romanticism and existentialism, he underwent in turn the intellectual influence of the *Arguments* group, of Barthesian semiology, of Althusserian Marxism, of French feminism, and finally of postmodern thought, leading him inexorably back toward aesthetics and even religion. From the start, Godard was unusually open to the fashionable and the topical. In itself, this openness was a strength, but its end result was to send his artistic and intellectual compass pointer swinging wildly around the dial. When Luc Moullet commented that it was easy to identify central themes in the earlier work of Godard, but that, in the 'late' period, the films proved much more difficult to categorise and describe in thematic terms, he was simply pinpointing the effects of this rapid and repeated change.[2] As with

1 Jean Cocteau, 'D'un ordre considéré comme une anarchie', address given at the Collège de France, Paris, on 3 May 1923. Published in *Le Rappel à l'ordre* (Stock, 1926).

2 Luc Moullet, 'Suivez le guide', *Cahiers du Cinema*, Special Godard supplement, 437 (November 1990).

Picasso, Godard's underlying obsessions and compulsions have surfaced in a protean array of styles and subjects.

Almost ten years have passed since I last wrote about Godard, at the time of *Passion* (1982).[3] During the eighties and into this decade, Godard's films have further developed an 'aesthetic' discourse, encompassing music, image, and text. Formal strategies have remained surprisingly constant, but quotation from the great works of the past has taken the form of providing classical reference texts to serve as an armature for a series of loosely linked episodes, fragments, and digressions. Beethoven quartets, the Gospel story, Shakespeare's *King Lear*, all have played this role. At the same time, the films are pervaded by a second layer of quotation and allusion, a complex interplay between text and image, and a proliferation of wordplay and metaphor. It is possible to see in these 'late' films many elements of earlier work, visible like archaeological strata, together with quite new elements and preoccupations – images of the local Swiss landscape, theological speculations, the appearance of Godard himself as magus and fool. But the climate of these films is no longer that of either modernism or political engagement. The urban, metropolitan, consumerist world of the sixties has now been decisively rejected, along with the values of 'modernity' and the politics of 'leftism'.[4] Nonetheless, Godard still sets his films in the present and still alludes to topical events. He is still fascinated by image technology. But there is a new type of mesh between past and present, in which the contemporary, instead of being pervaded by images from the past, is seen almost as an allegorical reworking of the past: airplanes are angels, the message of the Annunciation is delivered by videocassette, and Rubik's Cube is an emblem of cosmogony.

One of the strangest of these allegorical texts is 'Armide', an episode made for the British compilation film *Aria* (1987). Most of the directors are English (among them, Derek Jarman, Nicolas Roeg and Ken Russell), but they also include Robert Altman and Jean-Luc Godard. Each was asked to make a short film, without dialogue, set to an operatic aria. Godard chose, as his classical reference text, Armide's recitative aria from act 2, scene 5 of Jean-Baptiste Lully's tragédie lyrique *Armide*, commissioned by Louis XIV and first performed at Versailles in 1686.[5] The libretto, by Lully's long-time

3 Peter Wollen, '*Passion* 1', *Framework* 21 (Summer 1983). [In this volume, 94–7.]

4 Godard's distance from modernity is explicitly addressed in *Nouvelle Vague*, in which he speaks of a civilisation doomed to extinction.

5 Jean-Baptiste Lully's tragédie lyrique *Armide* was first performed at the Académie Royale de Musique, Paris, on 15 February, 1686. It was the last of a series he wrote for

collaborator, Philippe Quinault, is drawn from Torquato Tasso's *Jerusalem Delivered*. Armide is the daughter of the King of Damascus, whose realm is threatened by invading Crusaders from France. Through her beauty, she captivates and enslaves the Frankish knights, except for their leader, Renaud, who resists her charms and frees his comrades. Humiliated and burning with a desire for vengeance, she invokes spirits to enchant him and place him at her mercy. However, torn between love and hate, she is unable to deliver the fatal blow. This is the scene in which the aria takes place. Godard prefaces the film episode with lines from this aria:

> I yield to this Victor, by Pity I'm won ...
> My greatest wish that thou liest dead ...

For his film, Godard sets the story in contemporary times: in a gymnasium. The Crusader knights are represented by bodybuilders in shorts working out with elaborate machines. Armide and her companion are transmuted into cleaning women, attracted by the muscle men. The two women wear loosely belted housecoats, with nothing underneath. They set out mopping and dusting the floor and the equipment, moving on to polish the bodybuilders themselves. However, the men carry on with their disciplined workout, impervious to the women's charms, even when the women strip naked and pose in front of them. As in the opera, Armide threatens to kill a bodybuilder who ignores her, to stab him with a butcher's knife, but is unable to carry out her purpose. In the end, after further attempts at seduction, thoughts of revenge, and repeated frustration, the women are left behind as the bodybuilders march out in a parade line. Armide cries out 'Yes!' and 'No!' alternately and stands transfixed in a tableau with her companion. (In the opera, too, the enchantment is eventually broken and the knights leave, taking Renaud with them. But then Armide, in a rage, destroys her magic palace and is carried off by her demons.)

At first sight, we are confronted by a semi-pornographic discourse, in which servile women are shown as attracted by muscled men. They fondle themselves, touch the men, strip, and pose provocatively. The men are impervious and reject the desirous women. Thus, the normal conclusion of a pornographic video – the involvement of the women with the men:

Louis XIV, with Philippe Quinault as the librettist. In *Aria*, Godard uses the recording made for Erato in January 1983, conducted by Philippe Herreweghe and sung by Rachel Yakar as Armide and Zeger Vandersteene as Renaud, with the choir and orchestra of the Chapelle Royale, Paris. The album notes for this recording contain the libretto in the original French and in English translation. The two lines cited in the text are from this libretto.

perhaps an act of masturbation or fellatio – is never reached. In this sense, the film deliberately frustrates the expectations of the pornographic spectator/voyeur (who, like the filmmaker, we may assume is male). In the opera, Armide is torn tragically between love and hate, between an overpowering fascination with the phallus and a conflicting desire to castrate and decapitate the invader. In the film, although Armide remains the protagonist, the emphasis is shifted away from her interior conflict and the magical tragedy is reduced to a disenchanted tale of sexual frustration. Renaud and his companions simply ignore Armide, despite her seductive provocations. The implication is that the men are impervious to female desire because of their narcissistic relationship to their own male bodies, and this is sealed by their final bonding into an exclusive male group. It all ends as if the women have wandered by mistake into what is, after all, potentially gay porn, dooming them to frustration. Yet, in this misogynist world, homosexual desire itself is perhaps only the innuendo that conceals a deeper renunciation of all sexuality, each body trapped in the glass of its own narcissism.

'Armide' is reminiscent, in many respects, of two earlier films by Godard, *British Sounds* (1969) and *Numéro deux* (1975). In the first of these, two sequences are juxtaposed: workers on the assembly line at the Ford car factory in Dagenham, with a sound track of machine noise, and a naked woman descending a staircase, with a feminist discourse on the sound track. In 'Armide' it is as if these two sequences are combined into one. The sound track is broken up between fragments of machine noise and fragments of recitative (mainly, but not solely, the female voice). The image is of semi-naked women juxtaposed with men locked into machines, themselves 'machinised' as they pursue their discipline of rhythmically repetitive movement. The atmosphere is that of the factory assembly line, and their final departure, in a parade line, is like the stream of products leaving a factory, but the men we see are manufacturing not alienated commodities, but their own butch bodies. This self-production by the workers is like the production of a permanent and nonorgasmic erection, a 'phallicisation' with no fear of final expense or loss – no castration. The female voice, alternating between 'Yes' and 'No', is an ambivalent and divided voice, a split between accepting and rejecting this regime that excludes its enunciatrix.

In *Numéro deux*, the sexual overtures of the woman are rejected by her husband, exhausted by his mechanical work in the factory. As in a much earlier film, *Une femme est une femme* (1961), the first in which Godard breaks the music up into intermittent fragments, she then turns in frustration to another man, but whereas in *Une femme est une femme* (a loose remake of *Così fan tutte*) all ends happily with the reconstitution of the couple, in *Numéro deux* the husband is enraged and performs a violent anal rape on his wife. Here, it is the humiliated man who acts out his revenge on the body of the woman. In 'Armide', on the other hand, the men remain invulnerable, and the woman is doubly humiliated by her inability to carry out her revenge and kill the man she desires, but who refuses to acknowledge her. In psychoanalytic terms, perhaps we could say that while, in *Numéro deux*, the repressed fear of being the victim of anal rape by the male is acted out hysterically on the woman, in 'Armide' the fear of being the victim of castration by the female can be belittled, in fantasy, and turned against the woman through the image of the phallus as a narcissistic and magical object of male self-identification.

Godard, as far as I know, has never directly confronted male homosexuality as a central issue in his films. In 'Armide', we are as close to it as we get. It is hard to watch the film, as a cinephile, without thinking of Anger's *Kustom Kar Kommandos* or Cukor's *The Chapman Report* (on Godard's 'Ten Best' list for 1963). Godard's treatment of homosexuality, however, reflects a heterosexual ambivalence toward women, in which an infantilising voyeurism is combined with the acting out of an exaggerated misogyny, appropriating the imagery of homosexual desire as the signifier of the exclusion of the female from the male world. Ostensibly 'Armide' has a female protagonist, but, as in Howard Hawks's *Gentlemen Prefer Blondes*, the child-woman is exhibited within a tableau of male hypermasculinity. The governing antinomy in the film is that of 'soft and hard' (the title of a video that Godard made with Miéville earlier the same year, in which, once again, questions of gender are discussed). In Lully's tragédie lyrique, women are associated with love and desire, men with discipline and glory. In Godard's film, the women are associated with softness and wetness, with dripping mops; the men with hardness and tautness, with pumping iron. In one sense, of course, this scenario is a trivialisation. But it is also a defensive schema, an exaggerated reduction of sexual difference to a cartoon of stereotypical extremes unable to meet or make contact, a strategy by which to evade the terrifying consequences of contact. Godard's films resonate with the drums of the 'war of the sexes'. In 'Armide', the refusal to join battle is presented as the ultimate male victory.

It would be possible, perhaps, to read Godard's 'Armide' as a critique of patriarchy, seen as a 'homosocial' structure, a 'bachelor machine', based on the displacement of repressed homosexual desire into the self-contained male world of work, power and prestige. But, on the other hand, within the context of Godard's career, it seems more plausible to see 'Armide' as an elaborate defense against adult or assertive femininity, against feminine 'hardness'. Godard's late films valorise 'softness' ideologically, in contrast to the political 'hardness' of his Maoist period, in their love of the countryside and the beauty of nature. In a different, more questionable way, he valorises feminine 'softness' in his repeated choice of youthful actresses with firm breasts and flawless skins, soft but insipid. Powerful heroines, like Carmen or Armide (or, in another way, the Madonna), are reduced to the same innocuous model. What is important here is that 'softness', as signifier of femininity, is coupled with the tentativeness, confusion and servility displayed by the young women. In 'Armide' Godard gives the heroine a female companion, who is absent from the parallel scene in Lully's opera. Possibly this was suggested by Poussin's painting of Renaud and Armide, where Armide is restrained from murdering Renaud by an allegorical Amor. But more likely, it is a reminiscence of another, allied art-historical subject, the biblical story of Judith and Holofernes. Judith is a heroine who succeeded where Armide failed. In Godard's film, however, we are presented, not with a resolute heroine and her assistant, but with two ineffectual handmaidens, who can be distinguished only by the colour of their hair and their housecoats.

A pornographic subtext runs through Godard's films from the beginning, restrained at first by stricter censorship laws. The theme of prostitution is central to his early work, in which consumerism is presented as a kind of pornography: '*la civilisation du cul*'. At the end of the sixties, in *One Plus One*, aka *Sympathy for the Devil* (1968), and *Le Gai Savoir* (1969), pornographic discourse is transposed onto the sound track as well as appearing on the image track, and the fascination with the obscene and scatological is given a political twist. In fact, toward the end of the sixties the pornographic imaginary is a dominant dimension in Godard's increasingly apocalyptic vision of the world. Pornography, as in Pasolini's *Salo*, provides a vision of the world in which human relations are reduced to a cruel and abstract dialectic of pleasure and pain, of domination and subjugation. The emblematic artists of the sixties – Burroughs, Warhol, Godard – were all obsessed by pornography, and with the relationship between sexuality and an alienating commodity culture.

In 'Armide,' however, the mise-en-scène of pornography is set in motion, but enjoyment itself is blocked. Godard presents a world in which female desire, so threatening in so much of his early work, is doomed to disappointment by male indifference. Burroughs and Warhol, of course, had an explicitly homosexual world view, in which women were, by definition, unnecessary as sexual partners, and in Burroughs's view unnecessary *tout court*. In Godard's case, 'Armide' takes him over the edge into superficial 'camp', but the underlying framework of the episode is still heterosexual. Female desire is to be resisted and annulled through the displacement and renunciation of male desire. The male desires only to be the object of desire for woman and it is in this that his triumph lies, in the essentially heterosexual act of humiliating the woman who desires him and gratifying himself in her humiliation. The bodybuilders' indifference is felt as perverse, though necessary in its passive aggression. Yet, perhaps, this renunciation is the only solution Godard can now envisage to the problem of a destructive (and self-destructive) male sexuality.

However, Godard's fascination with pornography should also be seen as a formal feature of his work. Throughout his career, Godard has sought ways to distance himself from conventional narrative. In the sixties, he deliberately mixed Lumière with Méliès, fictional storytelling with documentary and cinema vérité, juxtaposing different narrative regimes. In *Le Gai Savoir*, he took a further step, toward the experimental film and the film essay or lecture. In the seventies, when he drew back from this radical avant-gardism, he began to introduce tableaux into his films. Pornography, of course, is based around the tableau. As Roland Barthes points out, in his *Sade/Fourier/Loyola*, it has a permutational rather than a teleological structure.[6] In this perspective, we can see Godard's leaning to pornography, not simply as a question of taste or choice of problematic subject matter, but also as a new strategy for de-composing conventional narrative, having exhausted most of the other options in his previous work.

Significantly, there is a single reference to the story of Renaud and Armide in Godard's early critical writings. In 1958 he went to the Festival of Short Films at Tours, where he saw Jacques Demy's first film, *Le Bel Indifférent*. This is a film version of a short dramatic sketch by Cocteau, which he wrote for Edith Piaf in 1940.[7] It is the monologue of a woman, whose beloved takes no notice of her. He ignores her words and herself completely, and, for most of the play, spends his time lying on the bed

6 Roland Barthes, *Sade/Fourier/Loyola* (University of California Press, 1976; originally published by Seuil, 1971). See especially the passages on the tableau in the section 'Sade I', and on the conveyor belt and the machine in 'Sade II'.

7 Jean Cocteau, *Le Bel Indifférent*, in *Oeuvres complètes*, vol. 8 (Marguerat, 1949). The monologue was written for Edith Piaf and first performed by her in 1940. *Renaud et Armide* was published in Paris by Gallimard in 1940.

in her room reading the newspaper, refusing to respond, impervious to her desire. Godard defended Demy's film in an article in *Cahiers* headed 'Ignored by the Jury', and, invoking Cocteau, likens the film to another play of his, *Renaud et Armide* (written the next year).[8] Godard must have been aware not only of the similarity in the subject matter of the two works, but of the transposition between heterosexual and homosexual versions. It is perhaps not surprising that Godard's 'Armide' should be so reminiscent of Demy's own later film work, in its visual style, its musicality and its use of choreography and recitative. However, the association with Cocteau is also suggestive: are not Godard's bodybuilders also transposed versions of Orpheus's motorcycle riders? Is Godard not transposing Cocteau's homosexual text to suit his own heterosexual dilemma?

In fact, I would argue that it is the spirit of Cocteau who reigns over Godard's recent films, especially through the idea of 'the eternal return', *L'éternel retour*, the reworking of classic and mythic texts in contemporary form. Cocteau, of course, is also the great French exemplar of the independent filmmaker, man of the arts, pursuing his uncompromising yet wayward journey through the wasteland of the cinema industry. Cocteau's own acquaintance with the story of Renaud and Armide came, I imagine, through the Michel Fokine ballet *Le Pavillon d'Armide* (first danced by Pavlova and Nijinsky), which was part of Diaghilev's repertoire. Godard's later works also echo the Cocteau of the Ballets Russes period, in their prolific borrowing from the other arts, their reworking of classical material in the garb of life-style modernism.[9] Cocteau and Godard both drape themselves in the mantle of the classics while extolling the charms of narcissistic youth.

It was precisely this strange mix of classicism and modernism à la Cocteau that first attracted me to Godard's films when he made his own debut as a filmmaker. I was living in Paris the year *À bout de souffle* came out and I went back to the cinema to see it many times. 1960! This was also the time of Samuel Fuller's *The Crimson Kimono*, and soon afterward came Budd Boetticher's *The Rise and Fall of Legs Diamond*. To me, Godard's *À bout de souffle* had the extraordinary merit of combining the Cocteau

8 Jean-Luc Godard, 'Ignorés du jury', first published in *Arts* 700 (December 1958), and 'Chacun son Tours', *Cahiers du Cinéma* 92 (February 1959), reprinted in Alain Bergala (ed.), *Jean-Luc Godard par Jean-Luc Godard* (Cahiers du Cinema, 1985), 152–5 and 156–63. The English translation, *Godard on Godard* (Da Capo, 1972), has detailed scholarly and critical notes compiled by Tom Milne.

9 For 'life-style modernism' in Cocteau's work, see Lynn Garafola, *Diaghilev's Ballets Russes* (Oxford University Press, 1989), especially chapter 4, 'The Twenties'; and Dore Ashton et al., *Jean Cocteau and the French Scene* (Abbeville, 1984).

tradition with the American B-picture tradition. *À bout de souffle*, too, was a small film, a film set on the fringes of the underworld, a grittily urban film, but with a difference: Godard's self-conscious modernity. Boetticher was actually mentioned in *À bout de souffle* (one of his films is showing at the cinema that Michel Poiccard, played by Jean-Paul Belmondo, dives into on the Champs-Élysées), but he was there alongside Apollinaire (whose poetry was dubbed over what should have been the dialogue from *Westbound*). This was certainly film made by an intellectual. Yet it wasn't purely in the Cocteau tradition, nor in the allied tradition of auteur heroes such as Rossellini or Bergman, however much their films were the preconditions for its possibility. It was a movie, as well as an art film. It wasn't simply rejecting Hollywood, aiming for a 'European' alternative, more cultured, more sophisticated, more sensitive. *À bout de souffle* was a 'refunctioning' of Hollywood, and, by implication, of American mass culture. It was more like a work of *détournement*.

The connections between Godard and Cocteau that stand out in 'Armide' have led me to re-evaluate the impact of Cocteau on Godard's career as a whole. Cocteau, after all, was the cinematic godfather of the *Cahiers* group and the principal example, in France certainly, of a director who combined a successful career with outsider status. My first view of Godard concentrated on his 'Americanism', linked to the auteurist rediscovery of Hollywood undertaken by *Cahiers du Cinéma*. Seen this way, Godard's early films, his Nouvelle Vague films, echoed important trends in my own English culture: the emergence of Pop art after the 'This Is Tomorrow' exhibition, for example. Richard Hamilton's painting *Interior I*, showing Pamela Knight in *Shockproof* (Douglas Sirk, from a Samuel Fuller script), followed soon after *À bout de souffle*, and seemed to echo its preoccupations. Lawrence Alloway, who was a critical spokesperson for the *This Is Tomorrow* group, was the nearest thing there was in England to the *Cahiers* critics, and a patron of the parallel English magazine, *Movie*.[10] In the end, as the sixties progressed, this cannibalising and reworking of American mass culture became more and more dominant in Britain. In the world of music, it produced the Beatles and the Rolling Stones. Indeed, English mass-cultural 'modernism' began to be hegemonic, in certain sectors, even within the United States itself.

10 See *This Is Tomorrow, Today: The Independent Group and British Pop Art* (Institute for Art and Urban Resources, 1987), the catalogue of an exhibition at The Clocktower, New York, curated by Brian Wallis.

Godard's films appeared as the products of a similarly cosmopolitan intelligentsia when compared with the much more 'domestic' and 'French' work of Claude Chabrol, Éric Rohmer, or François Truffaut, whose 'modernity' and 'Americanism' soon began to seem skin-deep. Indeed, ironically, Godard filled a gap left within English cinema itself, where the cosmopolitan sixties never found a native interpreter. (Expatriate American directors like Joseph Losey and Richard Lester wanted to make European art films – look at *Eve* or *The Knack* – only to be eclipsed by the real thing: Michelangelo Antonioni.) In this situation, Godard's films were the best possible substitutes for their missing English counterparts. *Performance* (Donald Cammell and Nicolas Roeg) and *Leo the Last* (John Boorman) did not appear until after Godard's own English film, *One Plus One*. But by then Godard had moved a long way beyond *À bout de souffle*.

In retrospect, I now see my 'Americanist' fascination with Godard's sixties films as one-sided. There were two further, often conflicting impulses at work in Godard's cinema, both of which were deeply French in origin. First, there was the strong strain of his own lifestyle modernism, which combined a journalistic sense of the topical with a more sociologically oriented mode of investigation and an attachment to the 'critique of everyday life', to use Henri Lefebvre's phrase.[11] It is this dimension of Godard's work that made him seem both a cultural 'barometer' and an emergent political critic. In cinematic terms, this strain owed a great deal to the films of Jean Rouch, which provided models of filmic urban anthropology, first in Africa, and then, with *Chronique d'un été*, made with Edgar Morin, in Paris itself. In intellectual terms, it was from the *Arguments* group, to which Morin belonged, that Godard drew most, but also, I am convinced, from the neighbouring, yet bitterly antagonistic, group of Situationists. Godard's films exhibit any number of Situationist characteristics – not only his topography of the 'society of the spectacle', but also, for example, the ideas of '*dérive*', of '*détournement*', and of plagiarism as a deliberate policy. Indeed, the films made by Guy Debord, the central figure in the Situationist movement, predate many of Godard's own later preoccupations and strategies.[12]

---

11 Henri Lefebvre, *Critique de la vie quotidienne* (Editions Grasset, 1947, and new extended edition, L'Arche, 1958).

12 The Situationists mentioned Godard adversely in three successive issues of *Internationale Situationniste*: no. 10 (March 1966), a discussion of the difference between *détournement*, as a Situationist practice, and collage, as practiced by Godard; no. 11 (October 1967), a programmatic article by René Viénet, noting Godard's alleged recuperation of Debord; and no. 12 (September 1969), remarks on Godard's 'false novelty' and 'belated and useless plagiarism', in the context of a juxtaposition of Godard's *Le Gai*

Secondly, there was Godard's profound and yet paradoxical attachment to the idea of art, both as a repertory of great works, an available cultural heritage, and also as an anarchic project in process, which simultaneously required the reinscription and destruction of that heritage. It is here that Cocteau's heritage also made itself felt. Like those of Cocteau, Godard's films showed a contradictory reverence for the art of the past and a delinquent refusal to obey any of its rules. This applied both to the cinema and to the other, older arts. Godard's films seem to be made in a consumerist version of Malraux's 'imaginary museum', a society full of posters and postcards of great paintings, records of great music, shelves of paperback books, and people who can quote instant lines of poetry to each other. But rather than seeing the consumer society as antagonistic to art, as did many antimodernists, Godard saw the pervasive availability of art as an integral part of consumerism. Art had left its sanctum to become a prominent feature of 'everyday life', alongside pinball machines and advertising posters. In this aspect of his work, Godard often seems to oscillate between a critique of consumerism and mass culture and a fascination with it. In this respect, too, Godard's work resembles Cocteau's. It was Cocteau, after all, who introduced the modern imagery of cabaret, café and sports arena to the world of the aesthetic spectacle, while distancing himself from it through constant allusions to the classics and 'high art', through a strategy of citations, rewritings and parallelisms.

Eventually, of course, Godard's trajectory took him on toward a leftist political commitment, crystallised by the events of May 1968, which threw his aestheticism into crisis. Everyday life itself became more and more politicised, until the streets were filled with militant demonstrations, and home, factory and film set became sites of political ferment. Unlike Cocteau, Godard did not recoil from politicisation. Indeed, his whole filmmaking career was bound up with a determination to be topical, to keep abreast of events (and particularly of the life-style of vanguard urban youth). Once this politicisation passed a certain point, it triggered a transformation of the whole system. Godard's cinema entered its militant phase. At first, this seemed likely to stabilise around some idea of 'Brechtian' or 'guerrilla' cinema, but it soon became clear that Godard's radicalism was impelling him toward a kind of 'Cinema year zero', although, even here, we feel echoes of earlier work: the Lettrists and

Savoir (1969) and Debord's *Hurlements en faveur de Sade* (1952). *Le Gai Savoir* shows Debord's title *La société du spectacle* in one of its close-ups of books. For Debord's films, see Thomas Y. Levin, 'Dismantling the Spectacle: The Cinema of Guy Debord', in Elisabeth Sussman (ed.), *On the Passage of a Few People through a Rather Brief Moment in Time: The Situationist International, 1957–1972* (MIT Press, 1989).

Maurice Lemaître's *Le film est déjà commencé*.[13] Cocteau broke with the Surrealists when they began to move to the far left, but Godard moved rapidly leftward with the Situationists and beyond, to join a Maoist groupuscule, as André Breton had joined the Communist Party.

Instead of the Romanticism of Poe, Dostoyevsky or García Lorca, it was the voice of Marxism-Leninism and Mao Tse-tung Thought that now overloaded the sound track of his films, providing an interminable and pitiless metalanguage, and a series of inquisitorial monologues, designed, like a Lettrist film, to provoke the audience. Yet, in many respects, elements of Godard's former strategies survived. Films were still structured in blocks and modules (often numbered), voices were divorced from characters, 'real people' were mingled with fictional roles, genres were mixed in the same film, dialogue was replaced by direct address to the camera/audience, cinematic devices and techniques were foregrounded, image track and sound track were filled with quotations. There was also a new emphasis on the semiotic character of the cinema, its codes and 'signifying practices', which were explicitly interrogated within the films themselves. Here we see the influence of Roland Barthes (another former member of the *Arguments* group), both in his inquiries into the rhetoric of the image and in his insistence on the necessity of verbal language to anchor the meaning of photographs.[14]

The films of this brief but intense period, which lasted from 1968 to 1972, were didactic and essayistic rather than narrative or dramatic. Even when there was a fictional 'story' it was subordinated to a more or less explicit 'master text'. However, following the breakup of the Dziga Vertov Group, this dominance of the 'master text' started to dissolve and, after Godard's removal from Paris to Grenoble and the beginning of his partnership with Anne-Marie Miéville, a new tentativeness began to be felt. At the same time, Godard began to be seriously interested in video as a form and to develop an ongoing semiotic inquiry, not only into the meaning of photographic images as such, but also into the specific differences of video and film, as opposed to television and cinema. This period saw a revival of Godard's interest in semiotic investigation and the contrast between the cinematic and the televisual sign. In *Ici et ailleurs* (1976) and *Comment ça va* (1976) Godard picked up threads that had been dropped since *Le Gai Savoir*. Although his films were still political,

---

13 See Maurice Lemaître, *Le film est déjà commencé?* (Editions André Bonne, 1952). The film itself was first shown at the Ciné Club du Quartier Latin, Paris, 7 December 1951.

14 See Peter Wollen, 'Godard and Counter-Cinema', *Afterimage* 4 (Autumn 1972), reprinted in *Readings and Writings* (Verso, 1982). Roland Barthes was asked by Godard to appear in a film as 'himself', but refused.

they lost much of the dogmatism of the previous period. In particular, his view of politics had changed and, in the wake of feminism, he now took into account the ways in which the 'personal' was intertwined with the 'political', a trend that eventually led him to the impasse of 'Armide'. His films and especially his videotapes now investigated the relationship between apparently 'personal' categories like 'love' and social categories like 'labour'. This was an extremely rich period in Godard's career.

Then, after 1976, when Godard moved again, this time from Grenoble to Rolle in Switzerland, his films took yet another new turn, toward a preoccupation with landscape, with metaphysics and with cosmic speculation. It is often assumed that this was because he was now living and working in the country, rather than the city. However, it is also possible to see the shift of emphasis as part of a much more general shift within French culture itself. Leading Marxists and structuralists began to abandon the master narratives and semiotic systems of the sixties. As the Enlightenment and 'modernity' were increasingly called into question, a process accelerated by post-1968 disenchantment, many French intellectuals turned away from 'knowledge-based' approaches to the humanities and toward the more speculative domains of aesthetics, philosophy and theology, or urged a decentralised vision of 'dissemination', 'rhizomes' and 'molecular' microstructures. Godard's films, too, abandoned the centre, not only geographically, but thematically as well, breaking down narrative into a mosaic of microelements. At the same time, there was also a clear and significant return to the tradition of Cocteau, in the development of personal mythologies and in a return to the classics, however heterodox the homage. Godard's revived classical aestheticism grew as his political commitment shrank.

As we look back on Godard's career, it is hard to find the red thread that unites his work, even though any one film or video is unmistakably Godardian. We tend to expect consistency in the work of an auteur, a single pattern of repetition and variation. But Godard has changed direction time and again, often seeming both to veer back and to advance simultaneously. In this respect, his career resembles that of his early model and mentor, Roberto Rossellini, who moved in turn from wartime propaganda to the founding classics of neorealism, then onward through the Ingrid Bergman cycle to the uncertainties of the late fifties and early sixties, and eventually, after *La prise de pouvoir par Louis XIV*, to the pedagogic biographies of his final period. It has proved hard for critics to respond with equal enthusiasm to every period of Rossellini's work. The early wartime films were often conveniently forgotten. Critical opinion divided sharply over *Viaggio in Italia*, when erstwhile supporters condemned Rossellini for abandoning neorealism, and others hailed him for enriching it with personal themes. His *Louis XIV* and his *Pascal* found him an entirely new generation of admirers, as well as bringing back some of the old, who now placed him alongside Jean-Marie Straub or, indeed, Godard himself, rather than with Luchino Visconti or Vittorio De Sica. The same heterogeneity is found in Godard's cinematic career, too, and consequently the same critical uncertainty and mutability. In France, critics have tended to line up for or against Godard in fixed battle order, but elsewhere only a few could follow all his periods with equal enthusiasm. Some looked back in nostalgia to the Nouvelle Vague and the sixties. Others regretted that he abandoned and disowned his 1968 political and avant-garde period. New admirers appeared to hail his 'late', Swiss films.

In 1964, just five years after he began work on *À bout de souffle*, Godard once more cited Cocteau in a review in *Cahiers*, this time as the author of *A Call to Order!*[15] After the ebb tide that followed May 1968, it seems Godard now felt the need for his own call to order. But his postmodern return to the classics, to religion, to opera, could not be so pure as Cocteau's. Troubled, as always, by confusing questions and fragmentary insights, Godard challenged the classical lucidity of his reference texts. Yet, as Cocteau observed, 'a masterpiece can never look like a masterpiece. It must necessarily be incomplete and full of defects, since it is the triumph of its errors and the consecration of its faults that make it a masterpiece.'[16]

Opinion is still divided as to whether Godard's 'late' films, however grave their errors and their faults, should be considered as masterpieces, even accursed and defective masterpieces. Yet, after seeing his extraordinary *Nouvelle Vague* (1990), a reworking of his own origins as classic reference text, I suspect that, once again, beneath the surface, something problematic, new and strange is already stirring that will compel another troubled critical reassessment at some time in the future. As if to unsettle both his admirers and his detractors, the perennial absolute beginner has given us yet another breathtaking and disconcerting debut.

* * *

Essay published in Jean-Luc Godard: Son + Image 1974–1991, *edited by Raymond Bellour with Mary Lea Bandy (MoMA, 1992).*

15 Jean-Luc Godard, '*Orphée*', *Cahiers du Cinéma* 152 (February 1964), an issue containing seven articles written in memory of Cocteau. Tom Milne's note in *Godard on Godard* (1972) is especially informative on details of Godard's debt to Cocteau.

16 See Cocteau, 'D'un ordre considéré', in *Le Rappel à l'ordre*.

Arrows of Desire

Here in Britain we are constantly bombarded by sombre bulletins reporting the sad decline, near-death and virtual disappearance of our national cinema. Occasionally some well-intentioned critic hails a commercial hit or middle-of-the-road 'quality' film as the first sign of a long overdue reversal of fortune. But deep down we all know that British cinema was dead almost before it was born. From the 1920s, British cinema was overwhelmed by American production and American imports; during the 1930s more memorable films were made by the British in Hollywood than in Britain; during the 1940s there was a brief, heroic period of hope, which launched the careers of Lean, Powell and Reed, before it was sadly cut short by the commercial collapse of the '50s. Britain then missed out on the New Wave, importing Losey, Lester, Polanski, Antonioni and Kubrick to take its place, and staggered onwards into the '70s in crisis and creative blight. After Harold Wilson lost his trade war against Hollywood in 1948, the writing was well and truly on the wall and by the time he became prime minister the film industry was only a minor concern, to be ineffectively succoured and propped up. Thatcher finally knocked the props away and that was that.

Of course, British cinema has had its shining moments, many more than are generally acknowledged. At long last, cinephiles are looking back at films like MacPherson's *Borderline*, Cavalcanti's *They Made Me a Fugitive*, and Hamer's *It Always Rains on Sunday* with new, re-enchanted eyes. But, on the whole, the commercial industry never secured its economic and institutional base, never developed the confidence in its central core that would have allowed it to undertake experiments and innovations on its fringe. In fact, it was not till the industry's collapse during the Thatcher period that innovative work began to prosper. Ironically, the near-death, virtual disappearance and sad decline of the industry, as defined by Wardour Street and its attendant press, coincided with the appearance, at long last, of an independent British cinema. This belated New Wave was rooted in the cultural renaissance of the '60s, nurtured through the '70s by public agencies such as the British Film Institute, and significantly funded in the '80s by a restructured television system. This was the context in which Derek Jarman, Peter Greenaway and Mike Leigh, for example, finally arrived on the scene and were recognised by the critics, if only because there was nothing left to look at. The history of British cinema turned out to be one of success after all – artistic success, in the true sense of the word – and it proved that the vocation and the talent and the skill were there, and that perhaps during all those decades of decline, they had simply been stifled.

What we are seeing now, however, is not so much the rebirth of British cinema, which would be a virtual impossibility, like the rebirth of Fordist manufacturing industry in general, but something quite different: the birth of a new type of audiovisual culture. The old distinction between a central, 'national' core of industry, studio and Wardour Street, which really counted, and a periphery or fringe of small, independent, even personal filmmakers, who could be trivialised, is no longer viable. 'Independence', in the old sense, has been more and more diffused throughout the whole sector. This first became obvious at the time when Channel 4 was set up and a multifarious and largely self-proclaimed 'independent' sector became conscious of itself as a lobby. The meaning of 'independence' was suddenly stretched to include vast media companies such as Carlton or Time-Life, on the one hand, alongside tiny agglomerates of 'avant-gardists' like the Independent Filmmakers Association [IFA], on the other. In between was an unruly array of would-be documentary filmmakers, sports programmers, low-budget feature film producers, media journalists and so on. Over the years these early aspirants have been crudely filtered down to 'realistic' proportions through the institutional sieve and it may well be that the '80s was basically a transition period which will lead us in the end to a newly stabilised core-periphery relationship. The old core, however, has still continued to crumble, as we can readily see by looking at the recent history of the BBC.

A crisis of the traditional core is also, necessarily, a crisis of the traditional periphery. If things look very different now to the IBA [Independent Broadcasting Authority], they also look very different to the IFA (or would, if it still existed). Once upon a time, there was a small, truculent and determined avant-garde in England, spearheaded by the London Film-Makers' Co-op and basically dedicated to spreading the gospel of late modernism, whether in its 'pure' aesthetic form or as an 'impure' amalgam with 1968 counterculture and gauchisme. Then came the second of the 'two avant-gardes' and the attempt, inspired by Godard, to build a bridgehead to a radicalised European art cinema. By bringing together, at the BFI, a broad concept of avant-gardism with the move to feature filmmaking, this trend helped to produce the context for the subsequent work by Greenaway and Jarman. By that time, however, the whole situation was already changing rapidly. The intense polarisation of mainstream core and avant-garde margin was disintegrating. With punk and 'New Romanticism', music and fashion began to seem like more viable oppositional subcultures than the traditional avant-gardes and to draw image-makers of all kinds into their ambit, particularly because, through music promos, the club scene and a new sector of the press, they also offered economic, institutional and critical support. Instead of a clearly coded mainstream and avant-garde, there was innovative, subversive, startling, transgressive, eccentric, critical and rhapsodic work across an expanded spectrum.

Effectively, the old 'avant-garde' (and rival 'avant-gardes') became diffused into a much broader universe of image-making activities. This development was accentuated by the appearance of a series of new technologies. First and foremost, of course, came video, no longer the preserve of network television. At first, video developed within the art world and alongside the film avant-garde. Film defensively stressed its differences from video (and its supposedly superior aesthetic qualities), while video, naturally enough, stressed its post-modernity and its exciting new range of technical possibilities. It was still, however, polarised against the television industry, just as film was polarised against the cinema industry. It was not until the appearance of music promos and the restructuring of the television industry itself that this began to change. Furthermore, increasingly sophisticated links between video and a rapidly advancing computer technology made it apparent that video was not simply a new medium, but part of a much deeper process of technological change, which presaged an entirely new structure of the audiovisual media and the moving image. At the same time, both the industry and individual artists began to use crossover techniques, blending video with film in new ways. At first, video was embedded into film, but later, as with Derek Jarman's exemplary work (and later Greenaway's), the two were more or less fused.

In selecting work for this Biennial, I found the two media were almost inextricably confused. Some work was shot on video and then transferred to film, other work was shot on film and then shown exclusively on television. Work which had been recommended to me as video turned out to be film and vice versa. Ideally the distinction between the two should be discounted. In practice, I believe it eventually will be, as film projection is finally phased out and replaced by flat screen HDTV. For the moment, however, work shot on video will be largely projected as video, even though the projected image quality is currently inferior even to that of 16 mm film and it would certainly be improved by transfer to film, if that were feasible. Some image-makers, of course, may justifiably prefer technically inferior quality on aesthetic grounds, just as you might prefer working in woodcut or linocut, or taking photographs with a toy camera, or composing for the kazoo. As we move towards a diverse audiovisual culture the technical specificities of different media will become grounds for aesthetic choice in different contexts, rather than distinct ontological categories. Meanwhile, if a majority (three to two in this Biennial selection) of image-makers prefer film to video, this is probably because it is easier to transfer film to video for television broadcast than it is to transfer video to film for screening in an auditorium. So, if I use the term 'filmmaker' from now on, this is because it is less cumbersome than 'moving-image-maker' or 'audiovisual artist', but it is equally meant to embrace video.

Meanwhile, for me the most striking development (and finally much more important than the choice between film or video) was the widening of the spectrum of genres and subcultures represented, coupled with the increased sophistication of formal strategies and the complexity and variety of the relationships between image and sound, and between form and content (traditional terms, I know, but still indispensable). In particular, I was struck by the strength and depth of gay filmmaking, of black and Asian diaspora filmmaking, of animation, and of personal documentary and diary filmmaking. These are, of course, very different types of category. The first represent work by specific groups with a range of particular cultural and political interests and concerns, while animation is a particular style of filmmaking defined by its mode of production (cross-cutting both film and video, although functioning somewhat differently in each), and the last category is more one of the genre, of an approach to filmmaking focused on recovery of the past and self-representation. For this reason, of course, these categories are frequently overlapping. As a result, we repeatedly find unexpected links and interconnections between filmmakers coming from very different cultural or production backgrounds. Robert Crusz, in his film *Inbetween*, made for Sankofa, goes back to Sri Lanka on a quest into his own family background in order to confront his identity as a diaspora filmmaker, finding also that perhaps the imaginary homeland of film itself is the one option left to him as he is caught in between other homes and lands. Stuart Marshall, in his self-financed video, *Robert Marshall*, travels to British Columbia in quest of his dead father in order to confront his own identity as an agent rather than a patient, constructing his own future as an HIV-positive video-maker by searching back into his past. Strategically, both of these filmmakers use home movies as a crucial element in their quest. John Akomfrah goes to Liverpool (for Black Audio Film Collective and the BBC) to make his video *A Touch of the Tar Brush*, to ask questions about the nature of British identity in the city where, in *Billy Budd*, Herman Melville described a company rollicking under the shadow of the street-wall of Prince's Dock circa 1800 'made up of such an assortment of tribes and complexions as would have well fitted them to be marched up by Anacharsis Cloots before the bar of the First French Assembly as Representatives of the Human Race'. Akomfrah presents the old-established cosmopolitan, mixed-race community of Liverpool as the forgotten utopian image of a possible Britain. David Finch, in his film *Stone Steps* (for the Arts Council) also goes to Liverpool, back to his old family home, to ask questions about the nature of the family in a globalised epoch in which Liverpool children leave home and engage in their own diaspora, now outwards from Liverpool, even as far as East Asia, and in which family and images are dispersed around the globe so that only the stars remain inaccessible.

These videos and films also bring to the foreground the changes that have taken place in our understanding of 'Britishness'. The guidelines for the Biennial take it for granted that the work chosen will, in some sense, be British. Obviously this is a problematic assumption: Made in Britain? Financed in Britain or by a British agency? Made in Britain by British citizens? By expatriate British citizens, living and working abroad? By non-citizens living in Britain? Although in practice, the guidelines proved loose rather than tight, the questions still remain. The whole concept of 'national cinema' (or 'national image-making') is one rooted in a historically specific way of thinking which reflects the rise of nationalism in the nineteenth century and its exacerbation in the twentieth. The reality is that with the globalisation of capital movement, communication and the movement of commodities, life-styles and peoples, nations are no longer the imaginary bounded entities which they were once proposed as being. In reality, of course, as John Akomfrah's video vividly reminds us, they never were like that. Britain had a considerable black population in the eighteenth century, and port cities, in particular, like London, Bristol or Liverpool, were always like valves through which the new and unfamiliar entered and then departed. Nevertheless the speed of transfers and exchanges has undoubtedly accelerated, both within Britain, from city to city as well as between city and country, and also throughout the world, between the global cities of the core and between the core and the periphery. Increasingly, people's lives are cast as unpredictable itineraries rather than as stable, fixed experiences. We can see this at work, not only in the videos and films made explicitly about diaspora, but also in work like Vonnie's *Justice Sucks*, a video diary which shows a life lived constantly on the move, uprooted, nomadic and disturbingly open-ended.

Vonnie's extraordinary Teenage Diary, made for the BBC Community Programmes Unit, tackles head-on the tensions between the personal and the private, on the one hand, and the institutional, the legal and the public, on the other hand. Made as part of a series in which teenagers were given the opportunity to make and control their own films, it relentlessly probes the limits of that control, taking the camera into situations where it is forbidden to tape, where Vonnie herself can hardly bear to return, where a terrible memory is conjured up by a blank wall and a single window, and where the power of the media is also used to empower Vonnie in her confrontation with the social services personnel who control her life. *Justice Sucks* is both formally inventive and also a moving and passionate exposé of the dysfunctionality of the family, just as, in a very different register – that of the animated fable – Marjut Rimminen and Christine Roche's scathing film, *The Stain*, provides its own poetic and unremitting indictment of family values. Richard Heslop's live action *Floating*, made for the BFI, returns to the theme of the family, reducing it to a grotesque and macabre travesty of human relations in which the family members pursue their own mad obsessions. And, in Tim Rolt's *The Vacuum*, a virtuoso mix of animation and live action made for Channel 4, a bizarre pseudo-family is created by means of its own household equipment, incorporating the cycle of death and birth into a fantastic world of domestic anomie. Chris Newby's *Relax*, another BFI film, confronts the possibility of disease and death – again the reality of AIDS – within the format of the dramatised personal diary, sparsely and with formal measure, while Jacqui Duckworth's *A Prayer Before Birth*, financed by GLA, documents the fatality of disability with unsparing, yet undespairing, images of agony and distress. Juliet McKoen's *Blood Sisters* also takes us into an intolerable world of excess and anguish. In some of these films, normality is stretched until it turns into absurdity. In others, the body is the site of a struggle between controlling and invading agents from outside, whether physical or psychological or institutional, and a fierce will to resist. Visual images and correlates are found for unbearable, intense bodily experiences with astonishing inventiveness and power.

The body is also the subject of videos and films as diverse as Mike Stubbs's *Man Act: The Sweatlodge* and Peter Greenaway's *M Is for Man, Music, Mozart*: both based around dance performances, the first creating an intense geometrical grid through camera position and bodily movement, the second subordinating the body as anatomical object to a largely frontal camera, setting it also within a typical Greenaway alphabetical series, which turns out to contain an allegory of the development of the arts from the resources of the flesh. Language, image and history also interconnect in Andrew Stones's *A History of Disaster With Marvels*, a savage indictment of scientific and technological pretension; while Sera Furneaux's *Anxiety/Rest* explores the relationship between word and image in the eerie context of the neurological textbook. For Paul Bush, in his film *Lake of Dreams*, another film made possible by GLA, the body is an analogue to the surface of the moon, lit with love and expertise, a pole of attraction and romance, while in Jayne Parker's *The Pool*, it is the object of examination and disclosure, part of the natural world, impassive and reptilian. Robert Sanders's *Bacon*, in contrast, reduces the body chillingly to the order of meat. Finally, in *Caught Looking*, made for television, Constantine Giannaris provides a blazon of gay erotic registers, in a brilliantly devised and executed simulacrum of the virtual reality of some impending computerised amusement arcade of sexuality. Perhaps this too, in its displacement of body into pure image, has a subtext of safe sex and flight from AIDS into a new mode of virtual sex.

In Constantine Giannaris's film the electronic theatre of eroticism is one which both speaks with an artificial voice and addresses the subject with a stream of pictograms and verbal text. The same is true of John Butler's *Leisure Society*. Audiovisual culture is increasingly becoming a multi-channel culture, incorporating live action image, music or electronic sound, natural or electronic speech, and verbal language in graphic form. The traditional film avant-garde always stressed the specificity of its medium, and films like *Lake of Dreams* or *The Pool* still display a fascination with film as such, at least in the care and precision of their making, although *Lake of Dreams* also shows an interest in new technology, transposing high romanticism into the idiom and media of the space age. A number of videos, on the other hand, use text, whether as an aesthetic motif, as a discursive tool, as a structuring device, or as a metalanguage. Commercial and vernacular forms of art have always used words in conjunction with images – in posters, in comics, in popular illustration, in ads and so on. Innovative periods in the 'high arts', such as those of Cubism or Pop Art, were also periods in which words started proliferating within the picture frame as artists attempted to incorporate new subject matter and new visual experiences into their work. It seems that video is going through a similar phase, both stimulated by new technology and responding to the ubiquity of text in the visual environment, both to comment on it and, in a certain sense, to aestheticise it.

Among the shorter works, one minute 'films' (videos!) made through the Arts Council for Channel 4's 'The Media Show', David Cunningham's *this moment*, also a text piece, and Vivienne Dick's *3am* comment on different aspects of time in strongly contrasting styles, while John Butler's *Leisure Society* combines the techniques of computer animation with text and music promo to create visionary satire. In general, music video has settled down into routine genres and state-of-the-art high-tech spectaculars with a stress on production values, but interesting work is still to be found, whether at the cheap do-it-yourself end of the scale, as with Gina Birch's *Loving Feeling* (with Dorothy), or, with much greater resources and big stars, as with John Maybury's *You Do Something To Me* with Sinead O'Connor (for the AIDS awareness Cole Porter spectacular *Red Hot + Blue*). John Maybury remains one of the most consistent British video-makers, moving between avant-garde, television and music industry. The Brothers Quay's *Are We Still Married?* (with His Name Is Alive) is an unexpected venture into the rhythmic possibilities of their disturbing animated world of eerie clockwork toys and ornate mechanisms. The Brothers Quay, of course, have led the revival of British animation, just as Derek Jarman has blazed the way for gay filmmakers, and their example has helped propel British animated film into the realms of the surreal and the magical. Kayla Parker's *Unknown Woman* brings together animation, feminism and myth, while Phil Mulloy's extraordinary *Possession* uses the Red Riding Hood story as a framework within which to develop a social critique, an allegory of the family and a series of wry reflections on animated filmmaking, using a style as vivid as it is minimal. David Anderson's *Door*, made commercially in 35 mm, also uses a fairy tale mode of narration, drawn from the pen of Russell Hoban, while showing a virtuoso, yet playful, technical facility, and, at the other end of the scale, Jayne Bevitt's *Some Dogs*, made when she was a student at the Royal College of Art, shows what can be done with slender resources, in an exhilarating comic meditation on the ultimate theme of death.

Finally, Alia Syed's *Fatima's Letter* brings together many of the themes and motifs I have characterised. It is both a poetic documentary of the Pakistani and Bangladeshi community of East London, seen mainly as they stand on the platform of the underground station, waiting for the train, then boarding or leaving it, shot in black and white with an extraordinary use of shadows and frames within the frame, and also a meditation on sexuality and the body, on the family and childhood, though indirect and metaphorical in its approach, rather than literal and straightforward. Reminiscent in many ways of the classic work of Maya Deren, it relies on building patterns of repetition and effects of choreographed movement created in the editing. It simultaneously creates a dreamlike world in which image flows into image and memory dissolves into imagination, and presents an ultra-realistic and meticulous depiction of an all-too-real world in its panorama of glimpses and glances and telling details. Finally, it is an exceptionally bold treatment of the relationship between image and word. When I first saw the film it was simply titled *Untitled* and it gradually became apparent that this signified, not only an uncertainty as to how to find an adequate title, but also an absence of subtitles for long stretches of the film in which the dialogue and voice-over were entirely in Urdu, until, after long delay, rolling titles began to appear, translating what had been heard earlier, but for those British viewers outside the Urdu-speaking diaspora, not hitherto understood, heard as intonation and rhythm, almost with the texture of music.

These films and videos, then, are formally innovative in many different ways, but all of them also confront issues of 'content' which are both fundamental and topical and impassioned. This new audiovisual culture is not reductively 'formalist', nor is it documentary or issues-oriented in the straightforward sense. It refracts an engagement with racism or AIDS, with family, body and sexuality, with identity and with justice, through formal strategies which accentuate rather than dilute the passion felt by the filmmakers. British cinema critics nowadays are prone to look back to the high romanticism of the 1940s to identify the golden age of the national cinema, a long-lost world of excessive melodrama and studio spectaculars. What I learned from selecting the work for the Second ICA Biennial was that the same passion and excitement can be generated by films made with a fraction of the resources, but with the same intense love of sound, movement and image. Moreover, this is quite compatible, not only with personal vision and formal experiment, but also with a commitment to a new vision of British culture, one in which there is an investigative sense of history, a critique of traditional institutions, an acknowledgement of the power of myth, romance and the marvellous, a fearless faith in personal revelation and self-examination, a restitution of the body to the centre of art, in the modes of both beauty and of tragedy, and a refusal to be constrained by the oppressive myths of Britishness and of identity as the criteria of a cruelly unproblematic logic of inclusion and exclusion. For the first time in many years, we can hail a new dawn for audiovisual culture in Britain, aware of its economic and institutional fragility, but aware too of the renewed hope it has already brought. In one area of British culture, at least, we have a future to which we can look forward.

Programme:

1

Robert Marshall Stuart Marshall
A Touch of the Tar Brush John Akomfrah
Justice Sucks Vonnie

2

this moment David Cunningham
Anxiety/Rest Sera Furneaux
A History of Disaster With Marvels Andrew Stones
Leisure Society John Butler
Man Act – The Sweatlodge Mike Stubbs
3am Vivienne Dick
Loving Feeling Gina Birch
You Do Something To Me John Maybury
Stille Nacht II: Are We Still Married? The Brothers Quay
Bacon Robert Sanders
M Is For Man, Music, Mozart Peter Greenaway

3

Stone Steps David Finch
Caught Looking Constantine Giannaris
Inbetween Robert Crusz

4
Some Dogs Jayne Bevitt
The Vacuum Tim Rolt
Door David Anderson
Possession Phil Mulloy
The Stain Marjut Rimminen and Christine Roche
Blood Sisters Juliet McKoen
Floating Richard Heslop

5
Unknown Woman Kayla Parker
Lake of Dreams Paul Bush
The Pool Jayne Parker
Relax Chris Newby
A Prayer Before Birth Jacqui Duckworth
Fatima's Letter Alia Syed

* * *

Catalogue essay published in Arrows of Desire *(ICA, 1992), accompanying ICA Biennial of Independent Film and Video 1992, also titled 'Arrows of Desire', programmed by Wollen.*

Interview on 'Arrows of Desire', ICA Biennial of Independent Film and Video

Ilona Halberstadt: *How did you make your selections for the Biennial?*

Peter Wollen: Partly, that's a practical question – and partly, it's theoretical. On the practical level, the ICA have a panel of consultants who submit viewing lists of work made over the last two years that they think was important. As the curator, I looked at all those works. But then, I asked the ICA people – Tim Highsted and Simon Field – about areas that seemed thinly represented in the consultants' lists. I was thinking of work from outside London, work from television, music videos and so on. I also asked my own friends and did my own research. I went to the *Time Out* office and looked through all their television listings for the two years and asked to see some work that was noted in those. In the end, I saw a lot of films and tapes, maybe three hundred.

Theoretically, I wanted to make a selection that was representative and diverse, that showed the depth and scope of independent film and video making in Britain, but also, of course, the quality. Yes, I know that talking about quality really takes us back to fundamentals. The classical problem is how to weigh your own taste against some transcendent standard, or, put more concretely, against the taste of the various cultures and subcultures that make up the independent film and video milieu, how to start out from your own personal preferences, but, at the same time, acknowledge the quality of work that you don't readily respond to yourself. Well, you do your best. I'm happy with the outcome. One of the video makers buttonholed me at the opening reception and commented that not all the tapes in the programme for which he was selected would please his own friends. Still, he said, after a pause, 'I'd have to say, they were all quality, though.' I was happy.

Do you see any emerging pattern of themes or genres or new directions?
Well, some areas emerge with a sharp profile – animation, for instance, and work by gay film and video makers. Also, there are a number of what you might call 'personal documentaries', work which is often explicitly autobiographical, and which goes beyond old categories like 'diary film'. Some of these begin to spill over into kind of 'essay films'. And because many of these film and video makers use clips from home movies or go and interview members of their family, there is a kind of intimacy and privacy to their work, which is then juxtaposed to an engagement with public issues and broad intellectual problems. Example? I was fascinated, and moved, by Vonnie's Teenage Diary, *Justice Sucks*, which came from the BBC's Community Programmes Unit. It was very personal, but at the same time she raised all kinds of political and ethical issues. She just switched from talking about the law to talking about love, for instance.

How do you see the relationship between television and cinema?
Cinema? What's that? None of this work is for the cinema, except in an extremely marginal sense. Some of it might show at festivals or at specialised venues. The cinema no longer has any central relationship with art. In fact, I would say that Britain is one of the few places that even has a residual art cinema. I'm thinking of Derek Jarman and Peter Greenaway. Who else is there, in other places? Ulrike Ottinger doesn't reach cinema screens. Paul Leduc doesn't. Hollywood is much too knowing to produce art inadvertently, like it used to. It can use art ideas, but that's not the same thing. Everybody's Albert Lewin. At best.

Television, on the other hand, is really important. A very high proportion of the work in the Biennial was made for TV or eventually screened on television – BBC2 or, to some extent, Channel 4. This is something specific to Britain too, certainly in comparison with the USA. I can't imagine seeing this kind of work on American television. Out! The best you can hope for there is Liquid TV on music cable. The real question is the relationship between television and the art world. The kind of work we are talking about exists on the sometimes overlapping margins of these two monsters – the media world and the art world. Here you have to distinguish between 'art world' and art – perhaps we need a new word. The old one is contaminated. These two spheres are the two poles of attraction, with their career commissioning editors and curators, their symbiosis with advertising and sponsorship, their ladders to success, their stars, their blockbusters and their niches. Artists have to negotiate them or fall into a kind of black hole. Because that's where the audience is.

How does that mesh with the relationship between video and film? You keep repeating 'film and video makers'!

I know. I ought to alternate it: 'film and video', 'video and film'. It is an increasingly irrelevant distinction. After I made my selection, I discovered that some things I thought were originally video were in fact film, and vice versa. I think even the technical differences in image quality are exaggerated – video seems inferior because people think of it as cheap and quick, so they don't spend money and time on lighting properly. Video isn't allotted the same production values. In any case, many people switch between one and the other, like I do, or use both in one work. They shoot on 16, or super 8, like Derek Jarman, and then go to video for effects, or they use video and then transfer to film. In the end, it's shown on TV or cassette. It's only in specialised screening situations, like the Biennial, where the two get separated, out of necessity, because the projection technology is different, rather than the production technology.

Independent film and video are often defined by lack of resources. Do you think this creates an aesthetic of its own, or maybe this is the wrong way of looking at the question?

People used to talk about the 'Cinema of Poverty', or Glauber Rocha's 'Aesthetics of Hunger', but that came from Cuba and Brazil rather than the capitalist core, and really referred to the problems of creating an industry. Evidently, if you don't have the resources you can't make Hollywood films, or even 35 mm films (although one of the films I selected did turn out to have been shot on 35 – an animation film). But you can make better films than Hollywood, let alone Pinewood, if that still exists. In fact, here the collapse of the film industry may even work to the advantage of independent film and video makers, especially through creating a new niche so that there is access to a new audience.

My impression of the work in the Biennial is that the aesthetic comes from the makers rather than from the resources. I don't think the *aesthetics* of this work would have been significantly improved with more money. This isn't to minimise the seriousness of the financial constraints that there are in Britain, and which are getting worse all the time. It certainly makes it more difficult to find money and it restricts the number of films and tapes that get made. It probably puts pressure on people to leave the independent sector for the mainstream or simply to give it all up. That's tragic, when there's so much talent and so much commitment.

Is there – what is the avant-garde now?
Well, there's a sense in which there will always be an avant-garde, in the 'cutting edge' sense of the term. There will always be artists who are experimenting with new means and pushing at the limits and expanding the potential of expression. In that sense, the Biennial is the avant-garde. But, in another sense, if you're talking about the classic avant-garde, explicitly polarised against the mainstream, with its apparatus of manifestoes and scandals and expulsions, I don't think that exists anymore. I think the Situationist International was the last classic avant-garde.

Now we have moved on from a war of position to a war of manoeuvre, if I can use Gramsci's distinction in a new context. In fact, as the art world has moved to the centre of the culture industry, absorbing the work of the classic avant-gardes, and putting a premium on innovation and 'opposition' as it did so, the whole situation has changed. It isn't as if there was the mainstream over there and the avant-garde over here, and never the twain shall meet. It's a question of opening up spaces in both the media and the art world and trying to create a viable area between them. It involves more pragmatic politics because there isn't such a clean break.

I thought about commercials a lot. In the end, I decided against including any, although I suppose music videos could really be counted as commercials, in which case I included three. One of these (John Maybury with Sinead O'Connor) was for an AIDS benefit and the other two (by Gina Birch and the Brothers Quay) were for virtually unknown bands, which hardly count. In that sense, the advertising industry has its weird margins too, just as the music industry does. And I also thought about the Labour Party's controversial NHS election ad, but decided against it. In any case, I would only have shown it if I could have deleted Neil Kinnock. I guess the real test case would have been if I had come across an ad which used the latest 'state-of-the-art technology' in a mind-blowing way, but I didn't see any that did.

As to whether it matters or not, yes, it does. The market constantly strives to instrumentalise and commodify everything of value. But I think it's unrealistic to think you can have entirely clean hands. I'm suspicious of purism. But sooner or later there has to be a line you won't cross and, in the absence of party discipline, you have to make your own judgements. Conversely, just as not every ad or music video is irredeemably complicit, so not every experiment is necessarily oppositional. It's a force field, in which judgements matter.

What is the relation between art and politics in your selections? Do they reflect the general malaise, the fragmentation of political groups – or rather is a certain new optimism breaking through?

Some of the work is clearly political. Green politics – Andrew Stones's *A History of Disaster With Marvels*; ethnic politics – or the politics of ethnicity – John Akomfrah's *A Touch of the Tar Brush* and Robert Crusz's *Inbetween*; attack on 'family values' – Marjut Rimminen and Christine Roche's *The Stain*, and Phil Mulloy's *Possession*; the politics of AIDS – Chris Newby's *Relax* and Stuart Marshall's *Robert Marshall*; post-Fordism – John Butler's *Leisure Society*. These are just some obvious examples that come straight into my mind.

But maybe what you're hinting at is that these are all concerns of the kind that used to be called 'single issue' politics, and that there isn't any cohesive sense here of politics as a master-narrative, as historically totalising. Or, put another way, isn't it just post-modern politics and is that real politics at all, in the traditional sense? Look at the way you couple 'fragmentation' with 'general malaise'... But I don't think that the unity imposed on diverse issues by traditional left politics was necessarily a good thing. I'm happy with a montage of politics. It's more realistic.

Perhaps I should try to clarify this one step further. I think it's possible, as you look at the work in the Biennial, to start making connections between different and very personal political stances, which are more fruitful than the kind of connections imposed by a totalising vision. For example, the connections between *Inbetween* and *Robert Marshall* lead us from ethnicity or AIDS to the family and thus through to *The Stain*. David Finch's *Stone Steps* relates to the family, but also, in a completely different way, to *A Touch of the Tar Brush*. Hopefully, this kind of richness and intricacy can help lead us to a better, more concrete, less abstract understanding of how different political issues and positions reverberate, and thus, in the end, to a more effective politics. It's another way of trying to link the personal with the political. Utopian, perhaps.

Why did you call the Biennial 'Arrows of Desire'?

As a counterblast to *Chariots of Fire*, of course, in an immediate way – by which I mean not just the film, trivial as it was, but a vision of British cinema which it came to symbolise because of its Hollywood recognition. The fact is that British cinema was unable to match Hollywood even in the immediate post-war period, when Rank tried, and it is completely unreal even to think about it now. Besides which, what would be the point? On the other hand, I think the work shown in this Biennial is definitely superior to its American counterparts.

Also, less directly, I think the allusion to Blake's Utopian *Jerusalem* is appropriate. Putnam was appropriating Blake via the Promenade Concerts and a completely decadent English chauvinism. Whereas I think the Biennial is truly in the tradition of Blake in its radicalism and its visionary intransigence. Utopianism again? Yes and no. I was in Mexico City in November, where the last, 1990 Biennial was screening. After the ICA, the programmes go on a round-the-world tour organised by the British Council. I was amazed by the enthusiasm of the audiences and by the coverage given in the press and on TV. It was completely unlike actually existing England, where of course neither the media nor the art press pay any attention. I had somehow got inured to the 'prophet in the wilderness' mode and was really impressed to find that, outside Britain, the work was seen more enthusiastically and, I think, more accurately, in terms of its real value.

Finally, is there an international style? Is it worth talking about the Britishness of this work?
It's international on one level and British on another, I guess, but I think both these terms are problematic and the work in the Biennial frequently pinpoints precisely that kind of problem. Look at Alia Syed's *Fatima's Letter*, for instance.

First, it's not made in an international style in the sense that the old Co-op filmmaking style could be regarded as 'international', despite national rivalries within the Co-op world. The Film-Makers' Co-op in Britain was obviously indebted originally to the American example and there was a kind of common understanding in New York and London and Berlin as to what avant-garde filmmaking was all about. *Fatima's Letter* comes out of that Co-op background. It often reminded me of Maya Deren. But Alia Syed has transmuted it into something quite new, which couldn't have happened anywhere except Britain, strangely enough.

British film and video making has turned out to be both very cosmopolitan and very local in ways which completely confuse our traditional understandings of terms like 'international' or 'British'. I don't think this is adequately captured by terms like 'multi-cultural' or even 'hybridity'. I was very struck recently reading books about the city (and most of this film and video making is definitely urban), such as Saskia Sassen's *The*

Global City, which is largely about London, and Manuel Castells's study of *The Informational City*.

They argue that we live in a new global 'space of flows' – flows of information, capital and labour – flows which run first between the dominant chain of global cities, and then to and fro between those cities and their satellites in the global hinterland, for which the cities serve as the command-and-control centres. Flows of capital themselves attract flows of labour, as workers, or those hoping to work, move into the satellites (Export Processing Zones and the like) and then into the global cities themselves, which become increasingly spatially and socially polarised. London, New York and Tokyo are the major triad of this chain of global cities, a kind of New Hanseatic League, as Saskia Sassen calls it.

In this New World Order of capitalism, the nation-state becomes increasingly irrelevant and enters into crisis, flailing about dangerously in search of a new role. The only viable form of resistance is to combine the local with the global, building new kinds of network, bringing together local communes from core cities and their hinterlands, to try and take back a measure of control from the transnational flows which currently control them. What interested me was the way in which films and tapes in the Biennial seemed to represent this kind of fusion of the cosmopolitan with the local. Plus an attempt to preserve and restore meanings which have been drained out of the outmoded idea of 'national culture', but are still necessary to us on a personal level.

So it is still worth talking about Britishness, but only if we see it simply as the place from which we fire our arrows of desire. And there is still a long way to go before they reach their targets. Right? I don't want to sound too Utopian.

* * *

Interview with Ilona Halberstadt, published in PIX *1 (1994).*

Perhaps …

Thirty long years have passed since I first wrote about Eisenstein for my book *Signs and Meaning in the Cinema*.[1] I was writing then in a very different context from the one in which we work today. The 1960s were the period when Russian art of the 1920s was rediscovered, and Camilla Gray's crucial book, *The Great Experiment*, published in 1962, had pointed out the links between Eisenstein and Constructivism – the Constructivist influence relayed through Meyerhold's stage sets and the connection between Rodchenko's Constructivist method of photography and Eisenstein's aim of 'catching movement at its height, the moment of maximum drama, obtained by a typically Constructivist low-angled shot'.[2] All this may seem elementary today, but it was eye-opening at the time. It made it possible to take Eisenstein out of the narrow context of film history and place him in the much wider context of artistic modernism. At the same time, it focused attention on Eisenstein's avant-garde credentials – his place alongside not just Rodchenko or Meyerhold but also Joyce or Brecht, a secure place in the history of modernism in the arts. For a film historian this was an important step. It now seemed possible to pry film aesthetics free from the deadly grip of realism, on the one hand, and Hollywoodiana, on the other, in order to create a new kind of film history, one that saw film as an art form, located (ontologically) at the crossroads of literature, music, theatre and painting. This need not altogether exclude popular cinema, but it would situate it in a much broader – and deeper – context, and point out the possibility of an alternative road.

1 Peter Wollen, *Signs and Meaning in the Cinema* (Secker and Warburg, 1969; 5th edition, 2013).

2 Camilla Gray, *The Great Experiment* (Harry N. Abrams, 1962), 253.

Indeed, Eisenstein's own reflections on the cinema supported this view. In writing about film art, he switched constantly between the lessons to be learned from Joyce, Scriabin, Kabuki and Kandinsky. Moreover, from my personal point of view, the filmic innovations of the 1960s, especially those of Jean-Luc Godard, seemed to show that an alternative road was indeed possible. Godard acknowledged his debt to Hollywood, just as Eisenstein acknowledged his debt to Griffith, but he too invoked Joyce, Hokusai and Mozart in his writing about film. At the same time, Godard defended Eisenstein's vision of *Que Viva Mexico!* against later pillage and travesty, insisting on Eisenstein's unshakable place in film history, and celebrating him (along with Welles and Murnau) as one of the three truly great directors. Godard deemed him 'the greatest editor in the world' (ahead of Alain Resnais); compared him to Tintoretto (for the colour sequences in *Ivan the Terrible*); advised us to love Eisenstein as much as Rouch; described his own homage to *Potemkin*, in *Les Carabiniers*, as 'proud, moving, Eisensteinian'; recounted with enthusiasm the reaction of an audience of children to Eisenstein's 'rapid, synthetic montage' in *October*; and described Eisenstein respectfully as both a great painter and a great choreographer.[3] This, of course, was before he switched his allegiance to Vertov and began to denounce his former master.[4] Nonetheless, it was Godard's defence of Eisenstein, running against the current of André Bazin and Christian Metz's attacks on montage, that reinforced my view that Eisenstein was not simply a great filmmaker but also a great artist in the fullest sense of the word.

And then, of course, Eisenstein was also a remarkable theorist and teacher. In 1964, Barthes's *Éléments de Sémiologie* appeared (translated into English in 1967). Eisenstein suddenly appeared in a new light – as a pioneer theorist of semiotics. Rereading his writings today, I think I was wrong to make such a rigid distinction in my mind, as I did then, between early and late Eisenstein, the Constructivist and semiologist versus the Wagnerian and symbolist.[5] At that time, I felt that Eisenstein's shift of emphasis from montage to synaesthesia, from Meyerhold to Wagner, was

3 Jean-Luc Godard, 'Chacun son Tours', *Les Cahiers du Cinema* 92 (February 1959); translated in *Godard on Godard* (Da Capo, 1972).

4 Godard signalled his allegiance to Vertov in 1969, following the attack on Eisenstein by Marcelin Pleynet in the Maoist-leaning film journal *Cinéthique*, translated as 'The "Left" Front in Art: Eisenstein and the Old "Young" Hegelians', *Screen Reader 1: Cinema/ Ideology/ Politics* (The Society for Education in Film and Television, 1977).

5 For insight into this period in Eisenstein's work, see Annette Michelson, 'Reading Eisenstein Reading *Ulysses*: Montage and the Claims of Subjectivity', *Art and Text* 34 (Spring 1989), 64–77.

a capitulation in the face of political and ideological pressures – quite comprehensible, in the circumstances, but not to be viewed uncritically either. Now I think that although there was a shift, politically modulated as prudence demanded, it was basically driven by developments in his own thinking, as he confronted the new reality of sound and colour as integral components of cinema and reconsidered, in response, his theories of 'ecstasy' and 'polyphony'. The idea of 'ecstasy', for instance, was already present in his early remarks on the emotional saturation produced in the spectator by the acrobat's death-defying somersault ('*salto mortale*'), and his theory of the 'monistic ensemble' was simply a reformulation of his views on the counterpoint of the visual and the verbal in the ideogram, one that now stressed the aspects of 'totality' rather than that of 'montage'. Indeed, the earlier writing could itself be seen as leaning too far toward a Pavlovian psychology and a 'machine aesthetic', which needed to be corrected by a shift in the opposite direction, as exemplified by his growing interest in ethnography and psychology as the foundation of 'inner speech'. On the other hand, I was probably right in thinking that Eisenstein often veered toward creating a mystical superstructure on mechanistic foundations.

Eisenstein's career as a theorist gives us, in fact, a much clearer picture of his goals and intentions than do the films themselves, too many of which have to be imaginatively reconstructed in the light of his writings. Of course, his production of Wagner's *Valkyrie* at the time of the Hitler-Stalin pact has to be seen in its political context. On the other hand, Eisenstein's interest in Wagner developed quite naturally from his thinking about audiovisual spectacle and he remained far from rigorously Wagnerian in his approach. Moreover, the cinematic production of *Ivan the Terrible* plainly exemplifies Eisenstein's assimilation of Wagner more accurately than the staging of the opera itself, which he regarded as yet another wretched failure to realise his vision. In many ways, I would now argue, Eisenstein's writings on aesthetics became more interesting as his career progressed and he moved beyond the problems of silent film to those of sound and colour. In the early writings, I can't help feeling, the idea of 'intellectual montage' served as a kind of substitute for the absence of verbal language, except in the form of subtitles – an often-neglected aspect of silent film to which Eisenstein paid close attention, in respect to both their content and their form, as well as their placement within the stream of images. Then, when sound first appeared, he toyed with the idea of substituting a form of 'narratage' for subtitles, seemingly along the lines of William K. Howard's 1933 Hollywood film, *The Power and the*

Glory, before consolidating his reading of Joyce and linguistics in a theory of 'inner speech' based on sensuous (and thus imagistic) thinking. In this way, dialogue was reduced to a subordinate role as the secondary exteriorisation of an interior reality which was the main subject of the cinema.

In fact, when we look closely, we can begin to see that Eisenstein's interest in literature – whether Dickens, Pushkin, Zola or Joyce – was largely directed toward its use of tempo in narration and its unscrolling, so to speak, of latent visual imagery. Eisenstein was interested in the way characters are portrayed through visual description. Thus Mr. Gradgrind in *Hard Times* is evoked through 'geometrical means', as Eisenstein puts it – his 'square wall of a forehead' combined with his 'square coat, square legs, square shoulders'. The character of Zola's Nana, on the other hand, is drawn through emblematic actions – her destructive nature is 'materialised' (Eisenstein's word) by the way she smashes up a *bonbonnière* of Dresden china. Dialogue is not seen as particularly important – hence, perhaps, Eisenstein's preference for Zola over Balzac, in the face of Marxist prejudice on the subject. In the case of Joyce, it seems that Eisenstein's approach concurred with that of Joyce himself – he is quoted as saying that only Ruttmann or Eisenstein could film his work, thereby confirming that montage was the essence of the books.[6] (Incidentally, Eisenstein admired Joyce as a master of montage in his own right, but despised Dos Passos, whom he saw as an imitator, influenced by the cinema, rather than prefiguring it.) This Joycean line of thought developed logically from Eisenstein's early preoccupation with intellectual montage. At the same time, however, he moved away from the role of montage as the agent of reason (as exemplified in his project of filming Marx's *Capital*) toward its capacity for arousing emotion, toward ecstasy as the final goal.

Writing to Esther Shub from Mexico in 1931, Eisenstein could go as far as saying that 'I'm no longer the slightest bit concerned with problems of montage. And, it's terrible to say, sound film even less.'[7] Instead, he said, he would 'like to work in the theater. In a good one, a real one. So strong is my reaction to the cinema.' It is as if words and filmic images had come to seem too removed from reality, too concerned with ideology. Cinema is reduced to 'fleeting little pictures – especially today with all its deafening noise or non-stop talk'. In Mexico, he tells his confidante, 'the living ethnography that surrounds me is far more fascinating than any cinema and especially documentary'. Perhaps it was in reaction to this *fading* of the

6 Marie Seton, *Sergei M. Eisenstein* (Dobson Books, 1978), 149.

7 Sergei Eisenstein to Esther Shub, 4 July 1931, in *Eisenstein 2: A Premature Celebration of Eisenstein's Centenary* (Seagull Books, 1985), 48.

film image that Eisenstein's mind turned momentarily, at least, toward the theatre, with its real bodies and real movement, rather than images and montage tempo. Or perhaps there is another way of looking at it. Perhaps it was not until Eisenstein turned his attention to the question of music that sound cinema genuinely seemed possible to him. Music creeps into his thought during the period of the transition to sound, at the end of the 1920s. First, he is intrigued by the use of the flute and the samisen in the Kabuki theatre, but before long he is beginning to see certain kinds of Western music as providing the model for his idea of 'overtonal' and 'tonal' montage, for the development of which he draws on the example of Debussy and Scriabin, in whose music he sees overtones functioning as 'one of the most significant means for [creating] affect'.

This approach to music ends up with his subsequent invocation of Scriabin, together now with Wagner, as a pioneer in the project of removing 'the barriers between the seen world and the heard world! To bring about a unity and a harmonious relationship between these two opposing spheres.'[8] At the same time, Eisenstein further developed his interest in Bach, who first appears as the protagonist of counterpoint but is now metamorphosed into an advocate of parallelism of 'movement' between sound and image, so that the music 'leaps' simultaneously with the verbal image of a leap in the words that accompany it. From one point of view, it might look as if Eisenstein were in the tradition of Viking Eggeling and other pioneers of ocular music – interested in creating a visual analogue corresponding to each sound – but there is a significant difference. Eggeling saw his visual analogues as necessarily abstract, whereas for Eisenstein they remained images drawn from figures and actions in the real world.[9] For Eisenstein, as we know from his charts of sound-image relationships in *Alexander Nevsky*, the sound-image relationship could be based on a kind of graph of the geometry of figures in movement, corresponding to a parallel graph of the 'sensed inner movement' of the music. The example Eisenstein offers is that of Disney's *Birds of a Feather* (1931), one of the Silly Symphonies, where the music appears to move back and forth in a wave-like fashion (it is a barcarolle by Offenbach) while the image of a peacock's tail reflected in a pool undulates 'musically' (Eisenstein's word) in concord with the accompanying sound.

8 Sergei Eisenstein, 'Synchronisation of the Senses', in *The Film Sense* (Harcourt, Brace, 1942), 87.

9 For the development of Eisenstein's adoption of the musical model, see Annette Michelson, 'Reading Eisenstein Reading *Ulysses*', and 'The Wings of Hypothesis: Montage and the Theory of the Interval', in *Montage and Modern Life 1919–1942* (MIT Press, 1992).

Of course, there is something shocking about the banality of this example, as there is about Eisenstein's later fascination with Disney's *Fantasia*. As Cavalcanti pointed out, Len Lye provided a much better precedent for sound-image relationships. Lye began with abstract forms, in the tradition of Eggeling, and then advanced to using abstracted and posterised dancing figures in *Trade Tattoo*. As I read the texts in which Eisenstein wrestled with the problem of audiovisual correspondence, I couldn't help thinking how strange it was that he so infrequently mentioned dance and dancers in this context. To understand why, we need to look into the 'Chapter about Dancing Lessons' in his autobiography, *Immoral Memories*.

Eisenstein hated his childhood dancing lessons and chronicles his utter failure to master not only the waltz but tap dancing too. The only dance he felt at all happy with was the foxtrot, which, 'in contradistinction to the dances of [his] youth, with their strictly prescribed patterns and rotation of movement ... was a "free dance," held together only by a strict rhythm, on the framework of which one could embroider any freely improvised movement'.[10] Isn't this the root of Eisenstein's underlying vision of cinema – the combination of free movement with a strict rhythmic framework? How could it be that it took him so long, that he left it too late, before he embarked on bringing dance and film together? In the same chapter, he describes his failure to learn to draw 'properly' as a result of a similarly stunting academic programme (in the bad sense of the word), 'the aridity of indestructible formulas and canons, both in relation to the movement of dance and of drawing'. As regards drawing, by adolescence Eisenstein managed to free himself from his childhood inhibitions, and in Mexico, he began to draw nonstop. Dancing, however, intimidated him long afterward, perhaps because its relation with sexuality was even stronger than that of drawing – drawing made it possible for him to be completely explicit about his homoerotic and sadomasochistic fantasies, whereas in films his predilections still had to remain veiled. Drawing was private and on paper. Films were in public and on the screen. Dancing, of course, involved real bodies and could be construed as even more dangerous.

Eisenstein's distance from dance is particularly striking because, during his lifetime, Russia was acknowledged to be the homeland of contemporary dance and Eisenstein's own career overlapped with that of Diaghilev and the Ballets Russes. In fact, as far as I can tell, Eisenstein only alluded to the Ballets Russes once in all of his voluminous writings, when he recalled

10 Eisenstein did, however, develop a very personal, even grotesque, style of solo dancing, a form perhaps of 'anti-dancing'.

seeing 'Fokine's *Aragon Jota* and Karsavina in *Chopiniana*'. This comes in the middle of a long list of great performances he had been fortunate enough to see, sandwiched between Chaplin, Stanislavski, Mistinguett, Nazimova, Mayakovsky rehearsing *Mystery Bouffe*, Gershwin playing *Rhapsody in Blue*, and so on down to Yehudi Menuhin and Rin-Tin-Tin. All the same, despite the dizzying eclecticism of the list, designed rhetorically to lead up to the apotheosis of Meyerhold as the performer who left the deepest impression of all, there is something slightly odd about his invocation of Fokine and Karsavina. In fact, *Chopiniana* was first performed in St Petersburg in 1907 and was then heavily revised, renamed and relaunched as *Les Sylphides*, which opened in Paris two years later in 1909. In both instances, the principal female dancer was Pavlova, although Karsavina also appeared in Paris, dancing a solo *valse* as the second *sylphide*. I have been unable to trace the Fokine. In any case it is hard to see when and where Eisenstein could have seen these performances, since they don't appear to match his childhood visits either to St Petersburg or Paris.

It is almost as if he felt bound to include the Ballets Russes, just that once, in passing and in the most mystifying manner! Of course, it is obvious why he would avoid mentioning the Ballets Russes in any other circumstance – they were, after all, an *émigré* phenomenon and it would have been politically tactless to speak about them. Moreover, Diaghilev was openly homosexual. His death occurred just a few months before Eisenstein visited Paris in 1929, so there was no longer an opportunity for them to have met, although Eisenstein did visit Cocteau, who, of course, had been one of Diaghilev's closest working associates, his bridge to the Paris art world and, in a sense, his successor. In fact, there was also a near miss in 1924, when Diaghilev himself had been hoping to revisit Russia. Mayakovsky, who was in Paris at that time, wrote to Osip Brik, suggesting that he might introduce Diaghilev to Eisenstein (along with Rodchenko and Lavinsky) as a suitable advertisement for the new Russia, failing which he should 'soften him with caviare', but 'if he doesn't like that, there's nothing to be done'. In the end, Diaghilev never came to Moscow, principally because the Soviet government refused to guarantee that Boris Kochno, his partner at that time, would be allowed to return again to Paris with him.

Nonetheless, there was one Russian who worked closely with both Diaghilev and Eisenstein. That, of course, was Prokofiev, who wrote the ballet music for *Chout* in 1921, for *Le pas d'acier* in 1927, and for *The Prodigal Son* in 1929, shortly before Diaghilev's death. In fact Prokofiev had first met Diaghilev in London back in 1914, where he played him his Second Piano Concerto and was commissioned on the spot to write a ballet score, a project interrupted by the First World War. Diaghilev saw Prokofiev as 'our future' and, after the War – and the Revolution – contact was re-established on a working basis. Diaghilev's affection for Prokofiev as his 'second son' (after Stravinsky) was great enough for him to risk *Le pas d'acier* even though it featured the revolutionary life of peasants, and proletarians danced on a Constructivist set. It is in this context that we should see Prokofiev's subsequent relationship with Eisenstein, which began after Prokofiev returned to the Soviet Union in 1932 and led to their collaboration on *Alexander Nevsky* and *Ivan the Terrible*, and also on Prokofiev's unrealised opera of *War and Peace*, for which Eisenstein served as a kind of consultant director, although he died before his work could be realised – after which his notes and sketches were used as reference materials for the eventual production. Eisenstein became, I would argue, a kind of substitute for Diaghilev in Prokofiev's career after he returned to the Soviet Union, commissioning him to write the scores for elaborate audiovisual spectacles. There is a sense, too, in which collaboration with Prokofiev led Eisenstein to see film performance in a more choreographic way.

The origins for this kind of collaboration lay, of course, in Eisenstein's work with Meisel on *Battleship Potemkin*. Meisel's role, sadly, has always been underestimated because *Potemkin* is still regarded as a 'silent' film, but, like *Nevsky* or *Ivan*, it could equally well be seen as an integrated audiovisual experiment. Eisenstein worked very closely with Meisel, as he did with Prokofiev, persuading Meisel, in Eisenstein's own words, 'to forego the purely illustrative function common to musical accompaniments at that time [and not only at that time! – P. W.] and stress certain "effects," particularly in the "music of machines" in the last reel.'[11] Following the success of the 'music of the machines', Eisenstein seems to have toyed with the idea that the sound track could be a kind of noise composition or montage, not unlike Vertov's early futurist cylinders. There is a sense in which *Potemkin*, with its stress on rhythm and tempo, both in the montage and in the music, could be viewed as a kind of Constructivist film musical – I have been tempted here to analyse the Odessa Steps sequence as a show-stopping dance number or early example of music video. After all, Eisenstein enjoyed film musicals – not just Judy Garland, but also *Stormy Weather*, with the Katherine Dunham dancers!

11 Seton, *Sergei M. Eisenstein*, 86.

It would have been easy for Eisenstein to transfer the montage techniques of the Odessa Steps sequence to dance film, as Maya Deren did in her *Choreography for the Camera* and *Meditation on Violence*, using montage to overcome the limits of gravity and physical agility and to counterpoint or regulate the rhythm of the dance.[12]

At the end of his life, Eisenstein seems to have become seriously interested in working with dance for the first time. He approached Russia's leading ballerina, Galina Ulanova, to see if she would play the Queen in *Ivan the Terrible*, but her other commitments prevented it. He did, however, go ahead with his first real dance sequence (discounting the folkloric *sandunga* in the Tehuantepec sequence of *Que Viva Mexico!*) which coincided, by good fortune, with his first experiment in colour. Then, in 1947, he began to work on a new project with Prokofiev, this time for a dance film of Pushkin's *The Queen of Spades*. A similar project discussed at that time was a dance film of *Carmen*, a work he had been thinking about long before, during his Proletkult days, now conceived with dancers who had worked with him on *Ivan the Terrible*. It seems that, at the end of his life, Eisenstein was finally moving toward the kind of film that, I believe, was already implicit in his theoretical writings. Why had it taken so long? Partly, it was because of his long-term unease at the idea of dance, an area of performance where he never felt fully in control. Instead, his interest in rhythmic movement was transferred away from the all-too-human body toward the more abstract realm of montage. Dance would have meant the introduction of the flowing line of his fantastic drawings into his cinema, as the trail of 'dynamic movement'.

Perhaps rethinking his experience in Mexico could have helped Eisenstein to lose some of his inhibitions on the screen as well as on the sketchbook page. I am reminded of the conclusions that Siqueiros (the great Mexican muralist) drew after his long conversations with Eisenstein in Taxco, where he was in criminal detention, conversations that led to the experimental 'cinematic' mural painted under his direction in Buenos Aires. In this work, Siqueiros tried to apply to mural painting what he had learned about cinema, just as Eisenstein had based his Mexican film on what he had learned from the muralists. Mural painting, Siqueiros concluded, could be dynamised by developing a new system of perspective that allowed for the movement of the spectator, creating forms to be seen by a spectator in movement, 'always corresponding to the infinite number of places from which the work could be viewed'. Siqueiros and his team

12 Maya Deren worked with the great American dancer Katherine Dunham and her company, and translated a dance world into a series of avant-garde films.

also filmed their mural, 'following the path logically taken by a spectator'. Perhaps Eisenstein might have reached the same conclusion and developed a camera that could follow a continuous flowing line, like that of his drawings, which danced as it worked, filming the movements of dancers to capture them within the fixed – or even dynamic – frame of the screen. Choreographing the long take, in counterpoint with montage, he could at last have realised his great dream of aesthetic totality – performative, audiovisual and kinetic.

* * *

Essay published in October *88 (Spring 1999).*

Knight's Moves

'Experimental film', 'Pure Film', 'Underground film', 'Co-op film', 'Avant-garde film', 'Counter-cinema'.... How distant all these terms seem from the vantage point of today, how dated, how nostalgic, how difficult to explain. I am afraid that, to make sense of them, I shall have to be shamelessly autobiographical, to go back over forty years or more in order to puzzle out the complex and confusing ways in which the theory and practice of avant-garde cinema developed and changed. 'Memory Lane' is always a treacherous path to follow, but it would be pointless to pretend that I was somehow an outsider looking back dispassionately on the intricate debates that flourished in the world of experimental film, during the 1970s in particular. Of course, these debates did not spring up from nowhere. The form they took was determined by a long previous history, going back many decades, and also by expectations of the future – this was a time in which I (and others) wrote drafts of guidelines for possible futures under the pretext of theorising contemporary film practice, looking for alternative ways of filmmaking.

It is futile – probably impossible – to try and define all the distinctions we might like to make between categories such as 'experimental film', 'avant-garde film', 'underground film', 'co-op film', 'counter-cinema' (my very own contribution) and so on. The history of experimental film is broken and diverse – rather, as in Viktor Shklovsky's image, it proceeded by knight's moves, going forward much of the time but always obliquely, sometimes aggressive, sometimes defensive, according to a strategy which was always difficult to define and second-guess. There are, however, some constants. Experimental film did not develop in an artistic vacuum; as well as its contrasts and connections with the commercial cinema, experimental film also had connections and contrasts with the other arts – painting, of course (itself a visual art), as well as music (another time-based art), and even poetry, particularly 'imagist poetry', but also 'typographic poetry'. In particular, the influence of painting and music often pushed experimental film towards animation as a working method and abstraction as a goal – Eggeling, Richter, Fischinger, McLaren, the Whitney brothers, and many, many others.

Experimental film has had a long history, spanning the entire twentieth century. At the very beginning of the cinema, every film was 'experimental' in a sense, and it was not until the feature film had fully crystallised that the concept of 'experimental film' began to take on a specific meaning of its own. Basically, the term began to be applied to all those films – and there were not very many of them – that differed in fundamental ways from the majority of films made as commercial ventures, as commodities. Right from the start, experimental films had a limited audience, an audience of aesthetes, intellectuals and radicals, a dedicated minority who were intrigued, even moved or thrilled, by the new, the unconventional, the difficult, the eccentric, the idiosyncratic. From the start, experimental films had one foot firmly placed in the art world (including the music world and the poetry world) and one foot, a little sheepishly, venturing into the film world, the world of the entertainment business. Experimental filmmakers were the oddballs, the innovators, the aesthetes, the explorers – marginalised but undeterred.

Today we have 'independent films', denizens of a kind of junior league of commercial cinema, designed for a more sophisticated and discerning audience than the blockbusters and star vehicles that dominate the market. But experimental films had quite different ambitions – they were designed to be demanding, difficult, even esoteric. From the very beginning the filmmakers were camp-followers of avant-garde art, aiming to integrate technology with aesthetics, to shake off the derogatory implications of the machine and insist that filmmaking could be as personal and idiosyncratic as music or poetry. From very early on avant-garde film was tied to the art world – Eggeling's abstract *Diagonal Symphony*; Richter's *Rhythmus 21*; Léger's *Ballet mécanique*; Man Ray's *Le Retour à la raison*, shown at the Dadaist 'Evening of the Bearded Heart'; Duchamp's *Anémic cinéma*; Buñuel's surrealist *Un Chien Andalou*, a film itself influenced by René Clair's Dadaist *Entr'acte*.... Buñuel's film was thus connected to the performance world through *Entr'acte*, and to surrealism through his admiration for Benjamin Péret. In the 1960s the connection of experimental film with the art world became even stronger, as artists like Andy

Warhol or Michael Snow became filmmakers, returning, in many ways, to the simplicity and the fascination with technique that characterised the very first films. The return to the past is typical of many experimental filmmakers of the '60s and '70s. Malcolm Le Grice's *After Lumière* remakes Lumière's own *L'arroseur arrosé*. Warhol's *Kiss* recapitulates, whether consciously or unconsciously, Edison's *May Irwin Kiss* of 1896. In 1968 Ken Jacobs made his *Tom, Tom, the Piper's Son*, a re-filming off the screen of Billy Bitzer's 1905 film of the nursery rhyme, re-filming as the camera wanders around the on-screen image, zooming in on details, making a film of a film, which Jacobs describes as 'a dream within a dream'. Looking back on it, I think that this is also true of *Penthesilea*, the feature-length film I made with Laura Mulvey in 1974, which not only incorporates documentary footage of a suffragette pageant, but is constructed by simply splicing together whole rolls of film, as if transported back into the period of so-called 'primitive cinema', before the invention of continuity editing. Experimental film, it seems, is constantly revisiting its past, not only the distant past of Muybridge or Lumière, but also the more recent past. The filmmakers of today draw on the work of their predecessors, the filmmakers of yesterday.

At the same time, the gravitational pull of the film industry can never be entirely discounted. After all, the Disney studio towered over the world of animation, as it still does today, and, for a number of filmmakers, making experimental films was a prelude to entering the industry. I am thinking, for instance, of René Clair, and also of Elia Kazan, who was one of the two actors in Ralph Steiner's *Pie in the Sky*. Similarly, many feature films have managed to find their way into the avant-garde canon – Wiene's *The Cabinet of Dr Caligari*, Pabst's *Secrets of a Soul*, Vertov's *Man with a Movie Camera*, Brecht and Dudow's *Kuhle Wampe*, Buñuel and Dalí's *L'âge d'or*, Cocteau's *The Blood of a Poet*, and so on. There is even a case to be made for *A Hard Day's Night*, inspired by Spike Milligan's absurdist *The Running Jumping & Standing Still Film*, or for the films of European art directors of the 1960s – Godard, of course, but also Rivette, Rouch, Straub-Huillet, Chantal Akerman and several others. In the 1970s there were many filmmakers who set out to make experimental features – the films of Yvonne Rainer, for instance, or those of Jon Jost, or even *Penthesilea* and *Riddles of the Sphinx*, which I co-wrote and co-directed with Laura Mulvey.

Another neighbour of experimental film has always been the documentary – especially the 'city film', beginning with Sheeler and Strand's *Manhatta* and Ruttmann's *Berlin, Symphony of a City* in the 1920s, and then continuing with Vigo's *À propos de Nice* and Ralph Steiner's *The City*, which was made in 1939. In England, John Grierson worked with Alberto Cavalcanti, maker of a classic avant-garde documentary of the 1920s, *Rien que les heures*, producing what we might well call experimental documentaries, such as *Night Mail*, with its voice-over poem, written by W. H. Auden, and working in counterpoint to the rhythm of the film's montage, its editing, as well as the rhythm of the pistons which drive the train. In his polemical book, *The Struggle for the Film*, written in the late 1930s, Hans Richter, best known as an abstract filmmaker, made the case for experimental documentary on both aesthetic and political grounds. For Richter, documentary was the true vocation of the cinema, as revealed by the first screenings of the Lumière brothers' films of the train entering the station, the workers leaving the factory.

After the war, the debates on documentary were thrown into confusion by the emergence of a self-confident group of filmmakers who were perceived by outsiders as 'underground filmmakers'. These filmmakers, however, saw themselves as an avant-garde in the (by now) classical sense of the term, especially those whose connections were largely with the art world, which also exerted a strong gravitational pull. Indeed the 'happenings' boom had placed performance right in the vanguard of the art world itself. Moreover, as David James has pointed out, poetry also exerted a significant influence on the film world.[1] Maya Deren, for example, claimed that her films, and those of others, were poetic and lyrical in their construction, rather than dramatic and narrative driven. Deren's own terminology distinguishes the 'vertical' and the 'horizontal', or, as we might put it today, the 'metaphorical' and the 'metonymic'.[2] In 1953, at the Cinema 16 symposium on 'Poetry and the Film', Parker Tyler (himself a poet) argued that there was a division between short films which worked with 'a surrealist poetry of the pure image', and longer films which accepted the responsibility of storytelling and sought to develop a cinema of 'poetry as a visual-verbal medium'.[3]

It is in this context that Stan Brakhage, many years later, could say that 'like Jean Cocteau, I was a poet who also made films'.[4] What becomes clear from all these disparate connections is that film is inevitably multifaceted – film and visual art, film and music, film and document, film and poetry – and that its potential can be developed in many different

1 David James, *Allegories of Cinema* (Princeton University Press, 1989), 29.
2 Ibid.
3 Parker Tyler, *Underground Film* (Da Capo Press, 1995).
4 James, *Allegories*, 29.

ways. Put simply, there can be no distinct ontology of film, only a range of possibilities. Perhaps Artaud was right when he suggested that at one end of the scale there was the commercial film, in which the world was broken down into units (shots) which were then combined into a sequence through continuity editing, and, at the other end, there was the documentary, which – as he described it – depended on capturing the unpredictable, the dynamic and still developing.[5] In fact, experimental film became divided between the carefully planned and controlled forms of 'structural film' and the unplanned and uncontrolled forms of films, which were, in effect, home movies, a subgenre of the documentary, in which the object being documented might be the effect of light as refracted through a translucent ashtray on the Governor of Colorado's desk.

I entered these debates in the 1970s, shortly before I first began to make films myself, in partnership with Laura Mulvey. The articles I wrote then were designed to justify the feature film format as a viable way of making an experimental film with a political argument. In fact, we made two feature-length films: the first – *Penthesilea* – made in Evanston, Illinois, in 1974, and the second – *Riddles of the Sphinx* –made in London, England, in 1977. Both *Penthesilea* and *Riddles of the Sphinx* were structured in segments without any continuity editing. The segments were rather like long chapters and were designed both to tell a story, schematically at least, and to raise a number of political issues, particularly feminist issues. Had they been conventional films they would probably have fallen into the category of melodrama – a grandiose film of *Penthesilea*, for instance, was an unfinished project of Leni Riefenstahl's and Laura Mulvey has observed that, made in another way, *Riddles of the Sphinx* could have been something like a Douglas Sirk melodrama, even a 'tearjerker' or 'weepie'.[6] The differences are budgetary, of course, but also stylistic, differences between one form of storytelling, well-polished and almost second nature, and another, consciously contrived and artificial.

Essentially they were experimental films, part of a series of films made in the 1970s – Chantal Akerman's *Je Tu Il Elle* (1974) or *Jeanne Dielman, 23, quai du Commerce, 1080 Bruxelles* (1975). Other significant films were Yvonne Rainer's *Lives of Performers* (1972) and *Film About a Woman*

5 Antonin Artaud, 'The Premature Old Age of the Cinema', in Richard Abel (ed.), *French Film Theory and Criticism, 1907–1939*, vol. 2 (Princeton University Press, 1988), 122–4.

6 Scott MacDonald, 'Interview with Laura Mulvey', in *A Critical Cinema 2* (University of California Press, 1992), 343–4.

Who... (1974), as well as the Berwick Street Collective's *Nightcleaners* (1975) and Jackie Raynal's *Deux Fois* (1976). These were the key films in what we might now think of as the avant-garde feminist breakthrough. Soon afterwards came Yvonne Rainer's *Journeys from Berlin/1971* (1979), a meditation on anarchism set both in America and Germany yet shot mainly in London. In this film, as in many of Rainer's films, friends of the director play crucial roles – for example, Annette Michelson plays the part of a patient, whose psychoanalyst at times refers to her on-screen as 'Annette'. At other times, he is replaced by a female therapist and eventually by Chad Wollen, then nine years old, who merely barks like a dog!

It was during this same period that Laura Mulvey's 'Fears, Fantasies and the Male Unconscious' (1973) was published, followed by 'Visual Pleasure and Narrative Cinema' (1975) – now a classic – and 'Film, Feminism and the Avant-Garde' (1978), as well as my own 'Godard and Counter-Cinema: *Vent d'Est*' (1972), 'The Two Avant-Gardes' (1975), and '"Ontology" and "Materialism" in Film' (1976). Six years later I wrote another polemical text, 'Semiotic Counter-Strategies: Retrospect' (1982), which concluded as follows:

> I want to return again to my early invocation of the names of Brecht and Breton, two emblematic figures in the history of the avant-garde. Brecht and Breton suggest two very different avenues for art, but I think that each insisted on things that are necessary – Brecht on understanding and explanation, Breton on freedom and the power of the unconscious. Each also had a vivid interest in popular art and entertainment and incorporated elements from it into their own work. It is also true to say that they both gave equal weight to form and content, to aesthetics and politics. Here is a quote from Breton, to the Paris Congress of Writers in 1935: 'In art we rise up against any regressive conception that tends to oppose content to form, in order to sacrifice the latter to the former.' And a quote from Brecht: 'Even an ivory tower is a better place to sit in nowadays than a Hollywood villa.'[7]

To put these texts in their proper perspective it is important to recapitulate the filmmaking context in which they were written. At the beginning of the 1970s a series of significant films were made, largely within the structural or structural/materialist tradition. In 1970 came Hollis Frampton's *Zorns Lemma*, Owen Land's *Institutional Quality*, George Landow's

7 André Breton, 'Speech to the Congress of Writers', in *Manifestoes of Surrealism* (University of Michigan Press, 1972), 240.

Remedial Reading Comprehension, Ernie Gehr's *Serene Velocity* and, in England, Malcolm Le Grice's *Berlin Horse*. The next year there was a group of much longer, very different films, including Brakhage's documentary of an autopsy, *The Act of Seeing with One's Own Eyes*, Michael Snow's extended post-structural film, *La Région Centrale*, and Frampton's *Hapax Legomena*, which came out in segments through 1971 and 1972. 1973 brought Peter Gidal's structural-materialist classic, *Room Film*, and Anthony McCall's installation film, *Line Describing a Cone*, while 1974 brought Michael Snow's very long work, *'Rameau's Nephew' by Diderot (Thanx to Dennis Young) by Wilma Schoen*.

Riddles of the Sphinx was much more systematic in its organisation. It consists of seven sections, arranged in a symmetrical pattern, 'ABCDCBA', with the central section consisting of thirteen 'chapters', each in the form of a 360-degree pan, the shortest about two minutes, the longest about ten. I saw the film again recently, when it was being screened in Vancouver, and I was struck by the way in which the pans perform two separate functions, formal and discursive. Each pan has its own tempo as it moves inexorably onward, without any perceptible change of speed, while new elements are constantly being revealed and their predecessors lost, rather like the continuous unrolling and re-rolling of a scroll. Within the circular space created by the rotation of the camera, objects, characters and events pass by without pause or interruption. The space is both flattened, pressing inwards, in interiors, and expanded, pushing outwards, in exteriors. The characters seem to be moving against the background of a frieze, only circular like a nineteenth-century panorama.

These effects were by-products of the choice and choreography of the film's camera movements, which, as in *Zorns Lemma*, combined serial units into a puzzle to be solved. At the same time, each pan acts discursively as a link between narrative events. This sounds like a very formalist description, but formalism was indeed crucial to the way the film was originally planned and envisaged. A film like *Riddles of the Sphinx* is designed to separate form from content, so that the spectator is simultaneously aware of each. Indeed, perhaps the most important riddle proposed by the film is that of how to reconcile form and content, and, if they cannot be reconciled, how to interpret that failure of reconciliation – one which, by all the evidence, must have been intended. In the case of *Riddles of the Sphinx*, form and content deliberately remain independent, unreconciled. Neither is dispensable but neither of them is dominant either. Form and content are simply on different tracks. At the time, we thought of this strategy as a kind of Brechtian device, a way of creating what Brecht called 'distantiation', forcing the viewer to step out of the story, out of any kind of identification, and to look at events as if from a distance, seeing them as issues to be dealt with intellectually, thought through, or argued out.

This Brechtian model was certainly in our mind, but I don't think it was exactly what we wanted to achieve. A closer model was that provided by Victor Shklovsky, the Russian literary theorist, who developed his own theory of estrangement – what is often translated as 'laying bare (or defamiliarising) the device'. The 'device' in this context refers to the particular stylistic and formal means that a writer uses in order to tell a story. In traditional storytelling the style and the technique are simply means to an end, to the author's success in captivating the reader and carrying her (or him) through to the end, to the conclusion or 'pay-off', without any disturbance or interruption. Shklovsky argued that when the stylistic or technical device was laid bare, it changed the reader's (or viewer's) whole relationship with the work, which came to be seen as something artificial rather than something natural. In Shklovsky's phraseology, the device can be seen as unmotivated, unrelated to the storyline, formally independent, like a 360-degree pan that doesn't follow the character or cut from one point of interest and involvement to another, so that 'we cannot provide a satisfactory realistic reason for its presence'.[8]

This is because, as commentators on Shklovsky have put it, the device (the series of 360-degree pans) exists simply to be noticed by the reader (or viewer). If we are made more aware of the technique than of its narrative function, it is 'revealed' or 'laid bare', seen as artificial rather than natural. Both *Penthesilea* and *Riddles of the Sphinx* are based upon the denaturalisation of technique. If technique is not revealed or foregrounded, the 'artistic devices' used tend to be 'automatised', taken for granted, so that the viewer remains unaware of the camerawork or the editing strategies as such. Shklovsky was interested in literary forms, such as the fable, which constantly remind us that we are reading a fiction and that we cannot mistake it for reality. This is somewhat different from Brecht's intention, which was to make us look at the characters and their actions objectively rather than identifying with them subjectively. Shklovsky's idea was that we should be as aware of aesthetic and technical qualities as we are of the story or the drama of the characters. We are deliberately made aware that the film has been constructed. In this sense, films like

8 Viktor Shklovsky, chapters 1 and 2: 'Art as Device' and 'The Relationship between Devices of Plot and Devices of Style', in *Theory of Prose* (Dalkey Archive Press, 1990).

Penthesilea and *Riddles of the Sphinx* were intended to function somewhat like poetic fictions, albeit fictions that pose questions.

There were two significant cinematic sources for these films. First, the segmentation and the chapter structure owed a debt to Chantal Akerman's *Je tu il elle*, which basically tells four separate stories, involving one central character, which the viewer is invited to compare with one another. Second, it also owes a debt to Jean-Luc Godard's *Vivre sa vie*, another film that has a chapter structure – explicitly numbered – so that instead of getting a continuous story we are given a series of disjunct tableaux. Again we are being asked to make our own connections, to provide our own interpretation, once it has been made clear that this narrative work is not going to be done for us, implicitly or explicitly, by the filmmaker – in this case Godard, who consistently preferred questions to answers. Yvonne Rainer too credits Godard as a source for an element of one of her films, although she gives Martha Graham and Virginia Woolf equal credit.[9] Her observation that 'Annette Michelson's non-naturalistic performance (in *Journeys from Berlin*) is totally appropriate' suggests a hint of Brechtianism too, although she also describes the text of the film as 'obviously a surreal kind of recitation', thereby introducing André Breton too.[10]

My 1972 essay on Godard and counter-cinema welcomed his break with the conventions of mainstream cinema, particularly his rejection of conventional narrative structures. For instance, he repeatedly questioned the process of filmmaking within the film itself, introducing digressions and interpolations that fractured the customary coherence of the narrative, separating the content of the sound track from the content of the image track and foregrounding the process of filmmaking within the film itself, often through the device of showing a film within the film, making the mechanics of filmmaking visible within the film itself, separating voices from characters or using Brechtian estrangement effects. These devices made new demands on the spectator, who was compelled to puzzle out the meaning of the film rather than receive it unreflectively. In a variety of ways, the spectator was encouraged to think about the film while watching it, to make a conscious effort of interpretation. Godard used many of the devices used by avant-garde or 'underground' filmmakers, but his purpose was quite different. When he showed scratched film in *Vent d'est*, it was intended as a sign of negation, of crossing out, whereas in other films 'noise' or scratching was foregrounded as an aesthetic gesture.

9 Mitchell Rosenbaum, 'Interview with Yvonne Rainer', *The Films of Yvonne Rainer* (Indiana University Press, 1989), 38.

10 Ibid., p. 39.

In *Journeys from Berlin*, as in *Riddles of the Sphinx*, we are reminded that we are viewing a fictional world and must not mistake it directly for reality, but instead try to understand how it relates to reality. At the same time, the aesthetic dimension of the work is foregrounded, rather than its narrative function. The narrative, as in a fable, is simply there to provide a set of examples, situations that the viewer is being asked to interpret, while simultaneously enjoying the formal and aesthetic qualities of the work. In this sense, the idea of counter-cinema is directed not so much against Hollywood films, which in fact often do 'lay bare the device' – for example, Hitchcock's *Rope* or a Busby Berkeley musical – as against André Bazin's call for 'realism' in the cinema, for the construction of an alternative world as real as the one that we are living in! The question Bazin asked himself was, 'What is cinema?' The truth is that the infrastructure of filmmaking – lighting, camerawork, editing and so on – exists in the real world, unlike the characters or the story. One of the main aims of counter-cinema was to challenge the assumption of on-screen realism by drawing attention to these off-screen mechanics, materials and processes of film, just as Brecht, working in the theatre, had drawn attention to the reality of the actor's stance or gestures.

In fact, a fascination with the mechanics of film, its material structures and formal devices goes back to the early years of film. Vertov's *Man with a Movie Camera* was made in the late 1920s, but it is already a film in which the camera is star, the hero of the film, and in which we see the processes of photography and editing as well as the projection of the film itself – a film within a film. The camera is also animated, so that it can walk on its three tripod legs like a self-willed robotic creature. *Man with a Movie Camera* has often been hailed as a direct precursor of the self-referentiality and foregrounding of technology which became a major feature of avant-garde filmmaking, in films such as Michael Snow's *Wavelength*, notoriously constructed around a single forty-five-minute zoom from one end of a New York loft to another. While there are some narrative incidents during the zoom – even a death – the zoom continues inexorably, so that soon the body left lying on the floor is no longer visible.

Wavelength was made in 1967. Interviewed slightly more than twenty years later, Michael Snow was quite explicit about his wish to lay bare the device. In his own words,

> I knew I wanted to expand something – a zoom – that normally happens fast, and to allow myself or the spectator to be sort of inside it for a long period. You'd get to know this device which normally just gets you from

> one space to another. I started to think about the so-called film vocabulary before I made *Wavelength* – with *Eye and Ear Control*. You know, what are all these devices and how can you get to see them, instead of just using them? So that was part of it.[11]

Shklovsky would have been delighted. He actually worked in a film studio, which he describes in his book *The Third Factory*, where he writes about the 'cuttings' (the individual shots, the minimal units of film) that 'are kept in the canvas-covered bins in the cutting room'.[12] He muses, 'I would like to film in a different way – to achieve a different rhythm. I love long strips of life. Give the actors a chance to show their stuff. Less tea, less cutting. All we can do is try.'[13]

Another significant film of this period was Anthony McCall's *Line Describing a Cone*, made in New York in 1973 and recently revived at the Whitney Museum. In many ways, it is a very simple film. There is a projector and a screen. On the celluloid there is a single point of light which is extended over twenty minutes, frame by frame, to become the circumference of a complete circle. As a result, the beam of light running from projector to screen becomes the surface of a cone that seems strangely solid and palpable, a kind of time sculpture, or as McCall has called it, a kind of kinetic light sculpture, until you try to touch it and your fingers pass clean through. To improve the effect McCall used to recommend the audience to smoke, but now that is no longer feasible. When I projected the film in a class, we used chalk-dust. At the Whitney, they created mist. Once again, the viewers' attention is drawn to process, rather than to image, inviting them to think about the nature of the projected image. In this piece, the projection beam itself is foregrounded rather than the image it projects; its reality is demonstrated. The beam of light, apparently the most insubstantial of objects, becomes visible as if it were a solid figure.

In the summer of that year, August 1976, McCall attended the Edinburgh International Forum of Avant-Garde Film, which brought together filmmakers from many different countries and with many different aesthetic (and political) positions, both from the New York avant-garde and from the post-Godardian counter-cinema. As a result of the provocative Edinburgh debates, McCall began to rethink his position as a filmmaker. In 1978, with Andrew Tyndall, a friend who was a journalist, McCall made *Argument*, a theoretically-oriented essay film, which was closer to

11 MacDonald, 'Interview with Michael Snow', *A Critical Cinema 2*, 63.
12 Viktor Shklovsky, *Third Factory* (Ardis, 1977), 77.
13 Ibid., p. 78.

the new wave of avant-garde political films being made in America and Europe than to structural film. In 1980 McCall developed this type of filmmaking further when he and Tyndall joined Claire Pajaczkowska and Jane Weinstock in making *Sigmund Freud's Dora*, a filmic dramatization of and commentary on Freud's text from a feminist point of view. *Dora*, like *Riddles of the Sphinx*, derived from the convergence of feminism, Brechtianism, '*Screen*' theory, 'new narrative', and the Godardian essay film. It was photographed by Babette Mangolte, who had previously worked with Yvonne Rainer and then with Chantal Akerman on *Jeanne Dielman*.

A principal source for *Riddles of the Sphinx* was Hollis Frampton's *Zorns Lemma*, a tripartite film whose title refers explicitly to mathematical set theory. It begins with a recitation of the eighteenth-century Bay State Primer's antique twenty-four-letter alphabet, followed by a series of twenty-four images, each repeated cyclically. Every image stands in for a letter of the alphabet and is on screen for just one second at a time – that is to say, technically, for twenty-four frames of film matching the twenty-four letters of the alphabet. Each time the images are recycled – images of breakers at sea or of eggs cooking or of painting a wall – one of them is dropped, until eventually none are left. Then, in the third sequence, human figures with a dog are seen crossing a snow-covered field, a sequence ending as the white of the snow merges with the white of the end leader, the film's own closing frames. According to Frampton, 'The film had its beginnings in pre-occupation with tension between graphic & plastic/flat vs. illusionistic elements in same space. The basic structure is one of a series of sets of sets, in tribute to Zorn' – or perhaps, one could say, the tension between the flat screen and the perspectival image.[14]

Films like *Zorns Lemma* or *Riddles of the Sphinx*, as well as many others, both take us back to the origins and pre-history of cinema itself, to Muybridge for example, and draw upon a like-minded circle of contemporaries. Already in the 1920s a kind of mutual aid had developed between filmmakers. Léger introduced Buñuel to Man Ray, who introduced Léger to Louis Aragon, still then a surrealist. They all attended the screening of *Un Chien Andalou*, as did Cocteau, who put Buñuel in touch with the Vicomte de Noailles, who agreed to finance *L'âge d'or*, in the same way that he had previously financed Man Ray's film *Les Mystères du château du Dé*. Max Ernst and Pierre Prévert appeared in the film, in the scene with the bandits in Catalunya. In making *Un Chien Andalou*, Buñuel had

14 Hollis Frampton, 'Notes on Zorns Lemma', in Scott MacDonald (ed.), *Screen Writings* (University of California Press, 1995), 56.

already worked for Jean Epstein on *Fall of the House of Usher*, and he also looked back to an earlier French avant-garde – the films he mentions specifically are Cavalcanti's *Rien que les heures* and René Clair's *Entr'acte*. Avant-garde filmmakers saw themselves as members of a community, with a common project.

A similar atmosphere prevailed in the 1960s in New York and in the 1970s in London. *Riddles of the Sphinx* was partly shot in Malcolm Le Grice's house – the kitchen scene – and partly in Steve Dwoskin's – the mirror scene. The editing room scene cites Mary Kelly's *Post-Partum Document*. The central character's young daughter – in the high chair, at day care, in the grandmother's garden – was actually the camerawoman's daughter. The whole history of the avant-garde is one not just of artistic or aesthetic connections but of social connections too. In fact these social connections are what make a movement possible – whether the surrealist film movement, or underground film, or structural film, or counter-cinema. Thus, in the late 1920s, when the idea of an alternative cinema really took root in America, those involved were the closely knit group who supported the 'Little Cinema' movement, an attempt by exhibitors to create a space for 'experimental pictures' or – a slightly different category – 'art pictures', such as Watson and Webber's *Fall of the House of Usher*, which premiered at the New York Film Art Guild in 1928.[15] At much the same time, in France, Germaine Dulac's films were screened through the emergent 'ciné-club' movement, and in England, in the 1920s, there was the London Film Society.

Half a century later, Anthology and Millennium in New York and the Other Cinema in London fulfilled much the same role, screening avant-garde features, including the premiere of *Riddles of the Sphinx*. It was in the 1970s that structural and structural/materialist film gradually extended in length and began to give way to the experimental and avant-garde feature film, as exemplified by Yvonne Rainer, by Mulvey-Wollen and by Chantal Akerman, as well as by Joyce Wieland, Jean-Marie Straub, Daniele Huillet (*History Lessons*, 1972) and the Berwick Street Collective's *Nightcleaners* (1975). It was in this context that I first wrote about the bifurcation of experimental film between the tradition of the Film-Makers' Co-op, on the one hand, and the avant-garde feature film, often with a political subtext, on the other. At the beginning of the decade, I was mainly preoccupied by the implications of Jean-Luc Godard's withdrawal from the usual goals and structures of the film industry, first on

15 Jan Christopher Horak, 'The First American Film Avant-Garde', in *Lovers of Cinema* (University of Wisconsin Press, 1995), 20, 21.

his own account and then in collaboration, notably with J. P. Gorin and Anne-Marie Miéville.

In 1974, when asked which filmmakers most interested me, I replied, 'Straub, Godard, Joyce Wieland, Michael Snow, Hollis Frampton for *Zorns Lemma*, Jackie Raynal for *Deux Fois*.' Then I added, 'I'm more interested in Hitchcock than before.'[16] So I would like to end with some observations about Hitchcock. In 1925 Hitchcock began to attend film screenings organised by the London Film Society at the New Gallery Cinema. There he developed connections and interests that stayed with him throughout his career, including an interest in experimental film. Many years later, he was inspired to make *Rope*, a film which shamelessly laid bare the device, through a miraculous series of long takes, running over many minutes. Yet the experimental dimension of *Rope* that moved Hitchcock the most was the machine that controlled the lighting of the giant cyclorama of New York that can be seen through the apartment window. The technician at the console could control the light to suggest the changing time of day. As night fell, the effect of sunlight was gradually diminished and replaced by electric lights as if from windows and neon signs. As Hitchcock recalled, 'By the time the picture went from the setting of the sun in the first reel to the hour of total darkness in the final dénouement, the man at the light organ had played a nocturnal Manhattan symphony in light.'[17]

I would like to conclude with a final reflection on the work of Viktor Shklovsky. Shklovsky was a literary critic, despite the time he spent working in a film studio, who argued that a literary work always consisted of the sum of its devices. Most authors attempted to conceal the devices, so that the reader was carried through the book without any friction, but Shklovsky championed, as I have noted, those books in which the device was foregrounded, laid bare. Shklovsky was not explicit about the political dimension of the 'estrangement' caused by laying bare the device – it was left to Brecht to stress that aspect – but he did insist on its theoretical and critical importance. In 1919 he explained that he 'sought a reinterpretation of literature that would stress the importance of purely linguistic elements and artistic devices: sounds and words, structure and style'.[18] He also stressed the role of the framing device – the significance of *Arabian Nights*, for example, in which the individual stories are framed within the story of Scheherazade, and the 'threading device', through

16 Peter Wollen, unpublished interview.

17 Alfred Hitchcock, 'My Most Exciting Picture', in *Hitchcock on Hitchcock* (University of California Press, 1995), 277–8.

18 Shklovsky, *Theory of Prose*, chapters 1 and 2.

which a series of separate stories or incidents are linked together through a common protagonist, as occurs in *Riddles of the Sphinx*.[19]

In the world of experimental film and counter-cinema, the language consists of its own, purely filmic, elements and artistic devices – devices such as the zoom, the pan, the projection beam and so on, as well as more abstract and conceptual devices such as the significance of counting twenty-four frames per second in relation to the twenty-four letters of the Bay State Primer alphabet. However, as Johanna Drucker points out in her fascinating book *The Visible World*, Shklovsky's writings did indeed have a considerable effect, not only on literature but also on visual art, particularly through their impact on typography, and especially in the case of avant-garde poetry in which the visual effect of the alphabet and its disposition on the page was as important as its verbal form and content.[20] I am sure that Shklovsky would have appreciated the artistic significance of such technological devices as the 360-degree pan, the zoom, the ten-minute take and the cone of light, artefacts that, rather than seamlessly hidden, were shamelessly foregrounded by a new generation of filmmakers. I am sure he would have approved of the insistent visibility of the filmic device, the shot as such, as much as he did the visibility of the material and mechanical devices of typography as instruments of poetry.

* * *

Essay published in Public *25 (2002).*

19 Ibid.

20 Johanna Drucker, *The Visible World* (University of Chicago Press, 1994).

II

Anti-Imperialisms

He That Shall Come

Lucien Rey

The installation of Europe throughout the world seemed, to the Europeans, to be the installation of order. In fact, of course, it provoked deep disturbances. European soldiers wrecked societies, European settlers seized land and livelihood, European missionaries stultified cultures. Dr Lanternari's book, *The Religions of the Oppressed*, translated from the Italian, describes one way in which indigenous people responded to the crisis which had overtaken them.

He documents the appearance, in America, Africa, Asia, Australasia and Oceania, of messianic religious cults, analyses their content and places them in their social and historical context. He shows a part of the reality obscured by the geometry and colour schemes of European atlases and chronicles the lives of an alternative set of religious heroes to those familiar in Europe. Instead of Livingstone, Schweitzer and Xavier, his protagonists are Handsome Lake, Simon Kimbangu and Te-Ua.

The advent of the Europeans, so clearly superior militarily, technically and culturally, discredited traditional rulers and priests. Their prestige crumbled away when it was seen how unfitted they were to meet the challenge set them. Yet the need for a leader was greater than ever. A messiah filled this need. He rallied the people and gave them new hope. Perhaps Dr Lanternari does not stress enough the *alternative* character of the messiah. He comments on the lack of any messianism in Japan. Yet surely this was precisely because the special circumstances of the Tokugawa shogunate allowed the emperor's reputation to remain unslurred by any capitulations to foreigners. He was therefore able, after the Meiji Restoration, to become himself the focus for national sentiment and resurgence.

Only one element of European culture was made available to the colonised peoples: Christianity. Indeed, it was thrust on them. They tried therefore to possess it for themselves, to adopt it for their own ends, to make it their own weapon. Thus many messiahs claimed to be Christ returned – but an indigenous, not European, Christ. They were impressed too by the Old Testament, where the troubles of the people of Israel seemed similar to their own. Dr Lanternari writes of the Maoris: 'The history of the Jewish people, taught by the missionaries as a model of religious strength and endurance, was learnt by the natives as a model of political action for modern times.' Others transformed the sacraments – into the eating of peyote, for instance – or imitated church organisation, like the Cao-Dai papacy in Vietnam.

Dr Lanternari points out that many cults acted politically, encouraging armed resistance. The Mahdi tried to drive the English from the Sudan; Wovoka's ghost-dance cult initiated the last Red Indian wars; the Hau-Hau of Te-Ua led the Maori Wars. He shows how abortive such rising proved to be and describes how, after defeat, the cults entered a second phase, more passive, accepting the inevitability of European presence. He gives as examples the supersession of ghost-dancing by contemplative peyotism and of Hau-Hau by the devotional Ringa-tu. Babism, he might have added, changed to Bahaism.

But this was not the only possible sequel. Cults also gave way to political parties proper. Dr Lanternari mentions the links the Kimbanguist church formed with KasaVubu's Abako party. The Black Muslims are being politicised now; attention has often been drawn to messianic remnants in Nkrumah's CPP. For, in the end, the political party achieved what the cult could not. The emerging indigenous elites drew the correct lesson from the success of the workers' movements in Europe. Their leadership could be sustained, effectively disseminated, directed towards long-term aims. The party leader sought to replace traditional rulers, drive out the European and regenerate the nation, just as the messiah had done. And he succeeded.

In his final chapter Dr Lanternari risks an analogy between the messianism of colonised peoples in the nineteenth century and the messianism of the New Testament itself. There are two crucial points, however, which he evades. First, Christ did not come from the masses – rural peasantry and hired labourers – but from the urban artisanate. So did most of the apostles.

Second, Christ's position could be seen as favouring the Romans. Certainly the Pharisees seemed to think it did. 'If we let him thus alone, all men will believe on him: and the Romans will come and take away both our place and our nation' (John 11:48). And the Pharisees, it must be remembered, were the inheritors of the tradition of the Maccabees, the leaders of antiRoman resistance – smouldering throughout Christ's life – and the guardians of the national interest and identity. There is other evidence too: Pilate's sympathy, Christ's fraternisation with centurions and collaborators, 'Render unto Caesar', the expulsion of the moneychangers.

Dr Lanternari's book is stimulating and comprehensive; its range of scholarship and depth of inquiry is astonishingly great. There are almost no flaws – though he does not seem aware that Ras Tafari was Haile Selassie's name before he seized power and that the Canudos Zien is portrayed in da Cunha's classic *Rebellion in the Backlands*. It demanded a translation and it deserves a readership.

* * *

Review of Vittorio Lanternari, The Religions of the Oppressed: A Study of Modern Messianic Cults, *trans. Lisa Sergio (MacGibbon and Kee, 1963). Published in* New Society, *5 December 1963, under the pseudonym Lucien Rey.*

The Revolution in Zanzibar

Lucien Rey

It seemed that the brightest spark in Africa had been snuffed when the news came through of the Tanganyika-Zanzibar *anschluss*. But it is now possible to be somewhat more sanguine.

First, the past. Zanzibar's political life has zigzagged violently from the start, but the zigzags have neither been unconditioned nor uncontrolled. The island's small size (both Zanzibar and Pemba are roughly forty miles from end to end; their combined population, split slightly in favour of Zanzibar, is only 300,000) and its peculiar social system gave its politics a special intensity and fervour – and a proportionately greater degree of mass participation and popular grasp of issues than would be possible in a larger, more sprawling and complex country. Hence Zanzibar's crash entry on to the continental and world stage.

What was the social system? The economy of both Zanzibar and Pemba islands is dominated by the production of cloves. Clove trees were first brought to Zanzibar by Sultan Seyyid Said, who was also the first ruler of the dynasty of Omani Arabs – he transferred his court to Zanzibar from Muscat in 1828. Since his reign Zanzibar's prosperity has been founded on cloves. Today they make up over 80 percent of exports; cloves and coconuts, often intergrown, account for almost three-quarters of acreage under cultivation. Yet the sharpest social antagonisms were not those in the clove plantations, between landlord and worker. Both islands must be looked at separately to find out why.

1. Zanzibar Island. There are three sectors. First, in the less fertile areas, the traditional villages of the indigenous inhabitants have survived: the 'Shirazis'. They have a subsistence economy; land has always been communally

held and very little has ever been alienated. Second, the clove plantations, now public property. Plantations ranged in size from half a dozen trees to several thousand. Sultan Said only allowed Omani Arabs to plant clove seedlings and the plantations remained almost entirely under Arab ownership. During the nineteenth century, until the British arrived, they were worked mainly by slaves. When the slaves were freed most returned to the mainland, but some stayed on as squatters, building homes on the landlord's land and guarding and tending his clove trees in return for the right to use the land for their own subsistence food production. Squatters were not allowed to plant clove trees themselves. Gradually, to fill the labour shortage caused by the exodus of slaves, there was a drift of Shirazis to the plantations and, in time, a third layer was added: Africans from the mainland. On a few 'rationalised' plantations squatters were turned out and replaced by hired labourers, but the great majority of landlords were unwilling to risk the disturbance of expelling their squatters. The squatting system meant that, even if the clove crop failed or could not be sold, the squatters did not starve. This helped to mollify landlord-worker relations. But, during the clove-picking season, there was a need for extra temporary labour, paid in cash, which was supplied chiefly by mainland immigrants who returned to Tanganyika after the harvest. Antagonisms did develop between indigenous workers and the seasonal immigrants, who were held to bring down wage rates for the harvest. This, together with landlord intimidation, explains why many squatters voted for the Arab-dominated ZNP (Zanzibar Nationalist Party). Third, Zanzibar City, the capital. Here lived, as well as the Arab and the Indian (commercial) elite in the Stone Town district, the proletariat and semi-proletariat of dockworkers, brickyard workers, household servants, etc. Many of these workers were mainland immigrants: they were a stronghold of the Afro-Shirazi Party (ASP). Their leader was Karume. The Afro-Shirazi Party was an alliance of this group with the traditional Shirazi villagers, who feared Arab encroachment on their rights.

2. Pemba Island. Pemba is much more homogeneous: the Shirazi villages have mostly died out and Shirazis intermingled with Arabs and owned clove trees. There is a historical reason for this. The people of Pemba had not been unwilling victims of Omani conquest, but had themselves appealed to Sultan Said to drive out their Mazrui lords, based on Mombasa. When he had done this, he allowed the Pemba Shirazis to plant clove seedlings alongside the Arabs. There were more Arabs on Pemba than Zanzibar, they intermarried and had no elite bastion there,

comparable to Stone Town. On Pemba, Arab and Shirazi landlords had a community of interests: the ZNP and the Pemba Shirazi ZPPP (Zanzibar and Pemba People's Party) went into coalition and formed the pre-revolutionary government. (They were helped toward electoral victory by rigged constituency divisions.)

It will be seen that the so-called ethnic divisions in Zanzibar reflect different *social* divisions, both in the two islands and in the three sectors of Zanzibar Island. Thus, at first, all the parties contained striking contradictions – since they campaigned on ethnic slogans – but after two principal splits (the Pemba Shirazis from the ASP to form the ZPPP; Babu's Umma from the ZNP) the social alignments became much more clear-cut. Shortly before independence, the polarisation between ZNP-ZPPP and ASP-Umma reached a new point with the amalgamation of the ASP and Umma trade unions, previously rivals: it was the Umma who had tried to swing the ZNP leftward by controlling its base against its elite – when they failed they took many Zanzibar City workers with them. The revolution, when it came, was not an ethnic, but a social revolution. This must be clearly understood if the meaning of the Tanganyika-Zanzibar union is to be assessed correctly.

Who made the revolution? Primarily, two groups together: the ASP Youth group, associated with Okello (though Okello was brought in for his military experience with the Mau Mau: he was not an originator), and the Umma commandos. It was the superior discipline of the commandos which saved the revolution from degeneration. Both these groups represented, first and foremost, the Zanzibar City proletariat – rather than the squatters or the Shirazi villagers. But after the revolution was assured, there was a general rallying of all the exploited against the Arab ruling class. The revolutionary government was able to put through at great speed measures nationalising the plantations, banks, etc. There was no foreign investment on the island, practically no industry. Most of what could be done was done, with general acclaim, in a very short time. But the revolution had small prospect of developing any further: the clove market was precarious, industrialisation for Zanzibar alone was impossible. The most that could be hoped for was a great increase in education and genuine mass participation in government – which would be a vivid example to the elite-ridden masses on the mainland.

But there was one other way forward: closer integration with the African mainland. Obviously this presented great dangers; there was a strong chance that any steps would lead only to the swamping and reversal of the revolution's gains. The closest ties which the ASP had with the mainland were with Tanganyika's TANU (Tanganyika African National Union, now the Tanganyika government party). Negotiations began: Babu, leader of the Umma, now merged into the ASP, took part. During the negotiations, it became clear that union was feasible; that Nyerere was not just out to reverse – even to sterilise – the Zanzibar revolution. Socialists have often distrusted Nyerere – for his Roman Catholicism, for his choice of advisors, for his conduct during the mutinies. But four factors weighed heavily: Tanganyika's exploited position within the East African Federation as a market for Kenyan goods; Nyerere's personal integrity and his distaste for the corruption now rife in Kenya; the discontinuity and doubt (largely over their concessions to imperialism in the suppression of the mutiny) which beset the Tanganyika government; Nyerere's friendship with the ASP leaders and respect for their socialist consciousness. As a result, they became confident he would not try to overthrow the gains of the Zanzibar revolution, but would welcome their participation in elaborating new policies – and a renewed political life – for Tanganyika. What of the future? The union began well: Zanzibaris were granted five cabinet posts – among them Babu in the key planning ministry and Idris Wakil, a young Shirazi, in Information. The Zanzibar army has not been disbanded and figured prominently in the May Day parade; there has been no restitution of private property; the East German consulate has not been dismissed. But the difficulties ahead must not be underestimated. First, Tanganyika is not at all like Zanzibar. It is a much larger country and is poorer. It has almost no working class; the trade unions have been suppressed; the rural economy and the society remain relatively unpenetrated. Second, so far TANU has probably not managed to become a genuine mass party – its weakness became especially clear during the mutiny. Government missions are now studying party structures in Guinea and Yugoslavia. But there will be great difficulties in building up a party and integrating Zanzibar into it – the Zanzibaris would become a tiny minority and it would be difficult to sustain the beneficent impact of their more formed political education. However, both Zanzibaris and Tanganyikans have shown a willingness to accept each other's pasts and to formulate common goals, based on achievements up till now. In Zanzibar almost all that could have been achieved, already has been: in Tanganyika, there is still much to be done. There is a good chance that the union will lead to the 'spreading' of the Zanzibar revolution in a much more effective way than could have been done by outside example or adventures. The revolution goes on, at a new level.

* * *

Essay published in New Left Review *I/25 (May–June 1964), under the pseudonym Lucien Rey. The 'Tanganyika-Zanzibar Anschluss' refers to the ratification on 26 April 1964 of Articles of Union between the Republic of Tanganyika, led by the government of Julius Nyerere and the People's Republic of Zanzibar, led by President Abeid Karumi, following the Zanzibar Revolution of 12 January 1964. The union resulted in the formation of the United Republic of Tanganyika and Zanzibar which changed its name to the United Republic of Tanzania on 1 November 1964.*

Aden

Lucien Rey

The collapse of Britain's interests in the Middle East promises to be spectacular. An uneasy shivering has been going on for years now and, as the end approaches, Britain's response becomes more and more convulsive. The scaling-up of military operations against tribesmen shows British 'decolonisation' in a cruel light. The gestures become more macabre as the grasp grows slighter.

What lies behind 'Operation Nutcracker'? The thumbprints of the sultans and sheikhs on the treaty which inaugurated the 'Federation of South Arabia'. And behind the thumbprints? The Aden military base: the Khormaksar airfield, the naval bunkering station, the network of storage tunnels inside the cliffs. And behind all that is Middle East oil.

Britain has invested heavily in the Aden base. Originally, it was only a staging post. It was not till the evacuation of Ismailia in 1954 that it was stepped up to anything like its present importance. Another boost was given as Kenyan independence approached: further miliary installations were built in Little Aden on the far side of the harbour. The base is still being extended. One drawback, for instance, is that naval and civil shipping have to share the port: it is thought that Britain intends to construct separate naval facilities.

Aden became a separate colony only in 1937; previously – since it was first seized in 1839 – it had been administered from India. But the colony was made up only of Aden town itself. The hinterland was divided into a Western and Eastern Protectorate: administrative entities whose reality was a quarrelsome conglomeration of petty sultanates and sheikhdoms. Aden had no industry except salt panning; later an oil refinery was built. Most employment came from the military installations. The protectorates were agricultural: the main crop was dates; some cotton is now grown in a few western states. They stretched for seven hundred miles along the coast, two or three hundred inland, but they are very sparsely peopled. Probably there are fewer than a million inhabitants and close on 300,000 of these are in Aden itself.

Aden was backward and Britain meant to keep it backward. In Aden a semblance of popular government was granted by, first, a municipality and later, in 1948, a legislative council. But the franchise was intolerably restricted; there were qualifications of wealth and of citizenship. To get elected, only a few hundred votes were needed. Special privileges were given to the Indian trading community. And so on. Opposition to Britain awoke slowly but once it had become conscious and organised it grew very rapidly. In 1954, Abdullah al Asnag founded the Aden Airways Employees Union. In 1956 the Aden Trade Union Congress was formed; al Asnag was General Secretary. And eventually, in 1962, the People's Socialist Party was inaugurated. The PSP is very largely the political wing of the ATUC. al Asnag is its president. Today the ATUC has a membership of 22,000, the PSP 33,000 (this figure is incomplete: many cells are clandestine and many members unlisted).

The PSP still looks on itself as a non-violent, social democratic party. It is proud of its ties with the Second International and the British Labour Party. It has limited its manifestations to strikes, boycotts and peaceful marches. For instance, when, in September 1962, the Aden Legislative Council was debating entry into the Federation, the PSP organised a march of protest, which was fired on by troops. It is said that the debate in the council chamber itself had to be broken off because so much tear gas was used that even the legislators were weeping. At any rate, the Federation went through in the end and the PSP leadership was jailed. It has become much clearer since to the PSP that peaceful, democratic evolution in Aden is very unlikely. But they are still reluctant to take to arms. The main support for violent struggle has come from the National Liberation Front, led by Qahtan al Shaabi in Cairo. Unfortunately relations between the PSP and the NLF are strained. (It should be said that alShaabi is close to UAR government circles.) Partly the PSP hangs back because they still cherish hopes that a Labour government in Britain will grant all their demands. But how likely is this? There would have to be a great deal of backtracking.

First, the Federation. The Federation started in 1959 with six states from the Western Protectorate; since then it has been enlarged, though it still does not include all states in either protectorate. Aden itself joined in 1963. The Federation has been beset with dilemmas from the start. A number of sultans were loath to join and had to be dismissed and replaced by their more malleable kinsmen. The Sultan of Lahej, by a stroke of ill luck for Britain, was not only the ruler of the most important state but also personally the best educated. Some of the cruder, less powerful sheikhs feared that he would manoeuvre his way into the paramountcy and finally, perhaps, the throne. They would not join unless he was dropped, so he was abandoned by Britain and replaced by his uncle. (He now runs a splinter opposition party from Cairo.) Thus a rough parity of incompetence and illiteracy was established.

It was difficult too to persuade Aden to join. Indeed, the Aden ministers who first signed the treaty have since all resigned in protest about the way things turned out. (Though one, Bassendwah, swallowed his doubts again.) Britain had to go to a great deal of trouble to find ministers willing to be drafted. Zain Baharoon, chosen as Chief Minister of Aden state, would have found it difficult to refuse; he runs the Brothers Trading Company, agents for Ford cars, Norge refrigerators, Zenith radios, etc. – lucrative concessions whose loss would be a bad blow. Another draftee was an agent for cotton insurance; another held a high post at the BP refinery; another was head of the United National Party (founded by deceased Chief Minister Bayumi) – the alleged tie-up between the UNP and the profitable *qat* monopolies granted by Bayumi is a talking point in Aden.

It can be seen that the federal cabinet is not very encouraging evidence for any claims that South Arabia is a fledgling nation which should be granted full independence under its present government. Indeed, they constantly quarrel even among themselves. For example, about a year ago an Egyptian-manned plane inadvertently landed on Mukayras airstrip in Audhali state. British soldiers from the British camp there prevented it from taking off again. However, the Audhali people insisted on greeting the Egyptian airmen with maximum hospitality and welcoming them effusively. The Sultan of Audhali, federal Minister of Internal Security, decided that he dare not risk trying to reverse the welcome his people had given and proposed in the cabinet that the plane and the airmen should be handed back to the Yemen. This was bitterly opposed by the Sherif of Beihan, a hard line supporter of the deposed Imam, who claimed that any decision was rightly his, as Minister of the Interior. Eventually both ministers – Internal Security and Interior – went so far as to send their private armies to fight it out. The British troops in Audhali were confined to camp. A stalemate was reached and the final decision was referred to

London. In the end, the airmen were returned to Cairo; the plane sent to Aden. This incident was typical.

Is the Federation reversible? Can the thumbprints be countermanded? Obviously this can only be done by ridding the whole area of the sultans themselves and abolishing their arbitrary powers. This means dismantling all the institutions which have been set up by Britain over the past years. Can this be done except by a popular revolution? Many leaders of the PSP are still confident that the sultans can be negotiated away. This seems very unlikely. Any attempt at reversing Britain's alliance with the sultans might easily lead to a civil war like that in the Yemen. As long as the Aden base remains, Britain would hardly be able to opt out of a civil war. In fact, Britain would have – more or less formally – to switch sides. At any rate, this is something qualitatively different from 'denegotiation'. A prime factor to be considered is the course which violence in South Arabia is likely to take: throughout what the PSP calls 'Natural Yemen' – the Republic and the British-occupied areas to the south. Violence is already well under way in the Federation; it will certainly spread.

There has always been violence in South Arabia and it has continued under British occupation. There have been constant tribal uprisings and British repression. The most recent outbreaks have been in Yafa, Mahra, Dathinah and Dhala states. In Yafa the tribes refused to enter the Federation and despite the deposition of their sheikh, they still remain outside. Yafa is a key state because it is in the Western Protectorate, near to Aden, and is on the Yemen frontier. In Mahra there has been unrest in the last year or two, ever since the US PanAmerican Oil Company started prospecting there and military roads were built to escort them. There have been several brief spells at 'pacification'. (There have also been attempts in Mahra to unionise the oil workers – many of whom have benefited from the ATUC in Aden.) Finally, there has been the rising of the five Radfan tribes in Dhala state. The Radfan tribes straddle the Yemen border and do not recognise any allegiance to the Emir of Dhala, nor to the Federation. Other tribes are known to have sent emissaries to the Radfan fighters, to get information about military problems and to co-ordinate their struggles. Britain knows that, unless the Radfan rising is quickly quenched, it will spread even further than it already has. This explains the fury of the repression.

Violence has another aspect in Aden itself. The culmination came with the bomb-throwing incident of 10 December 1963, when a bomb was thrown at the British High Commissioner, Kennedy Trevaskis, at Aden airport. Trevaskis and the Sultan of Fadhli were injured and two others killed. A union official, Khalifa A. Khalifa, was arrested and, though the charges against him were dropped, he has not yet been released. Even in jail he managed to top the poll in the October 1964 elections. There have been constant mass arrests, detentions without trial and deportations. Aden workers have been summarily rounded up, taken by truck to the Yemen border and dropped there. No provisions were made for their families still in Aden. The repression reached a new peak after the bomb incident, with the arrest of the whole ATUC and PSP leadership. The PSP has not yet been given the chance officially to contest an election: in the 1958 elections only 23 percent of 5,000 registered voters voted, though in 1964 the figure was 75 percent – out of 8,000. (Vacancies were filled between polls by turning the existing members into an electoral college and voting among themselves.) Its newspapers have been banned and its members victimised. Portraits of Nasser and black protest flags have been torn down. It is obvious that, in such a situation, the PSP cannot long remain non-violent.

Up until recently the Labour Party, though far from explicit, has seemed to be pursuing a moderate line on Aden. They have looked favourably on the PSP and encouraged them to think that a Labour government would bring in a new constitution, enlarging the franchise in Aden to return a PSP government and guaranteeing the PSP in Aden state against the power of the sultans in the protectorates. At the same time the base would be scaled down. (If need be, it could be shifted in part to Socotra – an adjunct administratively of Mahra state but, geographically speaking, a quite separate island of the Somali coast – and out to sea onto aircraft carriers, etc.) The base could be scaled down, it was thought, even if Libya was lost and even though Cyprus is problematic, to put it mildly. After all, there is still a base on Bahrain, on Masirah Island off the coast of Muscat, on Gan Island in the Maldives, there are still British troops in Kenya, etc.

Things look rather different now. The heavy British military involvement and the railroaded 'Constitutional Conference' have put the Labour Party in a dilemma. Their mild withdrawal policy now looks fraught with risks and repercussions. On the other hand, they are unwilling to break their tacit pledges to the PSP – particularly when the PSP is so embarrassingly linked with the Second International and the ICFTU. But already they have made the moves which would make the betrayal easier. They have backed the drive against the Radfan tribes, criticising it only on the grounds of military effectiveness. And they have said that the base is necessary 'for the time being'. A sector of the Labour Party has come out quite clearly for staying in Aden for a long while – at least as long as fighting goes on in North Kalimantan. What they must hope for is either a capitulation by the PSP – a readiness to permit the base to go on with minor alterations – or else the deep involvement of the PSP in violent opposition to Britain, so that they can be smeared and discredited in social democrats' eyes.

The PSP is certainly confused. Algeria is put forward, for instance, both as an example of accepting concessions along with independence (Mers El Kébir, the Sahara testing-ground) and also of armed struggle. Memories of Nasser's fiery speeches in Sana have made it difficult for them to accept the base. Also, of course, it is unlike other bases in that it completely dominates the town of Aden and is quite inseparable from normal municipal life; it is not a cut-off enclave. This too would make it difficult to accept; it is hard to see what independence could mean in such circumstances. Yet, despite all these pressures against capitulation, it cannot be quite ruled out. Moreover, the recently reported alliance between the PSP and the South Arabian League, dominated by exiled sultans, does not promise at all well.

There are one or two other questions that need to be put. First, what is the attitude of the USA? On the spot, there is close liaison between the Aden base and the US base at Asmara in Ethiopia. US fleets use Aden harbour. Within a wider perspective though, there are some contradictions between US and British interests and policies in the Middle East. The USA, for instance, recognises the Republican government in the Yemen and tries to foster good relations with the UAR. (It is particularly important for the USA not to seem to attack Cairo on two fronts: Israel and feudal monarchy.) Yet, on the other hand, widening the perspectives still further, there is a common interest for Britain and the USA in not sabotaging each other's more troublesome policies: Malaysia and Aden for Britain, Vietnam and Cuba for the USA. A certain quid pro quo of neutrality over these issues would seem attractive. Given all this, the USA can be expected to vacillate.

Finally, what is Britain's stake in the Middle East? Can it be dispensed with without radical social change in Britain itself? Some pointers: Middle East oil probably contributes roughly £100 million per year to Britain's balance of payments plus-column ('probably' and 'roughly' because of the notorious difficulty of interpreting oil company accounts); the sheikh of Kuwait is thought to invest about £35 to £55 million in London per year, which is rather over 10 percent of the liquid capital usually available; the Middle East supplies 50 to 60 percent of Britain's oil imports by value, at fixed prices, and ensures the place of BP in the international cartel. On the other hand, all this costs money to defend – though here again, it should be said that cheap oil makes other military operations, defending other interests, cheaper. It is obvious that there are very powerful sectors of British capitalism who have a strong interest in maintaining British military and political command in the Middle East to the last ditch. These are both industrial and financial interests: they comprise both those who wish – in what might be thought an old-fashioned way – to defend sterling and those in modern growth industries like petrochemicals, who might not usually be found in close alliance.

The struggle in South Arabia will go on. It may well lead to a general debacle of British interest in the Middle East. Such an outcome would certainly transform both the nature of the struggle and of the contenders. It is too early to say yet what would emerge.

* * *

Essay published in International Socialist Journal *1:56 (September–December 1964), under the pseudonym Lucien Rey.* International Socialist Journal *was founded by Italian socialist politician and journalist Lelio Basso in 1964, after a split from the Italian Socialist Party (PSI) that led to the formation of the Italian Socialist Party of Proletarian Unity (PSIUP). Wollen worked on the journal in Milan and Rome in 1964 and 1965. 'Operation Nutcracker' was the codename for the British military operation against the Radfani tribesmen and South Yemen's National Liberation Front, under the leadership of the military commander Ali Antar, in January 1964. Britain's heavy artillery and air attacks sought to crush the guerrilla warfare conducted by Radfani snipers throughout the Radfan mountains to the north of the port of Aden, the military base and capital of the British colonial protectorate of the Federation of South Arabia. 'Operation Nutcracker' intensified the 'Aden Emergency' of December 1963 declared by the British in response to the NLF's attempted assassination of the British High Commissioner, Kennedy Trevaskis, at Aden airport, which announced the 14 October Revolution of the NLF against colonial rule. Under the new Labour government, the British army escalated counter-insurgency operations, destroying villages and driving thousands of peasants into North Yemen. As armed resistance spread to yet more areas so did the British imprisonment, interrogation and torture of Yemeni rebels. In February 1966, the British announced the imminent withdrawal of armed forces; throughout 1967, the NLF seized control of more and more of the sheikhdoms and sultanates of the Federation. British troops finally withdrew on 29 November; on the evening of 29–30 November 1967, the People's Republic of Southern Yemen was born and 128 years of British rule came to an end.*

The Crisis in Sterling

Lucien Rey

Britain has long been losing ground in the struggle between the great capitalist powers. The Conservative government which presided over the last stages of the decline proved quite incapable of arresting it. A series of cycles set in, each of which left the economy weaker than the last. In 1964 the growth rate fell to 2 percent and a huge deficit began to build up both on capital and on current account. There was a disastrous influx of imports – not merely stocks, but semi-manufactured and even finished goods – and exports signally failed to improve. It was thought by many observers that the Labour regime elected in October would seek to reinvigorate the economy in alliance with the 'growth sectors' of industrial capitalism, in contrast with the discredited Conservative policy of alliance with the City, the stronghold of finance capital. The Labour left was warned to be on its guard against capitulation to the interests of growth industry; it was feared that the Labour government would only put through measures designed to rationalise and modernise the capitalist economy and then stop short. In fact, the capitulation has been much more drastic than that. The Labour government, it now seems, is not even going to pursue its target of 4 percent growth. It has capitulated to the City and to the international bankers. The stability of the world monetary system and the place of sterling in it are to have priority over any other objectives.

The Sterling Area is, of course, nothing else than the modern and morbid form of the old British Empire. It is the profane substructure for the sacred and holy superstructure of the Commonwealth. It is to save the Sterling Area that British troops are fighting in South Arabia and Borneo and Buccaneer fighter planes are sent to South Africa. Every time a Radfan tribesman is shot or a Singapore student imprisoned, sterling is a little safer. The surest defence of the Sterling Area means that Britain must keep its grasp over its three richest assets: Malayan tin, Middle Eastern oil and South African gold. Yet, despite all these riches, the Sterling Area is also a great handicap to Britain. It must be constantly defended, both on the battlefield and in the money market. And its nucleus and treasure-house, the City, embodies in itself attitudes, habits and priorities which weaken the domestic economic growth of Britain itself. Resources which might be devoted to domestic investment in productive and profitable industries have to be diverted in order to meet Britain's worldwide obligations, to pay for imperialist wars and so on. And Britain's status as a banking nation means that, according to the present system of international finance, a run on the pound can quickly mean the collapse of everything. At the same time, industrial capital has to contend with the backwash of the more or less unpredictable flows of money from country to country and currency to currency and with any number of ad hoc measures and regulators designed to cope with the disequilibria of these movements. It is no surprise that British capitalism is in a state of crisis and riven by contradictions.

As soon as the Labour government came into office, it was faced with the need to make immediate, grave decisions. Reserves were low and the trade balance was very unfavourable. Moreover, the very fact of the Labour government aggravated the situation. Many people, afraid that the new government might bring in various anti-capitalist measures, thought it wiser to move their money elsewhere. Others speculated that the pound would be devalued. And others felt that a catastrophe, if it could be threatened, might destroy the Labour government and lead to the return of the Conservatives to power. Consequently, it was imperative that the Labour regime should act decisively to correct the situation and to prevent sabotage. Before considering what they actually did, it is worth recapitulating some of the various courses open to them.

1. *Devaluation.* This is the solution preferred by certain groups in growth industry and by a few left-wing economists. It has the effect of discouraging imports and promoting exports; it also means a rise in the cost of living and a depression of real wages. It implies definite short-term discrimination against the working class. At the same time, however, devaluation is opposed by the City, whose income derives directly from sterling. In this instance, it was also strongly opposed by the United States, who feared repercussions on the dollar. On the whole, international bankers

dislike devaluation because they prefer stable, rigid rates. Devaluation is politically damaging in Britain because it is felt by many that the integrity of sterling is symbolic of Britain's greatness; this kind of chauvinism is deep-rooted in all classes. Finally, devaluation discriminates against other countries which hold sterling – both richer countries, such as Australia, and poorer ones, say, in Africa – and hence threatens the existence of the Sterling Area by making other countries less willing to hold sterling, for fear that their assets will be depreciated quite out of their control.

2. *Disguised devaluation.* In its most obvious form, this means import surcharges plus export subsides. However, this method is frowned on by all the various international trade organisations (export subsidies are considered particularly reprehensible; they often amount to dumping) and would sooner or later invite reprisals. They are therefore short-term measures. On the other hand, there are a number of possible schemes for doing much the same thing in a more sophisticated way, so that you cannot be accused point-blank. These include, for instance, waiving a turnover tax on exports, auctioning import licenses, etc. These more sophisticated schemes are evidently administratively complex; they could not be applied overnight and their effect would not be very rapid or very calculable. They are favoured, however, by groups in growth industry who are aware of the political and international arguments against devaluation.

3. *Deflation.* Deflation is the policy carried out by previous Conservative governments on the recommendation of City and Treasury opinion. The measures traditionally applied are to raise the bank rate, restrict credit, step up taxes on petrol or tobacco which are used as fiscal regulators, raise the level of unemployment. It has been effectively demonstrated that these methods do not work in Britain; that they have brought nothing but stagnancy. Moreover, they have meant constant assaults on the working-class standard of living. The Labour Party campaigned hard against these stop-go cycles during the election. However, deflation remains the favourite remedy of conservative economists, especially bankers, everywhere.

4. *Borrowing.* This again is evidently a short-term measure; it does nothing to put right fundamental weakness. There are two main sources from which Britain can borrow. First, from the IMF, which was originally dominated by the USA but is now, since the appearance of the American payments deficit and the formation of the Paris Club, the arena for

a deepening struggle over control between the USA and the Common Market countries, led by France. Second, from the central banks of other countries. The machinery for loans between Britain and the USA is comparatively advanced because of the mutual interest each has in shoring up the other's currency. Evidently, the more that is borrowed, whether in supplementary *tranches* from the IMF or in direct central bank loans, the greater will be the insistence of creditors on control and surveillance of the debtor's economy.

5. *Controls*. Physical controls over capital movements would need to be total and stringent. There would inevitably be a frantic search for loopholes, through Hong Kong, through spreading insurance risks, etc. Controls would undoubtedly be the most radical measure envisaged and would involve major social and economic transformations. They would create outright hostility between the government and very many capitalist interests; a freeze-up in private investment, for example, would have to be met by increased public investment. Controls would also undermine the Sterling Area even more seriously than devaluation; they could well lead to its disintegration. Those countries who could no longer withdraw their assets from London would not be inclined to send any more there. One unfortunate side effect would be the damage done to the development plans of many of the countries banking in London. They would have to be compensated by, for instance, vastly increased aid. Of course, very mild controls are advocated by some capitalist interests. Even the USA has retreated a little from convertibility with its Interest Equalisation Tax, and it also uses techniques such as computer stock control. But fiscal measures and indicative planning of this kind are only very marginal; only physical controls could be expected to have a major effect. Evidently, these are stern measures; import and exchange controls have to be enforced without fear or favour. It must be said that it is quite possible that various groups in the Labour Party would not be able to stomach them and might even bring down their own government.

It is clear that the decisions facing the Labour government were not easy; a lot of evidence suggests that Harold Wilson himself, an able economist with a strong sense of political realism, failed to appreciate how difficult they were. The crisis developed at an accelerating rate. It was met in six principal ways (not in precise chronological order).

1. *Credit from the IMF.* This was a routine drawing on immediately available credit. It did not indicate what the main lines of the new government's

policy would be. It did, however, reveal the strong position of the Paris Club vis-a-vis the IMF.

2. *A 15 percent import surcharge and slight export rebate.* This was as far as the government dared to go towards a disguised devaluation. It had two unfortunate effects. First, the emphasis given on the import surcharge gave it a deflationary effect, drawing off money to the treasury and raising the cost of living. Second, it discriminated against those countries who could not find alternative markets or were particularly dependent on Britain. Had Britain devalued, they would have devalued too and thus neutralised the effect. But there was no point in their following suit with import surcharges.

3. *Emergency budget.* The November budget had four main planks, but three of them were not to become effective until April the next year.

a) An immediate sixpence-a-gallon tax on petrol. This was a classic deflationary use of a fiscal regulator.

b) A deferred sixpence rise of the standard rate of income tax. The effect of this was to make the tax system more progressive and reverse the anti-egalitarian trend set in motion by the Conservatives.

c) Increased pensions next April, to be paid for by increased national insurance contributions and the tax rise. The delay of the pensions increase was clearly designed as a sop to deflationary pressures.

d) Unspecified corporations tax and capital gains tax proposals, deferred till next April. These, along with the redistributive tax and pensions proposals, were interpreted by hostile capitalist opinion as an irresponsible attack on profits, dividends, etc.

All in all, the budget was both deflationary and redistributive. The Chancellor seems to have hoped he would thus satisfy everybody; in fact, he angered everybody. The left complained about the deflationary postponement of pensions rises; the right objected to the enlargement of the welfare state in times of crisis. It is always the habit of capitalists to interpret a crisis as showing, not their inadequacy, but the need to win back their confidence by guaranteeing them better profits.

4. *Hints and rumours.* Throughout the crisis, the government, aware of the psychological aspects of economic behaviour, tried to create a favourable atmosphere, in which everyone would think well of them. They did this by making imprecise statements, in the hope that they would be taken

optimistically by all concerned. False hopes. The government was forced to pay the price for mystifying instead of clarifying consciousness. The City had to be reassured that there was nothing to fear from the new profits tax, West Germany that the Army of the Rhine was not going to be cut, EFTA (European Free Trade Association) that the import surcharges would soon be removed. But these open disclaimers disturbed opinion even more than the original subterraneous rumours. Worst of all, the Labour government made no attempt to explain its decisions to its own supporters; it could not – already half-knowing that it would capitulate. Yet, by this clouding of issues, it in fact made capitulation certain.

5. *A 2 percent rise in bank rate.* Late in the day, the bank rate went up. This was the government's first acknowledgement that there was a crisis in the capital account. Government spokesmen were at pains to point out that a bank rate rise was not necessarily deflationary; there was talk about a two-tier interest system. In reality, in such a situation, a 2 percent rise is deflationary; this was later underlined by a Bank of England letter about credit selectivity. However, here again, the Labour government became the victim of its own mystification. It was in fact, albeit grudgingly, putting through a deflationary policy under pressure. But because it put it through in fits and starts, denying all the time what it was doing (and many spokesmen probably sincerely believed their own denials), it failed to satisfy those who were putting on the pressure; at the same time, it demobilised those whose support might have made it possible to resist by refusing to put the alternatives clearly.

6. *Massive borrowings.* Even after the bank rate rise, the situation deteriorated. Attempts to stem the outflow of sterling by buying sterling with gold merely depleted the gold reserves. Finally, the government was forced to borrow £1,000 million. Nearly all this came from central banks, in eleven countries. A leading part in arranging the loans was played by the USA, which also made the largest contribution. The Labour government refused to allow formal surveillance of the economy as a quid pro quo for the loans; however, it is quite clear that informal pressure was and is very strong. The loans are only short-term; the very fact that the problem of their renewal is thus posed will obviously carry weight. However, the issue is blurred by the rivalry between the USA and the Common Market. The physicians who saved the 'Sick Man of Europe' did so because they were afraid the convulsions of his death might bring them all down. Meanwhile, they will continue to fight over his inheritance. All this will not

make Britain healthy, but it will give a little breathing space until either the USA or Europe feels strong enough to make an outright challenge. The policy of the Labour government is one of close alliance and a special relationship with Washington; this may enable them to resist direct economic pressures from Europe. On the other hand, it will certainly mean political concessions to the USA: Ascension Island was just a foretaste.

Thus the Labour government, ably assisted by the Bank of England and the Federal Reserve Board, checked the run on the pound. It was a famous victory. *The Economist* described it as 'a prime minister's prostration' and spoke of the Labour government as 'obliged last week virtually to hand over the management to Lord Cromer' at the Bank of England. Harold Wilson was dubbed 'Lord Cromer's poodle'. Meanwhile readers of *Tribune*, the traditional organ of the Labour left, were assured that 'the whole massive operation was conducted with quite extraordinary speed, skill and toughness by the Prime Minister and his colleagues', speculators had been 'given a beating' and foreign bankers had shown 'a much more sensible approach' than in the past. Indeed, the foreign bankers were all but paving the path to socialism. The British left never seems to learn. Only halfway through the Labour government's glorious first hundred days, it had instituted a deflationary policy, it had abandoned its cherished 4 percent growth rate, it had postponed welfare expenditure, it had asserted its devotion to imperialism 'east of Suez' and it had truckled to the City, the White House, NATO, etc., etc. What lessons can be drawn?

1. *The Sterling Area must be dismantled.* To persist in a policy of keeping sterling 'riding high' is to persist in a policy of imperialism. The struggle for financial supremacy merely reflects the imperialist struggle for world domination. The pathetic pride of the Labour government in having saved sterling is nothing less than pride at having been granted a further lease of life to ravage and exploit the world. The Labour left seems hopelessly confused about this. Thus Michael Foot writes in *Tribune* that 'the various governments, headed by the United States' – that is, the governments of the principal imperialist powers – who saved 'the purchasing power of sterling', acted with a sense of 'international responsibility'. The plain fact is that the only socialist way to prevent collapse was to impose controls, imperative planning and public investment. The Labour government made no steps in these directions at all. It merely profited from the imperialists' 'sense of international responsibility' in order to continue as an

imperialist power in its own right and to play its modest part, by saving sterling, in saving capitalism.

2. *There is no easy way out through international monetary reform.* The various plans to create a new world monetary system merely reflect the crisis in the present system and the need felt by the imperialist powers to carry on their struggle at a new level. Yet readers of *Tribune* are told, by Peter Shore, that

> the past week has seen a major development towards sanity in international currency arrangements. The swift mobilisation of a thousand million pounds to crush speculation against the £ is an experience which can and will be repeated to protect other currencies against similar speculative raids in the future. Indeed, it has opened up for the first time in many years the real possibility of making major reforms in our unstable international payments system.

It is difficult to imagine a more euphoric celebration of the power of international capitalism, culminating – as a socialist to socialists – with its final grovelling 'our'. What Shore is doing is to accept without question the view of an increasing number of bourgeois economists that world capitalism is suffering from a liquidity shortage problem, which explains its disequilibria. For these economists increased world liquidity has become the magic charm which entry into the Common Market used to be: the supernatural agency which will save sterling for good and remove the danger of another unpleasant crisis. The same views are also gaining ground in the USA, which is also suffering from a payments deficit, though not nearly so gravely as Britain. What Shore hopes, evidently, is that the narrow escape, not only of the pound, but also of the dollar, will lead the US government to throw its whole weight behind the demand for world monetary reform.

But what kind of reform? Ideas differ. At the OECD conference, shortly after the crisis, France pointed out that it was quite willing to relieve Britain of some of 'the burden of sterling'; its own projected Composite Reserve Unit currency would do just that, absorbing the old key currencies into a new unit embodying a high degree of European control and backing. The Americans, on the other hand, envisage a kind of super-IMF issuing a kind of super-dollar. Broadly speaking, as *The Economist* points out, the proposals are similar: 'the real issue is that of control'. At any rate, the crisis can be expected to deepen, since the present efforts of the USA to end its deficit and draw dollars back home will in fact mean less liquidity. Thus the USA, by trying to solve the crisis on its own terms, can only succeed in making it worse. The dogfights will get more vicious.

It is clear that any socialist government must insist on discussing these liquidity problems, not in a purely technical sense, but in the context of the distribution of world trade, as broached at the Geneva conference earlier in 1964. The issue at stake is not merely that of putting through a reform in the teeth of conservative bankers' opposition but of what the reform ought precisely to be. And, of course, who will have the power over any possible international credit institution, how its reserves will be provided, to whom it will issue credit, etc. What threatens is the emergence of an institution with financial power on an unprecedented scale; this cannot be welcomed indiscriminately. It is quite possible that contradictions among the great capitalist powers will in fact prevent such an institution being created; in that case we must be prepared for much sharper struggles between these powers, using monetary instruments as major weapons. It is doubtful whether sterling could survive such struggles independently; the signs seem to show that it would be absorbed by the dollar or else would completely collapse. There is scant indication that the British left is as yet beginning to face these problems.

3. *Withdrawal of sterling from the key currency system and demobilisation of the Sterling Area would mean radical transformations at home.* British capitalism is by now so intimately linked with the international capitalist system that an assault on one necessarily means an assault on the other. The way forward for socialists can be deciphered. But it will involve a long step-by-step process of building consciousness. By now the British working class and even Labour Party left militants are so thoroughly confused and mystified that there can be little hope of any immediate advance. But it must be made quite plain that the Labour government has capitulated, that it is deflating, and that this is the direct result of its determination to save the Sterling Area and remain a world imperialist power. The working class must not be sidetracked into wasting its energies on peripheral disputes, set in a context which it does not fully understand. In particular, close scrutiny must be made of four of the Labour government's stated next objectives.

1. *Incomes policy.* This must not be, in any form or on any pretext, a disguised and classically deflationary wage freeze, pay pause and so forth.

2. *Cutting foreign expenditure.* This should include ending wars in Malaysia and South Arabia and demobilising Britain's worldwide system of bases. It should also include disengagement in central Europe.
3. *Redeploying manpower.* 'Is it deflation if we reduce demand to help us re-deploy our manpower and use it as efficiently as other nations use theirs? (How do we move people from job to job in a blown-up economy, given a free society?)' Thus *The Financial Times*: a warning in itself.
4. *Encouraging exports.* Socialists must insist that this is done through imperative planning and public investment rather than private investment, subsidised by the government through incentive schemes and financed out of private profit.

Above all, socialists in Britain must prepare a long-term strategy; they must not entertain futile hopes of quick success. And they must remember that though it is easier to blackmail the left than the right with the fear of a Conservative government, the left must not perpetually allow itself to be blackmailed. Above all it must not let itself be demobilised at the same time.

* * *

Essay published in International Socialist Journal *2:7 (January–February 1965), under the pseudonym Lucien Rey. See previous bibliographic note to 'Aden'.*

Iran Today – and Tomorrow?

Lucien Rey

What is the political situation in Iran? What are the chances that the Shah's regime will be overthrown? First, we must consider the potential of the various opposition forces. These are partly political, partly sociological. Those which are primarily political have all already passed the pivotal moments in their histories in which they could unlock the situation on their own initiative and thus release their own potential at the time most opportune for themselves – least opportune, hence, for the regime. Today, though their potential does still exist – albeit much attenuated – they must wait for some other force to take the decisive action which will enable them to re-emerge on-stage from the wings. This new force, whatever it will be, is still primarily sociological, for the most part unaware of its destiny. Until it manifests itself, Iran will be in an interim period: the main political actors will appear to be the Shah and his close confederates, behind them the foreign capitalists, diplomats and generals; all other political action will be ruthlessly suppressed. But this *entr'acte* must not be mistaken for the end of the drama. Iran will one day be free.

First, we must consider the Tudeh (Communist) Party. As in so many other countries, communism first came to Iran as Bolshevism; Marxism has always been mediated through the special history of the Russian Revolution. For Iran, however, the impact of Bolshevism has been distorted by the facts of geography. Russia is Iran's northern neighbour; throughout the period of classical imperialism it was, with Britain, Iran's principal oppressor. The Bolshevik Revolution was, for Iran, not only an analogy and a model but a historical event of the utmost importance for the course of Iranian history itself. Had Iranian communism had its own Marxist heritage, or had any kind of wider Marxist perspective been available, it would probably have been able to cope with the difficult problems which arose. Perhaps if the first impetus of Iranian communism had not been so speedily and effectively suppressed and driven into exile an answer would have been found. (Sultan-Galiev, after all, had been not far across the border and his views expressed a very similar dilemma.) The ambiguity of Bolshevism for Iran still remains; one of the most encouraging signs of recent years is the insistence, among many young Iranian Marxists, of reinterpreting the history of the Tudeh Party and Russo-Iranian relations in full consciousness of this ambiguity.

However, despite all these handicaps, the Tudeh Party twice came very close to success in the decade after the end of the Second World War. Each time, sadly, they made a fatal mistake and, ironically, the second sprang from the recognition of the first. Both times, too, Tudeh Party policy became confused with Soviet government policy: this was another error, which was not recognised – or, at least, not openly and not in practice. Briefly, the situation was as follows. At the end of the war, an autonomous government was set up under Soviet tutelage in the northern province of Azerbaijan. The presence in Iran of the Red Army made Soviet influence in the capital very powerful. The Teheran government, under Ahmad Qavam, was emphatically pro-Soviet. It was backed by the Tudeh Party. The Soviet government agreed to withdraw the Red Army from Iran on very favourable terms: the Azerbaijan government was to be recognised by Teheran, the Tudeh Party was to join the central government with three cabinet posts, the Soviet Union was to be granted an oil concession. But, after a brief period of honeymoon between the Tudeh Party and Qavam, in the months immediately after the Red Army withdrawal, Qavam disregarded all his promises, smashed the Azerbaijan government, suppressed and persecuted the Tudeh Party and cancelled the Soviet oil concession. In six months Soviet influence in Iran diminished from military control of half the country to clandestine intrigue.

What went wrong? First, the Tudeh Party wrongly calculated that Qavam would not be able to break his word because to do so would mean relying on the army, which was under the Shah's control and not his. They estimated that the antagonism between Qavam and the Shah would preclude any reconciliation. But, in the event, Qavam did call on the army. The Tudeh Party drew the lesson from this that a prime minster from the old aristocracy, however hostile to the usurping Pahlevi dynasty, would always join with the Shah in the last resort, even if it meant his own personal eclipse. For this reason they distrusted Mohammad Mossadegh,

Qavam's cousin, when he became Prime Minister soon afterwards; they were reinforced in this distrust by Mossadegh's anti-communism and his tendency, like Qavam, to look favourably on America, as a power which could be used to break the Russian-British grasp on Iran. But Mossadegh also learned his lesson from Qavam: it was essential to wrest control of the army from the Shah. Almost singlehanded, with no organised political base, Mossadegh succeeded in this, but he was unable to consolidate his position. The Tudeh Party, who might have made all the difference, rallied to him too late and too hesitantly. Instead of earning victory, they earned martyrdom.

Second, the Tudeh Party, throughout this period, became too closely involved with Soviet interests. This was particularly the case after the collapse of their hopes when Qavam double-crossed them. There followed a purge in which a new, much more 'Russian' leadership was installed. During the next few years and throughout the Mossadegh period this leadership left Iran for exile in the Soviet Union. At the decisive moment, therefore, it was both out of touch with the immediate situation and only able to communicate through the Soviet embassy. These leaders still control the Tudeh Party from exile in eastern Europe. They are completely discredited.

However, it would be wrong to reject the whole tradition of the Tudeh Party or to think that it had no further potentiality. It has played a vital part in Iran's political and cultural history. It introduced Marxism to Iran and initiated a great mass of Iranians to entirely new political perspectives. And, in many ways, it was much closer to the particular history and culture of Iran than its purely political conduct and analysis would suggest. It incorporated much of the tradition of the Democrat movement of the beginning of the century and was to a great extent responsible for the cultural renaissance which Iran enjoyed during the forties; one has only to think of the novels of Bozorg Alavi or the plays performed at the Saadi Theatre. Moreover, not all its leaders left Iran; some refused to go. The heroic resistance of Khosrow Roozbeh after the royalist coup d'état is part of Iran's revolutionary history; his closing speech at his trial is one of the most remarkable documents of Persian Marxism. This part of the Tudeh Party's legacy still remains; though the party apparatus has been destroyed and discredited, this spirit still exists – in the cities and in the rural areas of Azerbaijan and Gilan – waiting to be tapped by some new force. And the same is true of the Tudeh Party's achievements in introducing Marxism and reviving Persian literature: they are the essential basis for any new progress.

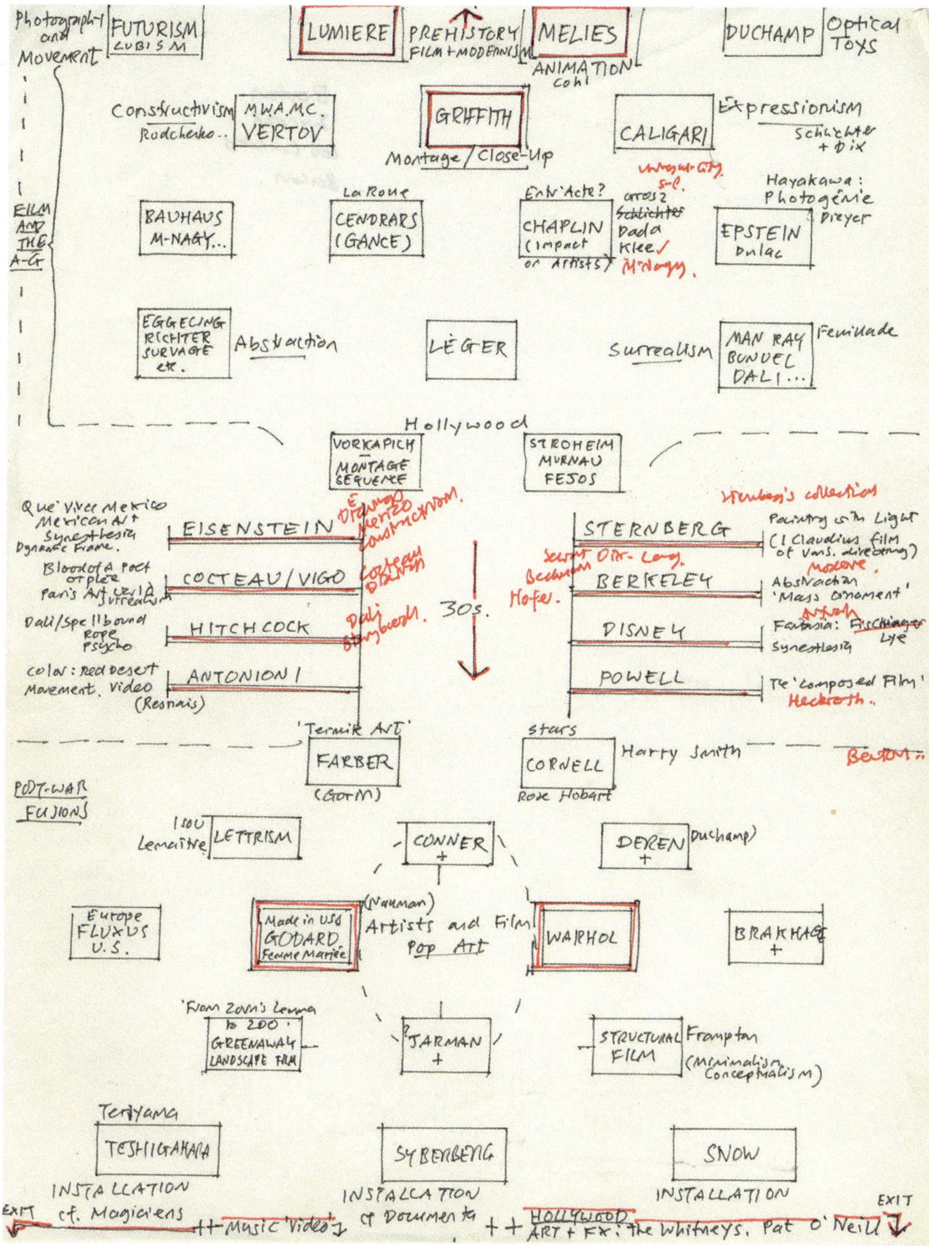

Diagram on the history of experimental film (undated)

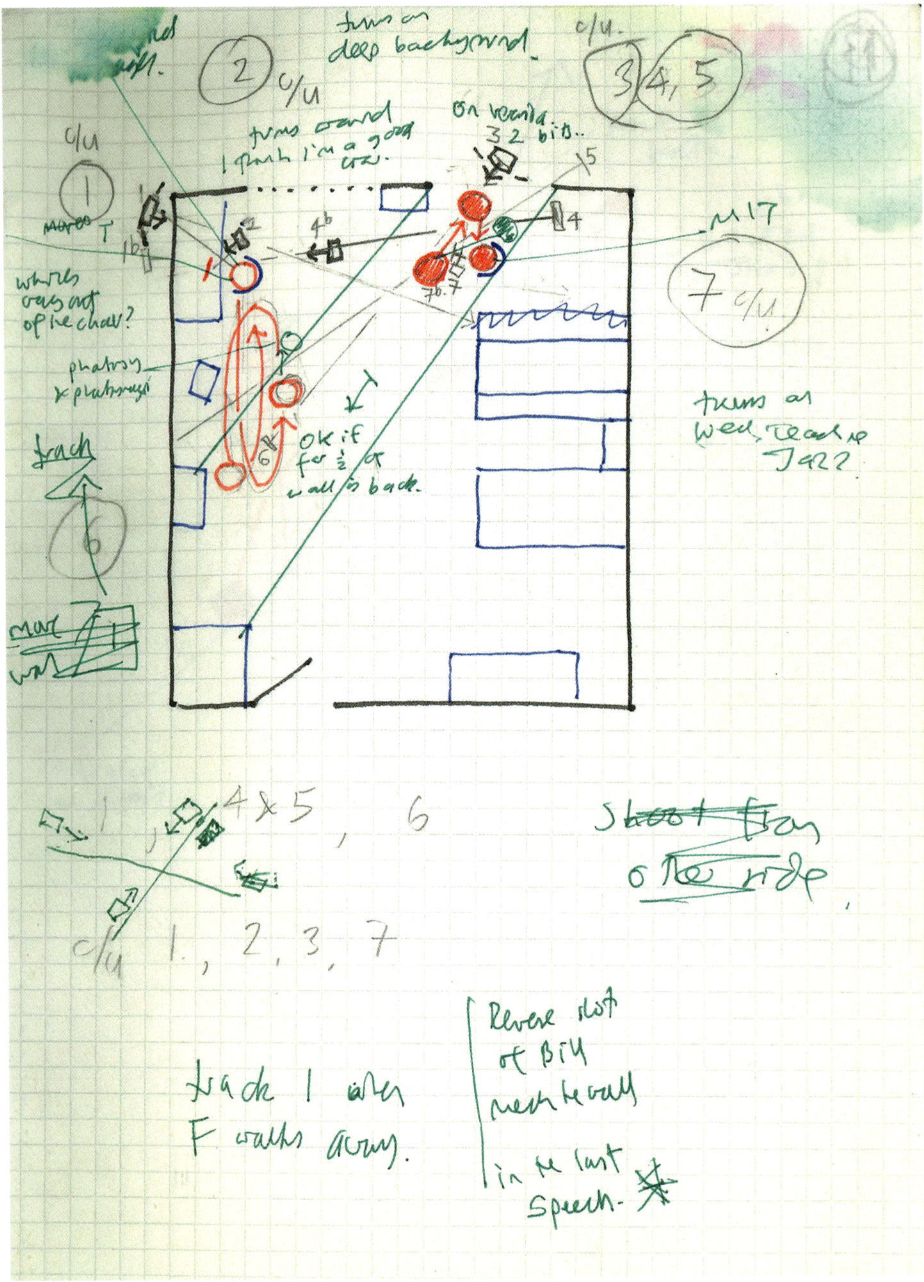

Shot plan for *Friendship's Death* (c. 1986)

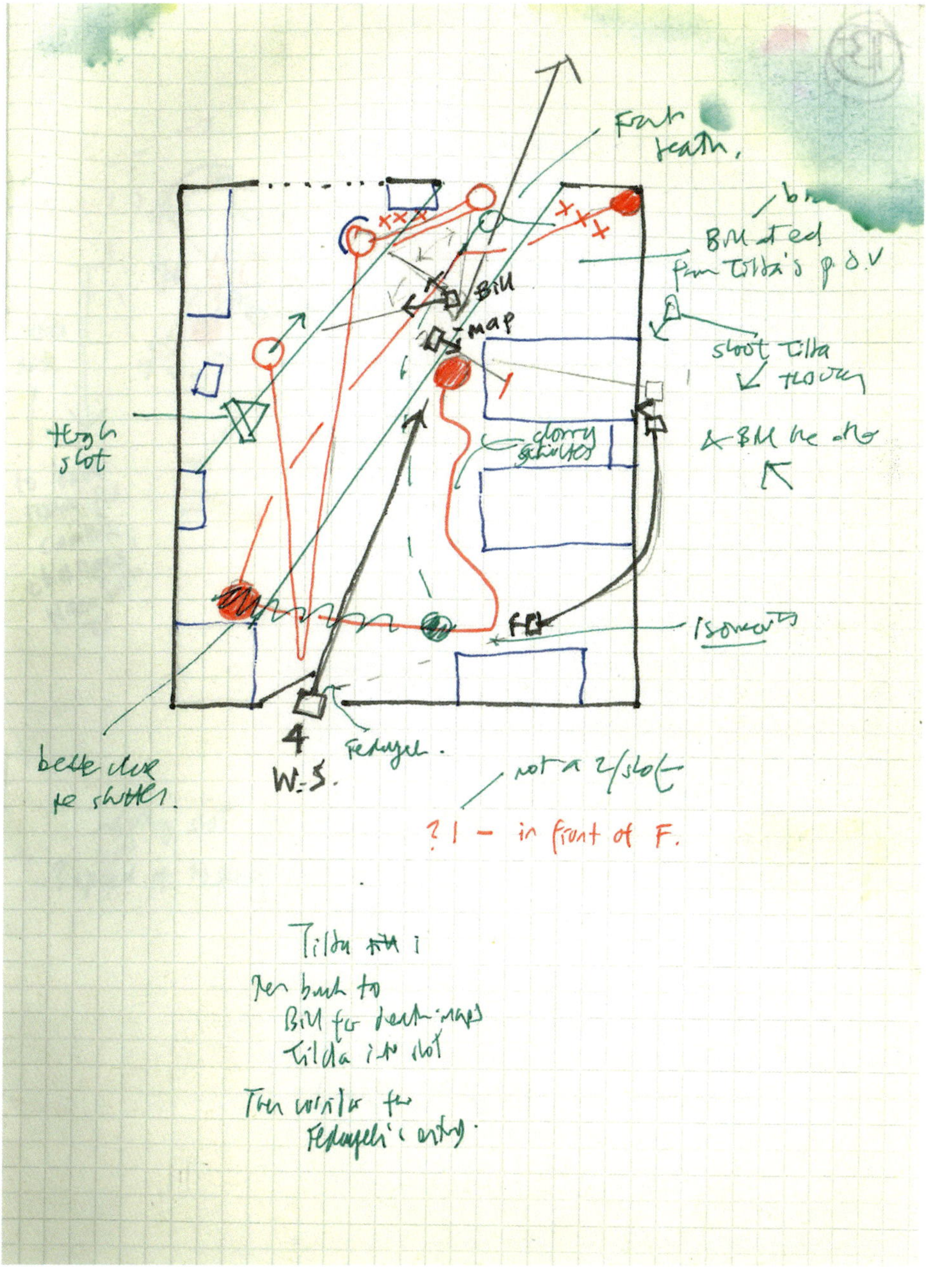

Shot plan for *Friendship's Death* (c. 1986)

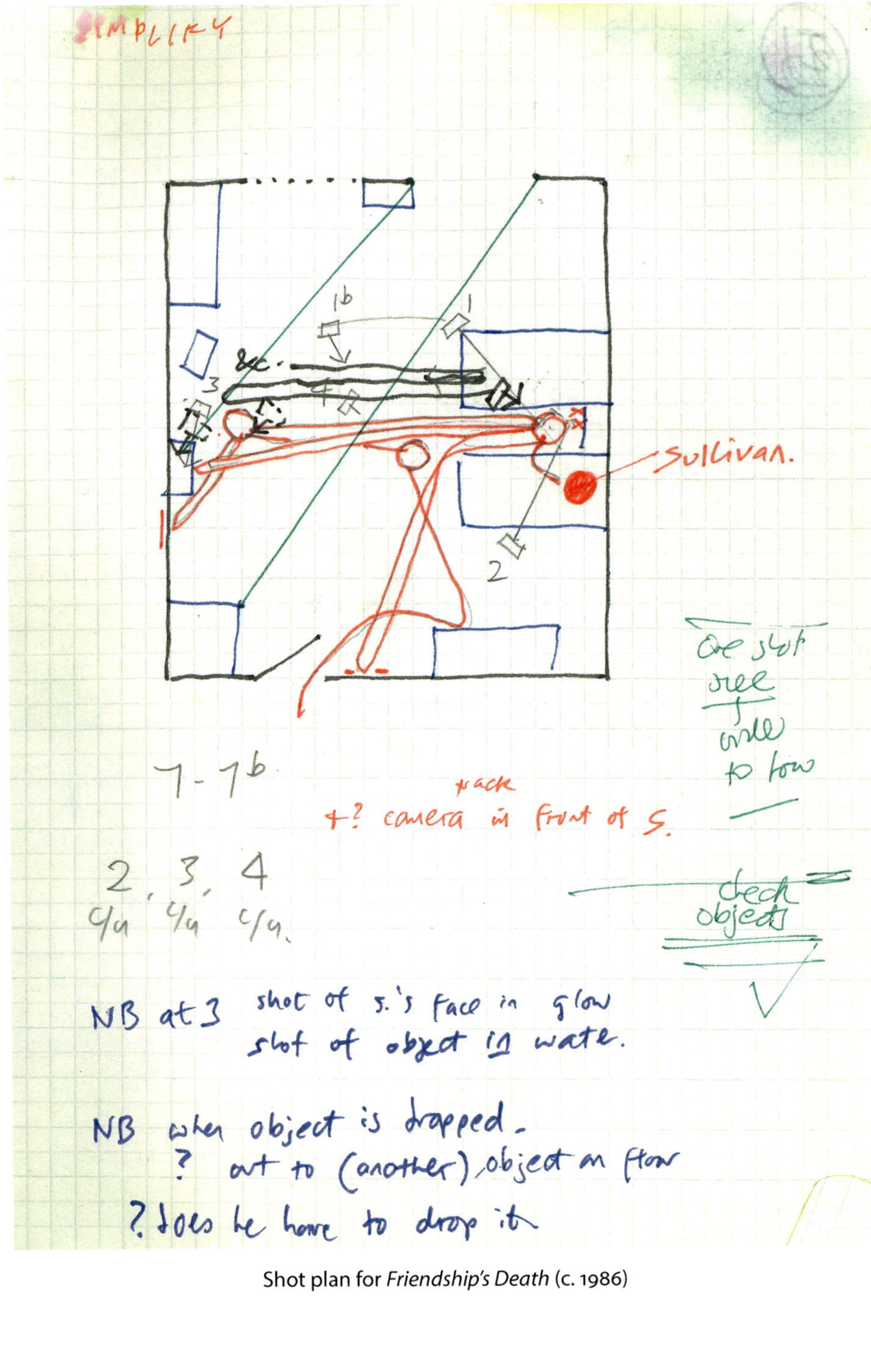

Shot plan for *Friendship's Death* (c. 1986)

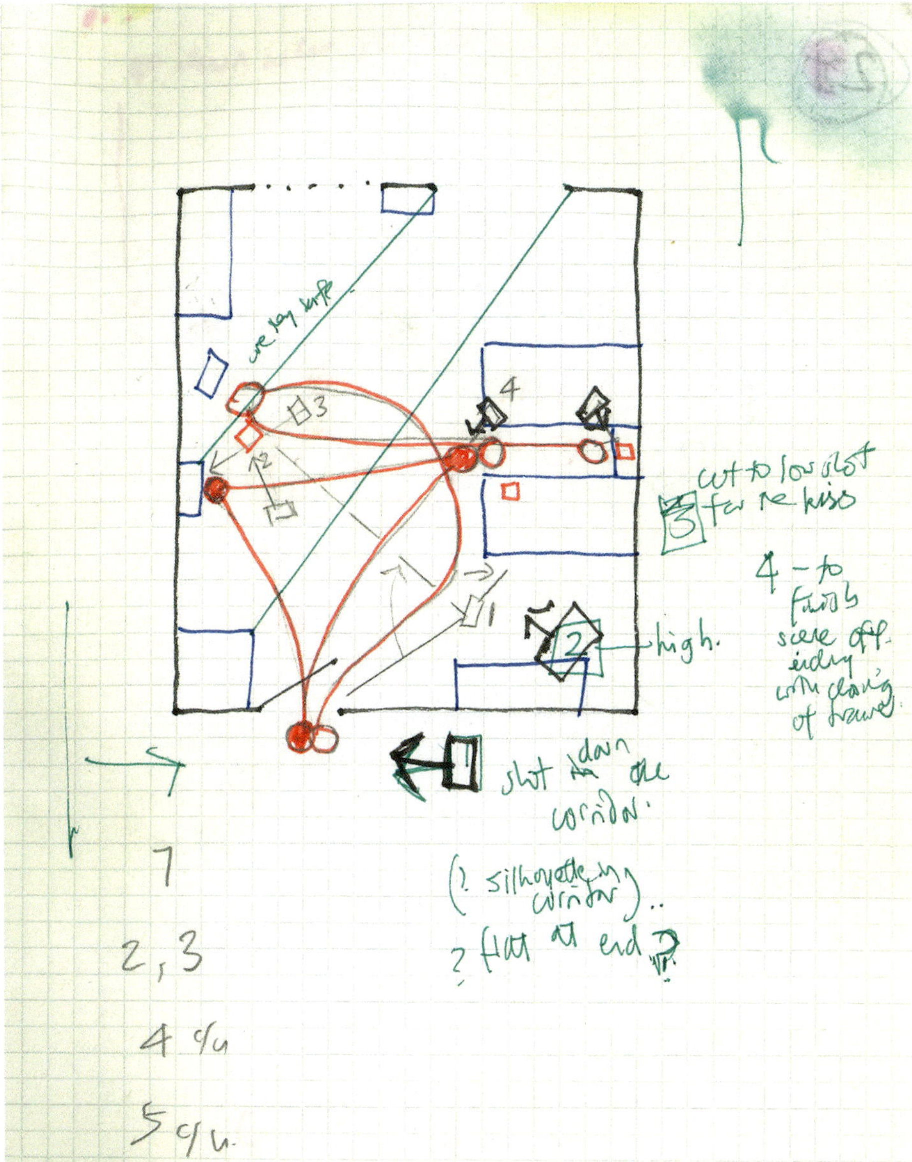

Shot plan for *Friendship's Death* (c. 1986)

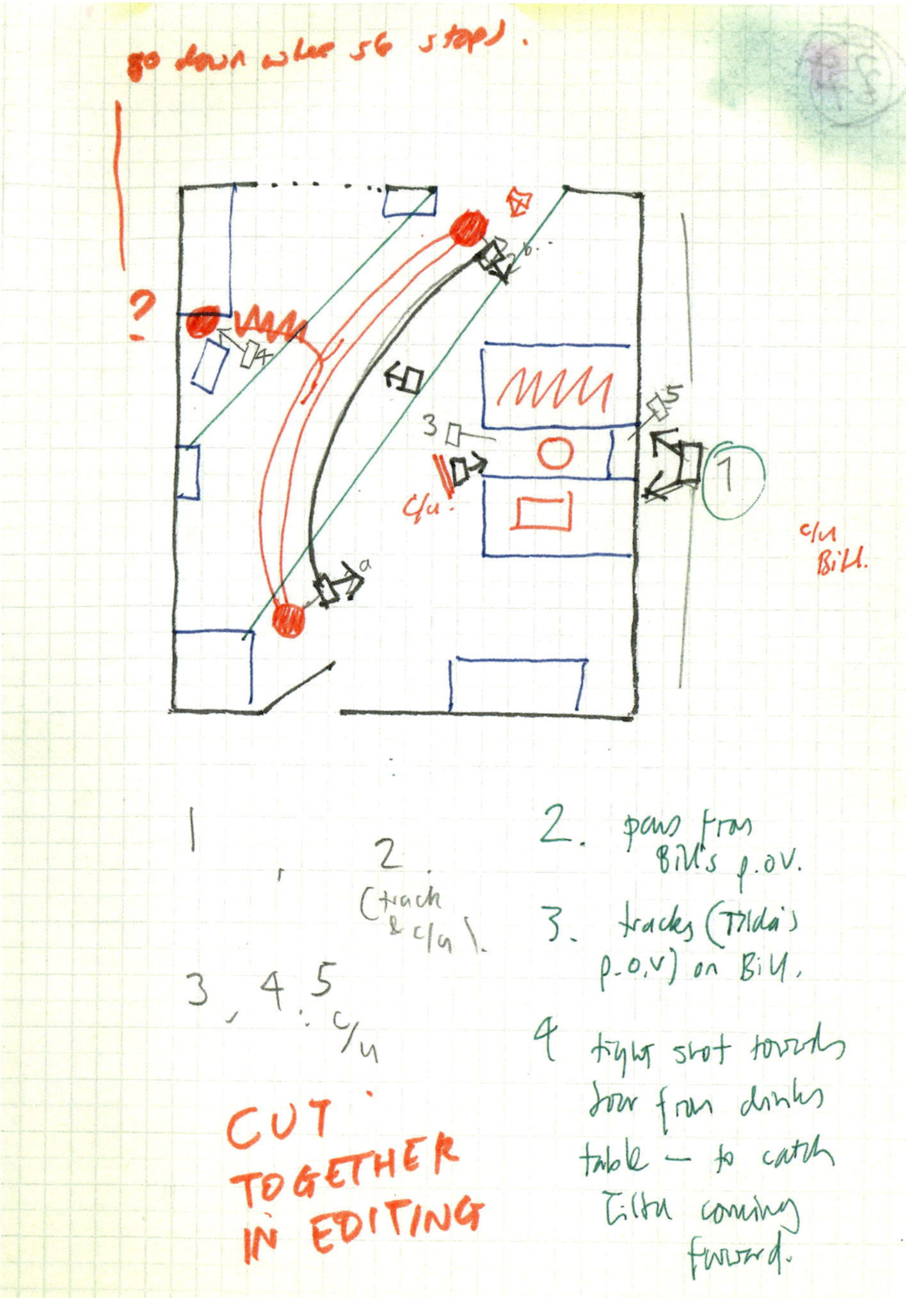

Shot plan for *Friendship's Death* (c. 1986)

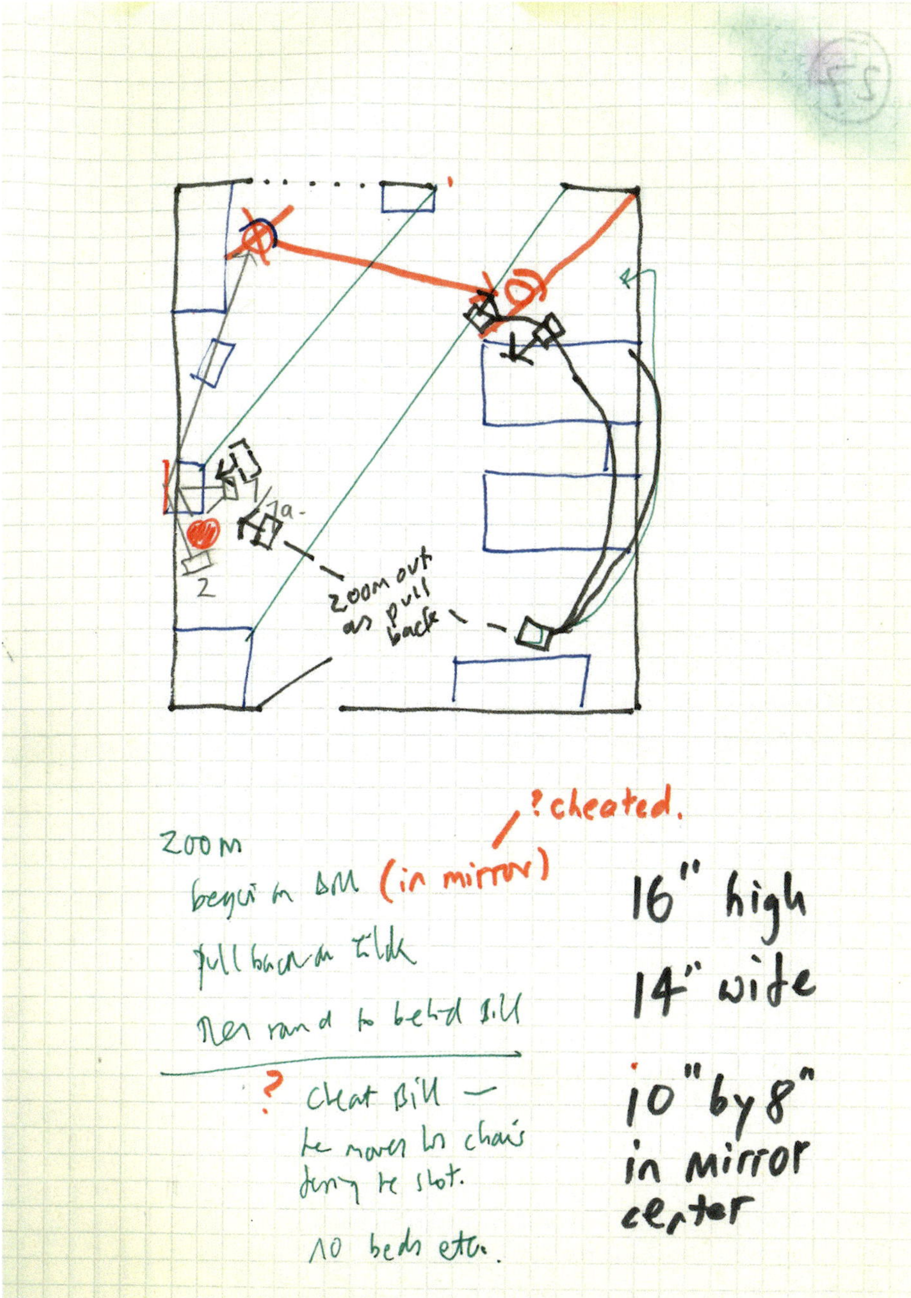

Shot plan for *Friendship's Death* (c. 1986)

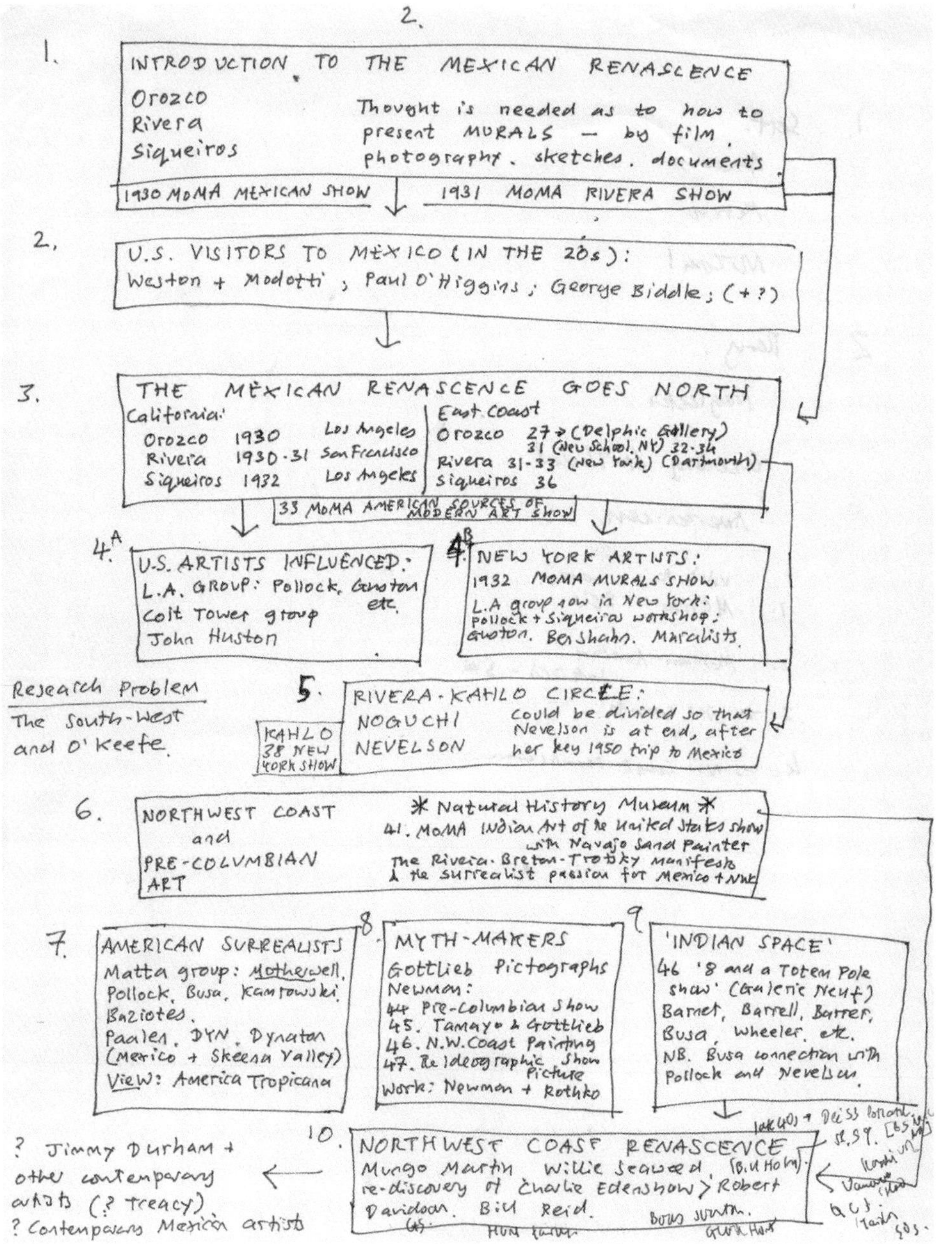

The Continent – sketch for an exhibition (1993)

The second major force in recent years has been the National Front, formally the political organisation of Mossadegh. In fact, however, it has never been anything but a loose conglomeration of very different and contradictory groupings, ranging from far left to far right, united principally by their antipathy to the Shah. Since the fall of Mossadegh, the National Front has been banned, except for a very brief period a few years ago. But during this period of what might have been underground work and organisation the secretariat in fact made little effort to keep the Front alive. After the coup d'état it fell into the hands of a group of ex-officials of the Mossadegh government and middle-class intellectuals associated with the Iran party who concentrated their campaigns almost entirely round trying to regain legality and the right to put up parliamentary candidates. This was an utterly fruitless policy. The most prominent National Front leaders also involved themselves, without any popular mandate, in negotiations with the Shah about the possibility of their entering the government; it is generally felt that they were considered an acceptable *équipe de rechange* by the Americans. This degeneration was brought to an end during the summer of last year when Dr Mossadegh – who is confined to his village – wrote a letter condemning their policy, pointing out that they were in danger of representing nobody but themselves and indicating an alternative line. The Front instead of being a unitary organisation controlled by the secretariat should be more of a confederation – each of the participating groups would nominate members of the directorate. This would have had the effect of shifting the Front to the left. The criterion for membership of the Front should be adherence to the slogan 'against despotism, against imperialism'. The Front should work with anybody who accepted this slogan. Mossadegh made his point clearer by reminiscing about the 14th of Tir, an occasion on which National Front and Tudeh Party members fought together in the streets to bring down an interim government during the Mossadegh period. This seemed to show an acceptance both of violence and of working with the far left. The National Front secretariat tried to suppress this letter, but it was circulated privately and its contents were soon well-known. As a result, the secretariat was politically nullified. However, no new leadership has arisen to take its place, although some inconclusive moves have been made in Europe. But the National Front too, although it never had any kind of coherent ideology, has an important legacy to pass on: the authority and charisma of Mossadegh himself, the most authentic hero of Iran's recent history.

Thirdly, there are various semi-socialist and social-democrat groups, the most important of which are led by Dr Baghai (Toilers Party) and

Khalil Maleki. Maleki was once a member of the Tudeh Party, but split in protest against too great Soviet influence. Since then he has moved rightward, attending Second International meetings in Europe and so on. However, he carries little political weight and is said to spend his time sitting in a room full of high-powered radios, tuning in to the news in various foreign languages. Only the tenuously related Socialist League has some influence, among exiles, mainly in Germany. It is difficult to see how there can be any resurgence of social democracy except through the agency of Hasan Arsanjani, a quite different and much more important politician. Arsanjani was the Minister of Agriculture responsible for launching the land reforms and later resigned in protest against the slow pace at which reform was being carried out and the obstacles put in its way. He is extremely popular among the peasants, who call him *Hasanjuni* (Darling Hasan). He is tolerated by the Shah and allowed to publish books and newspaper articles on socialism, a rare privilege. It is thought that if the political situation required a shift to the left, he would be the Shah's choice to cope with the crisis. He is known to be toying with the idea of founding a social democratic party, which would certainly absorb the remnants of Maleki's following; he supports, in his writings, restrictions on foreign capital penetration, higher tariffs, government encouragement of local industries, nationalisation measures and the expansion of the public sector to provide the dynamic for a 'mixed economy', tax reform, income redistribution, a new impetus to land reform, etc. – classical 'national-bourgeois' objectives.

If Arsanjani became Prime Minister, this would be both a setback and a challenge for the left. It would bring both new opportunities and difficult tactical problems. In my own view, the left should only support Arsanjani if he made a definite attempt to wrest control of the army from the Shah, and the left's campaign should concentrate on demanding a large cut in the military budget, an end of conscription, a reduction of the officer corps, reestablishment of civil control, an acceptable minister of defence and of the interior, and so on. And, secondly, the peasants should be encouraged to voice their maximum demands for the full implementation of land reform. (Although the problem of the peasantry is more complex than this: it is by no means, for instance, a single homogenous class. But there is no space here to discuss this question in detail.) It would be a serious mistake to support Arsanjani before it was clear that he was prepared to contest the Shah's authority. And it might well be a mistake to support him after he had contested it successfully. However, these questions are still very much in the future; at the moment, the regime has no pretensions towards differing from the Shah on anything or initiating any new reform measures. Nor have any of its ministers any degree of popularity.

Fourthly, there is the Muslim left. The leaders of this group, Professor Bazargan and *ayatollah* Taleghani, are both serving ten years imprisonment for criticising the regime. The Muslim left is rather ambiguous in its political attitudes, but it is of great importance because of the prestige of religion and its past role in Iranian history, when it has played a leading part in struggling against imperialism. In many ways the Muslim leaders are very conservative; they are inclined to oppose novelty and Western influence without any discrimination. But, on the other hand, they are intensely nationalist and resent the subordination of Iranian politics to foreign, imperialist interests. The non-Muslim left should certainly remain in close contact with these groups. They too, like the Tudeh Party and the National Front, are an essential part of the historic Iranian democratic and anti-imperialist movement. But they should also be encouraged to elaborate some rather more precise ideas about Islamic socialism than they have done hitherto; otherwise they cannot be expected to play a full part in social change. During the Mossadegh period, it will be remembered, the principal Muslim forces, led by *ayatollah* Kashani, drew back before the crisis reached its peak.

Fifthly, there are the nomadic tribes and the ethnic minorities. The two groups most often spoken of as possible sources of opposition are the Qashqai tribe and the Kurds. The Qashqai supported Mossadegh and rose against the government in 1963. One of their two exiled khans, Khosrow Khan, has been associated with the extreme left of the National Front – the group once centred around Fatemi, Mossadegh's Foreign Minister, since executed – but he is now more or less politically inactive. For a time it seemed possible that the tribes – Persia's traditional kingmakers, to whom the idea of overthrowing a dynasty is quite normal – might play a leading role in overthrowing the Pahlevi dynasty, that they had a natural revolutionary vocation. Whereas in China the peasantry have traditionally shaken the throne by their uprisings, in Iran it has always been the tribes. (Peasants have tended to emigrate: it was among Persian refugees working on the Baku oilfields that Marxism first reached Iran. Today they try despairingly to cross the Shatt al-Arab to Kuwait.) But the 1963 rising showed the weakness of the Qashqai's military position; they are not in a position to resist strafing by Sabre jets, particularly as they are too dependent on their herds. The Kurds are much better placed. But, at the moment, they are still preoccupied with the long and bitter war in Iraq. However, last summer a number of Kurds in Iran were gratuitously arrested and released at intervals, apparently as a warning. It was, in fact, in Iran that the Kurds did once have an autonomous republic – in which Barzani was Minister of War. They could well prove important.

Sixthly, there are student organisations, both within and outside the country. In Iran, student demonstrations are the most frequent expressions of protest against the regime. They have been ruthlessly suppressed; paratroops have invaded the University and student leaders been beaten and arrested. (On one occasion, students barricaded themselves in the CENTO-sponsored nuclear physics department, but this did not stop the soldiers forcing their way in and breaking everything up.) But, by themselves, students do not have the strength to make decisive changes. Their political opinions and allegiances are manifold; in Iran, the level of political education is low. Abroad, this is not the case: Iranian students are among the best organised and most well-informed. They do invaluable work, particularly in the United States, in giving information on the true state of affairs in Iran. It is among students abroad that the most serious effort is being made to renew the National Front and overcome old sectarian quarrels.

Recently, a burst of machine gun fire, supposedly aimed at the Shah, led to the resumption of a reign of terror in Iran. The palace guard responsible was cut down on the spot. Later, a group of young graduates, associated with the student movement in Europe, were arrested and charged with plotting the incident, their loyalty corrupted by reading booklets by Mao Tse-tung. The SAVAK secret police is notorious and, in this instance, they had reasons to be especially zealous. Only a few months previously the Prime Minister was shot dead on his way into the Parliament building. General Pakravan, then in command of the SAVAK, a cultivated man with a taste for verses, was promptly dismissed and replaced by Colonel Nassiri: force was to replace finesse. The new leadership was eager to prove its 'efficiency' and victims were speedily found. The Shah, well satisfied, flew off on a tour of Europe and South America. This distressing incident is typical of the blind fury of the regime: it has served only to stiffen student opposition and resistance and cruelly victimise a few unfortunate scapegoats.

Finally, there is the peasantry. Recently, since the announcement of land reform, there have been a number of riots and disturbances in the countryside, usually taking the form of peasants driving out unpopular bailiffs, seizing land not scheduled for distribution and resisting the gendarmerie sent to restore order. It is clear that these outbreaks cannot be really effective until they are co-ordinated and given a coherent purpose. However, the tasks of organisation are very hard and though a start has been made in studying the complexities of the situation, there is still a long way to go. Reasons for peasant discontent are extremely diverse and the same slogans and methods of agitation often cannot be used even in two adjacent villages. For instance, in villages where land has been distributed, the landless peasants are dissatisfied; in villages which the reform has not reached, the middle peasants. Again, compensation has been paid to landlords in accordance with their previous tax returns. This clever scheme has had unexpected results. Where there has been a 'good' landlord, who in the past treated his peasants well and also paid his tax returns honestly, the peasants are now worse off: they have to fend for themselves, the paternalist landlord is replaced by the moneylender and their instalment dues are high. But where there was a 'bad' landlord, the peasants are satisfied: they are no longer ill-treated and, since tax was evaded, they have very low repayments to make. There are countless quirks and discrepancies of this sort. This means that the peasants are certainly in a very turbulent state, their consciousness has been radically changed and they have become aware of their rights, but, on the other hand, it will be difficult to organise any widespread peasant solidarity in effective action.

In the next few years, new organisational forms and political movements will certainly appear in Iran. At first, these movements will probably have difficulties in rooting themselves in a situation in which opposition has been fragmented and demoralised by previous defeats and repression. But, by drawing on the rich revolutionary legacy of Iran's past – the Gilan republic, the trade unions on the oilfields, the Tudeh Party, the Azerbaijan experience, the Mossadegh period – and analysing and identifying themselves with the new social forces which are arising in the turmoil of Iranian society, struggling to create their own future, they will be able to gather strength and once again challenge the regime. In Iran, there are millions of peasants who are for the first time realising their own potentialities and seeing life in new perspectives; they will continue to demand a full and genuine agrarian reform. And there are hundreds of thousands of urban workers and unemployed who can only escape from insecurity and misery if Iran is given an economic dynamic which the present regime has shown itself incapable of promoting. These suffocated social forces will certainly find a political expression. Iran is a rich country, culturally and in economic resources. Its apparent somnolence hides frustrated energies which, when they are released, will sweep away the Shah and his tyranny.

* * *

Essay published in International Socialist Journal *2:9 (June 1965), under the pseudonym Lucien Rey. See previous bibliographic note to 'Aden'.*

Guilt by Association

Lucien Rey

For many years, the Iranian Secret Police have been angered by vocal opposition to the regime on the part of students in Europe. Recently, a golden opportunity came their way to intimidate dissident students by threatening them with the firing squad when they returned home. In April last year a young conscript opened up with a few bursts of fire in the direction of the Shah, whose light by Divine Providence remained undimmed. After several months of research, interrogation and torture, the Secret Police succeeded in forging the tenuous links by which they could throw responsibility for the assassination attempts, not where it belonged – on the cruel and oppressive regime which so easily and frequently produces desperate illuminés and gunmen – but on a small group of intelligent and politically alert students who had been active in student associations at British universities and technical colleges. They were put on trial on charges of conspiracy to assassinate the Shah and illegal membership of a communist association.

The linkage was contrived as follows: Shamsabadi, the palace guard who had made the attempt on the Shah's life and who had been mown down on the spot, had come from Kashan, a town south of Teheran noted for being the political base of Allayar Saleh, for a long time the only opposition deputy in the Persian Majlis and one of the leaders of the anti-governmental National Front. While in Kashan, Shamsabadi had been fairly active in pro-Saleh political groups and had, apparently, agitated in favour of better work conditions, higher pay and so on. Above all, he had nurtured a deep hatred for the Shah. In Kashan, he had known Ahmad Kamrani, who, shortly before the attempt, had moved to Teheran and, being lonely, had sought out acquaintances from his hometown.

Among them was Shamsabadi. Kamrani did not meet Shamsabadi often, but on one occasion, Shamsabadi confided that he intended to kill the Shah. Kamrani did not respond. Anybody who has lived in Teheran will confirm that there are countless Persians who would confess to a personal wish to kill the Shah. However, Shamsabadi's confidences were enough to get Kamrani the death sentence.

Kamrani, after arriving in Teheran and taking a training course in radio mechanics, had been given a job at the Arj factory by Engineer Mansouri. Mansouri had previously studied in England, at Manchester University, where he had been sent on an oil company scholarship. The link between Kamrani and Mansouri is the crucial connection, joining the group of acquaintances from Kashan with the group of acquaintances from English student circles. Mansouri himself was interested in politics but proved, under interrogation and during the trial, the least stable of the defendants, chopping and changing his story considerably. At one point, soon after his arrest, he was taken to the Shah's palace and, confronted with the Shadow of Allah in person, he grovelled and broke down, later retracted and re-retracted. In any case, Mansouri discovered Kamrani's interest in politics, which they discussed together and, as a result, Mansouri visited Kashan to meet various dissidents whose names Kamrani had apparently suggested. On one occasion, Kamrani mentioned to Mansouri that he knew a palace guard who intended to try and kill the Shah. This conversation led to Mansouri being sentenced to death. Mansouri is said to have judged that there were both advantages and disadvantages in the assassination of the Shah. He asked to be kept informed.

At Manchester, Mansouri had known Parviz Nikkhah, a former president of the Iranian Student Society in Britain. Nikkhah was politically active and astute. It is quite clear that it was Nikkhah whom the Secret Police were determined to have condemned. On his return to Iran from England, Nikkhah had kept in touch with Mansouri and two other students from English universities, Mansour Pourkashani from Manchester and Firouz Shirvanlou from Leeds. Together, they had intended to initiate studies and research into the socio-political situation in Iran, particularly the effects of the land reform, with a view to possible future political action. They had felt handicapped in their political discussions in Europe by lack of knowledge about the real situation in Iran and wished to make good this deficiency.

The problems facing Iranians in opposition are great. Since the repression and massacres of the fifties, which effected a hiatus in opposition continuity while not conferring any special status on the survivors – with the single, ambivalent exception of Mossadegh – it has been practically impossible to envisage building up an opposition organisation. Consequently, most oppositionists have had to put faith in a mechanico-spontaneous solution, whereby the course of the land reform programme, imposed mechanically by the regime, would itself create a spontaneous demand for a different kind of land reform. Revolutionary intellectuals could then insert themselves into this wave of practical criticism of the regime, bringing with them the theoretical critique they had elaborated in isolation. This seems to have been roughly the course which Nikkhah wished to follow. It did not involve any premature dramatic shocks – which would only unsettle the peasants and probably cement their loyalty to the throne – or organisational initiatives. As Nikkhah constantly emphasised during the trial, the situation demanded intellectual work and study, carried out personally.

Nikkhah's defence was the most interesting episode of the trial. Nikkhah was able to point out that he did not know anything of Shamsabadi's existence, let alone his intentions, nor did he know Kamrani. The prosecution's case seemed to be that Nikkhah had exercised an unwholesome political influence over Mansouri, which led him not to attempt to persuade Kamrani to attempt to dissuade Shamsabadi from carrying out the resolve which he had formed of killing the Shah. Evidently, this is not a conspiracy: it is guilt by association – and very tenuous association at that. However, military courts can be expected to ride roughshod over such niceties. The true case against Nikkhah can be seen from some of the prosecutor's outbursts:

> The standpoint of the Iranian nation and its basic ideology has illuminated our future road most clearly. Any deviation from this road, which is the road of the salvation, victory and greatness of Iran, will be impossible. Iranian youth should take heed and realise that if they deviate from the way of truth, this is the terrible fate that shall await them. It is, of course, incumbent on parents and families to give the lead in enlightening and guiding their children and youth, who are the main capital for the future of our country. If they are concerned about the well-being of their children, then they must warn them before they fall into the abyss of dissent and deviation, the consequences of which can be nothing but misery and destruction for them.

In the face of this kind of rhetoric, Nikkhah conducted himself with great calm, constantly insisting that the prosecutor return to the point:

Nikkhah's alleged involvement in an assassination plot. He defended his right to draw up what were known as 'the Kashan theses', a statement of the socio-political situation in Iran, which he intended to send out of the country to a friend in Europe. This, he insisted, was the private result of his personal research, which he had shown only to a few personal friends. And he stood by the only direct political activity attributed to him: the circulation of leaflets supporting a strike of Teheran taxi drivers. He insisted that it was permissible to oppose the incorrect policies of the government. This did not amount to setting up illegal organisations. However, notwithstanding the doubt surrounding all the accusations against him, Nikkhah was sentenced to life imprisonment, later reduced on appeal to ten years.

What lessons can be drawn from the government's response to the assassination attempt and its conduct of the conspiracy trial?

1. Opposition to the regime in Iran must arise within the existing, internal structures of the country. Students returning from abroad are too visible to the Secret Police. They must be able to submerge themselves in the opaque structures of villages, tribes and city slums. Yet this must not mean fragmentation and atomisation. Particular attention must be paid to means of unifying thought and action less easily perceived and traced than leaflets, pamphlets and so on. This means a careful study of the media of popular communication: travellers, pilgrims, performers, etc., and the nodal points of the grapevine: shrines, markets, 'garden parties'.

2. External opposition still has a key role to play. Largely as a result of pressure from outside, lengthy accounts of the trial were published in the Teheran press. For the first time, considered and forceful opposition voices – albeit from the dock – could be heard in Iran. This has had a very important effect in Iran. And among students abroad, while some have been intimidated, many have realised that it is possible to stand firmly against the regime and maintain morale even while in the hands of the Secret Police.

3. A new phase of the struggle has opened. For the first time, the significant and heroic opposition figures have been, not aged anachronistic leaders such as Mossadegh or the heads of the Tudeh Party, but young, flexible and undogmatic university graduates. They have provided a

new focus. In the future it will be much easier for the Iranian oppressed to develop their own strategy of liberation, untrammelled by the shackles of the past.

* * *

Essay published in New Left Review *I/35 (January–February 1966), under the pseudonym Lucien Rey.*

Dossier of the Indonesian Drama

Lucien Rey

For all but six months the world has awaited news of the fall of President Sukarno, his position gravely threatened by the ascendancy of the army and the attempted physical obliteration of the Communist Party. Yet throughout this period Sukarno refused to surrender, deploying his persuasive diplomatic skills to baffle and brake the army commanders and permit once again hopes of the impending re-entry of the Communist Party into civic life. He even proved adroit enough to dismiss the Minister of Defence, Abdul Haris Nasution, unquestionably the most powerful of the generals, at a time when the army was loudly celebrating its grasp over power and the massacre of its political opponents. Certainly the story is not yet finished. The vacuums which have been formed may be filled by still unsuspected forces; new contradictions may crystallise; new relations between firepower and diplomacy emerge. But the time has already come when it is possible to look back on the events which triggered off the political oscillations of the last six months with some degree of detachment, the first shock past.

The mainspring of the forces which briefly seized power in Djakarta on 1 October last year were dissident officers and troops from the Seventh (Diponegoro) Division of the Indonesian Army, stationed normally in Central Java. A group of junior officers from this Central Java Division had apparently become disenchanted with the conduct of the top army command. They accused them of corruption, falling into decadent and luxurious habits and, most seriously, dragging their heels over confrontation with Malaysia. They also suspected undue American influence. Accordingly they determined to rid the nation and the revolution of these parasites. The junior officers concerned were not necessarily left wing; some of them appear to have definite anti-communist records. They were however highly conscious of what they considered the proper duty of the army and its role in the Indonesian Revolution. They bore some resemblance to the Young Officers in Japan or, say, their counterparts in Turkey today.

However, it is one thing to sit and plot in Semarang or Jogjakarta, another to be in a real position to act. But opportunity presented itself. One of the junior officers, Lt Col Untung, was transferred to the Presidential Guard (Tjakrabirawa Regiment) in Djakarta, as a Battalion Commander. More than that. He was put in charge of arranging a historical pageant for the march-past on Army Day. This was crucial; it enabled the plotters to move battalions sympathetic to their aims into the capital for the parade. They now had troops available on the spot, not hours away in Central Java. The plotters set about perfecting their plan. In particular, they won to their side the Commander of the Guard at the Halim Airbase, just outside Djakarta, Flight Major Sujono. Control over the Halim Base would give them both a secure operations centre and a means of keeping contact with Central Java. They also involved a Brigade Commander from the local Fifth Division of the Army, Colonel Latief. Finally they made preparations to use armed auxiliaries being trained at the Halim Airbase as part of the projected Fifth Armed Force. These auxiliaries were mostly volunteers from the Communist People's Youth; the Fifth Armed Force, inaugurated about three months previously, was designed in effect to give the PKI (Indonesian Communist Party) a military presence. In the event, this unauthorised involvement in the affair was to cost the PKI dear.

The plot was put into action in the early hours of 1 October. The initial stage had three parts. First, action was undertaken to seize seven top army generals at their villas and bring them to Halim Base. These generals were named as members of the clandestine Generals' Council, which had been prepared to take over the state in the event of Sukarno's death or, indeed, should any other favourable opportunity suggest itself. There are strong signs of the existence of at least a close clique; the exclusion of the KOSTRAD Army HQ Commander, General Suharto, from the list of seven was due to the fact that such a clique did exist, but he was not a member of it. His omission was to prove disastrous to the plotters; it is hard otherwise to imagine why he was overlooked. Those to be arrested included almost every other top staff officer, including the chiefs of intelligence, finance and political activity. Second, key installations in the city centre were to be seized: the Presidential Palace, the radio station, the telephone exchange, crucial road intersections. (For some reason, the KOSTRAD Supreme Army HQ was neglected.) Thirdly, various other personalities, including Sukarno himself, were to be brought to Halim.

The Coup Moves into Action

At about 3:15 a.m. seven armed groups, ranging in size from roughly twenty to a hundred men, left the Halim Base for Djakarta. They proceeded to the villas of the seven generals and, in all cases, succeeded swiftly in overpowering the guards. After that, however, they met with uneven success. Three of the generals were killed during the raids. General Yani, Minister-Commander of the Army, lost his temper when refused permission to bathe and change out of his pyjamas. He stormed back into his bedroom and was shot down through the glass door. General Harjono heard the intruders coming, switched off all the lights and tried to overpower the first man to come through the bedroom door. He was shot. General Pandjaitan lived in a two-storey house, unlike the others. After a great deal of shouting up and down the stairs he eventually agreed to come down when his family was threatened. Besides, his Sten gun had jammed. However, he put up more resistance in the front yard and was shot.

Three more generals were successfully bundled into trucks and taken off to Halim. General Suprapto had recently had some teeth out; he was unable to sleep and, hearing dogs bark, went down to the front door, where he was seized. General Parman thought the next-door house was being burgled and went down into the garden to investigate. He was seized in the front yard. General Sutojo was arrested in his bedroom and blindfolded before being taken to the waiting truck. These arrests were completed shortly after four o'clock. But by far the most important general, Abdul Haris Nasution, the Minister of Defence, managed to escape. The intruders successfully disarmed his lookouts and quite extensive guard, as well as the guard of his neighbour, Dr Leimena, the Second Deputy Prime Minister. They then entered the house. General Nasution's wife, hearing the noise of doors opening and shutting, went to see what was happening. When she opened the bedroom door she saw a soldier standing there with a gun. She slammed the door shut and told Nasution. He insisted on looking for himself and nearly got shot. The soldiers outside started to try and break the door down. While they were doing this, Nasution's sister appeared with his daughter and asked to go into the room herself.

When the door was opened, the soldiers opened fire again; the young daughter was fatally wounded. Meanwhile Nasution had made his getaway and managed to scramble over the garden wall into the next-door Iraqi embassy. He was shot at as he got over the wall and fell down the other side, breaking his ankle. He then lay still, in the Iraqi embassy garden, for about three hours until the coast seemed well clear. The intruders had lost Nasution. However, they did seize his adjutant, Lt Tendean, who looked vaguely like Nasution in the dark. He was disarmed, thrust into a truck and driven off to Halim.

The second part of the plan was achieved without incident. By the time the three still living generals and Lt Tendean arrived back at Halim, the crucial installations of Djakarta were in the hands of the plotters. The third part also went well. Sukarno was at the house of his Japanese wife, Dewi. Untung went there, told the President that the top generals had launched a coup and asked him to come to Halim for the sake of his safety; the Air Force and the presidential guard had remained loyal. Sukarno agreed. The second personality asked to come to Halim was Omar Dhani, Commander of the Air Force. For some time Dhani had been at loggerheads with the Army; he himself was disliked by the top army staff and regarded as a creature of Sukarno's; tension had got worse since the Air Force was supposed to be in charge of the North Kalimantan action, from which the Army was suspected of withholding its full cooperation, and also since the Air Force had agreed to train and officer the Fifth Armed Force, seen as a direct PKI threat by the army staff. Dhani eventually agreed to go to Halim. As well as Dhani, Brig. Gen. Sabur, Commander of the Presidential Guard, was also fetched. The fourth personality seized was D. N. Aidit, chairman of PKI. Some mystery surrounds Aidit's presence. It seems that the plotters must have calculated as follows: since our military support is, in fact, relatively thin – two paratroop battalions, elements from the Guard, elements from the Air Force, some armed auxiliaries – we need Sukarno's backing. For this reason, he must be brought to Halim. Once he has agreed to back us, presumably over the radio, we shall need street demonstrations in support. We therefore need Aidit too. Moreover, it will also be as well to have him safely at Halim in order to paralyse the PKI until Sukarno has openly backed us. Otherwise we might be pre-empted by unplanned-for PKI action. This explanation – obviously only a reconstruction – would explain the point of arresting Aidit, bringing him to Halim and then, as far as can be seen, holding him incommunicado, while at the same time being quite friendly towards him.

Clearly, the plot was something of a gamble on the hope that Sukarno would back the plotters before the power vacuum in the army was filled in some other way. This was not a futile gamble. Sukarno came very close to playing along, close enough indeed to singe his wings. Later, Flight Major Sujono suggested that he was indeed implicated. However, two things went wrong. First, General Suharto swiftly seized command of the Army and acted with considerable competence. Second, Sukarno, casting around for a suitable new army commander – obviously Untung himself was out of the question – picked on General Pranoto instead of General Suharto.

The Alarm is Given

Suharto was wakened by neighbours at about half past five, told shots had been heard and a number of generals and other personalities appeared to have been abducted. Soon afterwards, a colleague came and confirmed the news. Suharto got in his jeep and drove himself to the KOSTRAD headquarters, arriving about 6.30. Having confirmed that Yani had been abducted he assumed command of the army and set about contacting fellow officers and representatives of the other armed services. General Umar, the Djakarta Territorial Commander, had already been alerted by Nasution's family and had done some rather listless reconnoitring. He was able to tell Suharto that the Presidential Palace was under the control of troops commanded by Brig. Gen. Supardjo, Commander of the 4th Combat Command from Mandau, West Kalimantan. (Supardjo had flown into Djakarta on receiving a go-ahead telegram saying that his daughter was gravely ill. However, he had not reported his arrival in Djakarta to anybody. It was now clear to Suharto that junior officers were acting illegally.) Umar put himself under Suharto's command. Suharto also got in touch with the first deputy to the navy commander and the Djakarta police commander. They agreed to keep their troops confined. Suharto next set about identifying the whereabouts of all the various army battalions supposed to be in Djakarta. Most of them, he ascertained, had turned up as expected at Senajan for a rehearsal for the army parade. However, parachute battalions 454 and 530, from Central and East Java respectively, were missing. These also, judging from insignia, seemed to be the battalions holding Merdeka Square, the Presidential Palace, etc. Suharto also ascertained that the Air Force was being evasive when he contacted them. He did not yet know however the whereabouts of the President, the status of the *coup de force* or the role being played by the Halim Base.

At 7:00 a.m. the first Untung broadcast came on the air. (They had to wait till 7:00 because it was only then that national broadcasting began.) In this broadcast, the 30th of September Movement, under the command of Lt Col Untung, was credited with saving the President from a Generals' Council coup. In particular, generals were accused of the fact that they 'lived in luxury, led a gay life, insulted our women and wasted government funds', as well as plotting to overthrow Sukarno. However, the broadcast laid very little stress on Sukarno himself. Nobody hearing it would imagine that Sukarno had thrown himself behind the 30th September Movement. Evidently he was playing for time. His first priority was to re-establish contact with the outside world; information at Halim, all sifted through Untung, was inadequate for making vital decisions.

Accordingly, a number of messengers were sent out, summoning advisers to confer with the President. Most of the top civil officials of the state were out of Djakarta at the time. Subandrio, accompanied by Njoto, one of the top PKI leaders, was in Sumatra. Charul Saleh and Ali Sastroamidjojo, leaders of the Murba and Nationalist Parties, were in Peking; Lukman and Sakirman, the other top PKI leaders, were in Semarang, Central Java; Abdulghani, the second leading Nationalist, was also out of town. But Sukarno did manage to get in touch with Leimena, the Second Deputy Prime Minister, about mid-morning. He also managed to accumulate at Halim the Minister-Commander of the Navy, since dismissed by Sukarno, and the Minister-Commander of the Police.

It now began to look as if things might go the way the 30th September Movement hoped. At 9:30 a.m. Omar Dhani signed a statement throwing the Air Force behind the coup. Although this was not then released, it was a strong card. Sukarno was beginning to feel his way towards a diplomatic outcome. At 1:15 p.m. a broadcast went out announcing that the President was in control of the situation, read by Sabur's Deputy Commander of the Presidential Guard and signed by Sabur himself. About the same time, the President issued an order appointing General Pranoto Acting Commander of the Army, under the President and on a day-to-day basis. Pranoto was a former commander of the Central Java Division, whose term of command had been cut short by Nasution. He was now third assistant to Yani, with responsibility for personnel. All this pointed to a situation in which Sukarno would soon re-emerge, the 30th September

Movement would be – presumably – rewarded and the leftward turn in Nasakom would be consolidated. However, Sukarno had not personally committed himself to anything.

Suharto at the KOSTRAD HQ

At about this time, possibly a little earlier, messengers from Sukarno had reached Suharto at the KOSTRAD HQ. It seems likely they were forwarded there by Umar or were looking for Pranoto. Suharto was now able to sum up the situation. During the morning he had managed to subvert most of the 530th (East Java) Battalion by sending former officers (mostly from the West Irian campaign) to talk to them. He felt confident he could do the same with the 454th Battalion, given time. He now knew that the Halim Base was the centre of the 30th September Movement operations. This meant he would have to tread carefully as far as the Air Force was concerned; there was a possibility Djakarta would be bombed. But, on the whole, militarily speaking, he was in a position to be confident. Also he now probably knew that Nasution was alive, though hurt and in hiding. He must have suspected that the other six generals were all dead. At any rate, he refused to let Umar and Pranoto go to Halim, remarking later that 'we had already lost quite enough of our generals'.

Conversely, when the messengers returned, it became clear that the 30th September Movement, and – in other terms – Sukarno himself, were in a position to feel depressed and pessimistic. Sukarno's interest was to disinvolve himself from Untung as swiftly as possible; perhaps he had already gone too far. Untung himself was clearly in desperate straits. At 2.00 he had issued another proclamation over the radio, announcing the formation of a Revolutionary Council, made up in an apparently random fashion of the names of top armed forces commanders, various political personalities, youth leaders, journalists, a university rector and so on, all mixed up promiscuously with some of the actual plotters. This proclamation, strangely, did not mention Sukarno at all. Perhaps this was because Sukarno had instructed them not to, as the price for possible future support; perhaps because they realised he was lost to them and tried instead to make a bid for as many other elements as they might possibly rally. Then at 3.30 they released Dhani's morning statement of Air Force support: this appears something of a last throw. It was clear the crunch was coming. At 4.00 Sukarno sent for his children and had them flown to safety in Bandung. By 6:00 much of the 454th Parachute

Battalion had followed the 530th into Suharto's hands. The rest were withdrawing towards the Halim Base; some Communist Youth auxiliaries, wandering blindly into Merdeka Square, were rapidly mopped up. Also at about six, after an ultimatum, Suharto won control of the radio and the 30th September Movement went off the air. By 7.00 Suharto had all key installations in Djakarta under his control. About this time further messengers left Sukarno; their aim, in effect, was to find out what Suharto's conditions were. He indicated that Sukarno must disassociate himself from Untung; in fact, he must leave the Halim Base. Accordingly Sukarno left Halim for his out-of-town palace at Bogor. Suharto asked a colleague to check Sukarno's arrival. At 9.00 Suharto himself went on the air announcing his full control.

Flames in Central Java

At the Halim Base, things must have looked gloomy indeed. However, there was still some hope for the 30th September Movement. Following the 7:00 a.m. broadcast, a number of their colleagues, including Col Suherman, head of army intelligence in the division and probably the brains of the coup, had seized control in the principal cities of Central Java. By evening Semarang, Jogjakarta and Surakarta were all in the hands of junior officers associated with the 30th September Movement. (There had been one blunder: the Division Commander, General Surjo Sumpeno, had managed to get away and had reached the military academy at Magelang.) The stage was now set for the second, brief, eventually tragic act. At about midnight the President's Jetstar flew into Halim Base. It contained the Air Force second in command, who had been with Subandrio in North Sumatra. (Subandrio himself had sagely decided to stay put.) More consultations took place. Soon afterwards two planes left Halim for Central Java, both Hercules transports. One, which landed at Semarang about 1.30, contained Untung. The other, which arrived at Jogjakarta at about 2.00, contained Omar Dhani and D. N. Aidit. By dawn the Halim Base had fallen to Suharto.

By this time, Untung and his associates were effectively finished. There was really no hope that Central Java could be held once Djakarta had fallen. Untung was a good soldier – the first officer parachuted into West Irian – but himself no politician. Faced with general falling morale, he went into hiding. Some days later he was arrested. Dhani, on the other hand, could still save himself. The essential thing was to brief the Air

Force, bring back dissidents into line and ensure no provocation was given the army. Consequently, he flew from field to field, having talks, finally returning to the Semplak Airfield, near Bogor, at 4.00 that afternoon, immediately proceeding to the Palace to be with Sukarno.

The PKI is Compromised

Aidit was in by far the most difficult position. How far was the PKI compromised? How far could it pull itself clear? In fact, as we now know, all was already lost. The PKI had already been fatally compromised in the following ways:

1. The involvement of People's Youth auxiliaries in the abduction of the generals, the occupation of installations in Djakarta and – most serious of all – the killing of the three generals who had survived arrest. These three generals had been shot at a place called Crocodile Hole, within the perimeter of the Halim Base, a few hours after their arrival there. One of them and also Lt Tendean, mistaken for Nasution, were beaten up with rifle butts. After execution they were thrown into a well to join the corpses of the other three generals previously killed. Involved in all this were auxiliaries undergoing training at Halim Base, from both the Communist People's Youth and the Communist *Gerwani* women's movement. The executions were given a kind of ritual character by singing and mass firing at the dead bodies. There is no hard evidence however of disfigurements or other atrocities. The auxiliaries involved definitely appear not to have been acting under any kind of PKI instructions, but merely to have been obeying, in a blind way, the Air Force officers who were their military superiors at the Halim Base.

2. The involvement of People's Youth elements in the rising in Jogjakarta, where they demonstrated against the Generals' Council, covered the town with pro-30th September Movement placards, seized the radio and so on. Again, they do not seem to have been acting under any kind of PKI instructions. More serious, in some ways, was the support given the coup by the Communist mayor of Surakarta, Utomo Ramelan. This was a stupid political mistake. The PKI paid the price for backing a 'popular' man for mayor instead of a more politically trustworthy cadre.

3. An editorial, hedging violently but nonetheless indicating support for the coup, appeared in the main PKI newspaper, *Harian Rakjat*, on 2 October. It had gone to press the previous afternoon. More explicit was a cartoon published at the bottom of the front page, mentioning the 30th September Movement and associating the Generals' Council with the CIA. It is difficult to explain these blunders. It is possible of course that the paper was set up, awaiting the go-ahead from some responsible PKI leader, found on the presses in that state by the Army when they seized the works and finally printed deliberately by the Army in order to discredit the PKI. On the other hand, it was not a suitable editorial whichever way you look at it: there is no point in hedging for 90 percent of an editorial if you let slip a *parti pris* in the other 10 percent. It is all the more strange since another PKI newspaper, *Kebudajaan Baru*, managed to confine itself to a short item in a box, reading:

THE SITUATION IN THE CAPITAL

> The situation in the capital today remains calm. Life continues as usual. The streets remain crowded with traffic, offices continue work as usual. So also street vendors, shops, schools and so on.

4. Later, Njono, head of the PKI in Djakarta, was to make – and withdraw – a confession to the Army, admitting PKI complicity in the coup. However, this confession does not bear examination. It is full of obvious flaws. People were said to have been at meetings they could not have attended; others who would have attended are omitted. No concrete actions are attributed to the PKI; all depends on the coup being a master plan in Aidit's head. Of course, since the PKI did nothing whatever on the fateful day, it is difficult to invent a role for them. Stress is laid on the hapless volunteers at the Halim Base who, as we have seen, did nothing but act blindly and confusedly throughout: certainly they did not behave like people playing a crucial role in a well-laid plot, backed by a two-million-strong party. In fact they were pathetic dupes.

5. Aidit's own presence at the Halim Base was compromising to some extent. However, the Army has not used it since: perhaps because they have not yet cooked up a satisfactory story; perhaps because it would be embarrassing as far as Sukarno was concerned and anyway would have to be squared with his version. Subsequently Aidit may have made a mistake in heading for Jogjakarta. He might have done better to stick

like a burr to Sukarno. As it was, by the time Lukman and Njoto arrived at Bogor, the anti-PKI campaign was well under way. Aidit never made it back at all. However, Aidit immediately on his arrival set about trying to ensure that PKI members stayed at home, did nothing to provoke the Army and confined themselves to following the political path trodden by the President at Bogor. He got immediately in touch with Sujono Atmo, the young pro-PKI acting governor of Central Java, with Utomo Ramelan, PKI mayor of Surakarta and with top PKI leaders Lukman and Sakirman, who were staying in Semarang. After talks, they got into Lukman's ministerial car and drove round Central Java making efforts to put down any PKI demonstrations which had flared up. Aidit also tried to requisition a plane to fly to Bali, another PKI stronghold, but by now opportunist officials were getting rather chary of him and he was unsuccessful. However, in his major endeavour he was indeed successful: there were no further PKI manifestations in Central Java and the renewal of control by General Surjo Sumpeno was not resisted. On the 5th Lukman set off by car for Bogor. Aidit tried to get a plane, failed and set out by road. He was almost certainly arrested on his way back and shot.

Undoubtedly it is unnerving that a party of the strength of the PKI can be so destroyed as a result of what seems a malign twist of fate. The main problem of course was that once Sukarno's unquestionable authority had been blemished, there was no armed shield which the PKI could rely on. Evidently the party was aware of its potential weakness; this lay behind plans to create the Fifth Armed Force. (Plans, of course, which backfired, as we have seen, in a quite disastrous way.) Nevertheless, what is really astonishing is the lack of any contingency planning.

What happened when Aidit was taken from his home by soldiers of the presidential guard in the middle of the night? Nothing. There seems to have been no contingency plan whereby, for instance, Njono – head of the PKI in Djakarta – was informed and in a position to put prearranged instructions to effect while awaiting renewal of contact with Aidit or else Lukman or Njoto. The party press was left completely uncertain of what to do, no effort was made to find out what the People's Youth were doing and re-establish a proper command chain, it seems that no contacts were made with the SOBSI trade union federation in case street demonstrations might be needed. The PNI (Nationalist Party), in contrast, held two top-level meetings on 1 October, one at 10:30 a.m., the other at 6:00 p.m., presided over by Surachman. Again, Lukman and Sakirman – equally in the dark – heard the Untung broadcast while having breakfast in Semarang. They do not seem to have left the house all day. It is difficult to think that they had any idea of what they might do. They seem to have just waited for Aidit and then, later, concentrated on getting to Bogor for the 6 October cabinet meeting. This was particularly unfortunate since the PKI knew that it might any day have to act in an emergency: if for instance Sukarno died or if Nasution launched a coup. In its ignorance and bafflement, it seems to have been mesmerised and paralysed.

The Anti-PKI Massacres Begin

The outcome proved to be disastrous. The Army swiftly inaugurated an anti-PKI campaign in Djakarta; Nasution was the main man behind this. The crucial events were the discovery of the six generals' bodies and the death of Nasution's daughter. These were used to start an immense propaganda campaign against the PKI, magnifying every small detail of its association with the 30th September Movement and pinning all kinds of horror stories on it. Armed mobs were encouraged to take advantage of this anti-PKI climate. Pogroms began. In Central Java the anti-PKI campaign took longer to get off the ground. Surjo Sumpeno had re-established control of Central Java by 6 October, using the same methods as Suharto had: splitting the opposition by cajolery and ultimatums. Both he and Sujono Atmo issued appeals for calm and a return to normality. It seemed that the counter-coup had been completed without bloodshed. However, almost a fortnight later, on 19 October, an army victory parade in Semarang, and the coincidental discovery of two army officers' bodies, were the signal for a wave of repression to start in Central Java. The tide of massacre eventually spread throughout Indonesia. Reliable estimates suggest that as many as half a million PKI members and sympathisers have been slaughtered. The Army stands triumphant above this swamp of blood and death.

Practically the whole of the top leadership of the PKI has been killed. The only Politburo member to escape was Adjitorop, who was in Peking for health reasons. Aidit was shot probably in the last week of October; his execution was never announced, presumably in order to prevent him from becoming a martyr figure. Lukman and Njoto managed to hold on longer, having taken refuge in the Presidential Palace at Bogor. They were removed on 30 November and shot about two days later, in the square of the naval academy. But the slaughter did not stop with the Central Committee; it went all the way down. In Bali reliable estimates put the figure killed at 150,000. Whole Balinese villages have been depopulated.

After Bali, the scene of the worst massacres has been in East Java and North Sumatra. The technique has been for the army to enter a village, force the headman to give names of all PKI members and sympathisers, round them up and then let the extremist right-wing Muslim and Christian mobs know when they are to be released. As they come out of jail they are chopped up with bill-hooks and machetes. The number killed far exceeds the casualties in the Vietnam War. The scale has been even greater than the French massacres in Madagascar or the Baath *ratissage* in Baghdad. These massacres have struck down totally unarmed people: men, women and children. They have not followed blindly in the aftermath of riots. They have been properly planned, organised and executed.

It is difficult to see what the future of Indonesia will be. Sukarno was left, despite all, still in a position to manoeuvre, though his former great charisma and freedom of action was impaired. And the PKI, of course, has experienced decimation before, at the time of the Madiun Affair in 1948. Meanwhile, the country has been plunged into economic chaos, bloodshed and resentment. From such a cauldron, anything might bubble up. Perhaps the one thing that we can now be certain will not occur is the orderly and peaceful progression to power of the PKI as Sukarno's heir.

In a country such as Indonesia, where power is centralised in the capital, and where the popular forces, if they are not to confront the Army openly in civil war, must rely on intricate diplomatic manoeuvres, then it is always possible for a vital pivot to be suddenly and unexpectedly upset and the whole precarious system to be shattered. Then nothing remains except crude armed confrontation: in the case of Central Java at the outbreak of the repression, army tanks against the bamboo stakes of hopeless PKI villagers.

It is easy to conjecture what might have happened if Aidit had not been almost alone in the capital and then held incommunicado or perhaps if Sukarno had named Suharto and not Pranoto as Acting Commander of the Army. But all we can really say is that the PKI was wrecked by the sudden brusque emergence of forces into the political arena which had been brewing silently in the officers' clubs of Semarang and Jogjakarta, forces it was unable to cope with because unable to predict. It is hopeless to suppose that the revolutionary forces will always have perfect vision. As consolation, we can only imagine what will be recreated and recrystallised from the ruins of the PKI in the opacity which remains.

* * *

Essay published in New Left Review *I/36 (March–April 1966), under the pseudonym Lucien Rey. In this text, Wollen reworked Benedict Anderson and Ruth McVey's document 'A Preliminary Analysis of the October 1, 1965, Coup in Indonesia', known as the 'Cornell Paper', into a 'highly abridged and more accessible version'. See Douglas Kammen, 'World Turned Upside Down: Benedict Anderson, Ruth T. McVey, and the "Cornell Paper"',* Indonesia *104 (October 2017), pp. 5, 8. In a private email dated 15 July 2020,* New Left Review *editor Perry Anderson stated that Wollen undertook 'an original redaction of the Cornell document entirely in his own words'. According to Robin Blackburn, the Dossier was attributed to Lucien Rey because 'the real authors still hoped to visit Indonesia'. See also Benedict R. O'G. Anderson and Ruth T. McVey, with the assistance of Frederick P. Bunnell, 'A Preliminary Analysis of the October 1, 1965, Coup in Indonesia' (Cornell Modern Indonesia Project, Interim Reports Pub. 52, 1971, and Equinox Publishing, 2009).*

Was Christ a Collaborator?

Jesus of Nazareth lived in a time of political turmoil. Between the lines of the Gospels, which are our main source of information about him, this comes through loud and clear. But it is never brought to the surface. The last thing that the writers of the Gospels wanted was to drag in politics. They wanted to extract Jesus from his real historical situation and put across a universal message, which could apply to anybody. Above all, they did not want to tie Jesus in with the fate of the Jewish people who, at the time of writing, had just been crushed by the Roman legions after a bitter resistance war.

However, the actual situation in which Jesus lived is plain enough. In 63 BC, Palestine was conquered by a Roman army, led by Pompey, and made part of the Roman province of Syria. Pompey, accompanied by his military staff, strode into the Holy of Holies of the Jerusalem Temple, which had been defended by its priests after the reigning king had opened the gates of the city to the invaders. From that moment on, until the final showdown 133 years later in 70 AD, the history of Palestine is mainly a history of Jewish resistance to Roman rule. It was a hopeless resistance which took place during a time which fundamentally was one of Roman expansion. Jesus of Nazareth lived right in the middle of this period and, despite his well-known attachment to the otherworldly, he could hardly have been blind to what was going on.

Palestine's Strategic Role

The situation was not an easy one for the Romans. Palestine – Judea, as the Jewish part of it was called – was one of a chain of small states, stretching from Armenia down to Egypt, which formed a buffer zone between Rome and the Parthian Empire to the east, based in Persia. Palestine was a crucial link in the chain because it bordered Egypt, granary of Rome. Parthia was the second major power of the region, and it was never conquered by Rome. Indeed, it several times inflicted defeats on the Roman legions, routed them and captured the eagles which were their battle standards. So Palestine was a sensitive area. A Jewish uprising could count on Parthian support. Indeed, in 40 BC, only about twenty years after Pompey's invasion and not very long before the birth of Jesus, this was exactly what happened. The Roman puppet regime was overthrown and a new king installed, with Parthian support. The Parthians, moreover, unlike the Romans, took care not to desecrate the Temple. Their position was more or less like that of the Indians in Bangladesh, a foreign power aiding a national movement for its own purposes.

The Romans reacted quickly. They ditched the old lot of puppets and brought in a new candidate, Herod, who was about thirty at the time. Herod's father had been the strongman, main pro-Roman in the old regime. Herod himself had been military governor of Galilee, the northern part of Palestine. When the Parthians came in, he managed to escape to Egypt and eventually got to Rome. There he was crowned king of Judea. With full Roman backing he returned, taking Jerusalem with the help of the legions in 37 BC, and promptly executed the rebel leaders. The anti-Roman king, Antigonus, was crucified, the first of tens of thousands who were to be executed in this way by the Romans or their puppets. Once on the throne, Herod stuck to it until his death in 4 BC.

It is not certain exactly when Jesus was born. All we can say is that it was during the reign of the Emperor Augustus, who died in 14 AD, and that during Jesus's adult life Augustus's successor Tiberius was on the throne. Jesus may have seen the end of Herod's reign, as an infant. Certainly the events which followed Herod's death must have impressed him, either as childhood memories or as stories which were told him as he grew up.

Herod's Death

Herod's death produced a crisis. Herod had been servile to the Romans and cruel and extortionate to his own people. He was loathed and hated. Naturally, when he died there was general rejoicing, and the national movement came to the surface again. There had already been rumblings shortly before the end of his reign. A student demonstration, more or less led by two Pharisees, Judas and Matthias, had culminated in the tearing down of the Roman eagle which Herod had displayed in the Temple to please his masters. The ringleaders were burned alive. When Herod finally died, there was an uprising in Jerusalem. The procurator, Sabinus, the top Roman official in Palestine, immediately moved troops into the capital to maintain law and order and also to seize Herod's treasury. During the festival of Pentecost, fighting broke out between pilgrims to the Temple and these Roman troops. Sabinus was pinned down in the garrison.

At the same time, there was another armed uprising in Galilee, led by a partisan leader called Judas, known as the Galilean, whose father had been executed by Herod for insurgency. This was a large-scale uprising in which the partisans took Herod's palace in Sepphoris and seized the arms which were stored there. Sepphoris was only a few miles from Nazareth, where Jesus spent his childhood. About an hour's walk away, in fact. The Romans had to send two legions, that is, twelve thousand troops, down from Syria to suppress these revolts and rescue Sabinus. During the fighting the Temple was badly damaged and Sepphoris was completely destroyed. When the Romans had restored order they crucified two thousand rebels.

Twice the Size of Northern Ireland

Palestine is a comparatively small country. Herod's kingdom of Judea was not much bigger than Wales, about twice the size of Northern Ireland. It did not extend so far south as Israel does today but it covered a fringe of what is now Syria and Jordan. The population, about five million probably, was not homogeneously Jewish. The Jews were concentrated in the Jerusalem area – Judea proper – and in Galilee, to the north, where they were fairly recent settlers. In between was Samaria, where the Samaritans lived. The Samaritans had their own religion which was a variant of Judaism. For example, they did not recognise the Temple, but had their own holy place on a mountain in Samaria. In the towns there were a number of Greeks and Hellenised Syrians or Phoenicians, who had first come in the wake of Alexander's armies and now identified with the Romans. Herod had encouraged further immigration of Greeks and had built a number of new towns for them, including a new port and capital, Caesarea, which nationalistic and pious Jews would not live in because it was dominated by irreligious monuments, such as a theatre and a racetrack.

The divided country, split by national and religious differences, had some of the features of Northern Ireland or Cyprus. The Jewish national movement took a religious form; it was religion which bound the nation together. The leaders of the Zealots, as the guerrilla partisans were known, were often ultra-religious and religion was one of the two main issues around which opposition to the Roman occupation crystallised. There were riots over the pagan eagle desecrating the Temple, as described above: later, after the Romans had adopted direct rule, there were more riots under Pontius Pilate over the same issue. There were uprisings in the late thirties, only a few years after the crucifixion of Jesus, when Emperor Caligula wanted to put up a statue of himself in the Temple. Ten years after that there was a big riot when a Roman soldier on guard on a roof overlooking the Temple made an obscene gesture to the pilgrims.

Imperialist Taxes

The second issue was economic: the Roman tax appropriations. Rome did not tax its own citizens but relied on wringing what it could out of subject peoples. The system was laid down officially and then the actual tax collection was left to private enterprise, on something like a tender basis. Roman troops backed up the tax-collectors. Naturally tax-collectors were regarded as collaborators with the Romans and there were frequent attempts to sabotage the system and boycott it. Quirinius's census in 6 AD was designed by the Romans to help implement tax collection and it provoked widespread resistance and armed struggle, which was not subdued for some time, right during the childhood of Jesus. Once again Galilee was a focus of the revolt, but this time there was heavy fighting in the south as well, led by a shepherd called Athronges. Thousands were killed by the Romans during this period.

Direct Rule Starts

The census was particularly resented because it marked the beginning of direct rule by Rome. The puppet regime was abandoned by the Romans shortly after Herod's death. His son was exiled after the procurator was given full powers, in Judea at least. In Galilee and in South-East Syria, the Golan Heights area, two other sons of Herod were allowed to stay on as autonomous rulers. Generally speaking, the Romans changed procurators quite rapidly. Pontius Pilate, who lasted nine years, from 27 to 36 AD, was an exception to the rule. Pilate was intensely hated and this loathing shows through all the Jewish source documents which remain. He was both harsh and corrupt. When he took money from the Temple treasury there were massive demonstrations against him. He suppressed them by putting troops into the crowd in plain clothes, and with concealed weapons, who suddenly leapt into action at a given signal. In the Gospels, there are references to the killing of Galileans, always troublemakers, and to riots in Jerusalem at the time of Jesus's death, while the word used to describe the two 'thieves' crucified with Jesus is the same generally used to describe guerrillas, rather like 'bandits'.

The Pharisees and Armed Struggle

However, the real struggle built up from the forties onwards, culminating in a full-scale national uprising in the sixties. At the same time, the national struggle began to crosscut with an increasingly overt class struggle. The traditional ruling class in Judea consisted of an interlocking bloc formed by large landowners and the hereditary high-priestly families who controlled the Temple. The Sadducees were members of this bloc. They were challenged as religious authorities by the Pharisees, who were rigorists, organised on a strict entry basis into cells, led by scribes, graduates in theology, but also including elements from artisan and even labouring backgrounds. It was the Pharisees who welded the Jewish nation together into a religious-political force. Many of the Zealot leaders were Pharisees who had decided to move into a phase of armed struggle.

The mass of Zealots, however, came from the people, from small towns and villages. This period was one of an overall movement in the countryside towards large estates, throwing small peasants, many of them in debt, off the land. There were a large number of slaves in Judea at the time and these made up part of the guerrilla armies. There was also an increasing number of hired hands, who are often mentioned in parables in the Gospel. The surplus of labour meant that they were usually employed on a casual basis. There was naturally a drift from the country into the towns and an increasing amount of employment in small craft industries.

Jesus and the apostles came from artisan families; Jesus was a carpenter, working with lumber imported from Lebanon, and many of the apostles were fishermen, owning their own boats. We know from other sources that the fishing industry was thriving in Galilee at the time and there was investment in pickles for use in exporting fish. Jesus did not come from the masses, who were either living off charity – there was an efficient dole system in operation – or else were day labourers or slaves. Neither, of course, did he come from the priestly caste or from a rich business or land-owning background. He was a petit-bourgeois.

Kidnapping and Assassination

The ruling class throughout this period became increasingly compromised with the Romans. It was the Roman procurator who appointed the high priest, usually a matter for bribery. In return, the high priest acted as a Quisling, maintaining law and order in Jerusalem – a sensitive area for Romans – with his own Temple police, and handing over troublemakers for trial. Yet at the same time, the Temple and its high priest were the main symbols of national consciousness. In the end, class feelings came out into the open. Zealots kidnapped a Temple official and, like Tupamaros, held him ransom for the release of political prisoners. Assassination of collaborators was stepped up, until a high priest was struck down too.

When, in the sixties, resistance gathered momentum, there were particularly troubled economic circumstances. For years extensions to the Temple had provided employment in Jerusalem and these suddenly halted. After riots, the programme was set in motion again in the form of paving the city streets. At the same time, there were complaints that the high priestly families, who had equipped themselves with armed gangs, were marauding in the countryside extorting 'tithes' on which they had no claim. Matters came to a head in 66 AD when, after a huge tax boycott, the Roman procurator looted the Temple treasury to make up the deficit. There was an immediate Zealot uprising. The Romans' main force withdrew and the remnant left behind were massacred. One of the first acts of the Zealot regime was to destroy the record of debts – freeing the masses from the grip of moneylenders and landlords. A new high priest was elected by lot, which fell to a peasant, an impoverished member of the priestly caste, an act regarded as outrageous by ruling-class opinion.

The Left is Isolated

During the four years between 66 and 70 AD there was all-out war. A whole Roman expeditionary force, comprising two legions and several thousand auxiliaries, was wiped out. The Romans lost over 5,000 infantry and 480 cavalry. This victory led to the setting up of a national government representing all aspects of religious opinion, both Sadducees and Pharisees, and even Essenes, the monastic group who produced the Dead Sea Scrolls. The Zealots opposed this government, which they regarded as class-based and potentially collaborationist. They were quite right.

The Jewish commander in Galilee, Josephus, who was a Pharisee, spent more time harassing the Zealots than preparing defences against Rome. When the Romans arrived, under Vespasian, he capitulated on the spot and became an open collaborator. Later he wrote a history of the events to justify his completely treacherous role. The backbone of resistance was led throughout by the Zealots who fought to the last in Jerusalem and then in the mountain fortress at Masada. When the Romans took Jerusalem in 70 AD, under Titus, hundreds of thousands were butchered and the city levelled. Josephus recounts how at one point the Romans ran out of wood for crosses and, when they had enough, had to search for empty spaces to put more crosses up in. It is in this context that the crucifixion of Jesus and the writing of the Gospels must be seen.

Where Did Jesus Stand?

It can hardly be believed that he was as oblivious to what was going on around him as the Gospel writers make out. Roman reprisals must have struck the families of Jews known to him in the area. One of Jesus's own disciples, one of the twelve, was Simon the Zealot, who presumably participated in one of the uprisings.

Reading the Gospels, the picture presented in the main is that of a passive collaborator. Although Jesus was condemned and executed by Pontius Pilate, every effort is made to clear him of any real responsibility. Crucifixion was not a Jewish method of execution. It was the Roman punishment for political crimes. Spartacus was crucified, for instance.

Whereas the Jews had responsibility for ordinary crimes and for religious offences, the political crimes went to Pilate. Yet the Gospels claim that Pilate washed his hands of the affair, protested Jesus's innocence, could see no wrong in him and was only pressured into crucifying him by the high priest and his lobby.

Jesus himself is represented in a pro-Roman light. For example, he is described as friendly with tax-collectors and collaborationists. He heals the child of a Roman centurion. He advises not simply going along with the authority of Rome under duress, but going twice as far as required. And, of course, the most important incident recounted concerns the payment of tax. 'Render unto Caesar that which is Caesar's and unto God that which is God's.' In the Gospels, this is presented as a particularly cunning reply which outwitted the Pharisees who asked it. In fact, it is not at all equivocal. It plainly supports the payment of taxes to Rome. The whole question of taxation was the burning issue of the day. On this issue, Jesus took a pro-Roman stand and backed the claims of the Imperial power.

Keeping Jesus Clear of Judaism

The counterpart of this pro-Roman attitude of the Gospels is the persistent denigration of the Pharisees. The Zealots, as such, play no part in the Gospel story at all. They are simply suppressed verbally, as the Romans suppressed them militarily. But the Pharisees are very much in the forefront. They are used as straw men who feed Jesus the straight lines which enable him to score off them. The purpose of this, as far as the Gospels are concerned, is clearly to distinguish Jesus and the Christian community from the Jews and the Jewish cause. In almost every case, it is a disagreement with Judaism which is stressed, so that Jesus can be distanced from his own people. Stories like that of the Good Samaritan are heavily promoted to the same end.

A number of scholars have tried to rescue Jesus from this pro-Roman presentation, especially in recent years when, after Auschwitz and Belsen, commentators on the Gospel have at long last become sensitive to its anti-Jewish bias. In particular, the episode of Jesus's trial has been gone over in detail and it has been admitted that Rome and not the high priest was responsible for his execution – as a political offender.

Pilate was not a weak administrator who was likely to allow the high priest's lobby to pressure him against his better judgement.

Pacifist Sentiment

This line of reasoning has led some writers to go as far as claiming that Jesus was actually pro-Zealot and sympathetic to armed struggle. This interpretation means discounting the great slabs of pacifist sentiment which fill the Gospels as nothing but post-Fall of Jerusalem PR, put in by the fawning Evangelists eager not to rub Rome the wrong way. In contrast, episodes like driving the money changers out of the Temple are stressed, and the fact that Jesus was arrested by an armed patrol and one of his disciples drew his sword and resisted arrest. Indeed, Luke describes how Jesus apparently instructed his disciples to buy swords just before the arrest, though he quickly adds that two would be enough.

It is certainly true that there are patches of anti-Roman material in the Gospels which may get closer to the attitude of Jesus, or at least the early followers, than the Gospel writers do. For example, the story of the Gadarene swine seems to have an anti-imperialist gibe hidden away in it. Jesus exorcises an evil demon, who is called 'Legion', and the demon then enters a herd of pigs who plunge over a cliff. The Roman occupation troops were known as 'pigs' by the Jews, so the moral is pretty clear. But conversely, there is a definite strain of anti-Temple feeling in Jesus's preaching. He is critical of a number of Temple institutions, particularly the financial institutions, and more than once criticises the various ways the Temple made money: donations, taxes, commercial transactions and so forth.

Above all Jesus did not in any way advocate violent resistance to the Romans, but believed that it was necessary to undergo a spiritual change in readiness for the coming of the Kingdom. He conceived of this change in a way which brought him up against the Pharisees, because he was an anti-traditionalist in his attitude to the Jewish religious law. Ethically, he was a purist, but not in a legalistic way. Judging from his numerous parables about vineyards, labourers and husbandmen, he was fully satisfied with the existing relations of production, including slavery, and the general economic set-up, though he was distrustful of the rich. He seems to have felt that the Temple should not be in any way a secular institution, either commercially or politically.

Jesus was Not Subversive

In itself, there was little that was subversive in Jesus's preaching and, in this sense the Gospel writers were right to portray him as a passive collaborator. But his fate was sealed when he began to attract crowds, partly because of his feats of healing, partly because he was a compelling orator. The Gospels several times tell how he tried to get away from the crowds and give them the slip, anxious about the outcome, as well he might be.

Pontius Pilate's last official act for example, in 36 AD, only two or three years after Jesus's execution, was to massacre a crowd of Samaritans who expected a revelation on their holy mountain. Anybody who gathered large crowds was in danger of being halted in their tracks for political reasons. In Rome the careers of sports and theatre stars were abruptly stopped when they began to acquire supporters who were too vocal or demonstrative.

Religions of the Oppressed

It is quite usual for messianic and prophetic religious movements to spring up in times of political upheaval. Jesus can be compared with the new movements which sprang up as part of the response to the advance of European imperialism: Peyotism and Ghost-dancing among the American Indians, Ringatū among the Maoris, Hòa Hảo in Vietnam. These movements attempt to break out of the confines of an apparently hopeless historical predicament, by stressing a glorious otherworldly role for the followers of their prophet. In a time of political turmoil, they appear dangerous to the authorities, anxious to suppress anything which might develop into a threat, usually cynical and ignorant, and inclined to err on the side of ruthlessness rather than mercy. They are put down and, if the circumstances are right, a new cult based on the prestige of martyrdom springs up.

The Man in the Middle

The real strength of Jesus's preaching lay in his ability to respond to conflict without being sucked into it. He was the man in the middle. Not only was he in the middle of a class conflict but of a national liberation struggle. He was able to find something to say which made sense to all kinds of people without ever coming down on one side or the other. This still is his strength. The discontented, the disaffected, the wretched of the earth could respond to him. So could tax-collectors and Roman soldiers.

In part, this was because he chose out of preference to speak in riddles and parables, to tell stories rather than make statements. But partly too it was because he had a talent for the ring of truth, for words which sounded right, which pushed everyone a little bit further together. He walked a verbal tightrope which he wove as he went along. And he could back it up with a quotation every time. It is precisely because he had this ability to reconcile conflicting aspirations, that he sometimes seemed subversive. But in the long run anything that covers over contradictions by appealing to both sides always favours those in power, and Christianity still does.

* * *

Essay published in 7 Days *9 (22 December 1971), Christmas issue.*

Contradiction

The concept of contradiction is one of the cornerstones of Marxism. 'The unity (coincidence, identity, equal action) of opposites is conditional, temporary, transitory, relative. The struggle of mutually exclusive opposites is absolute, just as development and motion are absolute.' Lenin's words can never be stressed enough. Marxist science and Marxist philosophy do not envisage a world in which identity is paramount, subject to the laws of formal logic, given to each of us in a way which is immutable or static or repetitive or which can be changed only as a continuum changes, by a series of adjustments. Marxism is about struggle, about rifts and ruptures, about crisis and revolution. It alone, in Lenin's phrase, can furnish 'the key to "leaps", to the "break in continuity", to the destruction of the old and the emergence of the new', which are the essential characteristics of history. In a word, it is about contradictions.

The dialectic, the logic of contradictions, had its origins in Greek philosophy, but made its decisive appearance in the modern world in the writings of Hegel. Hegel lived at the time when the bourgeoisie, so long contained within the limits and constraints of an age of absolute monarchs, first trod confidently upon the political stage. The French Revolution and the conquests of Napoleon left an indelible mark upon a generation, Hegel among them. These political events coincided with the discovery of history by the bourgeoisie, a discovery which showed itself in many varied aspects: in the revival of the Gothic, in the decipherment of the Rosetta Stone, in the further undermining of the Bible. In Hegel, this discovery found expression in a new turning in bourgeois philosophy. Hegel could find no interest in empiricism or the old rationalism, in the problems of the philosopher confronted by the timeless world of sense perceptions or innate ideas. He sought instead to elaborate a philosophy of history.

In order to produce his new system, however, Hegel found he had to dispense with many of the old shibboleths of philosophy. In particular, he had no use for the old, syllogistic logic, which had survived as a mainstay of philosophy since the time of Aristotle. In 1914, when Lenin was reading Hegel's *Logic*, he noted down, 'Quoting, on p. 125, the "famous" syllogism – "all men are mortal, Gaius is a man, therefore he is mortal" – Hegel shrewdly adds: "Boredom immediately descends when such a syllogism is heard approaching."' And in the margin, Lenin added, 'True!' In the place of the boring, wooden, petrified logic of Aristotle, Hegel developed a new, dialectical logic. For Hegel, however, this logic had a special, mystical role to play.

Hegel set the dialectic to work within an idealist framework. He conceived of history as the process in which man – the whole species, humanity as such – attained more and more rational consciousness of his own activity, drawing step by step away from the inanimate and contingent world of nature – the very lowest levels of the pyramid – until, in the end, man would finally reach complete self-consciousness and the whole of history would culminate in a world of pure rationality, more than this even, in unity with God (the '*Idea*'). Each step taken on this journey involved the negation of the step which preceded it: hence the need for a dialectical logic of contradiction. Each act of negation – which was both an act of Consciousness and consequently an act of history – brought mankind closer to its goal when the process of development would dissolve into what Hegel called, in a mystical phrase, the negation of the negation.

Hegel conceived of his logic as a 'concrete logic'. Negation, for Hegel, was not an abstract category which signified non-identity, as in formal logic. It was an act of the mind which was at the same time realised in history and was indeed the motor of historical development. History could only move forward because mankind was able to criticise, to oppose and hence to transform what had gone before, thus advancing in a kind of zigzag spiral towards the still centre. It was Hegel's view that, at the time he lived, the goal was virtually in sight: the Prussian state, the Christian church, etc., were not in need of negation and were the antechamber to the rule of reason. Not surprisingly this assertion quickly called forward a prompt negation and the critique of Hegel began in earnest. One of those who joined in this criticism was the young Karl Marx.

The general trend of 'left Hegelians', from the nineteenth century up until today, has been to assert that Hegel tried to stop the cable car too early, before mankind had really reached the top of the mountain. One more negation was necessary, as the proletariat achieved consciousness of its own role in the drama, as the representative of humanity in its final transformation, of its own consciousness, thus of its own activity, thus of the world. For some time, Marx's own view was something like this. However, in time, Marx made a decisive break with the Hegelian tradition, while still retaining the essential conception of a dialectic, now put to work within a materialist framework. The key to this break was a complete change in the attitude towards labour. Hegel had seen labour as the means by which man carried out his rational decisions; man thought about the world, acted on the world through labour and in this way further developed his reason. Marx, in contrast, saw labour as a material necessity; it was through labour that life was maintained and needs met.

Value, for Marx, was produced by labour and realised by use; it was not produced in the mind and then realised by labour. Once Marx's thought had diverged in this way from Hegel's, he was drawn towards economics, the study of the organisation of production. It was here, in his confrontation with Adam Smith and Ricardo, the leading bourgeois economists of the time, that Marx was able to benefit conclusively from the intellectual tool provided for him by the dialectic. For Marx, in his analysis of the capitalist economy, was able to show how this mode of production, by its own structure, by its own 'logic', contained a fundamental contradiction. Adam Smith and Ricardo had believed that the economy worked in a way which could harmonise the interests of all the members of a society, by increasing productivity through a division of labour which was in the best interests of all. Marx showed how this increase in productivity was, in a capitalist society, made possible only by the appropriation of surplus value, produced by surplus labour, by the owners of the means of production, capital goods, machinery, etc. The division of labour that Smith and Ricardo commented on was fundamentally a division between those who sold their labour power and those who bought it. The struggle of the capitalists to continue appropriating more and more of the surplus in order to be able to invest in order to compete was bound in the end to lead to intensifying crisis and eventual breakdown.

Thus for Marx, the contradiction between the forces of production and the relations of production was the basic fact of capitalist society, which was reflected politically in the class struggle and the development of revolutionary politics. This contradiction, however, was not something which developed smoothly or continuously. Development, for Marxism, is always uneven development; the 'connection and transitions', in Lenin's phrase, between different levels of a social formation cannot be reduced to a simple formula.

It was Lenin who, first and foremost, showed the connection and transitions between the economic level of society and the political. His whole political career was based on two fundamental works of economic science, one on the development of capitalism in Russia, the other on the development of imperialism in the world. It was Lenin too who, much more than Marx had done, deepened the concept of uneven development and directed penetrating attention to the contradictions which divide ruling classes among and within themselves, as a result of this unevenness:

> There are no miracles in history or nature, but every abrupt turn in history, and this applies to every revolution, presents such a wealth of content, unfolds such unexpected and specific combinations of forms of struggle and alignment of forces of the contestants, that to the lay mind there is much that must appear miraculous.

Lenin's political analysis was based without hesitation on the two concepts of contradiction and combination, with combination as 'relative' and contradiction as 'absolute'. It was precisely his mastery of the dialectic, not as an abstract dogma, but in application to specific situations, seen within a universal context (that of world imperialism), that enabled him to react so swiftly and unerringly to the news from Russia. In 1914, when he was asked to write an encyclopaedia article on Marx, Lenin read Hegel's *Logic* and noted: 'Aphorism: It is impossible completely to understand Marx's *Capital*, and especially its first chapter, without having thoroughly studied and understood the whole of Hegel's *Logic*.' The same might be said about the Bolshevik revolution: it would not have been possible without study of Hegel's *Logic*.

Twenty years later, in the red base of Yenan, Mao Tse-tung was staying up all night reading books of philosophy, including, Edgar Snow tells us, Spinoza, Rousseau, Hegel and others. Above all, he was impressed by Lenin's *Philosophical Notebooks*, with their copied-out extracts and comments on the *Logic*. The fruit of this work was the series of lectures Mao gave at the Red Academy in Yenan, later revised and published as the article *On Contradiction*. In this text, Mao encapsulates and crystallises what he had learned both from his own political practice and from his reading of Hegel, Marx and Lenin. Mao stressed two elements in particular. First, he made the new connection with military theory which his own experience had prepared him for. Mao's concept of contradiction is reflected in his theories of revolutionary war, the shifting tactics made necessary by the development of the situation, the interlocking forms of struggle appropriate to a war of 'jigsaw pattern'. Second, Mao developed the distinction between 'antagonistic' and 'non-antagonistic' contradictions, first suggested by Lenin in his notes on Bukharin's book, *Economics of the Transitional Period*. Lenin, in this brief, private comment, insisted that contradictions must continue after socialism was built, but need not be antagonistic. Mao took up this point to argue that antagonistic contradictions could only be solved by their intensification, by violent struggle, but that those which were non-antagonistic, such as between the post-revolutionary peasantry and proletariat, could be solved by peaceful means.

Thus, for Mao, it was necessary not only to specify the various transformations of contradictions, which at any point was primary and which was secondary, which forces were merging and which dividing, but also which were antagonistic and which were non-antagonistic, so that the appropriate form of struggle could be undertaken. Mao's political practice too was based both on a general economic analysis of China's position as a semi-feudal, semi-colonial country but also on an insistence on analysis of each specific situation in its concrete conditions, understanding what specific position each aspect of a contradiction occupies, what concrete forms it assumes in its interdependence and in its contradiction with its opposite, and what concrete methods are employed in the struggle with its opposite, when the two are both interdependent and in contradiction, and also after the interdependence breaks down. Lenin (in his crisp attack on articles by Lukács and Béla Kun in *Kommunist*) meant just this when he said that 'the most essential thing in Marxism, the living soul of Marxism, is the concrete analysis of concrete conditions'.

More than ever today we can see the need for dialectical study of the world situation, at a time when the alignment of forces is visibly shifting and many new and unexpected transformations are taking place. The touchstone for Marxists must always remain Lenin's insistence that struggle is absolute, the struggle of mutually exclusive opposites, of the masses against the ruling class, whether in Vietnam, Ceylon or Northern Ireland. It is for the masses that the materialist dialectic was produced, the instrument of their struggle to appropriate knowledge of history and society, and armed with this knowledge, to bring the contradictions of capitalism and imperialism to the breaking point. The concept of contradiction is their weapon in this struggle.

* * *

Essay published in 7 Days, *17 (23 February 1972).*

Two Weeks on Another Planet

1. Arab & Palestinian

PETER WOLLEN: The film began from the fact that I was in Amman in September 1970. Basically I was doing political journalism right up to the time I began filmmaking, although I wasn't a journalist in the sense of being a member of the international press corps. After the war and the Israeli occupation of the West Bank, the Palestinians were driven into setting up their headquarters on the East Bank, inside Jordan, in Amman. It was really the beginning of the organisation of the modern PLO. The lesson that the Palestinians drew from the war was that they could not rely on the Arab regimes and that they had to have an effective organisation of their own, their own political power.

As the Palestinian political organisation grew stronger, they began to threaten not only Israel but the Hashemite regime in Jordan. What developed was a situation of dual power in Amman in which the Palestinians controlled not only the camps but large sections of the city downtown, while the Jordanian army had control of the tops of the hills and the countryside and other sections of the city. This very unstable situation was inevitably headed towards armed conflict, which finally broke out in September 1970 – Black September – when the Jordanian army advanced into the Palestinian-held areas and into the camps and there was heavy street fighting. The Palestinians were driven out, to regroup later in the Lebanon. It inaugurated a new phase of Palestinian history in which the Palestinians became the victims, not directly of the Israelis, but of the Arab regimes and other Arab forces.

2. Woman & Machine

The original short story 'Friendship's Death' was one of a whole series of stories I wrote for Emma Tennant's magazine, *Bananas*, in the mid-70s. *Bananas* published a lot of science fiction writers – J. G. Ballard, Thomas Disch, Angela Carter, John Sladek – and since I wanted to write about this particular experience in Amman, I put the two together and wrote it as science fiction. The original extraterrestrial, Friendship, was a man. At a certain point, I came to feel there was something about it which wasn't working. Maybe in retrospect it was because it was turning into a kind of buddy movie. So I decided that I would make a complete change and turn the extraterrestrial into a woman. Because the imagery of machines is mainly a masculine one, it raises more questions, it presents the idea of a robot in a more unexpected way.

There is a tradition of the female robot, in Villiers de l'Isle-Adam's *The Future Eve*, in *Metropolis*, and Capek's *RUR*, which is the original robot play, in which there is what he calls a robotess. When I decided to change the gender of the robot, I went back and looked at those earlier models. I don't think *Friendship's Death* has much in common with *The Future Eve*, which is a different kind of fantasy structure, but it has a side in common with *RUR* and *Metropolis*: the machine as slave and the potential of slave revolt. In *RUR*, when the robots become self-conscious, they begin to act politically.

3. Man & Machine

The starting point is the metaphor of the alien, which is then supported by the discourse about homelessness and the Palestinians as people condemned to be alien because they don't have a homeland. Then there is the robot side, and a more general set of questions about machines and human beings. I wanted to call into question the whole human attitude towards machines – that machines are simply neutral tools – and to suggest that in an age of increased computerisation you cannot just continue thinking of machines in that way. Since the industrial revolution, we have had an immensely rapid development of machines. To the point, as is said in the film, where the fate of the whole human species is hanging on the decisions of machines, smart computers of one sort or another which are going to make decisions about thermonuclear war. It's an age-old question, the relation of humans to technology, and I wanted to look at that from a new angle.

4. There & Not There

In the journalist, I wanted a figure who was sympathetic, but who also had some of the journalist's traditional cynicism and wit. In a way, I saw it as a sequel to *The Passenger*, with the obvious difference that *The Passenger* is a road movie whereas this one is about being trapped, not being able to get out rather than constantly moving on. I wanted a journalist who was sympathetic, intelligent, humorous, a bit abrasive. In some ways falling within the stereotype of a journalist, but in other ways falling outside.

In *The Passenger*, the journalist is confused about his own role in relation to the reality he's supposed to be reporting. This one doesn't have those particular worries, but he becomes confused about his own role in relation to the extraterrestrial. So there is a similarity. But he doesn't have the same kind of ontological problems! Those are displaced onto the extraterrestrial. He has a home somewhere else; the extraterrestrial has also come from somewhere but has lost any possibility of returning, whereas in the end he can always go back home. That kind of being there and not there is built into the role of journalist.

5. Inside & Outside

But again I wanted, in *Friendship's Death*, to refract it all through the extraterrestrial; what's going on outside in the street is refracted through her perception of it more than through the journalist's, so that it's different from other recent films about journalists in wars – *The Killing Fields*, for example, in which Bill Paterson also appears. The central focus is not on the journalist but on the extraterrestrial. It's a kind of additional distancing device.

Her relationship to 'outside' is different from his. Throughout the film, she goes to the window and stands there completely unworried, whereas whenever something happens outside he starts backing away from the window, taking obvious precautions. Similarly, she is in the light all the time, whereas he tends to be in the shade. He draws the shutters to keep the outside out, he's consciously staying away from the outside and trying to cut himself off from it, because it's danger.

6. Politics & Death

When she first arrives, she is the envoy who is ready for MIT and the United Nations. Her identification with the Palestinians comes from the fact that she is forced to think about her own situation in a way that she wouldn't have been if her mission had gone according to plan. She has to improvise, she has to think through a completely unanticipated situation without any contact or help from base. She becomes fully autonomous. It's her growing consciousness of her own autonomy that eventually aligns her with the Palestinians.

Then she begins thinking through what it is to be human. What are her differences from humans? What would it be to become human, since she is on Earth and cannot go back to Procyon? What's the possibility of becoming human? And the decision to become human is necessarily a decision about death. It has a political aspect, but it also has a tragic aspect. She foresees the massacre to come. Accepting death doesn't mean she doesn't want to survive. You can want to survive and still accept the possibility, even the necessity, of death.

7. Look & Light

Her change from diplomatic envoy on arrival to Palestinian fighter at the end is charted through changes in costume and dress. There is a kind of technical reason for it, too. If you have a film which is about two people in two rooms, if you have that kind of constancy throughout the film, you have to have some principle of variation as well. One way of doing that is through changes in the 'look' of the character, the costume and make-up, etc. Another way is to vary the lighting, so that it goes through a series of changes, according to which room you are in, whether the window is open or whether there are shutters or blinds, according to the time of day, and then you get to paraffin lamps, to candles, to darkness.

Three things come through the windows: light, sound, and at one point a bullet. I thought very carefully about those, both light and sound, about what comes in from outside. What is most important about your awareness of the outside is the sound. It gets noisier, the sound of war becomes more intensive. There is quite a lot of street sound too, but like the war sounds it is stylised. I wanted an overall sound pattern to the film, which would be integrated with the music so that there isn't a complete divide between the effects track and the music track. To get that you obviously have to stylise the effects track to a certain extent. The camera positions were worked out during rehearsals. For each scene, there was a line drawn on the rehearsal room floor, to show where the light fell. Then the moves were worked out with the actors; their performances were choreographed to show a series of different views of the rooms.

8. Two Images

I decided to go for two kinds of images: some memories from earlier in the film and scientific imagery. The scientific footage comes from radio astronomy and from medical technology, mostly to do with the cardiovascular system, rheological graphs and that kind of thing. It relates to the science-fiction imagery of the robot. I focused that around blood, because it seemed to me a central image in the film – the moment when she looks at her hand and says 'blood'. One difference between the biological and the electronic is in terms of liquids, pre-eminently blood, and then there is the relationship of blood to death.

Why the idea of the crystal at the end of the film? Structurally it is a replacement. I had to find something to use instead of Friendship's 'translation' of Mallarmé in the original story. I didn't regard it as Friendship's definitive statement. It is like a pad on which she has been jotting down some odd notes, doodlings, things that seemed to her worth recalling. I didn't go for words, because there had been so many words earlier in the film. I wanted the sound to be dominated by the music track rather than have dialogue again. There is an echo of Friendship towards the end in the journalist's daughter who helps to decode the crystal. I didn't want everything to be totally pessimistic. The Palestinian poem by Samih al-Qasim, which is used at the end, is not pessimistic although it is very tragic.

9. Two Weeks

I knew it would be a cheap film, a film I could make in two weeks. I've always wanted to work in a studio. There was an artistic reason, that it was a story about people trapped in a hotel. I was interested in the idea of reflecting on a war while you are trapped inside. Then, of course, I knew I couldn't shoot in the Middle East. Thirdly, there is an obvious economic reason. It was difficult to convince people that I could film anything like that in two weeks, but I knew you could.

I've always been interested in a certain kind of virtuoso filmmaking, like the 360-degree pans in *Riddles of the Sphinx* or the video on location in *The Bad Sister*. Here you have the problem of doing a film in two rooms, again it involves a certain kind of stylistic and technical challenge. *The Bitter Tears of Petra von Kant* was one model of a film shot in one room. *The Saga of Anatahan* is a model of a studio picture in which you take something that at first sight doesn't seem like a studio subject, like a war, and do it in the studio. *Friendship's Death* has a similar kind of stylisation, control over the lighting, the cinematography, the performances, and so on.

10. Then & Now

I don't think of it as being any great break with my past. This is a film that is dealing with something that I have been thinking about for a long time, how do you make a political film? I was thinking in some way about what a Hollywood studio picture looked like. But it clearly isn't a Hollywood film or even an art film in the normal sense. In fact, the references, the classicism of it, disqualify it from being an art film, because art films are not made that way. So although it is not an avant-garde film in the sense of the '360-degree-pan' model, it is an attempt to come to terms with questions of politics, aesthetics and cinema.

We are not in the same period as those happy days when The Other Cinema was just opening. Obviously, we are working in a different situation. There is no purpose in being doctrinaire, believing one should be doing now what you were doing then. Not only have the terms of financing and the audience changed, but the terms of debate about these questions have changed. There is an overall continuity. I wrote about von Sternberg back in the '60s. I knew Sam Fuller made films in two weeks. This is a 'B' movie, it's the BFI's 'B' movie. I was thinking about Val Lewton at RKO.

Postscript: A & B

One of the strengths of what has been happening in Britain is the possibility of a lot of 'B' movies which have done well. *Letter to Brezhnev* is a 'B' movie, so is *My Beautiful Laundrette*, Derek Jarman's films are 'B' movies. I prefer these to the 'A' movies which have been touted as the strength of British cinema. I think it's a very interesting phenomenon of the last few years, these small, low-budget films that have a certain kind of energy and political edge.

* * *

Interview with Simon Field. Published in Monthly Film Bulletin *646 (November 1987).*

Introduction to *Wedding in Galilee*

Wedding in Galilee (1987), the film we are going to see in a few minutes, is remarkable for two quite unique reasons. It's the first feature made by a Palestinian director. And it was made in Palestine itself, in what was once Palestine, but now of course is divided between Israel and the occupied territories. I heard about Michel Khleifi's film some time before I first saw it. I'd just completed a film about the Palestinians myself and friends mentioned *Wedding in Galilee* to me and urged me to try and see it. When I finally got the chance, I was deeply moved. I hadn't really anticipated how good the film was going to be.

The first thing that struck me about it was the absence of animosity towards the Israelis, the military governor and his troops, who rule the lives of the Palestinian villagers. Of course, you're constantly aware of the Israeli occupation, but it's treated with a great deal of subtlety and humour, obliquely, ironically. It's a film which wants to understand everybody's reasons, to show the better side of people without ever minimising the injustice and lack of freedom felt by the Palestinians. It's about their struggle, but it's not an aggressive film, quite the reverse. It calls for justice, but also for understanding.

Second, it's a film about a wedding. There's a story which grips you as a story should and propels you towards a climax. There's always a threat, a possibility of violence, but the wedding itself is always the centre. The film lovingly portrays the spectacular beauty and ritual of the occasion, almost like a documentary, a strange and poetic documentary. Michel Khleifi wants to show the intricate detail and richness of Palestinian life, all the strands which go to make up a living culture. The film keeps moving sideways, away from the main spine of the plot, to introduce a new character, to dwell on some sensuous image, to conjure up an atmosphere of dream and ceremony.

Thirdly, and in some ways this is the most striking thing of all, the film is about the women of the community, their hopes and fears, their strength. At the centre are the bride, her mother, the groom's mother and his sister. They are the hub, the heart of the wedding, and of the village community. To show us who the Palestinians are, the strength of their resistance, Michel Khleifi looks at the women of the village rather than the men, who are more often living in the past, or else mirroring the machismo of the Israeli army. The women come from different generations. They have different outlooks and ambitions. For they are united by a double bond, as Palestinians and women, suffering the power of Israel and patriarchy.

Michel Khleifi was born in Galilee, in Nazareth, and left Israel when he was twenty years old in 1970. Now he lives and works in Brussels. For him, making *Wedding in Galilee* was a return to his home from exile, a chance to recreate the community in which he was brought up, one which he loves and honours, but from which he has acquired a critical distance. Of course, it's impossible for a Palestinian to avoid politics. At a film festival in Italy, Michel Khleifi opened a press conference on his film by making a joint statement with the Israeli filmmaker Amos Gitai, calling for the rights of Palestinians to be recognised, for a just peace. For me, this symbolised how resistance can be accompanied by reconciliation.

Wedding in Galilee is not an easy film to sum up in a few crisp sentences. It deals with issues and problems which are too often oversimplified, and it deliberately sets out to avoid clichés and easy rhetoric. It's a film which finds emotional depths where they are not expected and beauty and dignity where they are often overlooked. It's a film which was difficult to make, bringing together technicians, actors and actresses from outside with those from inside, both Palestinians and Israelis, professionals and real people. It's a very courageous film, it doesn't shirk issues, but it doesn't belabour them. It resists the temptation to sloganise or caricature. It celebrates the everyday and the sensuous, pleasure and beauty, in a land at war, plagued by severity, discipline, abstraction. Perhaps it's a utopian film with its generous hopes. Certainly, it's not a film you will easily forget.

* * *

Introduction to Wedding in Galilee *(Michel Khleifi, 1987), video recorded for broadcast on BBC2* Film Club, *10 December 1988. Transcribed and previously unpublished.*

Iraq

In the morning, when the orange of Zuleika was placed at the rim of the dish of the horizon, and the light by sleight of hand had conjured away from the quicksilver blanket of the sky the imprint seals of the stars, the Ilkhan Hulagu ordered the army to carry the torch into Baghdad.

– Wassaf, account of the fall of Baghdad, 1258

The bus is crowded. At my side,
a pilgrim sits, intent, with close-cropped hair,
singing all day of how the martyr died
in Karbala, in the great square:
'Tanha beh maidan miravad'…
The words are ringing in my ears. I feel
the sticky fear as we drive through Baghdad,
city given no chance to heal,
wounded city where brother killed
brother. Mute city. Those who tell
the truth are slaughtered, voices stilled,
bones snapped, in cell after dark cell.
They curse informants and, in the dawn light,
begin to count the minutes till the night.

The Ba'ath is a fire-storm that burns
vindictively, malevolent and blind,
raging, veering, consuming as it turns
close friend and bitter foe. Consigned
to defeat, Sunni, Shi'a, Kurd

gather in London, where an exiled friend
asks, 'Tell me, is it really true? I've heard
you knew Khalid. It meant the end
of hopes for us when Khalid died.'
Land without hope, study your fate:
death faces you on every side.
In a great arc, the bombers wait.
A world away, statesmen conspire to rain
destruction, then restore the Ba'ath again.

This is war. Look! There on the screen,
the idling motor, buried in the sand,
radiates heat. I look – you die. Unseen
watchers scrutinise their prey. Fanned
by the dry wind, crouched, parched, unfed,
conscripts cry and flinch under the full moon.
Satellites wheel in orbit overhead.
Sound rumbles through the bunker. Soon,
they will be targeted by smart
bombs. Then, intense, the killing field,
the land-air battle, the fine art
of death, the turkey shoot. They yield,
stay put, run, and are destroyed. It worked out
the way it was planned. Massacre and rout.

Like a dream, it happened so fast,
there was no time for stress, no time for pain.
There was a feeling of relief. At last,
America was feared again,
manhood and pride restored. No slam
dunk missed the basket. No restraints, no shame,
no dark memories stirred, no Vietnam
syndrome, no protesters to blame.
The long-awaited ground attack
met light resistance only. Theme
music. Headline News. Troops entering Iraq.
It happened all so fast, like a strange dream.
The yellow ribbons can come down. It's time to smile.
Here in L.A., the war seemed so worthwhile.

'Yes, yes, they somehow managed to survive...
Watching bombs fall on TV, I felt sick that day
sick with fear. My youngest brother's still alive...
A soldier – he's epileptic, but he was drafted anyway...
They smuggle things out somehow and the news
was mailed to friends in Sweden from Bombay!
It's terrible, the way you lose
touch and at last, when the war ends,
the Red Crescent provides phones, just
so families can get word through,
but we can't use them. We don't trust
the lines. Calls could be traced to you...'
The orange of Zuleika was now placed
at the dish's rim and all there was laid waste.

Where Khalid died, Bush's new exclusion zone
feigns to protect new rebels in the reeds.
Saddam, they say, avoids the telephone:
if Enemy Intelligence succeeds
in picking up his voice, a complex feat,
he's dead, killed by high penetration shells
reaching beneath the layers of concrete,
killed by the impact, burned up by the heat.
The martyrdom of Hussein in the square
still echoes down the centuries of blood
where now 'Satanic' planes control the air
so that George Bush can soar from the marsh mud,
finish the job, complete the task, the scheme
to introduce a U.S. backed regime.
Think of the polls, the votes. Think of the flag.
Think of the reeds, the body in the bag.

[P.W., Written during the first Bush regime].

* * *

Poem, 1992. The name Khalid refers to Wollen's friend, Khalid Ahmed Zaki, the Iraqi Communist revolutionary who was killed by Iraq's armed forces in June 1968 while leading the guerrilla campaign of the Popular Front for Armed Struggle against the Arif dictatorship from their base in the Southern Marshes of Iraq. Transcribed from a word-processed document in Wollen's archive. Previously unpublished.

John Wesley

I do not think there is much doubt that the major childhood influence on my view of history was that of John Wesley. I was brought up in a devout Methodist household. My father was a Methodist minister and my mother, although she had a strong leaning towards the Quakers, was a lifelong member of the Methodist Church. On top of this, my father was something of a Wesley scholar and, in fact, at the end of his life he became Curator of the Wesley Museum at the City Road Chapel, Methodism's principal shrine. I well remember the shelves in his study, lined with Wesley's sermons, with biographies of the great man and earnest commentaries on his works. Later in life, perhaps inevitably, I became a renegade, an unbeliever and an unrepentant sinner. Nonetheless, I had been stamped in many ways with the mark of Methodism, however much I might disown it, including, of course, its influence on the ways in which I rebelled.

Without any conscious effort on my part, I imbibed from my father a particular view of Wesley's life and legacy, and their lasting importance. In fact, it survived somewhere in my mind as a somewhat vague, but still powerful impression, and it was only recently that I began to flesh it out by researching Wesley for myself. Somewhat to my surprise, I must admit, I discovered that the Wesley presented by my father was arguably much more accurate than the dominant images of Wesley current among either Methodists or independent scholars and historians. My father's Wesley was a radical thinker whose deepest beliefs carried implications for what was later to be called the 'Social Gospel', implications which dovetailed with my parents' fervent commitment to the left of the Labour Party, to Bevanism and subsequently, Bevan having defaulted, to the Campaign for Nuclear Disarmament.

Academic scholars and historians tend to locate the rise of Methodism in relation to the social and political upheavals associated with the first wave of the Industrial Revolution and the political radicalism of a period which saw both the American and French Revolutions, a period of considerable turmoil within the British Isles themselves. Élie Halévy's *The Birth of Methodism* was first published in 1906 and his conclusions have set the agenda for many historians ever since.

According to Halévy, Methodism, or evangelicalism in the broad sense, with Methodism as its avant-garde, helped to save England from a French-style revolution at the beginning of the nineteenth century. E. P. Thompson brought a personal animus to the debate in his dismissal of Wesley as an anti-Enlightenment thinker and his assessment of Methodism as a block to political radicalism, a displacement of sexual energy into religious terror and a training-ground for the work discipline required by the capitalist labour market. (Thompson, like me, was the son of a Methodist minister.) More recently, Jonathan Clark, coming from a quite different background, has placed Methodism within the 'loyalty tradition' of deference to king and state, rooted not so much in traditional Dissent as in Tory nonjuror political ideology, and even Jacobitism.

I was presented with a very different version of early Methodism. The Wesley revered by my father was a fervent denouncer of the rich and powerful, a constant friend of the poor and the oppressed, a lifelong opponent of the status quo and, in effect, a crucial figure in the development of the English Enlightenment, before it was reduced to a purely secular phenomenon. This was a Wesley who could be aligned, in twentieth-century terms, with a Lansbury or a Gandhi. It was a Wesley whose mantle fell on William Blake and William Morris – twin heroes, paradoxically enough, for Edward Thompson as well as for my father. As always, the truth turns out to be more complex than any single version can suggest. Wesley was a complex and paradoxical figure, whose legacy was contradictory and confused as different followers drew on different aspects of his thought and conduct. The Society of Methodists began to fragment very quickly after Wesley's death and it was not reunited until the early 1930s, by which time almost all passion was spent, except in the case of a few recalcitrants like my father. Even within each strand of Methodism – Wesleyans, the New Connexion, Independents, Primitive Methodists, Free Methodists, Bible Christians, Quaker Methodists, Christian Revivalists, Ranters, Magic Methodists – there were different threads and tendencies, ravelling or unravelling in different contexts.

The book which most closely endorsed my father's particular view of

Wesley was *Good News to the Poor*, written by Theodore Wesley Jennings and published in 1990. In essence, Jennings puts the case for Wesley as an early exponent of liberation theology. Jennings confesses that at his seminary, where he was studying to enter the ministry, he 'found the whole business of eighteenth-century Christianity unspeakably boring and the preoccupations of the founder of Methodism tedious in the extreme', having had enough hagiography foisted on him as a child. He still avoided Wesley when he began to teach in a seminary himself and it was not till he found himself in Mexico City, at the Methodist Seminary of Mexico, that he was finally persuaded to teach a year-long required course on Wesley's sermons. Already interested in Latin American liberation theology, he was astonished to find that Wesley's teaching on economic issues was unmistakably radical and that, in fact, from the beginning, Methodism has chosen to reject Wesley's own most deeply held convictions about what Jennings has called his 'evangelical economics'.

It is widely recognised by Wesley scholars that John Wesley built his concept of the church, as it should be, on the foundation of his understanding of the 'apostolic' or 'primitive' church, the church before the Constantinian era, when Christianity became the state religion of the late Roman Empire, proclaimed as such by the Emperor Constantine. Begun, in its original perfection, at Pentecost, the church fell from grace when Ananias and Sapphira disregarded the precept to hold goods in common and kept some back as their own private property (Acts, 5:1–11). Wesley noted: 'Mark the first plague which infected the Christian Church; namely, the love of money!' Later, as he wondered about the reasons why the churches at Smyrna and Philadelphia had not been overwhelmed by corruption (Rev. 2:8–11 and 3:7–13), he concluded that 'it seems, because they were less wealthy... So that these, having less of the world's goods, retained more the simplicity and purity of the gospel.' As for the conversion of Constantine, Wesley wrote that,

> persecution never did, never could, give any lasting wound to Christianity. But the greatest it received, the grand blow which was struck at the very root of that humble, patient, gentle love, which is the fulfilling of the Christian law, the whole essence of true religion, was struck in the fourth century by Constantine the Great, when he called himself a Christian, and poured in a flood of riches, honours, and power, upon the Christians... Then, not the golden but the iron age of the Church commenced.

Throughout his writings, Wesley describes the desire for wealth and the love of money as the gravest threats to true Christianity. 'Most of those in England who have riches love money, even the Methodists; at least those who are called so. The poor are the Christians. I am quite out of conceit with almost all those who have this world's goods.' Or:

> On Friday and Saturday, I visited as many more as I could. I found some in their cells underground; others in their garrets, half-starved both with cold and hunger, added to weakness and pain. But I found not one of them unemployed, who was able to crawl about the room. So wickedly, devilishly false, is that common objection, 'They are poor, only because they are idle.' If you saw these things with your own eyes, could you lay out money in ornaments or superfluities?

Or, again, in a familiar political context:

> When I came to Belfast, I learned the real cause of the late insurrections in this neighbourhood. Lord Donegal, the proprietor of almost the whole country, came hither to give his tenants new leases. But when they came, they found two merchants of the town had taken their farms over their heads; so that multitudes of them, with their wives and children, were turned out to the wide world. It is no wonder that, as their lives were now bitter to them, they should fly out as they did. It is rather a wonder that they did not go much farther. And if they had, who would have been the most at fault? Those who were without home, without money, without food for themselves and families? Or those who drove them to this extremity?

On another occasion, Wesley defends the actions of a mob who, 'without striking or hurting anyone', took stockpiled corn from the harbour and sold it in the market 'at the common price', rather than see it exported.

Passages like this could be reduplicated over and over. The fact is that Wesley was strongly in favour of the redistribution of wealth, strongly critical of merchants, lawyers and people of wealth and quality in general. In fact, Wesley's vision of the Pentecostal Church clearly assumed that, in a truly Christian society, goods would be held in common and distributed according to need. He was strongly committed to human rights – an early opponent of slavery, a deprivation of the liberty 'to which an Angolan has the same natural rights as an Englishman'. Wesley was also fiercely critical of the actions of the East India Company, condemning his own countrymen without the slightest hesitation:

> What consummate villains, what devils incarnate, were the managers there! What utter strangers to justice, mercy, and truth; to every sentiment of humanity! I believe no heathen history contains a parallel. I remember none in all the annals of antiquity: Not even the divine Cato, or the virtuous Brutus, plundered the provinces committed to their charge with such merciless cruelty as the English have plundered the desolated provinces of Indostan.

In fact, as it became institutionalised, the Methodist Church preferred to forget the radicalism of Wesley's economic teaching. Under the leadership of his successors, the Church became increasingly involved in the world of power and wealth which Wesley had disdained. To a great extent this was because the Church became fearful of governmental action directed against it during the period after the French Revolution and during the Napoleonic Wars. As a result, the Conference – the ruling body of the Church – and the President, its leader, took steps to lobby Parliament and ingratiate itself with the government of the day. At the same time, draconian discipline was exercised within the church itself to prevent any involvement in politics by preachers or other church leaders. By politics, radical politics was particularly intended – after Peterloo tough measures were taken to stamp out any public criticism of the authorities which might be associated with Methodism. The process had begun by which Methodism increasing came to win 'respectability' as a politically conservative institution, rather than a wayward evangelical and nonconformist sect summoning up memories (and fears) of the Commonwealth days.

In this sense, Edward Thompson was absolutely right in seeing Methodism as a force for order rather than disorder. At the same time, however, it should be realised that the official policy of the Church reflected the judgements and interests of its leadership and local elites rather than those of the whole body of the church. The attitudes of professional preachers were different from those of the part-time lay preachers, and the attitudes of chapel trustees – typically the richest and most powerful members of the flock – were different from those of the poorer members. In fact, Methodism quickly began to split into different churches after Wesley's death, as subordinate currents were expelled or went their own way. Perhaps most significant of all was the foundation and rapid surge of the Primitive Methodists, whose growth rate during the first two decades of the nineteenth century far exceeded that of the official 'Wesleyan' Church. In fact, as one might expect, the Primitive Methodists were far closer to Wesley's model of what the church should be than were his official heirs.

My father greatly admired the 'Prims', as he called them. In fact, I was taken as a child to visit Mow Cop, the symbolic founding place of Primitive Methodism, located between the Potteries and the silk-weaving town of Macclesfield, where my father was then working. A local wheelwright, Hugh Bourne, had chosen Mow Cop as the site of an open-air revivalist meeting held on 31 May 1807. Essentially the meeting at Mow Cop was the first English example of an American-style 'camp meeting', an idea introduced by the visiting American evangelist, Lorenzo Dow, who was not above quoting Tom Paine in a sermon. Bourne's movement drew on the Independent Methodists who were strong in Macclesfield, the 'Kilhamite' Methodist New Connexion, centred on the West Riding of Yorkshire, and the so-called 'Magic Methodists' of Delamere Forest in Derbyshire, who saw visions and went into trances. The Quakers of Warrington were also an important influence on Bourne.

The Primitive Methodists essentially represented lay defiance of the Methodist Conference and a return to the evangelical roots of Wesley's ministry. They were particularly strong in rural areas where the Church of England was closely tied to the landowners and active on the magistrate's bench, as well as in weaving and mining communities, then the spearhead of the working class, still artisanal rather than fully proletarian in nature. They were known as 'Ranters' by outsiders, who thus explicitly connected them to the Commonwealth days, and, although they were not directly engaged in political action, they created a tradition of working-class public speaking, self-education and organisational experience which later fed directly into the nascent labour movement. The Primitive Methodists finally reunited with the Wesleyans in the early 1930s and, as a result, lost much of their unique quality. Nonetheless, it was through Hugh Bourne and the Primitive tradition that Wesley's more radical message was passed on through the nineteenth century. Mow Cop, I was taught, was second only to the Foundry, as an originating moment.

Selected Bibliography

Bebbington, D. W. *The Nonconformist Conscience.* Allen & Unwin, 1982.

Cornwall, Robert D. *Visible and Apostolic: The Constitution of the Church in High Church Anglican and Non-Juror Thought.* University of Delaware Press, 1993.

Hempton, David. *Methodism in British Society, 1750–1850.* Hutchinson, 1984.

Howse, Ernest Marshall. *Saints in Politics: The 'Clapham Sect' and the Growth of Freedom.* University of Toronto Press, 1952.

Jennings, Theodore Wesley. *Good News to the Poor: John Wesley's Evangelical Economics.* Abingdon Press, 1990.

Lester, Muriel. *Entertaining Gandhi.* Ivor Nicholson and Watson, 1932.

Postgate, Raymond. *The Life of George Lansbury.* Longmans, Green, 1951.

Purcell, William. *Portrait of Soper.* Mowbrays, 1972.

Reuter, Timothy, ed. *The Greatest Englishman: Essays on St Boniface and the Church at Crediton.* The Paternoster Press, 1980.

Thompson, E. P. *Witness against the Beast: William Blake and the Moral Law.* Cambridge University Press, 1993.

* * *

Essay transcribed from word-processed document in Wollen's archive. Previously unpublished.

III

The Continent: Re-Narrating 'American' Art

Frida Kahlo and Tina Modotti

Co-written with Laura Mulvey

1. On the Margins

André Breton went to Mexico, as to a dreamland, to find there that magic 'point of intersection between the political and the artistic lines beyond which we hope that they may unite in a single revolutionary consciousness while still preserving intact the identities of the separate motivating forces that run through them'.[1] Fatal point, we may think as we survey its histories in this century: art corroded and destroyed by politics; politics smothered and sweetened by art. Yet the hope is necessary. Breton found it particularly in the paintings of Frida Kahlo, in Mexico, in 1938, work which blended reverie, cruelty and sexuality – the surrealist virtues, whose enchantment was heightened for Breton by the connection with Trotsky (then living in Frida Kahlo's 'Blue House', her self-portrait hanging on his study wall).[2]

Others found the point of intersection elsewhere. The critic of *30/30*, reviewing an exhibition of Tina Modotti's photographs in Mexico City in 1929, described how she had found 'a clear and concrete solution' to the problem of joining art with propaganda in her emblematic photographs of sickle, corn-cob and bandolier, and other combinations with guitars or the numbers 27 and 123, referring to the articles in the Mexican constitution concerning the ownership of land and the rights of labour. She had shown how 'we can make a social art without giving up pure

1 André Breton, 'Frida Kahlo de Rivera', in *Surrealism and Painting*, trans. Simon Watson-Taylor (Harper & Row, 1972).

2 Trotsky arrived in Mexico on 9 January 1937. He was met at the port of Tampico by Frida Kahlo, and stayed with her in the 'Blue House' until May 1939.

art', how the production of a 'pure aesthetic emotion' through plastic form can be combined with 'revolutionary anecdotism'.[3] Modotti took the formal lessons she had learned from Edward Weston and found a point of intersection with the revolutionary politics she had learned in Mexico.

Breton's hope, the dialectical unity of art and revolution, is one that has haunted the modern period. The fact that it is still no more than a hope for us today demonstrates that none of the solutions sought, by Breton or by others of different tendencies, succeeded with any degree of permanence. The initial *élan* at the moment of intersection has not persisted or been generalised. We are left with a series of talismans, clustered most often at certain places and certain periods – Soviet art of the immediate post-revolutionary years, Berlin Dadaism, French surrealism, the Mexican renaissance – to which we may turn back for encouragement and understanding. We need to know what has been achieved and how it was checked and deflected, to construct our own history in its own incompleteness. That is the purpose of this exhibition.

Why Mexico? An exhibition of work by Frida Kahlo and Tina Modotti automatically invites questions about 'marginality' – the status, in terms of mainstream art history as presented in books and museum displays, assigned to Mexican art and to women's art and (in Modotti's case) to photography. The centres of art history are in Europe and the United States; Paris and New York are the last links in a chain which reaches back through Rome and Florence to the classical civilisations of antiquity. Breaks and diversions are to be smoothed over or bracketed off, the 'heterogeneous' to be admitted only as an influence. In this way the originality, scope and richness of Mexican art have been overlooked or underestimated.

2. The Mexican Renaissance

It is important to remember that Diego Rivera during his second stay in Paris (1911–20) was one of the best and most original of cubist painters.[4] At the same time, in New York, the Mexican Marius de Zayas was central to the Stieglitz group, the first American avant-garde. He was a crucial

3 Martí Casanovas, 'Las Fotos de Tina Modotti, El Anecdotismo Revolucionario', *30/30* 10 (1929).

4 See Florence Arquin, *Diego Rivera: The Shaping of an Artist, 1889–1921* (University of Oklahoma, 1971). Rivera was born in 1886.

contributor to *291* and was its main link with Paris.[5] In the 1920s after Rivera's return to Mexico, the decade of the Mexican renaissance, there was an extraordinary surge of energy in the arts, which attracted foreign visitors and admirers – among them Edward Weston and with him, Tina Modotti, who stayed after his return to California. This was the decade too in which, while Alfred Barr Jr went to Moscow, René d'Harnoncourt went to Mexico City.[6]

Then, in the 1930s, the muralists were able to launch themselves 'up there', north of the border, with works and workshops which had an enormous effect, as one would expect of a movement which provided the example of a distinctive and energetic American version of modern art. Surely 'the crisis of the easel picture', which Clement Greenberg notes in 1948, had something to do with the impact of Mexican muralism?[7] In particular, Siqueiros had a crucial and direct influence on Pollock, who studied with him. What is truly remarkable is the way in which Mexican art was shunted into the shadows after the New York art world had achieved its triumph.

It is worth comparing the art-historical fate of the Mexican renaissance with that of Russian art of the 1920s. There are similarities between the two experiences. In both countries the example of cubism enabled artists independently to develop a specific culture of modern art. In both countries the overthrow of an *ancien régime* (Tsarism, the *Porfiriato*) and the recasting of the society after political revolution and civil war gave the avant-garde a particular vision of its *rôle*, to produce the new art for the new society.[8]

Through Rivera there were, in fact, close links between the Russian and Mexican avant-gardes. Rivera lived in the Russian art colony of La Ruche in Paris – he was the model for Ehrenburg's novel *Julio Jurenito* and was invited to the Soviet Union by Shterenberg after the October Revolution.[9] Later in the 1920s, on a long visit to the Soviet Union,

5 See Dickran Tashjian, *Skyscraper Primitives* (Wesleyan University Press, 1975), and Catherine Turrill, 'Marius de Zayas', in *Avant-Garde Painting and Sculpture in America 1910–25* (Delaware Art Museum, 1975).

6 Alfred Barr Jr became the first director of the Museum of Modern Art in New York in the year following his visit to Moscow in 1927–28. René d'Harnoncourt was his successor in this position.

7 Clement Greenberg, 'The Crisis of the Easel Picture' (1948), in *Art and Culture* (Beacon Press, 1961).

8 Porfirio Díaz was the last pre-revolutionary president of Mexico, whose regime extended from 1876 to 1911.

9 See Marevna Vorobëv, *Life in Two Worlds* (Abelard-Schuman, 1962), and *Life with the Painters of La Ruche* (Macmillan, 1974).

Rivera took part in the debates on the relation between avant-garde art and revolutionary politics. Rivera's visit to Russia was matched by those of Mayakovsky and Eisenstein to Mexico.

Recent years have seen a great revival of interest in the Russian avant-garde and particularly in the ways in which art and politics converged and clashed. Many of the same issues and problems arose in Mexico at the same time – the relationship of the avant-garde artist with the mass audience, the *rôle* of collective work, the relationship between art and craft, the absorption of cubism into a complex national culture, the relationship between propagandist content and innovative formal concerns, and so on.

Yet while the Soviet artists' and theorists' search for answers to these problems has been recognised as of renewed importance for artists and theorists today, the Mexican experience has been only superficially introduced into the debate. The work of Kahlo and Modotti focuses particular questions about art and politics – feminist politics, in the contemporary sense, as well as classical revolutionary politics – in ways which are fruitful for those concerned by the same kind of questions now, since the resurgence of a conscious feminist art.

3. Women, Art and Politics

The second issue of marginality posed by this exhibition is that of women's art. At this point, the focus of attention shifts away from the actual historical context in Mexico that influenced Tina Modotti and Frida Kahlo and moves towards the debates which have developed around feminist aesthetics. It is here that the importance of the juxtaposition between the two artists comes into relief. An exhibition of either artist alone would have asserted her individual importance, her specific contribution to an artistic practice (painting or photography) and to women's cultural traditions. But the decision to bring the work of Frida Kahlo and Tina Modotti together is based on something more than the fact that they have been unjustly neglected and that their art and their lives are of great intrinsic interest. The juxtaposition is designed to raise a series of ideas and arguments that are relevant to questions about women's art and feminist aesthetics.[10]

10 See, for instance, the periodical *Heresies*, New York, from 1977, which still provides the principal forum for debate on women's art and feminist aesthetics. [*Heresies* closed in 1993.]

Thus the contrasts, as well as the parallels, suggested by the work of both artists provide a starting point for the exhibition's line of interest and argument. The parallels: Both, obviously, are women artists of interest to anyone concerned with art from a feminist perspective. Both were influenced by radical tendencies in contemporary Mexican politics and culture. They were both politically militant. Both found or developed their own aesthetic from under the shadow of a male artist of international repute. Both implicitly challenge 'high art', dominant traditions. It is here that their work has an immediate excitement and interest.

Feminism has always been deeply concerned with questions about representation, with the politics of images. This concern is with the way that 'woman' has been used in male representation, and (the necessary other side of the coin) with women's relegation to a marginal area of culture, specifically excluded from 'high art'. So work on women's art has proceeded on two fronts, both of which are relevant here. First comes a process of archaeological excavation, uncovering women artists overlooked and forgotten by male-dominated criticism. Secondly, there is the confrontation of the questions of value posed by the split between high art and applied arts and the examination of the rationale behind the unbridgeable gap that seems to divide them. In the present context this last point doubles with the discovery of popular traditions of Mexican art during this period (the background to Kahlo's work) and with an avant-garde desire to bring art into dialogue with the modern world and its technology (a contributing factor to Modotti's use of photography as political reportage).

Both Kahlo and Modotti worked in 'dialects' rather than the language of high art. Modotti learnt photography from Edward Weston, whose aesthetic was based on the desire to raise photography from a lesser art and give it the status of high art. Tina's own work shows a steady movement away from this principle. She returned rather to the documentary aspects of photography. The content changed as her work developed but she never lost or compromised her formal aesthetic position. Frida Kahlo's 'dialect' was drawn from folk art and naive painting, both as part of a contemporary movement to the popular but also as a source of imagery and emotion that was very close to her own preoccupations. The contemporary political and cultural background is essential for an understanding of Frida Kahlo and Tina Modotti's work. But it is the present interest in radical aesthetics, in the breakdown of high art, in the breakup of art under the impact of other media such as photography, that gives the Mexican background an immediate relevance.

The relationship between the lives and work of both women raises the question of how women come to be artists. The Mexican revolution provided a special context, a stimulus. This is the contribution of history. But in each case, an arbitrary element entered into their lives, changing its normal course and directing them towards unusual choices. Both these elements relate to the question mentioned above: woman's body and its place in representation. Kahlo had an accident as a teenager that left her permanently in pain and unable to have children. Her paintings are a visual record of the effect this had on her. Modotti was a great beauty; Edward Weston fell in love with her and used her as a model. It was her journey to Mexico with him that changed her life. When he went back to the United States, she stayed on, joining the Communist Party and becoming a photographer in her own right. The perspective offered by feminism is in terms of this emphasis on the body, on woman's body as a particular *problem* both as the vehicle for childbearing and as an object of beauty.[11]

Their relationship to the Mexican cultural background was necessarily rather different. Kahlo was an important Mexican artist, given added prominence by the fact that she was married to Diego Rivera, the leading mural artist. Modotti was a foreigner, drawn to Mexico by the events taking place there (as so many foreigners were), arriving as Weston's companion, and then utterly changed by what she found. But this point only highlights the series of contrasts and differences that provide the basis for the second level of argument at stake here. It is here that the juxtaposition between the two became crucial. Through their differences they can spark off a new line of thought or argument (like montage in the cinema, where bringing two images together can produce a third idea in the mind of the spectator).

Looking at the work of Tina Modotti and Frida Kahlo side by side, with this hindsight, one is struck immediately by the contrasts between them. While both produced work that is recognisably that of a woman (Modotti sometimes less so than Kahlo), the stance taken up by each as an *artist* is very different. On the one hand Frida Kahlo's work concentrates primarily on the personal, the world of the interior, while Modotti's looks outward, to the exterior world.

She photographed the street, women and children in the streets, men at public political meetings. In total contrast, Kahlo's subject is herself. She painted her private world of emotional relationships, she found images

11 See the periodical *m/f*, London, from 1978, for a continuing debate on 'the discourse of the body'. [*m/f* closed in 1986.]

for her personal experience of pain and her tortured relationship with her body, her obsession with her own image. The types of work they produced, therefore, stand in apparent opposition to each other, suggesting two different roads for feminist art: a concern with social problems on the one hand, and private ones on the other. Two points can be introduced here to break down this apparent polarity. First of all, the feminist slogan 'the personal *is* political' recasts Kahlo's private world in a new light. Secondly, Modotti's work as a photographer can only be understood in the context of *her* private life and position as a woman. The intention here, then, is to switch over, or rather to blur the distinctions set up by the polarity between them and to bring out the ways in which Kahlo's work is political and Modotti's is personal.

Looking at Frida Kahlo and Tina Modotti's work in relation to their lives and experience as women it is clear that conscious decisions about artistic stance are only to a limited extent the result of conscious, controllable choice. Two other forces are of utmost importance: that of historical heritage and that of individual accident. The relation between these two can be described as that between the necessary and the contingent. The differences between a working-class Italian immigrant to California and a Mexican bourgeois intellectual are of great importance. These social-historical conditions contribute to the artist's stance, to Kahlo's desire to explore herself and her colonised cultural roots through her art, and to Modotti's desire to change the conditions of exploitation and oppression she saw around her, then to devote herself to the international working-class movement. These differences are clear and visible in the two women's places of birth and death.

4. Revolution and Renaissance

The Mexican renaissance was the progeny of the Mexican revolution, an event – or rather a historic phase – which is not easy to characterise or describe in simple terms.[12] The overthrow of the *ancien régime* of Porfirio Díaz unleashed uncontrollable forces and counterforces for nearly a decade of civil war, *putsch* and counter-*putsch*, peasant rising and landlord repression, convention, charter and constitution-writing. It was a period of mingled cruelty, surprise and hope in which great masses travelled through Mexico on military campaigns and many millions died, others

12 For a recent political analysis of the Mexican revolution, see Donald C. Hodges and Ross Gandy, *Mexico 1910–1976: Reform or Revolution?* (Zed Press, 1979).

surviving to march in triumph through the capital, wreak merciless vengeance on the defeated or thank their luck or their cunning.

There are five things, at least, worth emphasising about the Mexican revolution. First, it was a genuine revolution. It swept aside the attempts of political leaders to limit or control its effects. Peasants and workers played a leading role in breaking careers, changing *régimes* and, eventually, recasting the entire political order, inspired by schemes for their own betterment and the destruction of old enemies. In the end, after many checks and long delays, Mexico emerged with the power of the old ruling class broken. Its three pillars – landlords, army, church – were shattered and the institutions of debt peonage and the old *hacienda* system were destroyed. What took their place, however, was not workers' and peasants' power, not socialism, but a new type of state, answering many workers' and peasants' demands but nurturing an indigenous capitalism at the same time, under the harmonising protection of a civilian and lay bureaucracy.

Second, during the period of the revolution, organised labour fought on the opposite side to the most militant peasant forces. The House of the World Worker, the centre of the anarcho-syndicalist trade-union movement, enlisted with Carranza and Obregón, and battalions of workers fought against the armies of Villa and Zapata, who in different ways represented the aspirations of the peasantry. This meant that the labour unions were integrated rapidly into the new post-revolutionary structure of power after Obregón became president in 1920, long before land reforms of any scope were carried out. It was a division which made possible the deceleration of revolutionary impetus until both workers and then peasants could be integrated into the new state system.

Third, the Mexican revolution occurred before the Russian Revolution. The armies which fought their way across the country had many a *corrido* to sing and demands formulated in many a *plan*, but they had no revolutionary theory of a Marxist, or even socialist type. Nor of course did they have the Russian Revolution before them as a model; there was no Communist Party in Mexico till after the end of the revolution. The Constitution of 1917 was a compromise document, whose famous articles 27 and 123 offered in reality less than they seemed to promise. They produced radical liberalism rather than a step towards socialism, and democratic rights dependent on a state power which was destined to sediment into self-perpetuating one-party rule, though much less murderous and pervasive than that which came to prevail in the Soviet Union.

Fourth, the revolution made possible the release of a great surge of national feeling, the culture of *mexicanidad*. This aspect aligns it with the wave of Third World revolutions which have characterised the middle of the twentieth century: in Turkey, Argentina or Egypt, for instance. The wish to be rid of the *Porfiriato* represented in part a wish to assert national independence, in the face principally, of course, of the United States, which only sixty or seventy years before had seized and annexed the whole northern half of the country and had continually intervened in Mexican politics, both by military incursions and through diplomatic and economic pressure. In this sense, the Mexican revolution was a national revolution, disfigured and enfeebled by internal divisions and civil war. Certainly this is how the revolution is officially presented, with varying degrees of vigour.

Fifth, the revolution coincided with a cultural revival, not as much political as philosophical. In reaction against the positivism which had become an official part of Porfirian ideology, the succeeding generation, that of the *Ateneo* of 1909, embraced a militant, not to say Promethean, idealism.[13] The tradition of classical humanism and idealist metaphysics was harnessed to a mystical vitalism and voluntarism, which grew to epic proportions with the revolution. Vasconcelos, the Minister of Education in the early 1920s who launched the programme of mural painting and cultural renewal from which the Mexican renaissance developed, was a leader of the *Ateneo* and the promulgator of a visionary teleology of the cosmic man, in which Mexican nationalism was blended with elements of Saint-Simon and Bergson, in an exalted amalgam of art, will and the destiny of *la raza*.

It was Vasconcelos who summoned Rivera and Siqueiros back from Europe to play their part in the cultural programme he had planned. (Rivera had been in Europe throughout the revolution; Siqueiros had fought on Obregón's side in the Red Battalions of workers.) Modelling himself on the example of Lunacharsky in the Soviet Union, Vasconcelos launched a mass literacy campaign, a reform of the education system and state patronage for the arts, which were to display the new national culture on a monumental scale. It was Vasconcelos's good fortune to find in Diego Rivera, especially, an artist who could match his own grandiose ambitions with the appropriate energy.

13 'El Ateneo de la Juventud' (The Athenaeum of Youth) was an intellectual society founded in 1909 with the purpose of reforming Mexican culture. See: Carlos Monsiváis, 'Notas sobre la Cultura Mexicana en el Siglo XX', in *Historia General de México*, vol. 4 (Colegio de México, 1976).

More than any of the other artists involved, many of them of great talent and ability, Rivera set his stamp on the Mexican renaissance (to the exasperation of his rival, Orozco). He set about creating an art which would be modern, monumental and American, worthy of the revolution and with the ideological and political aim of impelling it further forward. Unlike his fellows in Russia, Rivera determined to stay with figurative art and to reject abstraction. As far as content was concerned, Rivera revived the lost genre of history painting, on an unprecedentedly vast scale – the scale of the revolution and eventually the history of Mexico from its first beginnings, through every period up to the present, combined in one massive composition. Formally, he fused a mural style derived mainly from the early Italian Renaissance (Giotto especially) with elements of cubism, of Gauguin and Cézanne, of the caricature tradition and of Mexican pre-Columbian and popular art.

While Rivera dominated Mexican painting of the 1920s, it is important to realise that there were many others who flourished at the same time, with widely varying styles and types of subject matter. Nonetheless it was the concept of a monumental civic art, displaying in public places the history of Mexico, in a modern but distinctively national style, drawing on Indian and popular forms, which came to represent the core of the Mexican renaissance. Rivera's aim was to reverse the current of art history so that instead of the exotic or the primitive feeding into European art, the reverse would happen: the lessons of European art he had brought back with him would feed into the native Mexican tradition.

These strands formed the background of both Frida Kahlo's painting and Tina Modotti's photography (in Modotti's case in tension with the influence of her teacher, Edward Weston). The contrast between their work – its smallness of scale, both in subject matter and actual physical size – and the monumentalism of the muralists is immediately striking. Yet this 'smallness' is deceptive. It springs in part from the traditional constraints of women's art, which the Mexican revolution had done nothing to loosen. Yet within these constraints they were able to produce work quite as innovative and explosive in its implications as the mammoth productions of their *confrères*.

5. The Interior and the Exterior

The slogan 'the personal is political' dates back to the days when the women's movement was organised around consciousness-raising. The phrase is emphatic and assertive. But in announcing what now *is*, it contains within it the residual ashes, the memory, of what previously *was not*. This argument has been forcefully restated in *Beyond the Fragments*:

> Before the women's movement, socialist politics like all other sorts of politics, seemed something separate from everyday life, something unconnected with looking after children, worrying about the meals and the housework, finding ways of enjoying yourself with your friends and so on. It was something professional for men among men, for the shop steward or the party activist. The activities of the women's movement have begun to change that as far as women are concerned. But it's meant a different way of organising which does not restrict political activity to the 'professional'.[14]

The phrase 'the personal is political' rejects the traditional exclusion and repression of the personal in male-dominated politics. And it also asserts the *political* nature of women's private individualised oppression. The main achievement of consciousness-raising lay in providing a structure for women to discover that their problems were no longer 'problems', no longer anybody's 'fault', but were political issues. Out of this immediate experience feminism revalued the private and the personal, challenging the division of the sexes into separate spheres.

These political arguments also influenced feminist aesthetics, and are relevant to any attempt to transform an experience of oppression into a theory of oppression. The principal question is this: what relationship should a new, feminist aesthetic have to the culture of oppression and marginality which has traditionally moulded women's artistic work? This marginality brings particular repercussions in its wake when it is attached to an ideological concept of femininity and the 'feminine sphere'. Here a metonymic chain of meanings and resonances come into play, fettering women's cultural possibilities. The chain is a series of loose, associative links: woman, stability, the home, private emotion, family, domestic labour and decorative arts. But these links can only acquire meaning in opposition to another chain: man, mobility, work, transcendence, politics, productive labour and art. Thus an opposition develops between the interior and the exterior, the private female and public male as though

14 Sheila Rowbotham, Lynne Segal and Hilary Wainright, *Beyond the Fragments* (Merlin Press, 1979). For another approach, see Elizabeth Fox Genovese, 'The Personal Is Not Political Enough', *Marxist Perspectives* 8 (Winter 1979–80).

the feminine sphere was there primarily to give meaning and significance to its opposite.[15]

Walter Benjamin comments on the institutionalisation of the public/private distinction around the home:

> Under Louis-Philippe the private citizen entered upon the historical scene… For the private citizen, for the first time the living-space became distinguished from the place of work. The former constituted itself as the interior. The office was its complement. The private citizen who in the office took reality into account, required of the interior that it should support him in his illusions. The necessity was all the more pressing since he had no intention of adding social pre-occupations to his business ones. In the creation of his private environment he suppressed them both. From this sprang the phantasmagorias of the interior.[16]

Benjamin omits to mention that these phantasmagorias could only exist under the management of a wife. The home, on the scale envisaged here by the private citizen, only materialises as an effect of marriage.

It can be argued that, as women had been 'relegated', so had their creativity. Woman decorated her sphere with applied arts; the personal, private and domestic are the raw material of her self-expression. There is a danger here that a creativity produced by a social condition (the interior/exterior split) should then be theorised as *specific* to women and naturally expressive of 'femininity' as such. There is an important difference between 'femininity as such' and exploring a sphere which is not only assigned to women in a social division of labour, but is neglected and despised by men. In this sense the domestic, and the private lives it generates, are like uncolonised territory or virgin soil, untouched by the masculine. There are several positions that feminist aesthetics can adopt in response to this quandary. Women artists can embrace the domestic and personal, accepting their sphere and using it as a source of imagery and experience, simultaneously paying tribute to the historic relegation

---

15 In *Old Mistresses* (Routledge & Kegan Paul, 1981), Rozsika Parker and Griselda Pollock argue that this secondary organisation of masculine/feminine antinomy into social and cultural spheres dates from the Victorian period, and comment, 'for women artists have not acted outside cultural history, as many commentators seem to believe, but rather they have been impelled to act within it from a place other than that occupied by men'.

16 Walter Benjamin, 'Louis-Philippe or the Interior', in *Charles Baudelaire: Lyric Poet in the Era of High Capitalism* (New Left Books, 1973).

of women. But this position can, and should, lead very quickly to analysis of the female condition rather than a celebration of it.

Frida Kahlo's paintings emerge directly out of her life – her physical suffering and her emotional suffering. Living and working within the confines of her childhood home, she took herself as the main subject matter of art and painted her own image and her immediate relationships. Her art forms a material manifestation of her interior experiences, dreams and fantasies. It also seems to act as a 'decoration' of her life and relationships in a similar manner to the way she decorated herself and her house with the colours and objects of Mexican folk art. She painted her friends' portraits and gave her self-portraits to friends (such as the one she painted for Trotsky).

This private, personalised world that gave rise to her art seems encapsulated by the fact that she often actually painted from her bed, the most private part of the private world of the home. Kahlo continually gives the impression of consciously highlighting the interface of women's art and domestic space, as though in her life (and in her dress) she was drawing attention to the impossibility of separating the two. However, her art also acts as an ironic, bitter comment on women's experience. The feminine sphere is stripped of reassurance. The haven of male fantasy is replaced by the experience of pain, including the pain associated with her physical inability to live out a feminine role in motherhood. This pain is shown not only in *Childbirth* (1932) and *Henry Ford Hospital* (1932) but also in the theme of a 'mask' inherent in her self-portraits. The masks fall away, revealing the wounds inflicted by physical illness and accident (her damaged spine, her fractured leg) merging with the wounds inflicted by Rivera, the pain caused by his infidelities, as, for instance, in *Unos Cuantos Piquetitos* (A Few Small Snips) (1935), where a man is shown inflicting the wounds on a woman's body.

In her *Self-Portrait with Cropped Hair* (1940), painted after Rivera left her in 1939, she makes yet another leap from the interior pain caused by her love for Diego to the wound left on the female body by castration. Here, surely, is a direct reference to Freud. Kahlo's painting seems to move through a process of stripping away layers, that of the actual skin over a wound, that of the mask of beauty over the reality of pain. Then moving, like an infinite regress, out of the physical into the interior world of fantasy and the unconscious. Perhaps the most important aspect of this stripping away is its implicit rejection of any separation between the real and the psycho-analytic, an assertion of the reality of forces and fantasies that are of all the greater significance because they cannot be seen. Her use of metaphor and iconography is the means that enables her to give concrete form, in art, to interior experience. In this sense she takes the 'interior', offered as the feminine sphere, the male retreat from public life, and reveals the other 'interior' behind it, that of female suffering, vulnerability and self-doubt. Frida Kahlo provides an extremely rare voice for this sphere which, almost by definition, lacks an adequate means of expression or a language.

Tina Modotti gradually transformed herself from being an object of beauty, used in the art of others, into a professional photographer. As Weston's model, assistant and, finally, artistic apprentice, her concept of photography was initially dominated by his aestheticism. Gradually her work shows her searching for her own direction, and gaining confidence as her political commitment changed her way of looking at the world. Her photographs do not lose their sense of form; but her priorities change.

During the period when she was deeply absorbed in Mexican political life, Tina's photographs reveal two rather different strands. These different approaches seem to reflect and comment on both the social and political division between the sexes and Tina's own position as a woman photographer. Politics was primarily the sphere of men. In her photographs of Mexican political life, Tina used her background of formal aestheticism to produce an ordered and abstract rhetoric of revolutionary imagery. Her 'slogan' photographs reflect this aspect of her work, but her photographs of workers and political meetings show the same approach. The use of formal patterns gives a sense of detachment from the people photographed and a commitment to the political idea expressed. She must very often have been the only woman at the meetings she photographed. On the other hand, a different approach produces another strand of work in her photographs of women and children. The images of hunger, the oppression of being a child and childbearing speak for themselves. The images are posed and composed but the gaze of the subjects themselves strikes directly into the camera and out of the print.

Tina's photographs are predominantly of people in public, exterior space. In her own life, she was continually on the move: an immigrant in one country, adopting the politics and culture of another, then, as an exile, travelling through Europe as a CP militant. She didn't decorate the places she lived in. Manuel Álvarez Bravo recalled, 'The walls of her studio were white and clean. Later she started to write some of Lenin's and Marx's phrases on them'.[17]

17 Manuel Álvarez Bravo, quoted in Mildred Constantine, *Tina Modotti: A Fragile Life* (Paddington Press, 1975), 112.

The fact that Kahlo and Modotti's choices were not developed within a consciousness of women's art defuses a polemic or antagonism between them. Furthermore the choices they made, consciously or unconsciously, were clearly linked to their own conditions of existence, class, sex, history, even chance, showing up the contingent aspects of artists' work that can so easily disappear under a cloud of genius. Particularly, what they wanted to do and what was possible for them to do, their desires and limitations, were defined by the fact that they were women, however different the kinds of work they produced may have been.

6. Roots and Movements I: Frida Kahlo

Frida Kahlo was born and died in the same house in Coyoacán, on the outskirts of Mexico City. The house is now the Frida Kahlo Museum. It is depicted in one of the paintings Frida Kahlo made of her family tree. The infant Frida stands naked in the courtyard, holding the blood-red ribbon which connects her to her grandparents. On her mother's side the ribbon leads up into the volcanic mountains of Mexico, on her father's, across the sea to an invisible Europe. The motif of the ribbon is echoed by the twisting form of the umbilical cord which joins Frida's foetus to her mother, superimposed on her bridal gown. Below the foetus, another twisting form, that of a sperm, is penetrating an ovum, which at the same time is being pollinated by a blood-red cactus flower. The imagery is typical of her work; not only is she placed in her family house but rooted in a landscape and, more generally, in the process of nature, participating in a compound animal, vegetable and mineral life.

In another painting, *Roots* (1943), Frida Kahlo paints herself stretched out on the *pedregal*, the volcanic rock of Mexico, leaning on one elbow, her hair loose, her long dress cut away to reveal an intricate web of branches growing in and through her body, each ending in a large green leaf and connected by root tendrils with the earth below. Artery, umbilical cord, root, tendril: in Frida Kahlo's paintings these symbolic connections merge into a single image as the life force is carried precariously between soil, stem and body along convoluted and precarious veins. In the *Self-Portrait as a Tehuana* (1943) the lace of her headdress merges into the fronds of plants in the background through a tracery of tendrils.[18] In *The Two Fridas* (1939) the vein which connects to a locket of her loved one, held

18 See Hayden Herrera, 'Self-Portrait of Frida Kahlo as a Tehuana', in *Heresies* 4 (1978–9).

in one hand by the 'Indian' Frida, is being severed with scissors by the hand of her counterpart, the 'European' Frida, so that the blood drips down onto her white dress.

It would be wrong to think of Frida Kahlo as cloistered or secluded, despite the injuries which physically inhibited her movements, and her intense attachment to her native home and land. In some ways it would be easily possible to exaggerate the 'rootedness' of Frida Kahlo. She travelled extensively in the United States, firstly with Rivera, then on her own account when she was recognised as a painter in her own right, and also for medical reasons. She visited Europe after André Breton returned to Paris full of enthusiasm for her work. Nor did she live continuously in the Blue House even while she was in Mexico. It was there that Trotsky lived and the Dewey Commission prepared its report on Stalin's trials and purges of the late 1930s.

Nonetheless, Frida Kahlo developed her own sense of 'rootedness' and 'Mexican-ness' to an extreme degree. She wore Mexican dress and Mexican jewellery, transforming herself, so to speak, into a Mexican artefact. She was noted especially for her use of Tehuana costume – the long dresses of the women of Tehuantepec in southern Mexico who enjoyed a mythic reputation for their personal and economic independence.

For a while, when she visited New York and Paris for her exhibitions, Frida Kahlo's style was even taken up in high-fashion circles, featured in *Vogue* and adapted as a 'look' by Schiaparelli.[19] In a way, this suggests how much artifice there was in her 'rootedness', the extent to which her presentation of self *como Tehuana* was inextricably bound up with masquerade and a taste both for the archaic and the ornamental.

The same structure of feeling and sense of style comes out in her choice of art-historical models and pictorial schemes. At first sight, Frida Kahlo's paintings could be taken for those of a 'naive'. There is an element of this appreciation in Breton's celebration of Frida Kahlo as a spontaneous surrealist. It is true, too, that she never had any formal tuition as a painter and was largely self-taught – she began painting as something to do while bedridden after the road accident which incapacitated her in 1925. Her first paintings could perhaps be properly called 'naive'. But after her entry into the milieu of the muralist renaissance and her marriage to Diego Rivera, it is clear that she could hardly have remained naive about the kind of artistic choices that she made, even if they were suited to a reliance on intensity and vigour of conception rather than technical skill or painterly touch.

19 See Bertram D. Wolfe, 'Rise of Another Rivera', *Vogue*, 1 November 1938.

The Mexican renaissance saw a revival of interest in certain specific forms of popular and traditional art: *pulquería* painting, *retablos* and *ex-votos*, traditional portraiture and popular prints, as well as a more general interest in folk art.[20] This aesthetic 'going to the people' served the aims both of popular nationalism and political radicalism, on the one hand, and of the modernist attack on academicism and the institution of 'fine arts' on the other. Popular forms were celebrated and praised by most of the leading Mexican artists of the time – Rivera, Orozco, even Weston – but nobody took them to heart as much as Frida Kahlo, who not only reproduced their conventions but found ways of assimilating their typical subject-matter in her own personal preoccupations and 'symptoms'.

Ex-voto paintings were particularly important to her. Dozens of them which she collected are still on display in the Kahlo house today. They were paintings made on sheets of tin to be nailed up in church as thank-offering after a miraculous recovery from accident or disaster.[21] They are usually in three parts. At the top is the figure of the saint, the saviour or the virgin, whose aid was invoked and who effected the miracle. In the middle is a graphic and often gory depiction of the disaster or affliction. At the base is a written inscription expressing gratitude and recounting the details of the incident. Frida Kahlo uses this form particularly directly in the painting titled *Marxism Can Cure the Sick* (n.d.), in which Marx is shown in the place of the holy figure and Frida Kahlo herself is being cured, throwing away her crutches. Other works, like *Henry Ford Hospital*, show the catastrophe in savage detail, without offering any hope of recovery or amelioration.

It is worth stressing that *ex-voto* painting was already long in decline when rediscovered during the 1920s. The paintings emulated by Frida Kahlo had their heyday in the mid-nineteenth century. *Pulquería* painting (murals on the walls of *pulque* shops, where the cheapest form of alcohol was sold) and popular printmaking still existed during the 1920s, though they were to become extinct very soon afterwards, except for conscious revival by artists – Frida Kahlo herself painted a *pulquería* with a team of students in the 1940s, when it was already a clearly archaising project. The discovery of popular forms was essentially a discovery of what was already in danger of being lost, their adoption by artists a conscious revival and prolongation beyond their normal historical span. Later *ex-votos*

20 See Jean Charlot, *An Artist on Art*, vol. 2 (University Press of Hawaii, 1972).

21 See Gloria Kay Giffords, *Mexican Folk Retablos* (University of Arizona Press, 1974).

showed an influence of 'chromos' and comic strips which is absent from Frida Kahlo's 'historicist' use of the type.

In fact, the 'historicist' aspect of modernism comes out with great clarity in Mexico. In the first place, 'ancient' history was chronologically much closer and also in many ways culturally closer. The archaism of the Paris avant-garde took painters either back beyond antiquity – to ancient Egypt or, as with Picasso, pre-Latin Spain – or else out to the colonies, to forms of art which were brought back to the metropolis as the cultural plunder of imperialism. In Mexico the situation was very different. Aztec culture was only centuries rather than millennia in the past. By the time that the Aztec capital of Tenochtitlan was taken and razed by the Spanish, Michelangelo had already completed the Sistine Chapel, and Raphael and Leonardo were both dead. Pre-Columbian is much more nearly co-extensive with pre-Raphaelite than with Egyptian or Mycenaean. The city of Tenochtitlan was founded in the thirteenth century and fell in the early *cinquecento* – the Aztec era was simultaneous with the Italian Renaissance, and the sack of Tenochtitlan by Cortés took place in the same decade as the sack of Rome by his overlord, Charles V.

Thus the murals of Giotto, Piero and Mantegna which Rivera and Siqueiros studied and sketched were directly contemporary with the Aztec civilisation to which they turned back in the 1920s. Moreover, the actual language of the Aztecs (Nahuatl) was still being spoken and the Indian substructures of Mexican culture ('idols behind altars' in Anita Brenner's phrase) were still clearly visible.[22] Finally the Indian peoples had at last re-entered the mainstream of Mexican history during the revolution. Zapata's demands for land reform were posed and understood as demands for a return to pre-conquest forms of village organisation. A political history was being discovered and revived as well as an artistic one. Just as in the English Revolution appeals were made to the Saxon past before the conquest and feudal rule identified with the Norman yoke, so in the Mexican revolution, appeals to the pre-conquest Indian past still had a political value. It is for this reason, among others, that it was possible for political and artistic avant-gardes to overlap in Mexico in a way that they never could in Europe.

Hence the artistic avant-garde, once the crucial decision had been taken to retreat from any move into abstraction, was able to use popular forms not as a means of facilitating communication but as a means of constructing a mythic past whose effectiveness could be felt in the

22 Anita Brenner, *Idols Behind Altars* (Payson & Clark, 1929). This book contained photographs by Modotti and Weston.

present. Thereby it brought itself into line with the revolutionary impetus towards reconstructing the mythic past of the nation. Though Frida Kahlo was not herself a 'history painter' like Rivera, she also worked from the point where 'avant-garde modernism', 'popular historicism' and 'mythic nationalism' met, in her own favourite genre – self-portraiture. Popular forms made it possible for her to develop a form of self-portraiture which transcended the limits of the purely iconic and allowed her to use narrative and allegory. In this way she created a mode of emblematic autobiography steeped in *mexicanidad*.

Frida Kahlo's roots in Mexico allowed her to participate in the avant-garde precisely because the Mexican revolution was not just the destruction of an old Porfirian, feudal, colonial past, but at the same time the creation of a new one, rooted in the suppressed pre-Columbian culture and the rejected popular traditions. In her painting *My Nurse and I* (1937) the Indian form of the nurse, reminiscent of an Aztec goddess, is fused with the colonial Catholic motif of the Madonna and child, using the popular non-academic form in which the child is depicted out of proportion in relation to the mother with an enlarged, adult head – a self-portrait in fact. Thereby she both allegorises her own life and represents a mythic Mexican history in formal as well as figurative terms. In the background drops, like the drops of milk from the breasts, are falling like rain or manna: thus the world of nature is given its role as nourishing mother. Autobiography is encompassed by history and history by nature.

7. Roots and Movements II: Tina Modotti

Tina Modotti's relationship to Mexican culture was quite different from Frida Kahlo's though she took part in the same artistic movement. Tina Modotti's life was (almost) nomadic – born in Italy, emigrated with her family to the United States, moved from San Francisco to Los Angeles and then from California to Mexico, expelled from Mexico on a ship bound for Rotterdam, political asylum in Berlin, flight to Moscow where her work for the Comintern sent her first to Paris, then to Spain, and finally flight again to France, after the defeat of the Republic by Franco and the Fascist forces in the Civil War, and a final exile, back in Mexico, where she died in 1942, only forty-five years old. The ten years or so which she spent in Mexico (first visit in 1922, a second more or less settled stay from 1923 to 1930, the final exile from April 1939 until her death) was the longest period spent in a single country during her adult life. It is also the period when almost all her work as a photographer was done.

While she was still in Los Angeles, Tina Modotti was part of a group interested in Mexico and Mexican art. Her first husband, the artist and poet Roubaix de l'Abrie Richey, died in Mexico during a visit in 1922. Tina Modotti went to Mexico City to join him, but he died of smallpox before she arrived. He had already made friends among Mexican artists and Tina Modotti too found herself increasingly drawn towards Mexico. In the autumn of the same year, after her return to the United States, an exhibition of Mexican folk art was sent to Los Angeles, and her determination to return grew. The next year she left again for Mexico, this time with Edward Weston, the photographer. Robo Richey had already urged Weston to come to Mexico, just before he died, and join him in what he called 'an artists' paradise'. Weston's ideas about photography were essentially decided before he left for Mexico. In the first place, he was in reaction against 'pictorialist' photography, with its lack of focus, its atmospheric effects and its imitation of etching and painting. He wanted a photography which was clean and sharply outlined. Weston revered the modernist slogan 'Form follows function' and he wanted photographic forms which followed the function of the camera in its capacity to record with detail and accuracy. But besides distrusting pictorialism, Weston also rejected documentary realism and avant-garde photography – Man Ray or Moholy-Nagy. Documentary was not art and avant-gardism was another way of seeking effect and using camera trickery rather than straightforward photography. Weston's particular contribution was to find a different path: photographing ordinary objects or locations in the real world, clearly and straightforwardly, in order to bring out the formal values normally overlooked; to see with a trained and artistically sensitive eye the abstract formal compositions and textures of light and shade which could be elicited from ordinary reality and capture them precisely and without interference or mediation on his photographic plate. It was this aesthetic legacy which Tina Modotti, as his pupil, apprentice and eventually colleague, was to inherit.

In retrospect we can see close analogies between Weston's ideals for photography and those of Renger-Patzsch and the 'New Objectivity' photographers in Germany, or post-cubist purism and *l'esprit nouveau* in Paris. But Weston himself was very conscious of his own Americanism, of the need to break with European models of art. In fact, this was the driving force behind his modernism. The connection between Americanism, photography and avant-garde art had already been made in New

York by Stieglitz, who took a similar line. At the same time he felt stifled by the philistinism he felt in Los Angeles, where both avant-gardism and the claims of photography to art were still worse than suspect. He was naturally impressed by what he found in Mexico City, where cubist artists, such as Rivera, had rejected the Parisian aspects of cubism without abandoning avant-gardism – and at the same time been given massive public commissions. Even better – Rivera and the other muralists accepted photography as an equal art form.

Weston, however, could not accept revolutionary politics. He retained his North American individualism and distrust of socialism. Tina Modotti, whose Italian immigrant family was already socialist, identified rapidly with the political aspects of the Mexican revolution as well as the artistic. She joined the Communist Party and was active in political campaigns – in support of Sandino, for instance, and in opposition to Mussolini. It was during this period in fact that she met Frida Kahlo, through the Communist Party (Frida Kahlo was then in the youth movement) and, according to Kahlo's biographer, Hayden Herrera, introduced Kahlo to Diego Rivera, also of course a party member at that time.[23] At any event, for Tina Modotti, Mexico provoked both a rapid politicisation and a rapid development as a photographer in the manner of Weston. These two dimensions of her life and work, however, were in tension and part of the fascination of Modotti's photography lies in her efforts to overcome this tension.

During his time in Mexico Weston's preferred choices of subject for his photography were female nudes, Mexican folk toys and artefacts, clouds, plant and architectural forms, domestic objects (such as the toilet bowl he likened to the Victory of Samothrace). He also did many portrait heads, though he had a strong dislike for the idea of commercial portraiture (his main source of livelihood for much of the time). Weston also undertook some commissions – to photograph *pulquería* paintings for the magazine *Mexican Folkways* and, jointly with Tina Modotti, to provide the illustrations for *Idols Behind Altars*. His human subjects, then, were limited mainly to socially neutral objects, though with a definite bias towards the 'classically' rather than ornamentally folkloric (where, as he saw it, 'form followed function').

Tina Modotti's style of photography is clearly indebted to Weston. Like him she used a large-view camera or a Graflex, slightly more portable but still necessitating a tripod. Her compositions were consciously

23 Hayden Herrera, *Frida Kahlo* (forthcoming, 1982). [Published as *Frida: A Biography* (Harper & Row, 1983).]

geometrical, or 'elemental' as Weston might have put it. She did not crop photographs and she went for the same clean sharp-focus look as Weston. She used the same printing technique (like Weston, she frequently made palladium prints). Some of her photographs are on the verge of abstraction, as are many of Weston's – one of bamboo constructed simply around the parallel verticals of the stems or one of the rims of glasses (though this photograph is a double exposure, something Weston would never have allowed himself. Indeed, he half remonstrated with Tina at one point in his *Daybooks* because she made a print negative).[24]

However, Tina Modotti soon showed a much greater range of subject matter in her photographs than is to be found in Weston's work. To begin with, she took her camera out into the street and photographed people there. There are series of photographs of women in Tehuantepec, of scenes of mothers with infant children, of the poor (especially children) in Mexico City, of peasants on demonstrations or reading the Communist Party paper *El Machete*. These photographs retain the same formal preoccupations as Weston's despite their very different subjects. The hats of peasants on a demonstration echo the same circular forms as the glasses on a table. The formal composition of a photograph of a pregnant woman holding a naked infant on her hip is arranged with great geometrical clarity and without showing the faces of either mother or child. The geometrical character of her compositions is shown at its clearest in four photographs originally published in *Forma* in 1927[25] and described there as illustrations for a book of *estridentista* poetry by Germán List Arzubide.[26] These are of telephone wires, a gas tank, a construction worker among girders and the corner of a staircase. All are composed with an emphasis on the geometrical outlines and tracings of their subjects. Except for the staircase, however, they are all scenes of modern industry. This is in accord with the tenets of *estridentismo* which of all Mexican art movements was closest to European constructivism and futurism in its emphasis on the urban, the modern and the industrial as well as the revolutionary. But it is quite unlike Weston's response to Mexico. Just before his journey south Weston had been photographing industrial scenes but in Mexico he returned to domestic subjects. Modotti also photographed workers loading bananas and carrying timber with the same formal concerns.

24 *The Daybooks of Edward Weston*, ed. Nancy Newhall, vol. 1 (Horizon Press, 1961).

25 See the magazine *Forma*, ed. Gabriel Fernández Ledesma, 10 (1927).

26 See Carleton Beals, *Mexican Maze* (Lippincott, 1931).

The most remarkable geometrical compositions which Modotti used were in her series of photographs which used as elements objects emblematic of the Mexican revolution; bandolier, corn-cob, sickle, guitar. In this series the subject matter is clearly not found in situ but the product of deliberate mise-en-scène. The choice is determined not for its denotation but for its connotation – there is a move towards conceptual as well as formal abstractions. The connotations involved are those not only of *mexicanidad* but also of revolution – the sickle (especially as a composed element) and the bandolier. Weston also, albeit with a slightly uneasy conscience, took to arranging his subject matter to bring out its formal qualities, but Modotti not only did this but also selected subject matter to reflect her political commitment.

After Tina Modotti was expelled from Mexico, on the grounds that she conspired to assassinate the President, she continued her photography in Germany (where it had already been published) but was discouraged by finding that photographers there used the Leica rather than the heavy camera she was used to. Her decision to abandon photography seems connected with her inability to change her whole style of work as a photographer, as the move from Graflex to Leica would have demanded, rather than simply assigning photography a lower priority in favour of direct political work. Workers' photography movements in Germany had developed around news magazines in an attempt to match the use of photography in the establishment news media. The preconceptions of this style of photography were completely different from those implicit in Tina Modotti's work, which had been much closer in many respects to 'New Objectivity' photography.

In Mexico, Tina Modotti had worked with Workers International Relief, the worldwide organisation founded and directed by Willi Münzenberg. WIR not only ran mass-circulation photo journals and magazines but produced films, both in Germany and the Soviet Union (the Dudow/Brecht *Kuhle Wampe*, for instance), and published books.[27] It was an enormously complex and far-reaching organisation which acted both as a propaganda machine and a patron of the arts. It was also financially independent, which gave Münzenberg the possibility of pursuing a more flexible policy than would have been possible if he had had to rely directly on either the German or the Soviet Communist Party for his operations.

---

27 For this period see Terry Dennett, Jo Spence (eds), *Photography/Politics: One* (Photography Workshop, 1979), and John Willett, *The New Sobriety: Art and Politics in the Weimar Period 1917–33* (Pantheon Books, 1978).

Münzenberg's talents as an entrepreneur were suited to an age of mechanical reproduction. Within the mass media, photography is just an element, juxtaposed with print, part of a layout, without the singularity which is the mark of the aesthetic object. Tina Modotti's background had trained her to see a photograph as an art object, to be looked at in its own right, with its own intrinsic value, rather than as one component of a wider mosaic. While in Germany her photographs were taken up and published in illustrated magazines; in Mexico they were shown in exhibitions, mounted and hanging on a wall, like paintings. This was not simply a question of art in opposition to journalism, but of quite different ways of contextualising and looking at photographs. In a famous essay Walter Benjamin supplied the theoretical arguments underpinning the priority which Münzenberg gave to the mass media, arguing in favour of the 'journalisation' of art. Benjamin says 'politicisation' rather than 'journalisation' but it is clear from his essay that he is really concerned with the latter and 'politicisation' is a supplement: 'In some cases today's films can also promote revolutionary criticism of social conditions, even of the distribution of property. However, our present study is no more specifically concerned with this than is the film production of Western Europe.'[28]

Faced with the pressure to 'journalise' her art, Tina Modotti gave it up altogether. She belonged, in a sense, to a previous epoch, in which photography was an artisanal product, closer, despite the modernity of its technology, to folk art or popular urban art than to the mass media. The photographer had a small studio or workshop, received personal commissions, held public exhibitions, and so on. The photographs took a long time to conceive and even to make as a result of the detailed attention paid to the making of each print. Benjamin assumed that, in a secular society, this kind of activity would most naturally be justified in terms of 'art for art's sake' or 'pure' art. Certainly Weston's example does support this assumption. But Tina Modotti showed how this kind of photography could itself be politicised, without necessarily being 'journalised'. Moreover, her work had a crucial influence on other artists: Manuel Álvarez Bravo, the leading Mexican photographer of the next generation, and Sergei Eisenstein, whose interest in Mexico was awakened by reading *Idols Behind Altars*. In fact, Modotti's 'emblematic' political photographs and her photographs of life in Mexico are analogous in a number of ways to Eisenstein's own practice – in terms of *typage*, the mode of composition and even the concept of 'intellectual montage'.

28 Walter Benjamin, 'The Work of Art in the Age of Mechanical Reproduction', in *Illuminations* (Fontana, 1970).

8. The Discourse of the Body

The art of both Kahlo and Modotti had a basis in their bodies: through injury, pain and disability in Frida Kahlo's case, through an accident of beauty in Tina Modotti's. Frida Kahlo sought an iconic vocabulary which could both express and mask the reality of the body. Tina Modotti, whose career began as a film actress and a model, redirected the look which had focused on her outwards when she herself became a photographer. Kahlo's art became predominantly one of self-portraiture; Modotti's one of depiction of others – predominantly women, but seen with an eye quite different from the one that had looked at her.

Frida Kahlo had about thirty operations in the years between her accident in 1925 and her death in 1954. In the accident her spine was fractured, her pelvis shattered and her foot broken. For long periods she was bedridden, in pain and incapacitated. She was unable to have the child she desired and suffered miscarriages and medical abortions. In some respects her painting was a form of therapy, a way of coping with pain, warding off despair and regaining control over the image of her crushed and broken body. Painting brought pleasure, hope and power over herself. It made possible both a triumphant reassertion of narcissism and a symbolisation of her pain and suffering. She painted originally for herself, and it was not really till Breton recognised the value and fascination of her work for others that she conceived the possibility of holding exhibitions and marketing the paintings.

The vocabulary which Frida Kahlo found and used was primarily that of traditional Mexican Catholic art, especially depictions of martyrdom and of the Passion. There is an explicit use of the imagery of the Passion: the wounds of the scourging and the crucifixion, the knotted cord, the ring of thorns, the simultaneous shining of sun and moon during the Tenebrae. The style and iconography are those of popular baroque, in which intensity of expression is given precedence over beauty or dignity, and like most popular forms there is an archaic, almost medieval aspect to the representation, a love of minute detail, a disparity between foreground figure and background setting, a disregard for proportion and perspective. The graphic is systematically favoured rather than the perceptually realistic.

In particular, Kahlo uses the device of the 'emblem'. In *Henry Ford Hospital* her body on the bed is surrounded by a set of emblematic objects, like those surrounding the crucified Christ in an allegory of redemption. Emblems and attributes are graphic signs which carry a conventional meaning, often in reference to a narrative subtext (attributes) or a common set of beliefs (emblems). At times, Frida Kahlo used complex allegorical schemes, as in *Moses* (1945), with an idiosyncratic personal iconography. Through the resources of emblems, she was able to transcribe her physical pain and suffering into a form of graphic language, which could be read by the spectator. The appeal is not to an imaginary identification with herself as subject of pain but as a symbolic reading of herself as vehicle for suffering as in *The Little Deer* (1946).[29] Hence the common reaction of horror rather than pity, itself associated more with 'low' than 'high' art.

Another mode of representing the body which she used was to draw detailed imagery from anatomical textbooks. Before her accident she had intended to study medicine and her injuries gave her a further reason for studying anatomy. Anatomical organs are often used as emblems – the bleeding heart of Catholic tradition, or the pelvis in *Henry Ford Hospital.* The accuracy of anatomical depiction contrasts with other stylistic aspects of her painting, drawn from an epoch and a *milieu* without precise anatomical knowledge. The effect produced is not only one of physical fragmentation and dislocation but also a kind of anachronism.

Beauty is another form of accident, one that is prized rather than feared. Yet it is one which can bring with it its own burdens. After her expulsion from Mexico, the ship on which Tina Modotti was deported docked in New Orleans and she was detained for eight days in the Immigration Station there. She wrote to Weston:

> The newspapers have followed me, and at times preceded me, with wolf-like greediness – here in the US everything is seen from the 'beauty' angle – a daily here spoke of my trip and referred to me as 'a woman of striking beauty' – other reporters to whom I refused an interview tried to convince me by saying they would just speak of 'how pretty I was' – to which I answered that I could not possibly see what 'prettiness' had to do

29 The metaphor of the 'stricken deer' has a tradition in Mexican poetry. See, for instance, 'Verses Expressing the Feelings of a Lover', by Sor Juana Inés de La Cruz (Juana de Asbaje, 1651–95):

> *If thou seest the wounded stag*
> *that hastens down the mountain-side,*
> *seeking, stricken, in icy stream*
> *ease for its hurt,*
> *and thirsting plunges in the crystal waters,*
> *not in ease, in pain it mirrors me.*

Trans. Samuel Beckett, in Octavio Paz (ed.), *Anthology of Mexican Poetry* (Indiana University Press, 1958). On the theory of the emblem, and Sor Juana's practice of it, see Robert J. Clements, *Picta Poesis* (Edizioni di Storia e Letteratura, 1960).

> with the revolutionary movement nor with the expulsion of Communists – evidently women here are measured by a motion picture standard.[30]

Ironic, in a way, that this letter should have gone to Weston who did more than anyone else to promote and perpetuate the legend of Tina Modotti's beauty, both through his daybooks and through the photographs for which she was model, culminating with the famous series of her lying nude on the *azotea* in 1924. Tina Modotti also acted as a model for Diego Rivera when he was painting murals in the Agricultural College at Chapingo in 1926. Earlier she had been an actress – playing the fiery Latin vamp in early Hollywood Westerns. When Tina Modotti herself became a photographer she photographed primarily women, but the contrast with Weston's approach could not be greater.

Weston became famous as a photographer of the female nude. He claimed that it was the formal quality of the shape of the female body which interested him and that any erotic motive (and there certainly was one, because he had affairs with the great majority of his models) was suspended in the photographic work. His particular form of voyeurism, of taking woman as an object of gaze, was justified in the terms of pure aesthetic form. About the comments of others on the erotic quality of his work he wrote: 'Others must get from them what they bring to them: evidently they do!'[31] implying also that an erotic interpretation might follow from the 'sexual suppression' he himself did not suffer from. The fact remains, however, that his nude photographs of Tina Modotti are often taken from above, looking down on her as she lies passively, sunbathing or asleep, on the ground, in a conventional pose.

Tina Modotti's photographs were not of 'beauties' but of peasant and proletarian women, marked by the conditions of their lives. Often they are mothers with small children, their bodies framed to emphasise not their own form but that of their interaction with the children. That is to say, they are represented in the process of activity and work, rather than isolated in a pose for the camera. The camera position is often below head height (it is only men who are photographed from above, partly to bring out the circular shape of their hat brims). In her photographs of women especially, the careful organisation of the composition is not allowed to override the directness of the look.

---

30 Letter from Tina Modotti to Edward Weston, quoted in Constantine, *Tina Modotti*, 175.

31 *The Daybooks of Edward Weston*, vol. 2, 32.

For Frida Kahlo beauty was inextricably bound up with masquerade. In her self-portraits, whatever the degree of pain implied, by tears or even wounds, her face remains severe and expressionless with an unflinching gaze. At the same time the mask-like face is surrounded by luxuriant growths, accoutrements, ornaments and familiars – a monkey, a doll, a hairless dog. The ornament borders on fetishism, as does all masquerade, but the imaginary look is that of self-regard, therefore a feminine, non-male and narcissistic look. There is neither coyness nor cruelty, none of the nuance necessary to the male eroticisation of the female look. The masquerade serves the purpose of displacement from a traumatic childhood of the subject herself, ever-remembered, ever-repeated.

Throughout Kahlo's work there is a particular fetishisation of nature, an imagery of fecundity and luxuriant generation which is clearly a defence against her knowledge of her own barrenness, one of the products of her childhood accident. Veins, fronds and vines often merge with the body itself. There are three modes of self-portraiture: the body damaged, the body masked and ornamented, the body twined and enmeshed with plants. In some paintings even the rays of the sun are incorporated in the web. Fruit in still lifes become part of the body, flesh-like, or like skulls with vacant eyes. It is as though compensation for her barrenness, and a defence against trauma, are condensed in pullulating images of cosmic and natural vitality sometimes counterposed with images of barrenness itself, of lava rock and broken ligneous forms.

In a sense, nature is being turned into a complex of signs. Similarly the body itself becomes a bearer of signs, some legible, some esoteric. Masquerade becomes a mode of inscription, by which the trauma of injury and its effects are written negatively in metaphor. It is as if the intensity of the trauma brings with it a need to transfer the body from the register of image to that of pictography. Thus faces are read as masks, and ornaments as emblems and attributes. This discourse of the body is itself inscribed with a kind of codex of nature and cosmos, in which sun and moon, plant and animal, are pictograms. At the same time this pictographic effect de-eroticises the imagery.

Hayden Herrera, writing about Frida Kahlo, writes of 'her nearly beautiful face in the mirror'.[32] The aptness of 'nearly' carries with it a covert recognition of the overt ruin seen in *The Broken Column* against which beauty has been constructed as a defence. It is the artifice, the masquerade, which produces the uneasy feeling of slight mismatch between ostensible features and ostensible subject.

32 Herrera, *Frida Kahlo*.

Tina Modotti, on the other hand, suffered from the inscription of beauty on her body by others. It is somehow appropriate that while Frida Kahlo is remembered for her jewellery and her extravagant costumes, Tina Modotti is remembered as one of the first women in Mexico to wear jeans.

It is the discourse of the body, together with its political and psychoanalytic implications, which provides a continuity for us with Mexico between the wars. The history of art, as Viktor Shklovsky observed, proceeds by knight's moves, through the oblique and unexpected rather than the linear and predictable. If the art of Frida Kahlo and Tina Modotti has appeared to be detached from the mainstream, this by no means entails any loss of value. In many ways their work may be more relevant than the central traditions of modernism, at a time when, in the light of feminism, the history of art is being revalued and remade.

* * *

Catalogue essay co-written with Laura Mulvey published in Frida Kahlo and Tina Modotti *(Whitechapel Art Gallery, 1982), accompanying the exhibition of the same name at the Whitechapel Art Gallery, London, 26 March to 2 May 1982, curated by Mulvey and Wollen in collaboration with Mark Francis. The exhibition toured to Haus am Waldsee, Berlin, 14 May to 11 July 1982; Kunstverein, Hamburg, 29 July to 12 September; Kunstverein, Hannover, 26 September to 7 November; Kulturhuset, Stockholm, 19 November 1982 to 30 January 1983; Grey Art Gallery, New York University, New York, 1 March to 16 April 1983; and Museo Nacional de Arte, Mexico City, 1 June to 31 August 1983.*

Eisenstein in Mexico

Each of the planned six parts of *Qué Viva México* was to be dedicated to an artist: Siqueiros, Charlot, Goya, Orozco, Rivera, Posada.

This film will bring together paintings by these 'patrons' of the film, as well as other material that inspired Eisenstein, such as the Weston and Modotti photographs from *Idols Behind Altars*, with surviving footage shot by Eisenstein. It will not, repeat *not*, seek to recreate Eisenstein's film, but to understand its origins and its structure. It will also use Eisenstein's drawings made in Mexico, which show scenes from the film at sketch stage and the development of Eisenstein's pictorial ideas. Though many of the materials were destroyed in the Cineteca fire, excellent replicas exist and other drawings not in that collection have survived.

This film should coincide with the exhibition of Eisenstein's drawings scheduled for MOMA (Oxford) December '86, Manchester March/April '87, and the Hayward, June '87.

Peter Wollen.

* * *

Treatment for unmade film, c. 1985. Previously unpublished.

Introduction to *J. G. Posada, Messenger of Mortality*

José Guadalupe Posada died in 1913, soon after the beginning of the Mexican Revolution. Although he had spent a prolific life as an engraver and etcher, working mainly for the penny press, he was not well-known or widely acclaimed. In fact, he was buried in a pauper's grave by neighbours, only one of whom was literate.[1] Even today very little is known about his life. His rise to fame, the growth of the Posada legend, is due to the generation of artists who changed the direction of Mexican art in the years after the Revolution. The painter Dr Atl, the most persistent early pioneer of modernism in Mexico, and the young French immigrant, Jean Charlot, one of the group of muralists around Diego Rivera, were the first to notice Posada's work in the new artistic context of the post-revolutionary years.[2] Charlot, who saw his first Posada prints in 1920, followed up his discovery, showed prints to other painters and wrote the first biographical and critical essays on Posada's work, in the early twenties. In time, other artists – including Rivera, José Clemente Orozco and David Alfaro Siqueiros – took up Posada's cause, often in hyperbolic terms, and acknowledged their debt, direct or indirect, to the humble popular printmaker. The legend was born.[3]

Now that Posada is respected, studied, collected and exhibited, we are aware of the breadth and range of his work. But his entry into art history

1 Antonio Rodríguez, *Posada* (Editorial Domes, 1977).

2 Ron Tyler (ed.), *Posada's Mexico* (Library of Congress, 1979).

3 Jean Charlot, 'Mexican Print-Makers I: Manilla', 'Mexican Print-Makers II: Posada', in *Art from the Mayans to Disney* (Sheed & Ward, 1939).

was due especially to the more lurid prints that he made for the small press owner and publisher, Antonio Vanegas Arroyo, who employed Posada to illustrate the topical ballads and sensational *canards* he wrote and hawked around the streets and at fairs, pilgrimages and public gatherings. Above all, it was the *calaveras*, vivid and lively skeletons and skulls with grinning teeth, dancing, cycling, playing the guitar, plying their trades, drinking, masquerading, which seized the imagination of artists and writers. The *calaveras* were produced to be sold on the 2nd of November, the Mexican Day of the Dead, eye-catching skeletons, accompanied by jocular and satirical verses, designed to entertain and enliven the festivities.

Originally, the demand for Posada prints came 'from below', from the poor and the illiterate. The new appreciation of them 'from above' formed part of a much wider discovery and re-evaluation of Mexican popular art and imagery of different kinds. Posada prints took their place alongside such other forms as *pulquería* paintings, the fantastic scenes painted on the walls of cheap dives selling *pulque* and other kinds of grog and rotgut, rather like inn signs, and *retablos*, the *ex-voto* paintings, usually on tin, which were nailed up on church walls to commemorate some miraculous recovery from disaster or escape from near death, due to the invocation of a favourite saint, vividly portraying the catastrophe in question and the rescue from it, in a kind of comic-strip-cum-naive style. Posada's etchings and engravings seemed in the same register, showing the same startling directness, grim humour and unpredictable imagination.

Moreover, in Posada's case, a crucial connection can be discerned between the *calaveras* and the art of the pre-Columbian period, with its own profusion of skulls and pressing reminders of death. Indeed, the roots of the Day of the Dead were customarily traced back beyond their explicit origin in Spanish Catholicism to an older, implicit connection with the ancient Indian cults of human sacrifice and bloodletting, with their grisly furniture of skull racks and bloody obsidian knives.[4] It may seem a far cry from the top-hatted cyclist or skirt-hitching fandango dancer of Posada's *calavera* to the cruel grandeur of the pre-Columbian priesthood and its rites, but Posada's tiny storefront workshop at No. 5 Santa Inés Street (now calle de la Moneda) was, after all, only a stone's throw from the site of the great Aztec temple pyramid of Tenochtitlan.[5]

The artists of the Mexican renaissance were in full revolt against a tradition of dependence on European, especially Spanish, academic art.

---

4 María Teresa Pomar, *El Día de los Muertos* (Fort Worth Art Museum, 1987).

5 Robert V. Childs and Patricia B. Altman, *Vive tu Recuerdo* (UCLA Museum of Cultural History, 1982).

They wanted to replace it with an art whose genealogy would go back before the Conquest, which would be original to Mexico, popular and authentic. Partly, of course, as with other nationalist and revolutionary movements, this led to a revival of interest in folk art, in Indian toys, costume and pottery, the traditional arts of the village. But it also extended to the urban vernacular art of Posada. Posada was a trained draughtsman and printmaker (he attended the municipal trade school in his native town of Aguascalientes) and an unabashed commercial artist, seeking employment wherever he could find it and carrying out the commissions offered him by editors and publishers. But, in some ways, this made him closer to the fine artists and avant-gardists who admired his work – they, too, were trained and working to order, though from a very different background and with very different aesthetic values and ambitions. Posada formed a link between the folk tradition and the art of the muralists.

Indeed, muralism was a particular mode of 'street art', which could be compared with popular printmaking. Many, though not all, of Rivera's murals were painted on exterior walls, designed to be seen and looked at by passers-by on some other business, not art lovers, private owners or museum visitors. Muralism was presented and defended as a public form. Catchpenny prints and broadsheets, Posada's works were public too, though in a different way. Their place was the street, where they were hawked and sold by pedlars to a popular and often illiterate audience. They were not collected or exhibited in galleries. They illustrated *corridos*, ballads and verses, just as murals decorated buildings, both outside the confines of pure art. Like Rivera's murals, they often had topical themes and competed for attention with striking images and compositions, seeking to please an unsophisticated public.

The muralists themselves turned their hands to printmaking, following the impetus given by Charlot's rediscovery of Posada. After the Syndicate of Revolutionary Painters, Sculptors and Engravers of Mexico was founded in 1922, it published a magazine, *El Machete*, which was modelled on the old penny press, with more woodcuts and illustrations than text, many of them illustrating *corridos* and verse lampoons. Siqueiros and Xavier Guerrero were the most prolific contributors, although *El Machete* also carried work by Rivera and Orozco. (Orozco had himself begun his career as a cartoonist, for the well-known magazine *Ahuizote*, so that he had a much more direct link to the world of Posada than the other artists.)[6] *El Machete* was, of course, an agitational vehicle, highly politicised

6 José Clemente Orozco, *An Autobiography* (University of Texas Press, 1962).

in its content and Posada, too, was often presented, retrospectively, as a 'political artist', although in fact political topics are relatively rare in his output and he was capable of doing both pro-Díaz and anti-Díaz, pro-Madero and anti-Madero cartoons, presumably according to the political preference of his employers.

Today we can see how the post-revolutionary artists, in their choice of muralism as a form and in their enthusiasm for Posada, reflected an extreme 'phase two' version of modernism, which rejected not only academic and figurative painting, but easel painting as a genre. The denunciation of easel painting was at its strongest in the Soviet Union, in the writings of Tarabukhin and Arvatov, and in the manifestos and propaganda of the Constructivist movement. Although this aesthetic developed separately in Mexico there were, of course, close ties between the two countries, and the left wing of Mexican artists looked to Soviet artists for an example. Rivera had been a member of a largely Russian-exile milieu when he was in Paris and maintained his contacts after he left. Indeed, when he visited the Soviet Union in 1928, he signed the founding declaration of the October group of artists, which brought together architects, muralists, poster designers, book illustrators and cartoonists, on an explicit platform of 'public art' (implying the end of easel painting).

In fact, in some respects Posada was more like Rivera and the others than they might have imagined. He was not a native intuitive genius, but a trained artist who altered and adapted his style to accommodate his public. If we look at Posada's early work we can see the influence of European engravers and print artists (such as Cham or Grandville). His prints are detailed, finished and technically sophisticated. It is only later that he simplifies his style, producing work which is much cruder but often more striking. In much the same way, Rivera simplified his work, abandoning both his beaux arts training and the highly sophisticated speculation and composition of his Cubist period, to produce images which many have thought crude and too fluently figurative, with a popular audience in mind. For Posada, the motive force was ultimately commercial, whereas for Rivera it was political, but the trajectories were similar.

Posada was far from being an amateur, like the *Douanier* Rousseau, to whom he has sometimes been compared.[7] Nor was he an anonymous professional – he signed his work, unlike many other printmakers (though not all of it). It was the signature, of course, which first enabled Charlot to find out more about him and categorise prints under his name. His

7 T. J. Clark, *Image of the People* (Thames & Hudson, 1973).

workshop, round the corner from the art school of San Carlos, which both Rivera and Orozco attended at different times, also became part of the Posada legend. Both of them describe frequenting Posada's shop when they were at art school, thus enabling them to cast Posada not simply in the role of hero or precursor, but also teacher. Both claimed a direct contact (probably true for Orozco, but false for Rivera, at least according to Charlot – and Rivera, of course, was a notorious fabulator and mythomane!).

In this sense, it is wrong to see Posada simply as an 'influence'. His name and legend were constitutive in the establishment of the Mexican renaissance: they symbolised both an alternative tradition and crucially, a chain of succession. This particular role assigned to Posada was important both in relation to Mexicanism and in relation to Modernism. It gave credibility to claims to be part of an authentically Mexican artistic tradition, crossing both the class gap and the historic divide of the Revolution itself and, at the same time, guaranteed the modernity of the tradition by aligning it with the revival of interest in popular imagery among the European avant-garde. It was a way of solving the classic dilemma of revolutionary nationalism – how to be popular, authentic, traditional *and* modernising, all at the same time.

The European avant-garde had been interested in popular imagery at least since the time of the art critic and historian, Champfleury, and his friend, the painter Gustave Courbet. Champfleury's *Histoire de l'imagerie populaire* was published in 1869 (though he had first written about popular prints long before, in 1850). Courbet's paintings, of course, date from the same period – *The Meeting*, painted in 1854, derives from a popular print of the Wandering Jew, which Champfleury also used as the frontispiece for his book.[8] The next wave of interest in prints was dominated by the newly discovered Japanese prints which decisively influenced the early phase of Modernism, though it was perhaps their exotic rather than their popular qualities which were significant for the artists concerned. A third wave comes after the beginning of Cubism – which brought with it yet another re-evaluation of non-canonical and 'primitive' forms of art. It is especially worth noting also the use of Russian *lubki* (broadsheets and chapbooks) made by the Golden Fleece and Donkey's Tail artists, especially Mikhail Larionov, Natalia Goncharova and, a little later, Kazimir Malevich.[9]

8 Falla et. al., *French Popular Imagery: Five Centuries of Prints* (Arts Council of Great Britain, 1974).

9 Alla Sytova (ed.), *The Lubok* (Aurora Art Publishers, 1984).

Larionov was also a collector of popular prints, including examples of the French *images d'Épinal* and Japanese woodcuts, as well as the Russian *lubok*, which were shown at a large exhibition of popular imagery that he organised, with Goncharova, in April 1913. Larionov was also a friend of Rivera and a frequent visitor to his studio, while they were both in Paris. In general, Rivera was well-informed on Russian popular art, due to the exhibition which Nathalie Ehrenbourg, another friend, organised for the *Salon d'Automne* in the autumn of 1913 (where Rivera showed his early Cubist paintings). Indeed, it has been argued, by Ramón Favela, that it was these Russian influences that first induced Rivera to introduce Mexican motifs, such as *serape* stripes, into his Cubist work.[10] Certainly too, they prepared the ground for his immediate enthusiasm for Posada's work when it was shown to him by Charlot on his return to Mexico. In many ways Rivera saw the Mexican Revolution, and Mexican post-revolutionary art, through the lens of the Russian Revolution and Russian art.

In the Soviet Union, however, artists who had been influenced by the *lubki*, such as El Lissitzky or Vladimir Tatlin, moved away from them stylistically towards a much more abstract visual style or else, pulling in the opposite direction, towards the use of photography as a print medium, rather than woodcut or engraving. Evidently, this reflects the much greater impetus of a 'machine' aesthetic in the Soviet Union than in Mexico, as well as the demand for a 'proletarian' rather than a 'popular' art. Although there are some parallels with work like that of the *El Machete* artists, such as Vladimir Mayakovsky's 'ROSTA windows', most Soviet artists, even though working with posters, broadsheets or illustrated books, moved away from the imagery of the *lubok*. Mexican artists stayed much closer to the folk tradition, to *mexicanidad*, and this ensured the survival and reputation of an artist such as Posada. While artistic 'populism' came relatively late to Mexico, it grew deeper roots and lasted longer.

It could even be argued that the posthumous fame bestowed on Posada reflects the problematic path followed by the artists of the Mexican renaissance as they entered the 1930s. Whatever they may have said in their political rhetoric, all of them, including Siqueiros, the most Stalinist, rejected 'Socialist Realism' stylistically in their painting. The origins of their art lay in their rejection of beaux arts academicism in the years of the *Porfiriato* and it was impossible for them to renege on this. On the other hand, their political commitments, the populist culture they had brought into being in the post-revolutionary years, had entailed a

10 Ramón Favela, *Diego Rivera, The Cubist Years* (Phoenix Art Museum, 1984).

rejection of abstract art and, indeed, 'difficult' minority-oriented avant-gardism in general. They tried to find a third path, both Modernist and figurative, without being avant-garde or academic (or academic-revivalist like socialist realism). In this context populism, a respect for the non-academic (because untrained) figurative forms of folk art, and especially of an 'urban' popular artist such as Posada, was intrinsic to their whole political and aesthetic strategy.

The Mexican artists set out to create an 'original' and independently Mexican version of Modernism and it is in this context that Posada has to be seen. Their interest in popular imagery is both a part of the broader discovery of 'low' and marginal art forms by Modernists and at the same time a specific reworking of Modernism, which in turn entailed a specific attitude towards an artist such as Posada. The relationship between Mexican and European Modernism was complex, delicate and fraught with danger. There is no doubt that without the influence of Cubism and Russian avant-gardism, Posada would never have been recognised and praised in the way that he was. On the other hand, Posada also stood in a different relationship to the artists of the Mexican renaissance than the artists of the *lubok* did to Larionov or Wassily Kandinsky, or the artists of the German *moritaten* to George Grosz or Otto Dix. Posada was seen not just in terms of fresh material which could be purloined for new forms or imagery, or even as a repository of popular wisdom and insight in an unspoiled form, necessary for the rejuvenation or even completion of art, but as an artist in his own right, a beacon, an emblematic figure who pointed the way towards a specifically Mexican Modernism.

We can see the tensions clearly in the 1930s when Surrealism began to be known in Mexico. In due course, Rivera, who had begun as a Bukharinite, began to align himself with Trotsky, and thus draw closer to the Surrealists, who had already aligned themselves with Trotsky, as early as 1929. This realignment reached its culmination when André Breton himself came to Mexico in 1938, though it broke apart very soon afterwards. In 1937 Breton had given a lecture on 'black humour' at the Paris *exposition universelle* of that year and, when he was introduced to Posada, he immediately saw his work as exemplifying 'black humour' in an unmistakable way. On his return to Paris he set about compiling an anthology of 'black humour', which he completed in 1940, though publication was prohibited by the Vichy regime. Mexico became a privileged place for Breton, a surrealist country *par excellence* and Posada its exponent of 'black humour'. For the first time, the Posada who had been discovered by a Frenchman (Jean Charlot) in the context of Cubism and the Mexican Revolution, now was introduced to Europe by another Frenchman (André Breton), this time in the context of Surrealism and the Occupation.

For a surrealist, it was as much the content as the form of popular imagery which attracted the eye and contained a surrealist charge. Surrealism had a special relationship with the cruel, the morbid and the grotesque. Breton had always loved and praised the works of de Sade, E. T. A. Hoffmann and Lewis Carroll. In creating a counter-tradition to academic classicism and realism, Breton drew heavily on the Gothic and the grotesque. One of his earliest heroes was Alfred Jarry, himself also an admirer and practitioner of the popular print, and in Posada's cuts he saw perhaps an echo of the absurd and horrible world of King Ubu.

Surrealist attitudes and tastes, of course, have permeated European culture, to the point of becoming commonplace and even anodyne. It is hard now not to look at Posada's prints in the way Breton pioneered and see there, first and foremost, the quality which Thomas Gretton has called 'blithe gruesomeness'.[11] Indeed, the appreciation and enjoyment of just such 'blithe gruesomeness' has become acceptable to an extent that would probably have surprised Breton himself, who was still aware of the shock value both of nonsense and of cruelty and morbidity. For Rivera, Posada's skeletons and skulls provided a link with the politically repressed world of the Aztecs, a symptomatic return of values and motifs repressed for centuries by post-Conquest rulers as 'Indian', but for Breton they represented a link with the death instinct, with the repressed impulses of sadism, with the unconscious. Allied to nonsense and to laughter, they threatened the bourgeois order of constraining reason and hypocritical virtue.

From a European viewpoint, the *calaveras* appear as the last, coruscating version of the mediaeval imagery of the *danse macabre*, the Dance of Death. Dating back to the fifteenth century, first appearing in fresco painting, then popularised in woodcuts, the Dance of Death is found, too, in Holbein's book of prints published in 1538. Before 1562 its Lyon publishers had already produced eleven editions and by the end of the century there seem to have been as many as a hundred authorised and unauthorised editions. The Dance of Death drew together strands from the *memento mori* tradition as well as the *danse macabre*, the depiction of a succession of partners for death ranked in order of social precedence, and crystallised a set of responses to the dreadful toll of plague, famine and war. Although it is rarely said, it is hard not to see in the Mexican

11 Thomas Gretton, *Murders and Moralities* (British Museum, 1980).

cult of Posada also a response to the horrors of the revolutionary wars, rather than the prefiguration of their political outcome.

After Holbein, the Dance of Death begins to lose its intensity, the sense of urgency that death may call anyone at any moment, whatever their rank, whatever their wealth, learning or power, from the Pope himself downwards, and the sense of physical decay and destruction that reduces every corpse, however beautiful or strong it once was, to the same stereotypical skeleton with grossly grinning jaws. The Dance of Death becomes a more conventional vehicle for moral tales or satirical lampoons, as with Rowlandson's eighteenth-century English version. The Romantic rediscovery of the sublime brought with it, as its shadow and counterpart, the grotesque and the nightmarish, and in Goya's *Disasters*, the Dance of Death is transposed into a different register. It reappears intermittently in its traditional form, but in general it becomes one of the elements in a more generalised art of horror, as with Ensor or Dix. Part of Posada's impact is due to the way in which he recaptures the threads of the traditional form, taking us back once again to the prints of Holbein and his contemporaries. The familiar mediaeval skeletons reappear, but in modern garb, in modern contexts.

'Blithe gruesomeness', however, takes us back not simply to the Dance of Death, which was far from blithe, but to the whole repertoire of nineteenth-century urban popular art – catchpenny prints, peep shows, panoramas, Punch and Judy, melodrama and fairground attractions. The heyday of the broadside in Britain came earlier than in Mexico, from the end of the Napoleonic Wars onwards, but the material and style were not very different.[12] The prints published by James Catnach at Seven Dials from 1813 to 1838 prefigure those published by Antonio Vanegas Arroyo between 1880 and 1917 in Mexico City. Catnach was phenomenally successful in the same areas as Vanegas – murder sheets, gallows literature, rehashes of famous events, breathless narrations of topical news, chapbooks and so on. He is said to have sold two and a half million copies of his broadsheet on the murderer James Rush and to have taken hackney coaches heavy with bags of coppers to the Bank of England.

Catnach's prints, like those of Vanegas, were made to accompany ballads and street songs, to be hawked at markets and fairs or wherever crowds might gather. Like Posada's work, they show lurid scenes of crime, in which murderers stab their blood-spattered victims with huge knives or demented mothers smash their baby's skull against the wall.

12 Leslie Shepard, *The Broadside Ballad* (Jenkins, 1962).

Like Vanegas and Posada, Catnach and his artists would use the same print again for a new story. The stress was on grabbing public attention, on gore and melodrama, rather than on naturalistic detail or historical accuracy. In fact, it seems that seventeenth-century blocks were still being reused during the nineteenth century. At other times, blocks would be cut up and recombined or empty space filled with any available vignette, just as Vanegas and Posada would do. The subject matter of broadsides also remained more or less constant through the centuries – murders, catastrophes, humour, spectacular political events, sports, etc. – and remain so to this day in the sensational press and even now on television. These, of course, were also Posada's staples.

It is interesting to note how the qualities of these prints have affinities with more respectable work, which runs parallel to them and often draws on them or parodies them in a sophisticated way. Thus there is a strong streak of 'blithe gruesomeness' in the work of Edward Lear or, more obviously, Harry Graham's 'Ruthless Rhymes', which also depend on a combination of comical grotesque doggerel with eye-catching and melodramatic illustrations. Alfred Hitchcock also descends from this tradition and in his work elements from popular imagery, the spectacle of crime and punishment, the fairground, the chamber of horrors and the melodrama are condensed into the narrative mould of the detective and adventure story. Hitchcock began his career as a commercial artist and always prized strong and sadistic visual effects. Posada prints have much in common with a wide range of nineteenth-century popular arts in many different countries. For instance, depictions of burning buildings, train crashes and executions were frequent in German *moritaten*, peep show pictures and panoramas, though these were painted rather than printed and show much more detail. George Grosz remembered seeing in his childhood a panorama of a fire in the Paris *métro* – 'Dozens of tiny scorched fleas rushed the exit in panic fear, while a crushed pile of those trampled down in the rush lay like so many burned matches in the carriage doorways or on the platform. In order to depict the entire gruesome scene the artist had drawn the people as the tiny insects they really are.'[13] Strangely enough, I have seen the same panorama (or one of another *métro* fire in 1903), but I was struck not so much by the insect-like appearances of the fleeing victims, but by their wildly waving arms, very reminiscent of the panic-stricken Mexicans in Posada's earthquake prints. Similarly his print of a volcanic eruption seems very like the panorama

13 Erika Karasek et al., (eds.), *Schilder, Bilder, Moritaten* (Staatliche Museen zu Berlin, 1987).

of Mount Pelée erupting that Grosz also saw and described, with 'human figures, clearly recognisable, spiralling through the air'.

Fires and railway disasters provided material simultaneously not only for Posada or for the German panorama painters, but also for the builders of Coney Island, the pioneering New York amusement park. In 1904 William H. Reynolds devised his 'Dreamland' park at Coney Island, which contained an electrical and mechanical display of the eruption of Vesuvius, the Galveston Flood and the San Francisco Earthquake, as well as a burning hotel with hysterical guests ('Fighting the Flames') and even 'The Leapfrog Railway' in which two cars full of passengers crash into one another only to find that though 'they have actually collided', one car has leapfrogged on specially designed rails right over the top of the other and the passengers who 'in breathless excitement momentarily anticipated disaster... yet find themselves safe and sound'. Exhilarating accidents, thrills and spills are the hallmarks of the Luna Park.[14]

Coney Island reminds us that catchpenny prints and broadsides were not only street art but also fairground art, alongside the rides, the puppet and freak shows, the trestle theatres and the ghost rides. Posada frequently uses the old fairground motif of the jaws of Hell, which goes right back to the literal 'grotesque' of the mannerist pleasure garden of Bomarzo in Italy. The *calavera* too is an element of the fiesta, a popular festivity with puppets, fireworks, special markets, drinking, dancing and extra-sweet 'fairground' food (sugar skulls instead of candyfloss or toffee apples). It is here, in the Luna Park or on the Day of the Dead, that 'blithe gruesomeness' leaves the realm of black humour and enters that of the carnivalesque, a ritualised realm of licence and role reversal, in which thresholds and frontiers (as between living and dead) are crossed and effaced.

As Peter Stallybrass and Allon White have argued, 'respectable' society feels a deep ambivalence towards the fairground and the carnival.[15] It needs to expel and to control the 'other' world of popular festivity and misrule, but at the same time it feels a secret fascination with it, projecting there its own disavowed desires. There is both a threat and an opportunity for vicarious excitement. Posada's prints carry some of the same ambiguity, especially as they become art objects and museum pieces. They both threaten the conventions of the art world, transgress its implicit rules and standards, and at the same time reinforce by both revealing and yet

14 Rem Koolhaas, *Delirious New York* (Oxford University Press, 1978).

15 Peter Stallybrass and Allon White, *The Politics and Poetics of Transgression* (Methuen, 1986).

holding at a distance, by reinvigorating without overwhelming. In many ways, the art world acts as a mediator between the world of carnival and fairground and the respectable world of high culture. It acts as a conduit, with one extremity in Bohemia, the other in the Academy. In Mexico, the influence of Posada made possible the mix of populism and modernism which the artists of the renaissance wanted. It gave them street credibility, so to speak, while they pursued their monumental ambitions.

Perhaps the artist most similar to Posada is the pioneer French film-maker, Georges Méliès. Méliès was born in 1861, nine years after Posada, and worked as an illusionist and caricaturist before beginning to make films in 1896. His period of success lasted till 1909, when changes in the commercial structure of the nascent cinema industry undermined his position. Méliès had relied on selling films to fairground cinemas, booths set up alongside the rides, freak shows and other entertainments. Again and again in his repertory of 'primitive' black-and-white films (often hand-tinted) we find echoes of Posada. He featured dancing skeletons and giant skulls, part of the legacy of the phantasmagoria and the magic show, as well as films of earthquakes, volcanoes (Mont Pelée), train crashes, aeronautics, comets, state events, folktales and monsters. Like Posada, Méliès was first forgotten, then rediscovered by a later generation. Much of his work was destroyed (indeed, he himself set fire to a store of his own films, not seeing any value in them) or survived only by accident.[16]

Posada and Méliès occupy a peculiar niche in art history, in a particular period of transition. They came after the woodcut and the stage illusion, but before the mass-circulation press and cinema. They were small-scale urban professionals, whose work was meant to entertain, not so much the masses as the crowd. They come right at the beginning of the age of mechanical reproduction, using up-to-date, even innovatory print techniques, but still tied to old systems of distribution and exhibition, which were swept away in their lifetime or soon after their heyday. They saw themselves as artisans, but in the face of the image industry, they were claimed as ancestors by professional artists – post-cubist painters, surrealist and experimental filmmakers.

One artist who acknowledged the influence of both Posada and Méliès was S. M. Eisenstein. Eisenstein first saw Posada's work in 1929 in Berlin, in the home of the playwright Ernst Toller, and then soon after he visited Mexico to make a film and saw many more of Posada's 'inimitable pages'. The first film Eisenstein saw, at the age of eight, was Méliès's film with a

16 Paul Hammond, *Marvellous Méliès* (Gordon Fraser Gallery, 1974).

dancing skeleton horse, presumably *The Merry Frolics of Satan*. Later he thought of Méliès's hand-tinting when he came to work on the colour sequences of *Ivan the Terrible*, and he paid tribute to Posada in the Day of the Dead section of his Mexican film. After all, as he once said, 'I have been attracted by bones and skeletons since childhood. An attraction amounting to a sort of malady.'[17] Eisenstein was fascinated, too, by shock effects, by incidents of bizarre cruelty, by simplified and eye-catching images. He was a devoted collector of caricatures, popular prints and imagery, and recycled his collection in his films, transposing engravings or etchings into film shots. Like the Mexican muralists, he drew on the urban carnivalesque tradition and monumentalised it. Like them, too, he wanted to be both modernist and populist. It is no wonder that he was so fascinated by Mexico and specifically by Posada.

Eisenstein's great theme in his twenties films (*Strike*, *Battleship Potemkin*, *October*) was the revolutionary crowd, a dynamic flux. They are dominated by street battles and slaughters and even the working class of *Strike* is pre-Taylor and pre-Ford, semi-artisanal, more like a revolutionary 'city mob' than a disciplined mass. Eisenstein is like the Posada portrayed by Leopoldo Méndez, the artist at work while he looks out through the window at the Anti-Reelectionist riots in the street outside.[18] E. J. Hobsbawm, in his classic *Primitive Rebels*, describes how the urban riot became a thing of the past, with industrialisation (perhaps he should have said Taylorism and Fordism), with the end of famine and food shortages in the industrialised countries, with changes in the cities themselves, separating the rich from the poor in specialised areas, separating residential, commercial, finance and government centres, developing suburbs, redeveloping slums, cutting thoroughfares through popular quarters.[19] Posada belongs to the old city of riots and street crowds, pre-revolutionary but culminating (as in Russia) in the Revolution which eventually transformed it.

The political heroes in Posada's prints are still bandits – rural rather than urban figures, perhaps appealing to the pilgrims and market-goers who travelled into Mexico City from the villages, to the Shrine of the Virgin of Guadalupe or to the market, the *zócalo* or the bullring. The world portrayed is that of the urban poor, *lumpen* street people and criminals or victimised artisans. Posada's years in Mexico City were during the time when the main political organisations of the workers were anarchist,

17 S. M. Eisenstein, *Immoral Memories* (Houghton Mifflin, 1983).

18 Manuel Maples Arce, *Leopoldo Méndez* (Fondo de Cultura Económica, 1970).

19 E. J. Hobsbawm, *Primitive Rebels* (Manchester University Press, 1959).

and indeed the anarchists, followers of Ferrés, were particularly strong among the *tipógrafos*, who formed a national Confederación de Artes Gráficas in 1912. Ferrés was cautious, stressing the need for education and 'consciousness-raising', countenancing militancy only after careful preparation.[20] It is in this kind of context that Posada should probably be placed politically.

It was only after Posada's death, as the revolution gathered momentum, that the Mexican working class began to take clearly militant actions, finally committing itself to armed struggle. Despite Rivera's rhetoric it is highly unlikely that Posada would have identified with Zapata. The urban workers fought with Obregón (as did Orozco, Siqueiros and Dr Atl, in various capacities). But in reality Posada was a pre-revolutionary artist, whose relationship with current and impending events was oblique and enigmatic. Perhaps the most we can say is that he demonstrated a vitality and exuberance which was clearly at odds with the belle époque formality and order of the Porfirio Díaz regime. His work gives evidence of a force and energy among the *menu peuple* of Mexico City which already threatens to overspill its allotted bounds. But rather than a force of contradiction in the Marxist sense, this was more like a force of excess. In Bataille's terms Posada and his public were fascinated by *l'informe*, the monstrous and marginal which threatened the imposed identity and limits of society.

In the last analysis, Posada's art was not political in the sense that later artists chose to give the term – propagandist, ideologically saturated, or even concerned principally with political themes and myths. It was a narrative art and, for that very reason, touched in all kinds of ways on political issues. Posada's prints did not exist independently. They were accompanied by verbal material of various sorts, mainly news stories or *corridos*, improvised narrative ballads celebrating some folk hero (or villain) or commemorating some exceptional event.[21] Like much popular art, broadside prints were only one element in a complex, hybrid discourse. There was no separation of spheres. Insofar as one code dominated the others, it was the abstract code of narrative, which was realised in different, simultaneous modes. The same story was told, in one striking 'headline' image and then again in a more diffuse and elongated song. For Posada, many of the words (and melodies) were written by Vanegas, and the two should therefore be seen not simply as employer and employee

20 John M. Hart, *Anarchism and the Mexican Working Class* (University of Texas Press, 1978).

21 Edward L. Tinker, *Corridos and Calaveras* (University of Texas Press, 1961).

but also as artistic collaborators in a hybrid popular form, the broadside or street gazette.[22]

In fact, it is clear that though Vanegas's style did not change greatly when Posada's predecessor, Manilla, retired, Posada's style did change when he began to work for Vanegas. This was not due just to the fact that Vanegas was the entrepreneur, the 'producer', or that he was the more forceful artistic personality. The key element in Vanegas's role is that he stood at the crossroads between the creators (including himself) and the street-sellers (who included his wife and family). In a popular form, this is the crucial position, the point of mediation between the street people, pilgrims and revellers who bought and used the prints and the versifiers and engravers who made them. Of course, the same kind of mediation also occurs in the mass arts, in the industrial spectacle, but there the mediations are much more extended and abstracted. Popular art of the kind produced by Vanegas and Posada involved close contact between producer and user, who were part of the same social milieu.

Thus Posada was working in an interzone between the popular but impersonal forms of the mass media or the muralists (whose work was one-off and whose commissions came from the top down, from government minister, ambassador or powerful capitalist) and the more personal but less popular forms of fine art and specialised production for collectors or connoisseurs. It is clear that the art world constantly draws on the popular arts for material or new forms, particularly at moments of crisis, and hence it is no surprise that Posada, who played an important role at the beginning of Modernism, is rediscovered again as Modernism is challenged and begins to fragment. Indeed, the evaluation of graffiti art in the seventies is reminiscent in many ways of the re-evaluation of the broadside print. Graffiti art involved a street culture, was seen as an expression of the urban poor and underprivileged, was both public and personalised. Like the print, it was highly stylised, designed to be eye-catching and was repeated, although manually rather than mechanically.

Finally, it is important that, despite the similarities we can see between Posada's work and that of European or North American popular artists, he was nonetheless Mexican. Earthquakes and volcanoes, shoot-outs with the police, the Day of the Dead, are all part of Mexican experience, then and now, and the vigour and exuberance of Posada's work springs from this particular reality. As we look at Posada, or graffiti artists, or the

22 Blas Vanegas Arroyo, 'Centenario de la casa editorial de Antonio Vanegas Arroyo', *Todos los Días* 9 (May 1980).

Kalighat painters and Battala printmakers of Calcutta,[23] painters from Shaba or Huxian,[24] *haj* murals or barbershop signs, we should take care not to deracinate the work, remove it mentally from its context. Instead, we should use the work to question the institutions and parameters of the Western world, to question its hierarchies, its values, its motives and its cults. Popular Third World art is not necessarily any 'purer', but it is different, it reflects different institutions and values, and its difference, as so often is the case, is inseparable from an imbalance of wealth and power. In this sense, Posada was indeed, as Rivera claimed, the artist of the poor and the dispossessed.

* * *

Catalogue essay published in J.G. Posada: Messenger of Mortality *(Redstone Press in association with the South Bank Centre, 1989), accompanying the exhibition of the same name at Modern Art Oxford, 28 May to 23 July 1989, curated by Wollen. The exhibition toured to Camden Arts Centre, London, 29 July to 3 September 1989; Cornerhouse, Manchester, 9 September to 15 October 1989; Gardner Centre, Brighton, 21 October to 26 November 1989; Chapter Arts Centre, Cardiff, 2 December 1989 to 7 January 1990; Warwick Arts Centre, Coventry, 20 January to 24 February 1990; Victoria Art Gallery, Bath, 3 March to 7 April 1990; and City Art Gallery, Plymouth, 21 April to 27 May.*

23 Ashit Paul (ed.), *Woodcut Prints of Nineteenth Century Calcutta* (Seagull Books, 1983).

24 Guy Brett, *Through Our Own Eyes* (Heretic Books, 1986).

The Continent – Letter to David Ross

Vassar College, Box 193, Poughkeepsie, NY, 12601, 30 March 1992

Dear David,

I had an informal talk with Elisabeth last week during which she asked whether I would be interested in working with the Whitney on an exhibition centred, as I understand it, on both the Mexican muralists and the art of the South-West, especially perhaps Native American painting. This could be extended to painters such as Pollock, who came from the South-West and were decisively influenced by both the Mexicans and by Native American art. I expressed my interest, but it was not completely clear to me whether this was really a South-West regional show, or one with a wider ambit. I thought it was extremely important to represent the way in which both Mexican and Native American art influenced American art overall, not just in the South-West, but also via the Federal Mural Painting programme, the collection of Northwest Coast (Kwakiutl, Haida, etc.) art shown at the Natural History Museum in New York, etc.

Here are some impromptu notes about the areas and artists the show might cover. This is not, however, a proposal. It is more of a cultural sketch-map, and I am aware that much more thought and research is needed. Also, there are practical problems with showing murals in an exhibition, but I believe there is enough surrounding material (sketches, portable panels, associated work, etc.) to make such a show viable. The murals themselves could be represented by photographic and film documentation, as well as being designated as site-specific exhibits in some innovative way.

So, here are the possible elements:

First, work by Mexican muralists in the United States. All of '*los tres grandes*' (Orozco, Rivera, Siqueiros) worked in the United States, originally in California, where they made their first inroads, but later in Detroit and on the East Coast. During the 1930s they achieved a limited ascendancy over North American painting. They not only brought the 'message' of mural painting, as a public art form, to the United States, but also a vision of 'American-ness', which re-validated the high art of the pre-Columbian period, and the vernacular forms which survived in the culturally depressed 'Indian' communities. This further led both to a 'roots revivalism' and to a renewed interest in *mestizo* forms which mingled or juxtaposed elements from pre-Columbian and Native American art with European modernism (cubism, expressionism, surrealism).

Many American artists themselves went on pilgrimages south of the border and others worked closely with the Mexican painters while they were in the United States, while a wider circle followed their work with interest and enthusiasm. Prominent Black artists responded quickly to the Mexican example (v., for example, Hale Woodruff's Amistad Murals, at Talladega College in Alabama, 1938) although the major muralist of the Harlem Renaissance, Aaron Douglas (135th Street Library, New York, etc.), drew on African rather than Mexican sources. Mexican American/Chicano artists themselves went back to the heritage of '*los tres grandes*' and the Mexican Renascence when they began to become a force in the North American art world in the 1960s.

Murals painted in the United States by *los tres grandes*:
Orozco: Pomona College, Claremont, 1930; New School, New York, 1931; Dartmouth College, Dartmouth, 1932–34.
Rivera: Stock Exchange Club, San Francisco, 1930; Sterne Home, Berkeley, 1931; School of Fine Arts, San Francisco, 1931; Detroit Institute of Arts, Detroit, 1932–33; Rockefeller Center, New York, 1933; New Workers School, New York, 1933; and later, City College, San Francisco, 1940.
Siqueiros: Chouinard Art School, Olvera Street ('Tropical America'), and the Murphy Home, all in Los Angeles, 1932; the Siqueiros Experimental Workshop, New York, 1936–37.
Jean Charlot, another of the historic muralists, painted a WPA mural in New York and later worked in Hawaii.

Among those who worked with Rivera were Ione Robinson (in Mexico) and Clifford Wright, Lucienne Bloch, Stephen Dimitroff, Ben Shahn and

Louise Nevelson (in the United States). Close associates of Rivera included Tina Modotti and Edward Weston, and, of course, Frida Kahlo, who painted a number of important works while in the United States.

Among those who worked with Siqueiros in Los Angeles were Luis Arenal, Sanford McCoy (Pollock's brother), Reuben Kadish and Harold Lehman. Arenal, McCoy and Lehman also participated in the New York workshop, along with Pollock. Kadish went with Philip Guston to Mexico itself where, with Siqueiros's encouragement, they painted a large mural in Morelia. Subsequently they painted a mural in Duarte, California, and Guston went on to become one of the most prominent FAP muralists.

Orozco worked alone, but was associated with the Delphic Gallery group of artists.

The example of the Mexicans had an obvious impact on the work of Thomas Benton, who painted his first commissioned mural at the New School, alongside Orozco. Benton's relation to the Mexicans was notoriously ambivalent and rivalrous, but, even while he rejected their work as foreign to the United States, he absorbed it and shaped his own mural painting style consciously counter to theirs. Benton was also the teacher of many of the Los Angeles group, including Pollock.

The Coit Tower murals in San Francisco, 1934, painted by Wright, Stackpole, Arnautoff and others, are the most striking example of the direct influence of Rivera. Indirectly, the Mexicans had an enormous impact through the efforts of George Biddle, who went down to Mexico, stayed with Rivera, painted Siqueiros's portrait, talked with Orozco, and returned to the United States to play the decisive role in setting up the Federal Art Project [FAP]. An old friend of Roosevelt, he wrote him in May 1933, citing the example of Rivera and the success of the Mexican muralists in launching a progressive, public, national art movement. Biddle himself painted a mural for the project in Washington, 'Society Freed Through Justice'.

Another important early development was the Museum of Modern Art's Murals exhibition held in May 1932. As Lincoln Kirstein (chair of the exhibition committee) noted, fresco painting had been developed 'by the great decorators from the days of the Tauromachies of Knossos, through Giotto and Michelangelo to Rivera and Orozco' and was now being revived in the United States, following the example of the Mexico City school. This show of portable murals included work by George Biddle, Stuart Davis, Georgia O'Keefe, Ben Shahn, and many others. It also included a photo-murals section, with work by Berenice Abbott, Charles Sheeler, Edward Steichen, and others. It was on the basis of this show that Davis and O'Keefe were invited to paint murals for Radio City Music Hall. Steichen also produced a photo-mural for the Center Theater in the same complex.

Davis went on to paint a number of murals, although he was more influenced by Léger than by the Mexicans, as were the group of modernist artists who later worked for the FAP (Diller, Browne, Bolotowsky, Greene, Criss, Xceron). Léger himself painted murals in New York, for the Rockefeller family and for the World's Fair. O'Keefe, unfortunately, gave up, under pressure from Stieglitz who strongly disapproved of 'that Mexican disease called murals'. Following this setback, she became closely tied to the South-West however.

Other significant murals, painted by artists who later achieved international recognition, were those by Arshile Gorky at Newark Airport, 1936, as well as one for the World's Fair of 1939 (and privately for the Riviera Club, Fort Lee, New Jersey, 1938–39); by James Brooks for La Guardia Marine Terminal, 1942; by Willem de Kooning for the SS President Jackson, etc. Pollock worked as an assistant to Job Goodman on a FAP mural and Nevelson taught mural painting for the FAP at a Brooklyn school.

Many others from the Rivera and Siqueiros groups also painted murals for the FAP, such as Lucienne Bloch and Marion Greenwood, who, with her sister Grace, had worked with Rivera in Mexico. Other artists from this milieu, such as Philip Guston and Peter Busa, also worked for the FAP. In a neighbouring field, Isamu Noguchi worked on public sculptural projects, such as a children's playground, during this period and Lloyd Ney's controversial Post Office mural in New London, Ohio, should not be forgotten. Of course, many other well-known artists worked in the easel painting section of the Federal Art Project.

As noted above, the Mexican muralists also directed attention to Native American painting. This too featured in the work of the FAP, through the Index of American Design and the establishment of workshops in the South- and Mid-West which encouraged Native American painters, whose work should certainly be rescued from oblivion.

There was also an important influence of Native American art on non-Indian artists. Pollock mythologised his few contacts with Indian culture during his early years, pored over the illustrations in the Smithsonian Institute's ethnographic reports, and went to see a Navajo sand-painter at work in the Museum of Modern Art. Pollock's breakthrough *Mural*, painted for Peggy Guggenheim, reflects Pollock's concern for the 'shamanistic' dimension of painting. (And also his involvement with the

Chilean Matta's project of an 'American Surrealism'.) However, Pollock, like many other of his contemporaries, was also decisively influenced by the Northwest Coast artists, whose work he studied at the Museum of Natural History.

Northwest Coast art was the most sophisticated surviving North American Indian art. It provided a counter-balance to Mexican pre-Columbian art, just as these two, taken together, provided a counter-balance to European art. At the same time, it provided examples both of mural painting (houses were painted externally) and of stylised forms, verging on abstraction. The society was relatively rich and remote enough to have maintained its cultural energy into the twentieth century, despite repeated onslaughts by missionaries and Mounties.

Among those especially fascinated by Native American and Northwest Coast art were John Graham, Adolph Gottlieb and Barnett Newman. Mark Rothko was also a frequent visitor to the Natural History Museum and the surrealists were devoted enthusiasts for Northwest Coast masks and artefacts. Through Wolfgang Paalen, for instance, who travelled to the Skeena Valley, Louise Nevelson became interested, and, on a trip to visit Rivera in Mexico, Nevelson also saw the Mayan stelae and sacred monuments which so influenced her own work, especially in terms of his own ideas about 'metamorphosis'.

Northwest Coast art also produced the 'Indian Space' group of painters – Will Barnet, Robert Barrell, Gertrude Barrer, Peter Busa and others – who showed together in the forties. Barnet and Busa, with Nevelson, also formed the Five O'Clock Club in opposition to the Abstract Expressionists. These painters drew on the Northwest Coast artists as American exemplars of a simultaneous interest in abstract form and mythological content.

Two other artists deserve special mention – Emily Carr and Rockwell Kent, who had direct contact with Native American culture and honoured it in their own work, although they painted in a very different style. Kent was also a controversial muralist, who incorporated a political message in Inuktitut into his work (advising Puerto Ricans to hold fast to their independence!).

Finally, important artists emerged during this period among the Kwakiutl and Haida themselves, such as Mungo Martin and Willie Seaweed, whose work should certainly be recognised alongside that of those who admired and learned from the artistry of their forebears. Their example led to the post-war flowering of contemporary Northwest Coast art, associated especially with Bill Reid.

I hope this all gives some indication of the way my mind is working and suggests the extent to which Mexican muralism and Native American art were at the heart of painting in the United States at a crucial historical moment. Each of them presented a model of a specifically American tradition. I look forward to hearing your response.

Best wishes,
Peter Wollen

P.S. Jean Charlot's classic book on mural painting is titled *From Lascaux to Disney*, and I also believe that any consideration of muralism should also include Disney, whose work can be seen as animated muralism as appropriately as animated film.

* * *

Letter to David Ross, Director of the Whitney Museum, 1992. The proposed exhibition, tentatively titled (among other names) 'The Continent', was never realised. Previously unpublished.

The Continent – Notes to a Sketch for an Exhibition

TOTEM AND TABU: OR *HOW AMERICA STOLE MODERN ART FROM ITSELF* (OR SHOULD WE SAY: *FROM ITS OWN OTHER*?) – OR. . . . . ? ?

NOTES TO A SKETCH FOR AN EXHIBITION,
LAYING THE NECESSARY GROUNDWORK FOR A FULL EXHIBITION PROPOSAL, AFTER FURTHER RESEARCH, THOUGHT, IMAGINATION AND DISCUSSION.

FIVE GUIDING PRINCIPLES:

1. This exhibition is historical. In other words, it tells a story. Consequently, although covering a lot of ground, it is selective in terms of the telling of that story. Its criteria are both aesthetic and narrative criteria. It should instruct and delight. It will need innovative presentation. It welcomes intellectual controversy.
2. This story is an old story with a new twist: the triumph of modern American painting. As we all know by now, this is the story of how American artists 'caught up with Paris as Paris had not yet caught up with herself' (and never did) or (seen from the anti-triumphalist point of view) 'how New York stole the idea of modern art'. Whatever the antagonism between Clement Greenberg and Serge Guilbaut, they certainly agree on one thing, blindingly obvious to them: America took from Europe in order to overtake Europe. This exhibition presents

a different point of view: it shows what North America took from Mexico, and from the artists of the Pacific Northwest, while it suppressed all consciousness of its debt.

3. The Mexican Renascence provided a crucial and inspiring model of what American art could and should be: an art which absorbed European modernism into a native American tradition, which respected Parisian cubism and Russian constructivism but also (and equally) American Indian artworks, which drew on the fresco painting of Giotto and Piero, but also on that of Chichén Itzá, which was both personal and public, historical, mythic, political and experimental. North American artists, latecomers, could draw on different aspects of this model. In Pollock we see a debt to muralism, especially Orozco, a debt to the North American Indian heritage, and a specific debt to Siqueiros from whom he acquired a version of experiment in art, consolidated for him later by another Latin American, Matta Echaurren.
4. North Americans had largely destroyed Native American society. Militarily defeated, Indians were herded into reservations and their culture shattered. On the Northwest coast, however, especially in British Columbia and Alaska, native peoples, the Kwakiutl, the Haida, and others, lucky and resilient enough to escape or deflect the main thrust of westward expansion, were able to maintain their rich artistic production into the twentieth century. In New York, artists inherited it through books and monographs, but, above all, through the collections of the Natural History Museum and the Museum of the American Indian, as well as through special exhibitions, such as the MoMA show of 1941 or the show organised polemically by Barnett Newman in 1946. Their artworks decisively influenced Gottlieb, Newman and Pollock, to take the three most obvious examples, and inspired both the Surrealists and, of course, the 'Indian Space' movement (which was fatally marginalised – for being too explicit?).
5. This story is not a straightforward, linear narrative. It advances, as all history does, obliquely, elliptically, by knight's moves, with gaps and leaps. This non-linear narrative, with its breaks and its uneven back-and-forth movements, must govern the form of the exhibition. At the same time, the story must be coherent, comprehensible – and compelling. The viewer should emerge with a new understanding – of the impact of Siqueiros, the trajectory of Pollock, the delayed-action release of Nevelson – and a new fascination – with Kwakiutl painting, with the strange career of Philip (Goldstein) Guston, or the legacy of muralism.

Peter Wollen
2 November, 1993

* * *

Preliminary notes for an exhibition, 1993. The text is from the same fax to Elisabeth Sussman as the Sketch for an Exhibition (see plate section in this volume), and follows immediately after it. Previously unpublished.

Masculinity: Siqueiros and Pollock

The relationship between Siqueiros and Pollock is well documented. Pollock worked in Siqueiros's experimental New York 'laboratory of modern techniques' during the early 1930s where he observed and participated in Siqueiros's art production. In particular, this involved the making of large-scale non-easel works, the use of industrial paints such as Duco, the spreading of surfaces on the floor in order to attack them from above and from all four sides, and the use of spray-guns and sticks dipped directly in the can to spatter paint, as an experiment in the creative use of chance. Pollock's participation followed naturally from his earlier encounter with Siqueiros's mural work in Los Angeles and from his subsequent relationship in New York with Thomas Hart Benton, the American painter most comparable to the Mexican muralists. Unlike Benton, however, Siqueiros was committed to experimentalism as well as to public art.

As well as observing Siqueiros's style of work, Pollock was also able to observe Siqueiros's personality. Siqueiros was deliberately and exaggeratedly macho in his public projection of himself. He attributed this to the influence of his grandfather, Antonio Alfaro, who had fought for Juárez against the European invaders in the mid-nineteenth century, a crucial period in Mexican history. Antonio Alfaro affected a piratical demeanour and a black *charro* costume (ceremonial cowboy clothing), rode horses, drove cattle, abused homosexuals ('*muchachitos – hijos de la chingada*'), believed children should be educated with the fist, abhorred religion and divided women sharply between the ideal types of mother and whore. José (who later changed his name to David, apparently in homage to the great painter and public figure of the French Revolution) got on badly with his father, who, in contrast to his grandfather, was devout, orderly, proper and conservative.

By the time he was at art school Siqueiros was competitive, truculent and given to violence. He soon became involved in a student uprising and, not long afterwards, answered the call to arms against the Díaz regime and joined the revolutionary forces of General Diéguez. Siqueiros remained proud of his revolutionary service throughout his life, telling stories about a time of uncanny violence and cruelty, killing for the sake of killing, peremptory executions, mass slaughter and reckless risk of life. In Europe, where he was sent after the revolutionary victory, as a reward for his military service and in recognition of his talent as an artist, he boasted endlessly about his experience of violence and terror, walking erect as a soldier should, with chest puffed out, and exclaiming that there were 'no homosexuals in Mexico, country of Pancho Villa'. In short, as Bertram Wolfe later described him, he was 'aggressively virile'.

Siqueiros's art reflected the same outlook: monumental, public, technological, dynamic, kinetic, full of huge, hyper-muscular, aggressively foreshortened figures. He rapidly became a leader of the Mexican mural movement, alongside Orozco and Rivera, and also a founder and militant within the Mexican Communist Party. He led armed groups during fighting against the Dorados, armed right-wing militias, who attacked the Communist Party, earning the title of 'El Capitán Sangre Fria' ('cold-blooded captain') for his exploits. Later in the 1930s, after his time in New York, he volunteered for service in the Spanish Civil War, where he became a colonel (a title in which he gloried for the rest of his life). His work in Spain was primarily in intelligence and, on his return to Mexico, still working for the Soviet GPU, he organised the first assassination attempt on Trotsky, which led to the murder of Sheldon Harte (the aide on guard duty at the time of the attack). Harte's body was found in a shallow grave on the estate of Siqueiros's brothers-in-law. In short, Siqueiros was not only, as Rufino Tamayo, the leading painter of the next generation, characterised him, a megalomaniac, but also a ruthless and unashamed killer.

'In the old days', he boasted while he was in Spain, 'we went to paint with pistols in our belts. They couldn't have stopped us if they had wanted to'. In New York too he carried a pistol. This was the man with whom Pollock struck up a close, indeed physical rapport, grappling and wrestling with him. Axel Horn, another comrade, summed up one incident as 'getting boisterous, the usual macho business… There was no animosity between them, but they ended up in a contest under the table. That pistol of Siqueiros's, maybe, was what set Jackson off.' Pollock was attracted to macho leaders, whose style he emulated. Siqueiros outdid any of the others. Next to him Tom Benton, for all his swagger, his misogyny and his endless abuse of 'fairies', must have seemed somewhat insipid.

It seems clear, from the recollections of friends and acquaintances, that Pollock himself was impressed by the machismo of Benton and Siqueiros and made efforts to emulate it. 'Jackson was always doing the Benton thing', Whitney Darrow recollected, and, more precisely, 'all that Benton smokestack and "tote-that-bale" kind of thing'. Larry Rivers remembered Pollock's wish to imitate his heroes 'not only for what they have done as artists but their reputation as men among other men'. Darrow characterised this as 'in the spirit of Americanism and the outdoors', Rivers as 'like American – in my background, with everybody European, I didn't have his rollicking, mother-fucking macho'. Clement Greenberg attributed 'that business of being masculine' to the influence of Jackson's brother Sande, who had introduced him to Siqueiros. Gerome Kamrowski recollected how 'the only time you saw a cowboy in Manhattan was when the rodeo was in town – except for Sande. And Jackson was right there beside him wearing jeans and boots.' Budd Hopkins noted how Pollock's success was based on the idea that he had 'the big macho American virtues – he should be rough-and-tumble American – taciturn, ideally – and if he is a cowboy, so much the better.' Patsy Southgate more than once compared him to Hemingway.

Pollock's macho posture is important not simply as a matter of personality or character, but because it was also reflected in his work and played a part in his success. Like Siqueiros his most successful work – the classic dripped and spattered abstracts – was on a large scale (though nowhere near so large as that of Siqueiros), exhibited the traits of dynamism and kineticism that Siqueiros also advocated, incorporated industrial materials into the process of painting and suggested to many a psychological climate of turbulence, violence and aggression, characteristics that Siqueiros himself saw as essentially American in contrast to European decadence. Pollock's work was described as 'explosive' and, by Greenberg, 'an eruption', 'full of energy', 'overpowering'. As early as 1947, Greenberg was introducing Pollock as containing a feeling which he characterises as 'radically American', invoking Faulkner and Melville as 'witnesses to the nativeness of such violence, exasperation and stridency'. Although Greenberg might lament Sande's bad influence on a personal level, he was prepared to laud the same qualities when applied to Pollock's art.

Siqueiros, unlike Pollock, had a programmatic view of Americanism, which he first outlined very early on in his career. He distinguished carefully between a nostalgically primitivist Americanism and a modernist, dynamic Americanism. While still in Europe, in 1921, he was exhorting Mexican artists, in futurist vein, to 'live our marvelous dynamic age! love the modern machine, dispenser of unexpected plastic emotions, the contemporary aspects of our daily life, our cities in the process of construction, the sober and practical engineering of our modern buildings.' At the same time he called for a return to Mayan and Aztec art, not in the sense of 'archaeological reconstruction', but through appropriating their 'clarity' and 'synthetic energy'. For Siqueiros the indigenous art of Mexico was the foundation for the aesthetic of the future, to which modern artists must return in order to create new and dynamic art-forms after four centuries of indecision and irresolution. Cubism and futurism provided an example, but the new generation of American artists nonetheless had to go beyond Europe, incorporating the monumentality, geometrical structure and 'plastic purity' of native pre-Columbian art.

In this view, America represented monumentality, dynamism and the future, whereas Europe represented domesticity, decadence and the past. Thus mural painting, as developed during the Mexican renaissance, was essentially a public art, whereas easel painting, to which European art had been reduced, was essentially private. It is clear that these antinomies between public and private, large and small, narrative and decorative, could easily be mapped onto a fundamental antinomy between male and female, so that America was seen as a young, active, outdoor male, whereas Europe appeared as an aging closeted female, already in her decline. In this way, Siqueiros's personal machismo could be aligned with his aesthetic theory and practice, under the banner of a progressive Americanism. His conversion to Soviet communism added a further dimension to this vision: it stressed the need for revolutionary violence and for mass power and, in the thirties, it aligned communism with 'twentieth-century Americanism'. Moreover, the history of Mexico – the struggle against the Spanish invaders, the liberation from Spain, the defeat of Maximilian, the overthrow of the *Porfiriato*, perceived as pro-European, the preference for Madero over Huerta as revolutionary leader – all predisposed Siqueiros's generation to an anti-European stance which persisted despite post-revolutionary tension with the United States. Siqueiros, along with Orozco and Rivera, found the United States a congenial place to work during the 1930s. The implicit dream was that of a united America, led by progressive governments (Roosevelt, Cardenas) which would serve as the antechamber to a new, dynamic society uniting the technological dynamism of the United States with the populist revolutionary zeal of Mexico.

Similar themes can also be found in Pollock's expression of his artistic goals. In his 1950 radio interview with William Wright, taped for the Sag Harbor station, but never actually broadcast, he directly linked his own technique as a painter to the significance of modern technology: 'It seems to me that the modern painter cannot express this age, the airplane, the atom bomb, the radio, in the old forms of the Renaissance or of any other past culture.' The 'past culture' which Pollock spoke of is clearly that of Europe – in the same interview Pollock points out that Chinese painters also painted on the floor, and elsewhere he alludes to the techniques of Native American sand-painters. Pollock was engrossed by the work of Northwest Coast and Navajo artists all his life, repeatedly visiting the Museum of Natural History in New York and somehow managing to collect all twelve volumes of the Smithsonian studies of the American Indian. At the same time, of course, he used industrial rather than art materials – rolls of cotton duck from John Boyle, usually sold for upholstery, commercial 'Rivit' glue from Behlen and Brother, Duco or Devoe & Raynolds industrial paint. In the radio tape, he also comments on his interest in mural painting – 'The direction that painting seems to be taking here – is – away from the easel – into some sort, some kind of wall – wall painting.' Specifically, he expressed an interest, as had Siqueiros, in using new, modern materials, plate glass sheets and plaster slabs. 'I think the possibilities of using painting on glass in modern architecture – in modern construction – terrific.'

Pollock's breakthrough work was the mural, nine by twenty feet, which he executed for Peggy Guggenheim at the entrance to her New York apartment. It was a work which he painted in a single night in order to meet the deadline he had been given six months earlier. Pollock himself described how his original outline was based on a series of visionary memories of a visit he and his brother Sande had made to the Grand Canyon in the fall of 1926. While there, they were taken on a hunting trip to shoot mustangs – wild horses – trapped when they came down a canyon to a watering hole. One of their companions, Robert Cooter, recalled, sixty or so years later, that 'they were beautiful horses, and I can't believe we could just shoot them and walk off. But we did. And I'm ashamed of it to this day.' The stampede which Pollock painted in 1944 was a cruel and tragic event in which he was implicated through his own violence, his own performance of masculinity, his own part in the slaughter of beautiful, long-maned, terrified animals. When he had painted the wild stampede, he set about obliterating every identifiable image, every trace of his shame. With this gesture, Pollock had finally discovered his way forward, the strategy which would lead him to success and greatness: work which substituted an interior energy and power, the resources of the unconscious, for the representation of exterior energy and power, the resources of realism in the service of politics. Innocence was lost and Pollock, at this critical moment, stepped beyond figuration.

Pollock continued to work on a large scale, and he would certainly have taken the opportunity of even greater monumentality if it had been offered to him. With his architect friend and drinking companion, Tony Smith, he hatched plans to include murals as part of Smith's architectural commissions, on the model of the Guggenheim mural. Smith and Pollock, with the help of Pollock's close friend Alfonso Ossorio, made serious efforts to obtain a commission to paint extensive murals for a Roman Catholic church to be designed by Smith, but, unfortunately, the idea never got off the ground. Ossorio was a major influence on Pollock at this time. Not only did he buy his work, arrange exhibitions for him and write a crucial catalogue essay, but he was also the link between Pollock and Dubuffet. He had recently completed an enormous mural for a church in the Philippines, which was an elaborate composition involving the church ceiling and its massive hanging beams as well as the focal section in the chapel's sanctuary, but the Catholic priests who met with Pollock, Smith and Ossorio were not impressed by this precedent. Nonetheless Smith and Pollock persisted in their plans. As late as 1955, Smith designed a building to house three of Pollock's mural-size paintings and persuaded his architectural client, Dr Fred Olsen, to buy Pollock's painting *Blue Poles* and place it in the Olsen house, effectively as an intrinsic part of its overall design.

Another friend, Peter Blake, who was a curator of architecture at the Museum of Modern Art in New York, was inspired by Pollock's work to try and create a museum in which the paintings would define the architectural space, rather than the other way round. He based his scheme on a design for an ideal museum by Mies van der Rohe, in which the artworks, free-standing or suspended from above, would themselves act as if they were the interior walls, rather than being supplements suspended on them. Working with Pollock and helped by Marcel Breuer, whom he had also interested in the project, Smith constructed a scale model of the museum, financed by Ossorio, who provided $1,000 for the materials. Pollock himself contributed miniature paintings and sculptures. Through their work on the model, Blake also obtained a commission for Pollock from Breuer, who asked him to paint a mural for a Long Island house he was designing for the Geller family. When the work was finally completed

Geller's wife dismissed the painting as 'a piece of junk' and no further architectural commissions emerged. Apparently undeterred, however, Pollock never gave up his dream of mural painting. Late in 1955, just a few months before his death, he was still experimenting with new miniature works for Blake's museum model.

Pollock's concept of a mural, of course, was very different from that of Siqueiros, but it clearly reflected his wish to go beyond easel painting. In this respect he was encouraged by Clement Greenberg, who enthusiastically endorsed the idea of large-scale painting. In 1945, he associated Pollock with 'boldness, breadth and the monumental'. In January 1947, he concluded a joint review of Dubuffet and Pollock by observing that 'Pollock points a way beyond the easel, beyond the mobile, framed picture, to the mural, perhaps – or perhaps not. I cannot tell.' Soon afterwards Pollock made an application for a Guggenheim Fellowship, noting that 'I intend to paint large movable pictures which will function between the easel and the mural'.

In January 1948 Greenberg continued this theme, writing in *The Nation* that, 'since Mondrian no-one has driven the easel painting quite so far away from itself; but this is not altogether Pollock's own doing. In this day and age the art of painting increasingly rejects the easel and yearns for the wall.' The very same month he wrote, in *Partisan Review*, that

> there is a persistent urge, as persistent as it is largely unconscious, to go beyond the cabinet picture, which is destined to occupy only a spot on the wall, to a kind of picture that, without actually becoming identified with the wall like a mural, would spread over it and acknowledge its physical reality. I do not know whether there is anything in modern architecture itself that explicitly invites this tendency. But it is a fact that abstract painting shows a greater and greater reluctance for the small, frame enclosed format.

In March he announced that French art (except for Dubuffet) was in decline and that American painting (as represented by Gorky and Pollock) was now at the centre of Western art. Two months later he published his celebrated essay on 'The Crisis of the Easel Picture', in which Pollock is cited, along with a group of other American artists, as working towards the destruction of the easel painting. A phalanx of American painters, including Pollock, were now marshalled against Dubuffet, the only French artist for whom Greenberg still showed any respect. Soon, however, Dubuffet would be described as showing 'the highest sophistication', 'erudition' and a 'very acute and civilised perception', qualities which are clearly meant to be contrasted with Pollock's 'powerful originality', natural and untutored. In the same way, Greenberg described French painting as 'finished', 'packaged' and 'tamed', as opposed to the raw, open and wild qualities which could be found in Pollock.

Pollock was himself influenced by his Americanist masters – Benton, Siqueiros and the Chilean surrealist, Matta – but he was careful not to disparage Europe, although he never went there, and he described his own art in cosmopolitan terms. Nonetheless, he plainly played the American card when it suited him and he did little to disavow the image of his personality constructed by the critics and the press. The tone was set by James Johnson Sweeney in his catalogue essay for Pollock's 1944 Guggenheim show: 'Pollock's talent is volcanic. It has fire. It is unpredictable. It spills itself out in a mineral prodigality not yet crystallised. It is lavish, explosive, untidy… risk… vitality… liberation… exuberance, independence and native sensibility.' Reading such a paean, in which Pollock is seen as an overwhelming force of nature, free, disorderly and uncontained, it seems that the artist is indeed being described as though he were a kind of mythic and virile America, pushing back frontiers, breaking with outmoded conventions, pioneering new ideas with energy and spontaneous enthusiasm. This myth also underlay Harold Rosenberg's proclamation of 'Action Painting' in his 1952 essay in *ARTnews*. As Rosalind Krauss later described it,

> Rosenberg's Action Painter was a literary hero, a larger-than-life figure out of American Tall Tales. His historic essay sought to make of the contemplative artist a hero of action. Both the emphasis of post-war existentialism on the *act* as the measure of man, as well as the end of radical rhetoric calling for political action in the climate of the Cold War, created a nostalgia for the Man of Action.

Siqueiros, of course, was an artist who prided himself on being an authentic man of action, a revolutionary, a soldier and, if need be, an executioner. Pollock was cast in a lesser role, that of artist as virtual man of action, confronting on his canvas the risks and dangers of the psychological arena. The myth of the artist as action hero was designed to fuse together the broken shards of Trotsky's revolutionary, Hemingway's bullfighter and Warshow's Westerner, to create a new hero of American masculinity out of the discredited remnants of the old. This new type of hero – in line with existentialist thought – was to be an anguished self-creator, whose personal struggle was worked through in the act of painting, a struggle which, in many ways, could only be self-punitive.

Masculinity is often structured in a paradoxical relationship with masochism. This is very clear, on two levels, within the work of Siqueiros himself. First, there are the extraordinary series of photographs he had taken of himself, and also his family and friends, arranged in various poses of suffering and torment. Second, there is the central importance of the depiction of suffering in the paintings themselves, for which, of course, the preliminary photographs – exercises in perspective and foreshortening – were originally taken. The fact that Siqueiros used himself as a model simply corroborates his own identification with tortured and martyred heroes. In essence, Siqueiros's work commemorates martyrdom. Despite its massive scale, insistent dynamism and aggressive monumentality, it is not triumphalist. If anything, it is defeatist. From the burial of the martyred worker in the National Preparatory School, through the crucified central figure in *Tropical America*, the martyred workers in *Portrait of Present Day Mexico*, his first portable mural, *Proletarian Victim*, the New York paintings, *Collective Suicide* and *Echo of A Scream*, the lynched Negro in *Cain in America*, the victims of fascism in the Electricians Union mural, the river of the dead in *Del Porfirismo a la Revolución*, the tortured hero in *Cuauhtémoc Redivivo*, the endless line of the oppressed in the *Polyforum* – in fact, throughout a career of political painting, the dominant note is one of unalloyed suffering and martyrdom, hardly alleviated by the occasional defiant revolutionary or hyper-muscular superhero.

In a pioneering essay on Lawrence of Arabia, Kaja Silverman has shown how masculinity and what Freud described as 'moral' or 'reflexive masochism' can be closely bound together. T. E. Lawrence, the self-appointed leader of an armed liberation struggle against the Ottoman Empire on behalf of the Arab nation, himself understood how the qualities of mastery and leadership, which made possible the identification of a mass of followers with a single individual, could be bound up with a masochistic desire for self-abasement. As Silverman describes it in her book *Male Subjectivity at the Margins*,

> Because reflexive masochism provides a mechanism for disposing of the subject's masochism without obliging him or her to renounce activity, it is ideally suited for negotiating the contradictions inherent in masculinity. It offers, in other words, a masochism, which is, if not without risk to masculinity, at least as free of any such risks as masochism can ever be,

in that it not only facilitates a sustained identification with activity, but disposes of the subject's masochism 'privately'.

Freud saw 'reflexive masochism' as a device by which the subject's own cruelty was turned upon himself 'without an attitude of passivity towards another person… The desire to torture has turned into self-torture and self-punishment' – into reflexive masochism. Silverman goes on to argue that this 'moral masochism' enables the subject to be both the one who inflicts pain on behalf of an exalted moral principle and the one who pleasurably suffers that pain. The leader dominates his companions both by the stringency of his standards and his action on their behalf, but also by his theatrical ability to bear more pain, to endure more suffering. Thus the 'feminine' implications of masochism are warded off and reversed into an instrument of masculinity. Pleasurable pain, self-inflicted, can 'function as the badge of leadership' and the guarantee of virility.

Siqueiros, of course, aspired to leadership over men in many fields: political leadership, military leadership, artistic leadership. In all three areas, he emphasised not only his role as dynamic leader but also his suffering and abjection. Siqueiros spent long periods of his life in prison or under house arrest – a lengthy term in the early 1930s, a brief incarceration after the Trotsky assassination attempt, another lengthy term in the 1960s – and also long periods in political exile, as the price of his release from jail sentences. Precisely as with Lawrence, this willingness to suffer, along with those whose cause he represented, guaranteed his credentials as their leader. The most interesting model here – a political, military and artistic model – is Cuauhtémoc, the Aztec leader who led the doomed Mexican resistance against the Spanish and died a terrible death under torture. Cuauhtémoc's suffering and martyrdom – his identification with his people – is much more prominent in the ways in which Siqueiros depicted Cuauhtémoc than is his resistance, precisely because it was his suffering that guaranteed his role as hero. In the 1951 mural, *Cuauhtémoc Arisen: His Torture*, the Aztec hero is being tortured by conquistadors clad in armour and bearing pikes and lances. In the 1961 sequel, *Cuauhtémoc Arisen: His Resurrection*, he himself is wearing the armour and has thrust his lance into the centaur which represents the conquistadors. As in the Christian myth, the passion is the guarantee of final victory, but, in Siqueiros's version, this victory is represented by a simple reversal of terms, from submission to triumph, from prostration to erection, from suffering flesh to cruel metal.

Pollock's case is more nuanced than that of Siqueiros. Pollock never set out to be a leader (he allowed himself to be cast in that role by others) and his relationship with masculinity was both less intense and more troubled. Many observers felt that Pollock's performance of masculinity involved an obvious element of uneasy posturing, of flawed theatricality. Thus Nicholas Carone observed that there was 'something wrong with the macho act' and Willem de Kooning commented, 'Jackson – yah, he would put on that tough guy act, you know?' Many friends and acquaintances – both old like Gerome Kamrowski and new like Ruth Kligman – made a comparison between Pollock and Marlon Brando or James Dean. Robert Motherwell compared him to 'Marlon Brando in scenes from *A Streetcar Named Desire*', except that 'Brando was much more controlled than Pollock'. Presumably, the comparison came in part from the sudden explosions of violence, in part from the exaggerated pose of masculinity, in part from the mumbling and inarticulacy. Both Brando and Dean, of course, also showed a penchant for masochism. Later, after the fatal car crash, the comparison could also play into the Pollock myth – Pollock as another troubled romantic rebel, too young to die.

However, the key element in the comparison, I believe, was that of theatricality. Many friends of Pollock have stressed the difference between his generous and gentle nature at some times and his violence and aggressiveness at others, often when drunk. Pollock's relationship with violence was plainly a troubled one. In many ways, as with Siqueiros, it served as a pretext for abjection – being beaten up or thrown in jail. But its function in relation to his art was plainly different in a number of crucial respects. First, it is clear that the turning point in Pollock's artistic career came with his entry into psychotherapy, in the late 1930s, and his subsequent turn towards inwardness and self-examination, as well as towards mythic reference and free association. His experience in therapy was given artistic validity by his encounter with surrealism. Pollock's violence became, so to speak, psychologised and channelled into the act of painting itself. Insofar as violence remained the subject matter of his work, its direct representation was obliterated. In fact, just as figuration gave way to abstraction, so depth and background gave way to surface and foreground. In this respect, Pollock was the polar opposite of Siqueiros, whose work was marked by an extreme three-dimensionality and aggressive perspective foreshortening.

Pollock's work lures the rapt viewer into a flat picture space, whereas Siqueiros's murals are projected outwards, through an elaborate perspective construction, to assault the mobile viewer within a complex architectonic space. Pollock's work is designed for viewing by an individual subject, whereas Siqueiros posited a mass viewer, moving through and past the work, on foot or in a vehicle. In this sense, Pollock's viewer is 'contemplative' and his work 'optical'. It has 'cult value', in the sense used by Walter Benjamin in his essay on 'The Work of Art in the Age of Mechanical Reproduction', whereas Siqueiros's work is 'tactile'. It produces a 'shock effect' on the mass viewer. Siqueiros, of course, was directly influenced by the kinetic strategies of Soviet silent cinema, clearly a model for Benjamin also. Eisenstein was of crucial importance for both of them.

Second, Pollock's work, because of its flatness and its abstraction, always hovered on the edge of decorativeness. Pollock himself worried about this and reacted negatively to the idea that he was a 'decorator'. From Dubuffet and Ossorio, he learned how to encrust and texture his surfaces, but as we can see from Ossorio's own work, this was an ambiguous lesson. It is important to remember that Pollock's path to success was paved, to a considerable extent, by the fashion press. It was in *Harper's Bazaar* that James Johnson Sweeney published his crucial article on 'Five American Painters', with a colour illustration of *The She-Wolf*, bought directly afterwards by the Museum of Modern Art. Serge Guilbaut describes this event, rather melodramatically, as a symbolic 'castration', through which Pollock was 'domesticated by the system of fashion' so that *The She-Wolf* was transformed into a 'lamb'! *Harper's* subsequently used Pollock paintings as backgrounds for fashion photographs, which played an important role in popularising his work. Indeed, it was through Alexey Brodovitch, art editor at *Harper's* and an early Pollock supporter, that Hans Namuth, himself a fashion photographer, was introduced to Pollock and given the contacts which enabled him to make his celebrated photo series and subsequent film of Pollock painting. Brodovitch also proposed a book collaboration with Pollock, which the painter welcomed. The decorative aspect of Pollock's art has been systematically downplayed precisely because it conflicted with the heroic role which was assigned to him. American painting needed signifiers of masculinity rather than effeminacy, of heroic struggle rather than women's fashion. Nevertheless, we should not forget that Pollock was the painter, not only of volcanic turbulence and the masculine sublime, but also of *Shimmering Substance* and *Lavender Mist*. It is not for nothing that Greenberg spoke of Pollock's work in the context of Matisse and late Monet.

In the last analysis, Siqueiros's faults – masculinity exaggerated to the point of kitsch – and Pollock's virtues – decorativeness energised by rebellious violence – are linked to their respective cultural situations.

Siqueiros came from a relatively peripheral and subordinate country with a history of victimisation. Mexican machismo derives from an obsession with male violence inseparable from the national myths of conquest, independence, the struggle for reform, insurgency and armed revolution. Siqueiros represented these myths in hyperbolic form and cast himself as a mythic character in a new revolutionary chapter. Pollock, in contrast, came from a large and powerful country with a history of military victory, violent westward expansion and the might of overwhelming armaments. He reflected the myths of the frontier and global power, but he also undercut and problematised them. National myths are inevitably bound up with questions of sexual pathology: monumentalisation of manliness, fear of effeteness, defence against guilt, identification with the suffering people, mourning and masochism. As a result, signifiers of masculinity, in the work of both artists, became inextricably entangled both with the private projection of self and with the public projection of a dynamic national culture.

* * *

Catalogue text published in German as 'Männerkunst: Siqueiros und Pollock', in Siqueiros/Pollock, Pollock/Siqueiros *(Kunsthalle Düsseldorf and Dumont, 1995), accompanying the exhibition of the same name, Kunsthalle Düsseldorf, 30 September to 3 December 1995. The English version is transcribed from a word-processed document in Wollen's archive. Previously unpublished in English.*

Global Conceptualism: North America – Exhibition Ideas/Notes/Proposal

Suggested preliminary list:

Shusaku Arakawa and Madeline Gins
Karl Beveridge and Carole Condé
Henry Flynt
Hollis Frampton
Harry Gamboa, Jr (Asco)
Guerrilla Art Action Group
General Idea
Helen Mayer and Newton Harrison
Robert Huot
Mary Kelly
People of Kitwancool
Yayoi Kusama
Les Levine
Lee Lozano
Yoko Ono
Adrian Piper
Faith Ringgold
Allan Sekula
Joyce Wieland
David Wilson

I have excluded from this list any artist who exhibited in the recent Los Angeles show, *Reconsidering the Object of Art*. I have selected work which addressed social issues and/or fell outside mainstream definitions of Conceptual Art. Based on artistic merit within these guidelines, women artists make up 50 percent of my choices, artists with Native American or non-Western backgrounds over a third, 'collective' artists nearly one third and Canadian artists one quarter.

I have tried to indicate the great variety of ways in which 'conceptual art' was realised. A large number of the artists worked in such marginalised areas as billboard art, book art, ecological art, film, performance, photography and poster art. Some of these artists' conceptual work is now very little known. Relatively few people may be aware of the work done by Robert Huot and Faith Ringgold when they were associated with the Art Workers' Coalition. Not many people remember that Henry Flynt invented the term 'concept art' or that he led the early boycott of MoMA in the '60s. The conceptual film work of David Wilson, founder of the Museum of Jurassic Technology, is largely forgotten. The conceptual (and political) performance work of Yayoi Kusama and Harry Gamboa, Jr, has only recently been rediscovered. Lee Lozano, often mentioned by Lucy Lippard as the leading woman conceptualist in the early days of the movement, is largely unknown. Mary Kelly's early work is usually categorised as 'feminist' rather than 'conceptualist', although the two are not mutually exclusive.

Arakawa and Gins's massive project, 'The Mechanism of Meaning', has been largely forgotten. Les Levine's work in relation to the Inuit people of northern Canada is not well known. Yoko Ono has both gained and suffered from her fame – we should look again at her work, including her performance pieces with Lennon. Allan Sekula is not usually considered a 'conceptual' artist but this seems anomalous – why are photographic series of water towers considered 'conceptual', but not series (with documentation) of factory workers?

* * *

Undated exhibition notes for North America section, curated by Wollen, of the exhibition 'Global Conceptualism: Points of Origin, 1950s–1980s', organised by Luis Camnitzer, Jane Farver and Rachel Weiss, Queens Museum of Art, New York, 28 April to 29 August 1999; Walker Art Center, Minneapolis, 19 December 1999 to 5 March 2000; Miami Art Museum, Miami, 15 September 2000 to 26 November 2000. Previously unpublished.

A number of changes can be seen between Wollen's proposed artists in this text and the final exhibition list, which is as follows: Eleanor Antin, Shūsaku Arakawa and Madeline Gins, John Baldessari, Theresa Hak Kyung Cha, Carol Condé and Karl Beveridge, Hollis Frampton, Harry Gamboa, Jr, Hans Haacke, Douglas Huebler, Robert Huot, On Kawara, Mary Kelly, Joseph Kosuth, Christine Kozlov, Sol LeWitt, Lucy Lippard, Lee Lozano, Yoko Ono and John Lennon, Adrian Piper, Martha Rosler, Seth Siegelaub and John W. Wendler, Michael Snow, Vincent Trasov (Mr Peanut), Lawrence Weiner, Joyce Wieland. Wollen's essay 'Global Conceptualism in North American Conceptual Art' was first published in the accompanying exhibition catalogue Global Conceptualism: Points of Origin, 1950s–1980s *(Queens Museum of Art, 1999) and republished in Wollen's essay collection* Paris Manhattan: Writings on Art *(Verso, 2004).*

A Trialogue on Arrows of Desire

Kodwo Eshun, Oliver Fuke and Nicolas Helm-Grovas

Kodwo Eshun: The thirteen texts gathered in 'Anti-Imperialisms', the second section of *Arrows of Desire*, the first seven of which are published under the pseudonym Lucien Rey, are written with a near-forensic attention to detail. These are articles and essays that analyse the political, military and economic crises of postcolonial, semi-colonial, colonial and imperial nation-states such as Zanzibar, Indonesia, Iran, the Federation of South Arabia and Britain, written for the left readership of periodicals such as *International Socialist Journal* and *New Left Review*. What is fascinating in 'The Crisis in Sterling' (1965), to take just one essay, is its anti-imperialist analysis of the first hundred days of Harold Wilson's new Labour government. Like Tom Nairn, Wollen approaches Britain as an imperial power confronted by an economic crisis that it cloaks in the reverential terminology of the so-called Sterling Area, which is nothing other than 'the modern and morbid form of the old British Empire'.[1] Fleet Street journalists traditionally treat the sterling crisis as a domestic issue; Wollen pursues its international implications. This anti-imperialist perspective gives Wollen an external perspective on Britain. From the early 1960s of 'Aden' and 'The Revolution in Zanzibar' through to 'Contradiction' in 1972, the vocabulary of anti-imperialism affords Wollen a grasp on the totality of imperialist capitalism as a world system.

Nicolas Helm-Grovas: For me, there's a strong Leninist dimension to these texts. They're about the balance of forces at a particular time and the manoeuvres of political actors. And also 'weakest link in the chain'

1 See 'The Crisis in Sterling' in this volume, 172.

analyses of imperialism. It's really good that you mentioned 'Contradiction', which is 1972, the same year that Wollen's essay 'Godard and Counter-Cinema' was published in *Afterimage*.[2] The lectures on Godard that we have collected here are from the period 1972–1974 when Wollen taught at Northwestern University. These dates are important because they underscore how counter-cinema is, in part, cinema understood in such a Leninist fashion, as the manoeuvring of political entities within cinema.

Oliver Fuke: In these counter-cinema lectures, he also introduces the distinction from Marxist theory, elaborated by Plekhanov and taken up by Lenin, between agitation, propaganda and theory and suggests that there are three levels of political film. In his analysis of the 1969 film *British Sounds* in these lectures, Wollen gives a detailed account of the soundtrack and uses a quotation which must be from Godard: 'This film is a sound which is opposing another sound: it is a revolutionary sound which is opposing a reactionary sound. But inside the film itself, there on the film-stock, this is expressed in the dialectics of the struggle between images and sounds.'[3] For Wollen during this period, the film is conceived as a kind of meeting-place in which these different struggles take place.

Nicolas Helm-Grovas: Yes, the film-text as comprised of political forces struggling against one another. We could definitely imagine that Wollen is influenced by Mao's essay 'On Contradiction', which he also talks about in his own essay 'Contradiction', in the way he articulates the antagonisms expressed in cinema, akin to Mao's discussion of principal and secondary contradictions. The Dziga Vertov Group period is, of course, Godard's Maoist period too.

Kodwo Eshun: What is peculiar about Godard, for bourgeois critics, is that he regards work on the theory of cinema as a political task. In the lecture on *British Sounds*, Wollen wants to analyse the politics of *British Sounds*, not 'in the sense of manifest content, which is both schematic & eclectic, but in the precise sense of the place of film as "political work"'. Understanding film in this way requires Wollen to turn back to 'some classical problems of Marxism' to gain insights into the questions posed by Godard that confront him in the present. The films of Godard and Gorin

2 Peter Wollen, 'Counter Cinema: *Vent d'Est*', *Afterimage*, 4 (Autumn 1972), 6–16, reprinted as 'Godard and Counter Cinema: *Vent d'Est*', in *Readings and Writings: Semiotic Counter-Strategies* (Verso, 1982), 79–91.

3 See 'Jean-Luc Godard: *British Sounds*' in this volume, 58.

compel Wollen to critically revisit historical questions of collectivity and autonomy in relation to the Communist Party, the coalitional form of the Popular Front, the historical examples of *Lef* and Mayakovsky and the dire legacies of Stalinism and Zhdanov's call for 'social realism'. Wollen even alludes, critically, to the example of the revolutionary writer Lu Hsun who led the League of Left-Wing Writers in 1930s China, anticipating the importance of Mao's ideas of cultural revolution and the practice of criticism and self-criticism so crucial for the Dziga Vertov Group.

Nicolas Helm-Grovas: The use of the term 'manifest content' from Freud's *The Interpretation of Dreams* suggests that 'political work' is analogous to what Freud calls the 'dream-work': the process by which 'latent content' (the unconscious material that is the impetus for a dream) is reshaped into what we dream and may remember. So it's the transformative structuring – or moment of production/transformation – that interests him, along the lines of Godard's distinction between 'making film politically' (emphasising the process) rather than 'making political film' (emphasising the product).

Oliver Fuke: Wollen is using Marxism and psychoanalysis together from quite early on. In the essay on counter-cinema, right towards the end, it's his engagement with psychoanalysis that allows him to register some critical distance between his position and Godard's regarding fantasy and fiction. He argues that 'desire, and its representation in fantasy, far from being the necessary enemies of revolutionary politics – and its cinematic auxiliary – are necessary conditions'.[4]

Nicolas Helm-Grovas: It's worth connecting Wollen's concern with narrative theory and narration in avant-garde film with the fact that these political texts are often narrative-driven, almost microhistories.

Kodwo Eshun: Yes; you could say that these texts are microhistories of the present: accounts of the military genocide in Indonesia in September 1965 to March 1966 or a political trial in semi-colonial Iran in November 1965. There is a way in which the levels of governmental deception and tenuous association recreated in 'Guilt by Association' (1966) recall the levels of imposture in *The Passenger* (1975), which Wollen co-wrote with Mark Peploe and Antonioni. Wollen uses his experience as a political

4 Wollen, 'Godard and Counter Cinema', 88.

journalist to fictionalise the figure of David Locke, the professional foreign correspondent at odds with his work, his marriage and his life. In interviews, Wollen and Peploe suggest that what ails Locke is an obscure ontological unease. There is, however, another possible reading. I think Locke epitomises a specific kind of white, male disenchantment with the Third World, which is played by and abstracted from the Chadian civil war of the 1970s. In a scene from the screenplay for *The Passenger* that significantly did not make the final cut, Locke's producer and friend retrieves pages and pages from Locke's cardboard file from which he reads to Locke's widow. Neither are sure whether Locke was joking or serious. I would suggest however, that Locke's sentences on the 'nonsense' of independence and the masquerade of Africanisation provide us with an insight into Locke's racial, political and ethical unease that Antonioni removed to render his dissociation more opaque.[5]

Oliver Fuke: *The Passenger* dramatises the stakes of people writing essays with commitment because you're exposed to disillusioned journalists who approach their work in cynical ways. The film has that scene, which Serge Daney liked, where the act or apparatus of journalism is critiqued.[6] The unnamed subject of the interview critiques the problematic framework animating Locke's questions.[7] He then turns the camera back on Locke, who looks startled, and says, 'Now we can have an interview, you can ask me the same questions as before …' You get an echo of this type of jaded journalist in *Friendship's Death* with Sullivan, who says that he's 'sympathetic' to the PLO but ultimately seems quite cynical.

Nicolas Helm-Grovas: We could say that one of the structuring absences of the 'Anti-Imperialisms' section of this book is *The Passenger*, which doesn't directly appear in any text. It connects to pseudonymity, because *The Passenger* is also about becoming someone else with a different name. Half of the texts in the 'Anti-Imperialisms' section are written under the Lucien Rey pseudonym.

---

5 See Mark Peploe, Peter Wollen and Michelangelo Antonioni, *The Passenger* (Grove Press, 1975), 78.

6 Serge Daney, 'Re-mise en Scène, or Restaging (Ivens, Antonioni, China)', in *Footlights: Critical Notebook 1970–1982*, trans. Nicholas Elliott (Semiotext(e), 2023), 65.

7 The screenplay reveals the figure interviewed by Locke as Rama Fadeda, the fictional rebel leader of the United Liberation Front. See Peploe, Wollen, Antonioni, *The Passenger*, 65–6.

Oliver Fuke: There's another scene in the film where Locke says, 'I used to be someone else. But I traded him in.' I always wanted to connect this phrase to Wollen's use of different writing personae which could, as it were, be exchanged, but it doesn't quite work because they weren't successive stages. He wrote under two pseudonyms through the same period, and it could be argued that, even after he started publishing in his own name, he continued to inhabit different personae or voices.

Kodwo Eshun: To publish such distinct texts under the names of Lucien Rey and Lee Russell in the same issue of *New Left Review* is like daring people to make the connection between the two names of the one person. Or is it three names? Lucien Rey, Lee Russell, Peter Wollen: how many readers made the connection between them?

Nicolas Helm-Grovas: A place is made for the political necessity of speculation, which returns with *Friendship's Death*, and a concern with thinking the position of the subject or enunciator in political (conventionally understood as rational) discourse, to the point even of inventing or fabricating such subjects. Practically, the Lucien Rey pseudonym was politically determined. Wollen was a deserter from military conscription in the UK. He graduated from Oxford University with an undergraduate degree in English Literature in 1959. He was one of the last people to be conscripted – conscription in the UK ended in 1960, with the last men completing their service by 1963. He did start the training, for some weeks, but was allowed to leave the military base to consult a doctor for an infected foot, and went AWOL. He went underground in London, and didn't see his parents or siblings for a very long time. In April 1960 he travelled to Paris, and in the autumn of 1960 he went to Iran. After he returned to London in 1961, he used the Lucien Rey and Lee Russell pseudonyms for his published writing, and was paid under the counter. In the middle of the decade he was living in Rome with Laura Mulvey and Jon Halliday, and working for Lelio Basso's *International Socialist Journal*. When they returned to London and he took up a 'proper job' at the British Film Institute, he was worried the desertion would catch up with him, but it never happened. (Much later, when he applied for a US 'green card' in 1993, he was again fearful that this history would catch up with him, as he was certain that US 'background checking' was much more efficient than the British version, but the connection was never made.) By 1967–1968 he starts writing under his real name. This is the more pragmatic dimension of his pseudonymity. But on a more conceptual level, 'Lucien Rey' is the introduction of fiction into journalism. Wollen writes these hyper-detailed factual texts, but there's a fictional authorial identity, a level of textual play. Especially because the names he chose contain references to other writers.

Kodwo Eshun: It is intriguing to note that, unlike his writings as Lee Russell, which he recalled more than once, most notably in 'Lee Russell Interviews Peter Wollen' for the fifth edition of *Signs and Meaning in the Cinema* in 1997, Wollen hardly, if ever, referred to the writings of Rey. That reticence gives the impression that he turned his back on those texts because he wanted them to be forgotten; that, however, would be an assumption neither confirmed nor denied by Wollen himself. I can imagine a dialogue in which Lucien Rey interviews Peter Wollen that would confront the writerly aspects of Rey's writing with the political aspects of Wollen's texts. An important text in which stylistic brio meets political nerve to spectacular effect is 'Was Christ a Collaborator?' published in *7 Days* for its Christmas edition in 1971. It's an anti-imperialist attack on the 'fawning' writers of the Gospels. Its title announces its heterodox mission. We know that Wollen drew on the work of Vittorio Lanternari's *The Religion of the Oppressed: A Study of Modern Messianic Cults* for this article because 'Was Christ a Collaborator?' revisits his review of Lanternari from eight years earlier, in *New Society*. 'Was Christ a Collaborator?' is one of those texts where it would be good to know more of Wollen's sources. In these early writings, Wollen rarely provides footnotes. This is not an academic text; it's a political takedown, meticulous in its attention to the concrete conditions of Palestinian life under Roman occupation.

Nicolas Helm-Grovas: It's an ideological analysis, and a materialist analysis – he discusses the Roman Empire, the Roman taxation system.

Kodwo Eshun: Yes; exactly, it's a materialist analysis that insists on the class position of Jesus of Nazareth. The historical Christ was not from the masses of rural peasantry or hired labourers. He was a carpenter working with 'lumber imported from Lebanon'. As with most of the apostles, he was 'a petty bourgeois' from the 'urban artisanate'.[8] Reading the Gospels for these details of labour and capital indicates Wollen's capacity to activate the scandalous, heretical dimension of Marxist demystification. Indeed,

8 See 'Was Christ a Collaborator?' in this volume, 158.

Wollen's writings for *Seven Days*, throughout its all-too-brief run from October 1971 to March 1972, go out of their way to dispel readers' expectations of dogmatic or economistic Marxism. 'Was Christ a Collaborator' is a shock to thought, whether or not you were brought up Methodist, as was Wollen.

Nicolas Helm-Grovas: Pasolini is another heretical Marxist.

Kodwo Eshun: One would expect Wollen to mention Pasolini but he rarely does.

Oliver Fuke: That's because of his film semiotics. He thinks that Pasolini has a conservative theory of film semiotics, close to André Bazin in its realist and romantic aspects.

Kodwo Eshun: I'm thinking also of the scandalising dimension of Godard's Marxism, which Wollen likes. The way Marxism is a shock to conventional thought.

Nicolas Helm-Grovas: Wollen is an avant-gardist. There's already an interest in shock from that. His interest in Surrealism, for instance. There's an overdetermination. Finally, I would say for this notion of heretical Marxism that combining semiotics and Marxism is a kind of heresy, as is combining psychoanalysis and Marxism.

Oliver Fuke: And the shock of feminism to Marxism. That's very important. Wollen was very open to that, and it separated him from lots of other Marxists at the time.

Kodwo Eshun: Multiple shocks conducted between anti-imperialism, psychoanalysis, semiotics, and feminism by, and on Marxism. Marxism as the reversible circuit along which flow the currents of these energies, impulses and forces.

Nicolas Helm-Grovas: Wollen as an avant-gardist is a good way of linking to his essay 'The Avant-Gardes: Europe and America', from 1981.

Kodwo Eshun: That essay, which appeared in *Framework*, looks back to the influential arguments of 'The Two Avant-Gardes' written for *Studio International* in 1975; it's a text that's part retrospective critique and part autobiographical polemic.[9] Wollen accounts for his role in the historical moment of 1975 by drawing out the 'programmatic strategy', the 'subtext' and the 'polemical drift running beneath the surface' of his most (in)famous essay. He begins with a reference to the debate between Malcolm Le Grice and P. Adams Sitney as the starting point that he sought to supersede in his 1975 essay.

Nicolas Helm-Grovas: Sitney's book on the American avant-garde, *Visionary Film* (1974), definitely has an anti-Europe slant. The whole narrative is that the avant-garde migrated from Europe to America after the 1920s. But Wollen isn't interested in simply a counter-defence of Europe. He wants to go beyond that polarity, to elaborate the framework in which the controversy takes place, and in a sense, to work at a meta-critical level, something he's already done in 1975 and does again, with an added self-retrospective aspect, in 1981.

Kodwo Eshun: Sitney acts as a useful foil against which Wollen goes into battle. Wollen's article in 1981 prompts Sitney to write an irate letter to *Framework*, to which Wollen responds in a ten-point rebuttal.

Oliver Fuke: Between 'The Two Avant-Gardes' and 'The Avant-Gardes: Europe and America', there's a need to clarify the stakes of the first essay, which had already become a very influential text on avant-garde film. But, six years later, there are also various things that Wollen thinks about differently. For example, he makes some points about *Tel Quel* and how this discourse, as with New American Cinema, contains different contradictory trends. Wollen also explicitly distinguishes between 'modernism' (concerned with 'reflexiveness' and 'semiotic reduction') and 'avant-garde' (engaged in 'semiotic expansion'), and, in a departure from the earlier argument, he identifies both tendencies *within* the first avant-garde. The influence of Peter Bürger's thought seems apparent here, though it is combined with other lines of argument. The schematic overview Wollen provides in 'The Two Avant-Gardes' had a crystal clarity that was helpful in many ways, but could be objected to in certain respects. At this 1981 conjuncture, as history has moved on, it requires this kind of rearticulation.

---

9 Peter Wollen, 'The Two Avant-Gardes', *Studio International*, 190:978 (November–December 1975), 171–5, reprinted in *Readings and Writings*, 92–104.

Kodwo Eshun: Wollen is undertaking what I would call an 'intertemporal' reading of 'The Two Avant-Gardes'. That entails looking back, from the vantage point of 1981, at the discrepancy between the future that Wollen and his allies worked to bring into existence in 1975, and the recent present after 1975 as it actually unfolded, and using the retrospective insights gained from the gap between expectation and actuality to assess the future for British independent film culture in the 1980s, which, in turn, helps to assess the point from which to intervene to support the avant-garde against the resurgence of reactionary forces in the present of 1981.

Nicolas Helm-Grovas: I think that by 1981 some of the claims Wollen makes in 'The Two Avant-Gardes' have become part of the basic discourse around European and North American avant-garde film, which is obviously different from saying that everyone agreed with them. But there's also been a political shift to the right. Wollen was very attuned to France: by the mid-1970s, you're already seeing the *nouveaux philosophes*, Bernard-Henri Lévy, André Glucksmann, etc., people recanting their Maoism. In any case, in the more reactionary moment of 1981, the positions of 'The Two Avant-Gardes', as they've been disseminated in the UK and beyond, have been stripped of some of the way in which in 1975, they're really also, if you take the idea seriously, a manifesto for the Independent Film-Makers' Association (IFA). The IFA was about a cinema of social practice, not only an interest in 'semiotic expansion', to use a phrase from the 1981 text. Even as early as 1981, there are already layers of reading and discussion over 'The Two Avant-Gardes'. There is a set of automatic or dominant narratives about the text, and he's trying to reframe it. There's a parallel between Wollen's positions on avant-garde film and on theory, where he always articulates two available positions, and then demonstrates that neither is sufficient on its own. He wants to outline a position that has elements of both, or that can dialectically mediate an antinomy. This is well-known with his argument about what he calls the two avant-gardes. The same is true of theory too. Because you have on the one hand Wollen's critique of a kind of theoretical idealism, which is what *Tel Quel* represents for him by now. This idealism is probably clearer to him because *Tel Quel* specifically has moved to the right. Philippe Sollers converts to Catholicism in the late 1970s, and in fact *Tel Quel* is dissolved the year after Wollen's essay. On the other hand, and this is also an effect of, or response to, the rightward lurch, there's a return of realist positions within film theory. Wollen sees these as merely reactive. In response to idealist semiotic theories, you get a return of pre-semiotic realist positions.

Wollen sees this return of realism and empiricism within Marxist theory more broadly: the excesses of Althusserianism lead to E .P. Thompson's *The Poverty of Theory* (1978). There is a wider anti-theory reaction.

Kodwo Eshun: Wollen picks up on that reactionary impulse to expel theory, banish semiotics and deport 'structuralism' from its 'infiltration of the universities and cultural institutions' in Raymond Durgnat's article 'The Death of Cinesemiology (With Not Even a Whimper)', which explicitly builds on Thompson's anti-Althusserian diatribe.[10] This sense of mounting a heroic struggle against the semiotic subversion of higher education foreshadows the so-called MacCabe affair, which epitomises the conservative fightback against the incomprehensible 'jargon' imposed on impressionable students, the undermining of intellectual standards and the seduction of fashionable Parisian theory. Wollen clearly senses a revitalised moral economy of anti-theory. This revanchist structure of feeling converges with the political situation in early-1980s Britain where Margaret Thatcher's appeal stems from her capacity to translate policy issues into a moral language that can animate a neo-McCarthyite resurgence 'designed to wipe out the aftermath of '68'.[11]

Nicolas Helm-Grovas: I would argue that Wollen is articulating a classical Marxist position about the mutually sustaining relationship between two perennial bourgeois philosophies or ideologies: idealism (or, relatedly, romanticism) on one side, and empiricism (or, relatedly, positivism or reductive scientism) on the other, ideologies that Marx says are seemingly opposed, but actually accompany one another to the 'blessed end'.[12] Neither can go beyond the antinomy that traps them and their opposite pole. In this context Brecht is again an important reference point for Wollen, as an artist who does try to overcome this antinomy – between an avant-garde idealism of the signifier and realism – dialectically. Wollen sees feminist filmmaking in a similar light.

Oliver Fuke: In 1975, Mulvey and Wollen had made *Penthesilea* and are looking to make *Riddles of the Sphinx*, whereas in 1981, Wollen can reflect back on the significance of feminist avant-garde film, particularly that

10 See Raymond Durgnat, 'The Death of Cinesemiology (with Not Even a Whimper)', *Cinéaste* 10:2 (Spring 1980), 10–13.

11 See 'The Avant-Gardes: Europe and America' in this volume, 91.

12 Karl Marx, *Grundrisse: Foundations of the Critique of Political Economy (Rough Draft)*, trans. Martin Nicolaus (Penguin, 1993), 162.

of Yvonne Rainer's and Chantal Akerman's feature-length feminist films. He says: 'The problems of the avant-garde began to seem more and more utopian, a vain struggle to hold back the tide of irrationalism. In fact, it was in the area of feminist film-making and feminist film theory that the line was best held. Feminism, of course, was itself in part a product of the political and intellectual upheavals emblematically associated with 1968. Feminism also demanded a critique of image and narrative in dominant forms of cinema which inflected it towards the avant-garde.' When he writes this six years after 'The Two Avant-Gardes' he's writing after the high point of political modernism. He's looking back and considering the impact of feminism for thinking film semiotics. That's quite crucial.

Nicolas Helm-Grovas: They were already citing feminist filmmakers when they were interviewed about *Penthesilea* in 1974, though.

Oliver Fuke: My argument though is that he can gauge the import of feminist film and feminist film theory at this point, and that allows him to reframe his argument, and to think about it all in relation to film semiotics. Whereas in that nascent moment in 1975, Mulvey and Wollen have made just one film. Akerman's *Jeanne Dielman, 23, quai du Commerce, 1080 Bruxelles* is about to come out or has just come out. They haven't met Rainer yet. That happens in 1976, but they've seen her first two films and think they are important. At that point, it's all just emerging. Lots of questions are being asked; new alliances are being formed. It's difficult to theorise so precisely. He doesn't even mention feminism in 'The Two Avant-Gardes'. But by 1981, he thinks that feminist filmmakers and feminist film theorists are doing some of the most important and critical work.

Kodwo Eshun: Wollen criticises film semiotics for its failure to develop 'flexible enough concepts to extend the scope of semiotics beyond the classical codes of Hollywood or art cinema' in ways that could 'feed directly into film-making'. Feminist filmmaking and feminist film theory are the exceptions to these problems; that's where Wollen sees a feedback between avant-garde film and theoretical work. When he refers to recent feminist films made in contexts where 'feminist theoretical writing has provided background and encouragement', he might well be referring to contemporary feminist theory films such as Lis Rhodes's *Light Reading* (1978), Sue Clayton and Jonathan Curling's *The Song of the Shirt* (1979), Sally Potter's *Thriller* (1979) and Jay Street Collective's *Sigmund Freud's Dora* (1979).

Nicolas Helm-Grovas: To return to what Kodwo said earlier about the position of Sitney here, and also in Wollen's reply: the proper noun is a very important figure in Wollen's writing. It works as shorthand for arguments and ideas. Names are a way of condensing things and specifying them quickly in order to lay out a landscape. So here there is 'Sitney', but also '*Tel Quel*', 'Le Grice'. The names condense wider trends. This is part of the diagrammatic writing style he often employs. A productive reductivism.

Kodwo Eshun: It's necessarily reductive, because if you accounted for their positions in detail you would never be able to launch an argument; you would have to qualify each determinate statement you make with caveats, modifications and exceptions.

Nicolas Helm-Grovas: Wollen doesn't only use this method for his antagonists, though – Brecht and Godard function in the same way. 'Godard' embodies for Wollen a whole set of principles and aspirations and methods in six letters, two syllables.

Kodwo Eshun: I agree. The polemicism, the oppositionality and the diagrammaticism engender a provocative and productive reductivism that summarizes complex positions. It's a way to schematise the field to map out the conjuncture that sets the terms for the intervention underway in the project at hand. That provides an insight into Wollen and Mulvey's turn towards the Mexican renaissance of the 1930s. Redirecting attention towards Mexico from the late 1970s opens a new geography of revolution that reorients their thinking throughout the 1980s and into the 1990s. It's striking to see that generative schematisation at work in Mulvey and Wollen's juxtaposition between the small paintings of Frida Kahlo and the photography of Tina Modotti that breaks with the monumentalism of *los tres grandes*.

Oliver Fuke: When searching for critical models where art and politics converged, the important point for Mulvey and Wollen, as Kodwo suggests, is about resituating the geographies of the avant-garde. In the catalogue essay, they are arguing that, in comparison with Soviet art of the same period, Mexican art has only been mentioned in these types of discussions in a very superficial way thus far. Mulvey and Wollen had spent time researching it, talking with Hayden Herrera and so on, and had reached the conclusion that the cultural practice of the Mexican renaissance provides a compelling model.

Nicolas Helm-Grovas: They start the catalogue essay on Kahlo and Modotti with Breton. Perhaps they start there because Breton is more famous at this time than Kahlo and Modotti. But what happens is that instead of maintaining this privileged place, Surrealism gets refracted through Mexico. Mexico decentres the reading of Surrealism. The focus on women artists similarly decentres. Just before this project, there are various texts and interviews by Mulvey of the late 1970s in which she frames her work in terms of debates in feminist aesthetics at that time. These are part of the same context, and the exhibition, book and film are an intervention in these debates.

Oliver Fuke: Feminist discourse on the body is important here and it's discussed at length in the essay.

Kodwo Eshun: Mulvey and Wollen cite magazines like New York's *Heresies* and journals like London's *m/f*; these periodicals mount an ongoing debate to which 'Mexico/Women/Art' (1979) – the first public outcome of their research on the work of Kahlo and Modotti – is responding. 'With Frida Kahlo', writes Wollen, 'there is a particular kind of relationship to folk and popular culture, an intense self-investigation and self-exposure (both through her self-portraits and her journals) and a prominence of the symbolic representation of the body. These are all the kind of things you get to see and read about in *Heresies* and across a whole range of women's art today.'[13] You can hear the preoccupation with a feminist politics of representation of the female body that Oliver mentioned running through the 1970s and 1980s and into 'Arrows of Desire' in the early 1990s when Wollen selects independent films, experimental videos and animations for their 'fearless faith in personal revelation and self-examination' and their 'restitution of the body to the centre of art'.

Oliver Fuke: I also think it's important to note that Sonia Boyce and Donald Rodney have spoken about the significance of seeing Kahlo's work, in the Kahlo and Modotti exhibition at the Whitechapel Gallery. In the mid-1980s, Boyce made some drawings that were directly influenced by Kahlo's work. Rodney also drew on Kahlo in many ways. He explored related topics, often with less of a personal focus, and derived formal ideas for mixed media works from her paintings. He quoted *The Broken Column* (1934), in *Britannia Hospital 3* (1988). Considering the relation

13 Peter Wollen, 'Mexico/Women/Art', in *Readings and Writings*, 110.

of both Kahlo and Modotti to Britain in 1982: the anti-imperial and anti-colonial aspect of their lives and art, and that of the Mexican renaissance more generally, seems important. It's the year after the Black People's Day of Action, and various uprisings against police harassment and racial attacks in Brixton in April 1981, Coventry in May, Southall, Liverpool, Manchester, Handsworth, Leicester, Bolton, Luton, Nottingham, Derby in July, Sheffield and Brighton in August 1981. The artists associated with the British Black Arts Movement are all beginning to make work.

Kodwo Eshun: I think Sonia Boyce and Donald Rodney's transformations and transpositions of Kahlo's bodily symbolism reward sustained study. Boyce has consistently spoken of the importance of Kahlo's work for her consciousness of herself as a politicised artist in interviews conducted in 1986, 1987, 1991, 1992 and 2002. In 2022, she recalled that her inspiration as a younger artist was 'discovering Frida Kahlo' in 'an exhibition with Tina Modotti'. I would argue that the 'complex of signs' assembled in Boyce's work, developed and elaborated from her study of Kahlo's paintings, extend and expand the 'discourse of the body' that provided a continuity with the Mexican revolution for the generation of Mulvey and Wollen. Similarly, studying Boyce's and Rodney's work today helps us to draw continuities and discontinuities between now and the early 1980s when Mulvey and Wollen were bringing Kahlo and Modotti together to ask questions about their moment. There's a critical sentence in their catalogue essay which speaks to this: 'We need to know what has been achieved and how it was checked and deflected, to construct our own history in its own incompleteness.' I find this formulation to be very powerful in its understanding of their present as a matter of forces checked and deflected by counter-revolutionary forces. It's a matter of using art as a vantage point from which to begin to see their historical formation, in the present, as the outcome of the contestation between earlier political forces.

Oliver Fuke: If you think about an earlier text like 'The Revolution in Zanzibar', it's an analysis of what has been achieved and what is still to be done. The impetus underpinning Lucien Rey's writing is transposed to a curatorial context to look at an artistic movement, what it accomplished and where it was derailed.

Nicolas Helm-Grovas: With 'Frida Kahlo and Tina Modotti' the mode is perhaps more montage than genealogy.

Kodwo Eshun: Montage places two times, two eras, two moments next to each other to get them to speak to each other in a language other than their own. The idea is that the 1930s to 1940s illuminates the 1980s even as the 1980s throws a light on the time between the wars. That's the tiger's leap of montage.

Nicolas Helm-Grovas: Yes, exactly. It's anti-historicist.

Kodwo Eshun: A curatorial strategy of montage deliberately excludes the decades in between, not because they're not important, but to highlight certain aspects that will be elided if you patiently reconstruct the concerns specific to each decade. A strategy of historicization will lose certain insights; the ambition is to sharpen those insights by dramatising them through montage rather than historicising them through genealogy or through the *longue durée* of the archive.

Nicolas Helm-Grovas: Again, reduction in order to clarify. But I also think that for Wollen, that kind of historicist thinking chains things together. It traps them. When there are just two moments there are more possibilities of combination and for speculative thought emerging in the spaces. It's like what Eisenstein says about sound, when he says that the problem with sound film is that the images have more inertia and it's harder to move them around. There's more weight to them, which reduces the possibilities for combination as a form of thinking the new.

Oliver Fuke: Mulvey and Wollen state that montage aims to undo the idea of a triumphant genius in exhibition-making. So there's a feminist dimension to that montage.

Nicolas Helm-Grovas: Maybe we could see Wollen's montage of David Alfaro Siqueiros and Jackson Pollock more than a decade later in a similar vein. That text takes up some feminist concerns but applies them to two male artists.

Kodwo Eshun: You could say that the theory film, as Mulvey and Wollen referred to their own films in the 1970s, allows them to pose the idea of a 'theory exhibition' for the 1980s. The transposition of montage from cinema into exhibition-making, as you have both suggested, enables Wollen and Mulvey to make a film from a series of feminist arguments about women's art addressed to the ways in which art history positions that art. If the 'Frida Kahlo and Tina Modotti' exhibition applies Eisensteinian montage to exhibition-making then Wollen's unmade film *Eisenstein in Mexico* reads like a proposal for an exhibition in cinematic form. What's critical about this cine-curatorial project is its disinterest in providing the missing images required to complete Eisenstein's *Que Viva Mexico*. Instead, it brings together the different kinds of images Eisenstein would have assembled to invoke *Que Viva Mexico* as a structuring absence around which orbit photographs by Modotti and Weston, footage shot by Eduard Tisse, drawings by Eisenstein and murals by Orozco, Siqueiros and Rivera. The aim is to assemble a visual study, in Nicole Brenez's sense, that brings audiences face-to-face with the images that evoke the absent presence of *Que Viva Mexico*. To confront audiences with the counter-revolutionary conditions that blocked the aesthetic revolution of *Que Viva Mexico*. Wollen's exhibition 'Posada: Messenger of Mortality' continues his preoccupation with 'an independently Mexican version of modernism'.[14] The catalogue essay on José Guadalupe Posada exemplifies a mode that Wollen deploys throughout the 1980s and 1990s. I think of it as a networked mode of narration in which he identifies expatriate friendships within milieus that facilitate aesthetic exchanges and political affinities.

Oliver Fuke: In 'Knight's Moves' Wollen says that movements are aesthetic and political but also social, the latter being an aspect necessary to understanding them.

Kodwo Eshun: Wollen emphasises the density of relationships between expatriate artists living and working in proximity with each other in a foreign city to draw out what we could call the social life of form.

Nicolas Helm-Grovas: A lot of Wollen's writings in that vein end up in *Raiding the Icebox*. The essays in *Raiding the Icebox* were written in the late 1980s and early 1990s, the same time as the Posada essay. This is a period in which Wollen is engaging or re-engaging with 'the popular'. I would say engaging for the first time rather than re-engaging, because when he writes about popular culture before that, like with Hollywood cinema, he doesn't approach it through the concept of the popular. Wollen was friends with Paddy Whannell, who wrote *The Popular Arts* with Stuart Hall in 1964. That book discusses John Ford and the Western genre. That's exactly the time Wollen starts writing about film for *New*

14 See 'Introduction to *J.G. Posada: Messenger of Mortality*' in this volume, 283.

Left Review, including writing about John Ford and other directors of Westerns. Yet Wollen approaches these by more or less ignoring the notion of the popular unpacked by Hall and Whannel. I think he's very concerned to avoid Hollywood cinema being reductively sociologised, and its aesthetic components thereby ignored or minimised, and to do that he simply brackets the concept of the popular. He can't let it in. By the end of the 1980s, he's able to return to this issue. By this time the theoretical discourse on the popular has become quite sophisticated in the work of people like Stuart Hall, or in a journal like *New Formations*, where Wollen publishes many of the essays that end up in *Raiding the Icebox*. One of the things that's most compelling in the Posada essay is the historical and theoretical argument. It's a more traditionally Marxist narrative than Wollen often provides, which is that Posada is situated at a very particular moment in the history of the forces and relations of media production: it's no longer artisanal folk art, but it's not yet mass media. It has elements of both, because it's printed but its form of distribution is being hawked on street corners. This underpins an argument about the work's form and its politics and ideology, which I think is really powerful.

Oliver Fuke: Wollen's thinking about Mexico culminates in his plans in the early 1990s for an exhibition, never staged, that went by several names, most notably 'The Continent'.

Kodwo Eshun: You could think about 'The Continent' from the opposition drawn between Clement Greenberg's triumphalist position on twentieth-century American art and Serge Guilbaut's anti-triumphalist critique. Those positions contest each other but despite that opposition, they still share the idea that America took modern art from Europe in order to overtake Europe. Wollen's point is that this shared presupposition suppresses all consciousness of the debt North America owes to the Mexican renaissance and the Northwest Coast renaissance in British Columbia, in Canada. That repression is psychic as well as artistic.

Nicolas Helm-Grovas: The approach is in a certain sense psychoanalytic.

Oliver Fuke: I think of 'The Continent' project as quite genealogical, taking founding myths of origin and showing how they're always, in a sense, multiple. Wollen's curatorial project would have foregrounded Mexican art and Pacific Northwest Coast art. It was intended to counterbalance the inflated importance European art has been given when thinking about artists like Pollock and to critique the role that critics have played in securing this narrative, as well as national myths more generally.

Nicolas Helm-Grovas: And also deflating the importance of US artists overall, I think. The term 'America' is a problem here. Wollen is clearly testing different names for his project, but seems most persuaded by 'The Continent'. When we wrote 'Re-Narrating "American" Art' in our section heading, we put 'American' in quotation marks, because if not that positions you in an allegiance that the exhibition is taking apart. Wollen's argument, implicitly at least, is that the Mexican and the US dominant national myths are different in that the Mexican one involves the incorporation of indigeneity in certain forms, whereas the US one involves the repression of indigeneity. The latter is a discursive repression but based in literal attempts at elimination, genocide. There are relationships to Europe in both myths. Greenberg sees Pollock as an heir to and culmination of a European tradition, but also as American and not European. What constitutes 'American' here is definitely not indigenous. It's something modern that's associated with the USA and pioneer myths.

Oliver Fuke: Although it is concerned largely with 'American' painting, by demonstrating its debt to Mexican art and Native American art, this curatorial project is also at the same time engaged in the process of questioning not only art-historical categories but also national myth and identity, or political self-understanding. As Edward W. Said was arguing in *Culture and Imperialism* (1993) at almost exactly the same time, 'imperialism', and we could add 'settler-colonialism', was rarely mentioned in accounts of United States history, culture and politics. This exhibition would have brought all of this up and presumably, if it had gone ahead, would have been quite an intervention.

Kodwo Eshun: It's a question of challenging the stability of whatever we think America is by calling it 'the continent'. There is a calculated indeterminacy: to which continent, exactly, does 'The Continent' refer?

Nicolas Helm-Grovas: Yes, it's a question of suspension. To a certain extent, the continent is geographic, but geographic boundaries are never purely physical. They're always about how that is divided politically and culturally; what constitutes a significant physical boundary is not simply objective or pre-discursive. Wollen's project contains artists from 'Canada' in the way it does 'Mexico' or 'the USA', but his work overall doesn't analyse the construction of the category 'Canadian art' in the way it does the other two. Wollen was interested in the art of indigenous people in the Pacific Northwest, in what is now commonly called British Columbia.

Kodwo Eshun: His engagement is with Haida artists of the Northwest Coast renaissance of the 1960s and 1970s, especially Bill Reid and Robert Davidson.

Nicolas Helm-Grovas: I think this was Wollen challenging the hegemonic, received notion of 'Canadian art', in which the art of First Nations people was excluded from modern and contemporary art and instead placed in the anthropology museum. Wollen proposed similar art for inclusion when he curated the North American section of the major exhibition 'Global Conceptualism: Points of Origin, 1950s–1980s'. Indeed the contrast between the way that exhibition straightforwardly named a particular area and how Wollen suspends naming in his own is striking. So the continent is also imaginary. I think an important reference point here is the Surrealist map of the world, published in Belgium in the magazine *Variétés* in 1929. The USA is basically eliminated apart from Alaska and Hawaii, territories that aren't connected to the rest of the nation. Most of Canada disappears, but Mexico stays. It's a new continent where the elements have a different weighting.

Kodwo Eshun: Wollen is making curatorial interventions that entail an interrogation of the institution of art history. We don't know why 'The Continent' was not realised. Whatever the reason, its cancellation exposes the limits of the Whitney Museum of American Art in the early 1990s. I think the documents we do have demonstrate the extent to which 'The Continent' sought to intervene in the dominant US-centrism of modern art in twentieth-century North America.

Oliver Fuke: He opens his proposal by saying this exhibition is historical. It tells a story, but that story is something of a counter-narrative to the dominant one that's been told hitherto. That's what he's trying to displace. Therefore, that involves him operating in this way. Exhibition-making, which is necessarily multimedia, can tell a complex story like this.

Kodwo Eshun: I agree. The documents we have enable us to envision the ways in which 'The Continent' would have afforded Wollen the form and the medium to transpose his argument for the intermedial ontology of film from the theorisation and the making of film towards the space of exhibition that would have tested those arguments through the curatorial strategies of montage.

Oliver Fuke: Let's consider finally the book's title, *Arrows of Desire*. This was the name given by Wollen to the series of independent films and videos he programmed in the early 1990s at the ICA. It included film-makers and video makers like John Akomfrah, Robert Crusz, Stuart Marshall, Jayne Parker and Alia Syed. Wollen states that he selected the title, taken from William Blake's Preface to *Milton: A Poem in Two Books*, as a 'counterblast to *Chariots of Fire* … not just the film … but a vision of British cinema'.[15] When I think about this title, I connect it with Mark Stewart and The Maffia's track 'Jerusalem', deployed in Black Audio Film Collective's *Handsworth Songs* (1986). It reworks tradition into new revolutionary sounds to counter persistent reactionary ones. Wollen does something similar with this phrase. By the time of the ICA Biennial, Wollen is arguing that an audiovisual culture has emerged operating between the art and media worlds, experimenting with new means and what he calls a 'montage of politics'. The new and heterogenous works making up this counterblast to nostalgic British cinema have, in a sense, taken a knight's move away from counter-cinema.

Kodwo Eshun: Wollen might well have known Mark Stewart and The Maffia's version of 'Jerusalem' from *Handsworth Songs*; after all, he wrote about Reece Auguiste of Black Audio Film Collective's *Twilight City* a number of times. I think the idea of the montage of politics enables him to register the ways in which independent and experimental films and videos in the ICA Biennial revisit, revise and rework signs of nationality, locality and cosmopolitanism in subtle yet significant ways that confound traditional assumptions of Britishness, hybridity, Englishness and diasporicity. I think there's a desire to complicate what counts as 'intimacy' and what signifies as 'public issues' in the films and videos he selects for 'Arrows of Desire'. These films constitute an 'avant-garde' but not in the traditional sense of an explicit polarisation 'against the mainstream'. It is a matter, instead, of studying the ways in which they expand 'the potential of expression'. It's significant, too, that Wollen doesn't use the phrase 'artists moving image' at this time. Instead, he's referring to the 'cultures and subcultures' of audiovisual media or audiovisual culture in relation to

15 See 'Interview on "Arrows of Desire"' in this volume, 127.

what he calls the 'two monsters' of television and the art world. The generality of these terms conveys the sense that the criteria for categorising, judging and thinking of the place of independent film and experimental video have diffused in ways hard to grasp according to established critical vocabulary. It is as if Wollen is using the vehicle of the Biennial, not only to bring himself up-to-date but to force film criticism and film theory to update itself, to account for the state of the British avant-garde in 1992.

Nicolas Helm-Grovas: It's also worth tracing the continuities between the work of the 1970s and what happens in the 1990s given that Wollen is so often associated with, and confined to, a 1970s cinematic and theoretical project. I'm reminded of the film *Godard 1980*, an interview between Godard, Wollen and Don Ranvaud filmed by Jon Jost. Godard is asked about *Sauve qui peut (la vie)*, his 1980 film which seems to represent a return to a more traditional form after his experiments with the Dziga Vertov Group and Anne-Marie Miéville in the previous decade. Godard says something to the effect that sometimes when you are walking around and exploring you end up crossing your tracks from earlier before going off another way. I see something similar in Wollen. When he turns again to Eisenstein in the middle of the 1980s, for instance, he does this from a different direction, through Mexico. And then when he writes about Eisenstein once more in the late 1990s, he speaks a lot about Eisenstein's missed encounter with dance, dance being a topic that Wollen had become more and more fascinated by from the end of the previous decade onwards. You could chart something similar with Wollen's returns to Godard.

Oliver Fuke: Exactly. At a very basic level, I really like the way that in each of the texts on Godard included in this volume, written at roughly ten-year intervals, Wollen refers to the last time he wrote about Godard. In this sense, they chart both Wollen's and Godard's overlapping paths. The first take on Godard's *Passion*, published in 1983, refers to the essay (and hence the lectures) on Godard and counter-cinema from 1972–4; 'L'Eternel Retour', from 1992, refers to his text on *Passion*. 'Knight's Moves', which is from 2002 and about experimental film more generally, slightly bucks the trend in that in reaches right back to 'counter-cinema' – a thirty-year gap! – bypassing the other two essays. Still, in each text there is a kind of palimpsestic layering. In 'Knight's Moves', Wollen describes how he and others 'wrote drafts of guidelines for possible futures under the pretext of theorizing contemporary film practice'. It really gives a sense of the urgency and passion that can be felt in the writing from the 1970s, the search for alternative ways of filmmaking.

Kodwo Eshun: Those returns to Godard and Eisenstein parallel Wollen's own returns to his participation in the debates over the future of avant-garde cinema of the 1970s. We've already seen this return in 'The Avant-Gardes: Europe and America' in 1981. In 'The Last New Wave: Modernism in the British Films of the Thatcher Era' (1987), Wollen argues that the importance of Greenaway and Jarman in the 1980s might be due, in part, to their non-participation in those debates on the avant-garde. Perhaps, he suggests, Greenaway and Jarman's distance from those debates liberated them from 'the baggage of past positions and pronouncements', allowing them to evade the role of 'political filmmaker' and enabling them to take up artistic positions from which emerged, eventually, their distinct anti-Thatcherist projects.[16] That reads to me like a coded self-criticism. Or perhaps a recognition that, as a theorist who makes films, he remains committed to those debates, those positions and those pronouncements in ways that set him apart from Jarman and Greenaway. In 'Arrows of Desire' (1992), Wollen recounts those debates in the Brechtian mode of a children's story that starts: 'Once upon a time, there was a small, truculent and determined avant-garde.' 'Knight's Moves', as Oliver suggests, revisits those debates, in 1999, emphasising the ways in which they were determined by the 'expectations of the future'. Across these essays, Wollen continually moves between the third and the first person, using the changing vantage point of each time of writing to invoke the ever-growing distance, for him and for us, as his readers, from the horizons of expectation that guided those futures past. These writings capture a specific structure of intertemporal feeling in which Wollen registers his changing position and his continued commitment. We read him as he ages, articulating the continually changing relations between futures, pasts and presents.

Nicolas Helm-Grovas: The phrase 'arrows of desire', as Oliver suggests, reconfigures the project of counter-cinema through a 'knight's move'. Arrows, after all, are weapons, suggesting that battlefield model of cultural struggle of the counter-cinema era. But the imagery of arrows is more romantic than would be permissible in that era, in which productivist, industrial metaphors dominate. And to speak of 'arrows *of desire*' is to

16 Peter Wollen, 'The Last New Wave', *Paris Hollywood: Writings on Film* (Verso: 2002), 181.

more strongly foreground the libidinal dimension of such a political and artistic project. Of course, post-1968 film theory was always a desiring discourse, strongly so, even if that desire was typically mediated through or took the form of a relentless intellectualisation of cinema. This is part of the passion that Mulvey speaks of in her famous reference to 'passionate detachment'.[17] However, with 'arrows of desire' there is almost a reversal of emphasis – the 'counterblast' takes place *through* desire. Yet this doesn't make it less political.

17 Laura Mulvey, 'Visual Pleasure and Narrative Cinema', *Screen*, 16:3 (Autumn 1975), 18.

List of Permissions

'Introduction to Two Mayakovsky Scenarios', first published in *Screen*, is reprinted by kind permission of Oxford University Press.

Three sets of lecture notes on Godard's films *Le Gai Savoir*, *British Sounds*, *Wind from the East*, and lecture notes on Godard and Counter-Cinema, courtesy of the Peter Wollen Collection, British Film Institute National Archive.

'The Avant-Gardes: Europe and America', 'Reply to Sitney', and '*Passion* 1' are reprinted by kind permission of *Framework, The Journal of Cinema and Media*.

'L'Eternel Retour' is reprinted by kind permission of the Museum of Modern Art, New York.

'Arrows of Desire' is reprinted courtesy of the Institute of Contemporary Art, London.

'Interview on "Arrows of Desire", ICA Biennial of Independent Film and Video' is reprinted by kind permission of *PIX*.

'Perhaps...' is reprinted by kind permission of *October*.

'Knight's Moves' is reprinted by kind permission of *PUBLIC: Art | Culture | Ideas*.

'The Revolution in Zanzibar', 'Guilt by Association', and 'Dossier of the Indonesian Drama' are reprinted by kind permission of *New Left Review*.

'Was Christ a Collaborator?' and 'Contradiction', first published in *7 Days*, are reprinted courtesy of Amiel Melburn Trust Archive.

'Two Weeks on Another Planet', first published in *Monthly Film Bulletin*, is reprinted by kind permission of *Sight and Sound*.

'Introduction to *Wedding in Galilee*', 'Iraq', 'John Wesley', courtesy of the Peter Wollen Collection, British Film Institute National Archive.

'Frida Kahlo and Tina Modotti' is reprinted by kind permission of Laura Mulvey, co-author, and the Whitechapel Gallery, London.

'Eisenstein in Mexico', correspondence regarding the proposed exhibition titled 'The Continent', 'Masculinity: Siqueiros and Pollock' in original English, and 'Global Conceptualism: exhibition notes', courtesy of the Peter Wollen Collection, British Film Institute National Archive.

'Introduction to *J.G. Posada, Messenger of Mortality*' is reprinted by kind permission of the Redstone Press, London.

'Diagram on the history of experimental film', '*Friendship's Death* diagrams', and 'The Continent – sketch for an exhibition', courtesy of the Peter Wollen Collection, British Film Institute National Archive.

Index of Films

Index of Names

Forthcoming from Verso

Knight's Moves: Selected Writings 1966–2003
Edited by Kodwo Eshun, Oliver Fuke, Nicolas Helm-Grovas

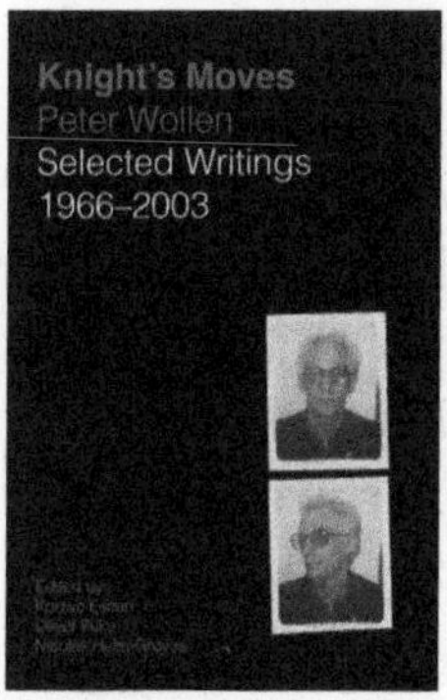

Knight's Moves: Selected Writings 1966–2003 gathers texts exemplifying Peter Wollen's deliberate disregard for received hierarchies between high art and mass culture, popular forms and the avant-garde. Taking up Viktor Shklovsky's notion of the 'knight's move' on the chess board – the simultaneous L-shaped movement characteristic of art and history – Wollen advanced unexpected connections and repressed affinities between areas of art, culture and politics habitually kept far apart. Bringing together nearly forty years of texts on the histories of dance and fashion with analyses of music video, graffiti, children's toys, gardens, cinema and postmodernism, and proposals for films and television programmes, *Knight's Moves* highlights Wollen's preoccupation with the promises and the problems of cultures of crossover, interzone, intersection and independence under twentieth-century Euro-American capitalism.

With an introductory essay by Nicolas Helm-Grovas

Fire and Ice: Selected Writings 1960–2004
Edited by Kodwo Eshun, Oliver Fuke, Nicolas Helm-Grovas

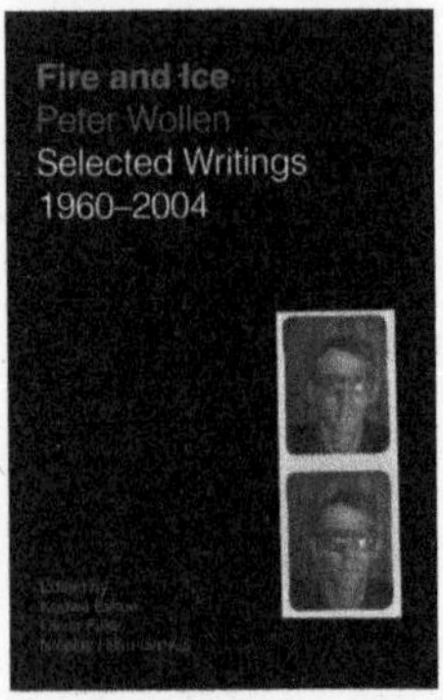

Fire and Ice: Selected Writings 1960–2004 derives its title from Peter Wollen's metaphorical contrast between the moving image and still photography. It assembles texts relating to Wollen's work as a filmmaker, his participation in the oppositional and independent film culture of the 1970s, and his engagement with the politics of psychoanalysis, feminism and the avant-garde. Presented alongside these are writings, notes and interviews about linguistics, semiotics and cinema, and experiments with speculative, poetic, critical, theoretical and science-fictional forms of counter-language. As a filmmaker, theorist and writer, *Fire and Ice* reveals Wollen's sustained invention of counter-strategies exploring, exploiting and undermining the division of labour between theory and practice.

With an introductory essay by Oliver Fuke